For WRH

Reviews of the First Edition

Thoughtful and thought-provoking. Readers will be alternately delighted or enraged by Dr Hakim's controversial arguments. But even those who remain sceptical of her conclusions will admire the way she has culled her evidence and the clarity with which she presents it.
Professor Gordon Marshall, Nuffield College, University of Oxford
(now Vice-Chancellor of Reading University)

According to the feminist lobby, women in general are an exploited group and the difference in their employment experience compared to men represents the outcome of male oppressive power rather than free choice. Using an unusually extensive range of data drawn from a number of disciplines and countries Dr Hakim explodes a number of myths. For example, women are not becoming so similar to men that gender differentiation loses its rationale. Apart from the dramatic increase in part-time work, female employment has not increased dramatically over the last 150 years. There is little evidence that housewives are exploited in the sense of working longer hours in total than men. Unpaid or voluntary work is undertaken as much by men as by women. Women's rates of labour turnover exceed those of men by 50%. There are important differences in work commitment and orientation with women less concerned than men to maximise earnings at the expense of working conditions. In short, this book should be essential reading for those interested in the operation of the labour market, including economists, psychologists and lawyers as well as sociologists.
Professor PJ Sloane, Jaffrey Professor of Political Economy, University of Aberdeen

This impressive review is essential background reading for all employment and discrimination lawyers.
Professor BA Hepple, Master of Clare College, University of Cambridge

This is the most important synthesis of research on women's work ... in a decade. ... All of it sets the mind buzzing with questions, thoughts, ideas and speculations in a way which few other books on this subject have achieved. ... It focuses attention where it is most needed – on the processes whereby women are excluded from the higher echelons of professional and managerial occupations. ... A key conclusion is ... the likelihood of increasing polarisation between work-centred and home-centred women in the 21st century.
Professor Peter Elias, Institute for Employment Research, University of Warwick.

The author's politically incorrect stance is fully backed with evidence and bibliography, and her book is clearly required reading.
Professor WS Siebert, University of Birmingham

The dreams of the women's liberation movement of 30 years ago have not been fulfilled. To some extent, as Catherine Hakim famously recognised, this may be because the aspirations of most women have never been the same as the agenda set by committed middle class feminists.
Pamela Meadows, National Institute for Social and Economic Research

If there is any economically literate guide to research and debate on trends in patterns of paid employment amongst women that is more clearly written than this, it could hardly offer more condensed yet comprehensive coverage than that offered here. ... No-one, perhaps, has a greater overall knowledge of her source material than Dr Hakim, and very few would be able to use it so adeptly.
Professor Michael Rose, University of Bath

Although I would not endorse its conclusions, I would recommend the book for its impressive array of material from many disciplines. (My own research) confirms the polarisation described by Hakim. ... She is right to point out that full-time paid work is not a route all would choose. Policies need to recognise the role of the unpaid worker and her entitlement to a share in the family cash, before, as well as after, any break-up.
Professor Heather Joshi, City University, now at the Institute of Education

KEY ISSUES IN WOMEN'S WORK:

FEMALE DIVERSITY AND THE POLARISATION OF WOMEN'S EMPLOYMENT

Second Edition

Catherine Hakim

London School of Economics

London • Sydney • Portland, Oregon

First published in Great Britain 2004 by
The GlassHouse Press, The Glass House,
Wharton Street, London WC1X 9PX, United Kingdom
Telephone: + 44 (0)20 7278 8000   Facsimile: + 44 (0)20 7278 8080
Email: info@cavendishpublishing.com
Website: www.cavendishpublishing.com

Published in the United States by Cavendish Publishing
c/o International Specialized Book Services,
5824 NE Hassalo Street, Portland,
Oregon 97213-3644, USA

Published in Australia by The GlassHouse Press,
45 Beach Street, Coogee, NSW 2034, Australia
Telephone: + 61 (2)9664 0909   Facsimile: +61 (2)9664 5420
Email: info@cavendishpublishing.com.au
Website: www.cavendishpublishing.com.au

British Library Cataloguing in Publication Data
Hakim, Catherine
Key issues in women's work: female diversity and the
polarisation of women's employment – 2nd ed
1 Women employees – Great Britain 2 Women – Employment –
Great Britain
I Title
331.4'0941

Library of Congress Cataloguing in Publication Data
Data available

ISBN 1-90438-516-8
ISBN 978-1-90438-516-8

Contents

Series Editors' Preface

The *Contemporary Issues in Public Policy* series aims to publish books which provide highly informed and comprehensive analyses of topical policy issues. This series has grown out of an earlier project by the same editors, *Conflict and Change in Britain: A New Audit*, which looked set to founder when its publishers, The Athlone Press, ceased operations on the retirement of its mainstay staff. We have been fortunate in finding, in the GlassHouse Press imprint of Cavendish Publishing, a new publisher keen to relaunch the series with a fresh steer. The main change will be the much greater emphasis of the new series on cross-national, comparative perspectives, both in their own right, as crucial for a better understanding of the issues under scrutiny, and for the light they shed on the situation in the UK.

Three developments have given added urgency to a more comparative perspective. First, the past decade has seen the quickening pace of globalisation and the engagement of nation-states in increasingly complex supra-national formations. Without subscribing to the view that this renders a national focus redundant – in some ways national frameworks have been strengthened by, for example, devolution – the shortcomings of a purely national focus are, in most cases, all too apparent. Secondly, the proliferation of international agencies and supra-national political and trade entities have led to data mountains of such variable quality that only the truly expert can make sense of the terrain. Thirdly, and to some extent consequently, a newfound populism and impatience with hard-won expertise have become increasingly evident in most media and much political representations of public policy issues. Against the appeal of gut reaction and electoral advantage, academic scholarship is all too often consigned to the margins or dismissed out of hand. The need for measured and dispassionate weighing of the evidence and theoretical clarity is all the greater in this context.

We are hence fortunate in having, as the first book in the new series, *Key Issues in Women's Work* by Catherine Hakim, a work which more than meets these considerations. First published in the parent series in 1996, the book rapidly gained acclaim as essential reading on a subject fraught with intense partisanship and immense complexity. Dr Hakim has not only revised and updated this second edition with exemplary thoroughness, she has also applied preference theory in a distinctive way to contest and, in key respects, to supplant theories of patriarchy and of rational choice theories which she finds seriously flawed. This greatly expanded second edition of what has already become a classic text is thus a markedly more formidable coverage of fundamentally the same themes and conclusions as her original book. Essentially, her principal verdict was and remains that, whatever their merits in the past, feminist theories of labour market discrimination can now play only a negligible role in explaining occupational inequalities by gender. It is worth emphasising how rare an achievement it is to challenge a well-established paradigm in any field without unduly belittling or grossly caricaturing the opposition: the standard straw man technique. Dr Hakim is a tough but fair critic of theories whose defenders must marshal equally convincing analytical and empirical resources if they are to continue to be plausible contenders for influence in the processes of policy debate and policy making.

David Downes and Paul Rock
London School of Economics
August 2004

List of Figures

List of Tables

List of Cases

Barber v Guardian Royal Exchange Assurance Group (Case 262/88) [1990] ICR 616 ECJ; [1990] IRLR 240; [1990] 2 All ER 600

Bilka-Kaufhaus v Weber von Hartz (Case 170/84) [1987] ICR 110 ECJ; [1986] 2 CMLR 701; [1986] 5 ECR 1607; [1986] IRLR 317

Commission v France (Case 312/86) [1988] ECR 6315

Francovich v Italian Republic [1992] IRLR 84

Kalanke v Freie Hansestadt Bremen (Case C-450/93) [1995] ECR I-3051; [1995] IRLR 660

Marschall v Land Nordrhein Westfalen (Case C-409/95) [1997] ECR I-6363

Meade-Hill and Another v The British Council [1995] IRLR 478

R v Secretary of State for Employment, ex parte Equal Opportunities Commission [1994] IRLR 176 HL

R v Secretary of State for Employment, ex parte Seymour-Smith [1994] IRLR 448 DC

R v Secretary of State for Employment, ex parte Seymour-Smith [1995] IRLR 464

Rinner-Kühn v FWW Spezial-Gebaudereinigung GmbH & Co KG (Case 171/88) [1989] IRLR 493 ECJ

Stadt Lengerich v Helmig [1994] ECR I-5727 ECJ

Acknowledgments

I thank Duncan Gallie for providing special tables from the 1992 PSI survey of employment in Britain which were used in Table 4.8. I thank Sheila Jacobs for providing special analyses of the 1980 Women and Employment Survey from her DPhil. thesis, including the analyses that provide the basis for Tables 5.3 and 5.4. I thank Simon Burgess for providing special analyses of the General Household Survey data used in Table 5.7. I thank the Office for National Statistics for allowing me use of the 1% Longitudinal Study, and members of the LS Support Programme at the Social Statistics Research Unit, City University, for assistance with accessing the data which is used in Table 6.3. I thank ONS and the ESRC/JISC/DENI programme for creating and providing access to the 1% and 2% Samples of Anonymised Records from the 1991 Census of Population, the ESRC Census Microdata Unit at the University of Manchester and the Computing Service staff at Manchester and ULCC and the London School of Economics for help with processing these huge datasets which provided the basis for Table 6.2. I thank Bob Hepple for comments on an early draft of Chapter 7. I am indebted to Norman Stockman, Norman Bonney, Xuewen Sheng and Masami Shinozaki for bringing the Chinese and Japanese surveys used in Tables 4.6 and 4.7 to my attention.

The following appear in this book by permission:

Tables 2.1, 2.2 and 2.3 reprinted with minor changes from Hakim, 'Workforce restructuring, social insurance coverage and the black economy', *Journal of Social Policy*, June 1989, by permission of Cambridge University Press.

Tables 4.3, 4.5, 4.8 and 4.10 reprinted with minor changes from Hakim, *Models of the Family in Modern Societies: Ideals and Realities*, 2003, by permission of Ashgate Press.

Tables 3.3 and 5.2 reprinted with minor changes from OECD *Employment Outlook 2002*, with permission of the OECD.

Table 6.1 reprinted with minor changes from Hakim, 'Explaining trends in occupational segregation', *European Sociological Review*, September 1992, by permission of Oxford University Press.

Tables 6.4 and 6.5 reprinted from Hakim, 'Segregated and integrated occupations: a new framework for analysing social change', *European Sociological Review*, December 1993, by permission of Oxford University Press.

Table 6.6 reprinted from Hakim, 'A century of change in occupational segregation 1891–1991', *Journal of Historical Sociology*, December 1994, by permission of Blackwell.

Figures 1 and 2 reprinted from Main, 'The lifetime attachment of women to the labour market' in *Women and Paid Work*, 1988, by permission of Brian Main and the Institute for Employment Research, University of Warwick.

Abbreviations

BCS	British Cohort Study
BSAS	British Social Attitudes Survey
CPS	Current Population Survey
DI	Dissimilarity Index
EC	European Commission
ECHP	European Community Household Panel
ECHR	European Court of Human Rights
ECJ	European Court of Justice
EEOC	Equal Employment Opportunities Commission (of the USA)
ESRC	Economic and Social Research Council (Britain)
EU	European Union
FES	Family Expenditure Survey
FTE	Full-Time Equivalent
GHS	General Household Survey
GDP	Gross Domestic Product
GNP	Gross National Product
ILO	International Labour Office of the United Nations
ISSP	International Social Survey Programme
LFS	Labour Force Survey
MTBA	Multinational Time Budget Archive
MTUS	Multinational Time Use Study
NCDS	National Child Development Study
NES	New Earnings Survey
NLS	National Longitudinal Surveys (of Labour Market Behaviour)
OECD	Organisation for Economic Co-operation and Development
ONS	Office of National Statistics
OOPEC	Office for Official Publications of the European Community
OPCS	Office of Population Censuses and Surveys
PSID	Panel Study of Income Dynamics
RSS	Royal Statistical Society
SAR	Sample of Anonymised Records (from the British census)
SNA	United Nations System of National Accounts
TUC	Trades Union Congress
USA	United States of America
WES	Women and Employment Survey

Abbreviations used in tables

..	Data not available
*	Less than 0.5%
FT	full-time
PT	part-time
M	males, men
F	females, women

Chapter 1
Explaining Women's Subordination

Are women today oppressed? Or do they now have the best of both worlds – taking jobs when they like, on an equal basis with men, but retreating to the sanctuary of the home to revert to their other role as homemaker and mother whenever they please? What makes women's employment distinctive? This book is about the choices women make, the diversity of these choices, and their consequences.

There are good reasons for optimism. History looks quite different when viewed from women's perspective. World War Two may have been traumatic, but it was nonetheless beneficial for women, breaking down job barriers and creating new openings. The 1960s brought the contraceptive revolution, giving women independent control over their fertility and opening up the option of voluntary childlessness. The 1970s and 1980s brought equal opportunities legislation that produced a 10% increase in women's earnings as compared with men's in Britain and the USA. The 1980s also brought the impact of European Union (EU) policies and European Court of Justice (ECJ) decisions insisting that the principle of non-discrimination between men and women, in particular in all aspects of pay, had to be fully implemented throughout Europe. With the decline of the manufacturing industry in Europe after World War Two, modern economies shifted towards greater emphasis on service sector industries, all offering more congenial work environments to women. Recent developments have created a new and beneficial social and economic situation for women.

On the other hand, the potential for change does not seem to have borne fruit. Men and women are still segregated in different occupations, with women concentrated in what is often described as a 'job ghetto' of low-grade, low-paid work. Sex differentials in earnings of 10%–20% in Europe and Australia, 20%–30% in the USA, and 40% in Japan still remain, even if these are smaller than before (OECD, 2001: 139; Padavic and Reskin, 2002: 123). Men seem always to have the upper hand, so that it is more of a struggle for women to get what they want. In practice, it is argued, women remain disadvantaged and dissatisfied with their lot.

This book offers a more empirically grounded review of developments in recent decades than is offered by most current texts on women's employment, and thus a more informed assessment of the main theories accounting for women's social and economic position today. It presents a new analysis of women's position in the labour market and of the social changes currently under way in all modern societies. The focus is on women's choice between paid employment and full-time homemaking, and on women's position within the workforce. The choices women make seem to be changing, prompting vigorous debate over the nature of the changes, and whether sex differences in lifestyles are finally disappearing

The focus is paid employment in the market economy and the terms 'work' and 'employment' are used interchangeably throughout the book for stylistic variation and simplicity. As the next chapter demonstrates, strictly speaking, work covers a broader range of activities than employment. Similarly, the terms sex and gender are used interchangeably, for stylistic variation, and because there is a perfect overlap for the vast majority of people. Strictly speaking, gender refers to the meanings that societies and individuals ascribe to female and male categories defined by sex.

Key issues in women's employment

Is it really necessary for women to go out to work to gain equality with men? Are they not doing enough work in the home and raising children? It is often argued that women's work has been systematically undercounted and undervalued, giving a false impression of women's contribution to the economy: first, that national statistics fail to fully reflect the hidden wage work of women – as family workers, in home-based employment and in the informal economy; secondly, that national statistics do not even attempt to record women's domestic work, caring work and voluntary work. Chapter 2 reviews the evidence for these two arguments and finds them not proven. It shows statistics on unpaid work are readily available and rarely show women doing more of it than men.

The alternative view is that women have been gaining economic equality with men as levels of female employment rose steadily from the 1950s onwards. Women's gains have been men's losses, as women steal men's jobs and feminise them. Men are displaced, socially as well as economically. Chapter 3 examines the feminisation of the workforce and finds that jobs have been defeminised as well as being demasculinised. Apart from the creation of a segregated part-time workforce, there have been no substantial changes in the level of female employment for over 150 years.

Do women really want paid employment? It has become received wisdom in recent years that they do, that any differences that might have existed in men's and women's work orientations, work commitment and ambitions have now faded away. Women want interesting jobs and well-paid work just as much as men, but are prevented from getting them by discrimination, overt and covert. Chapter 4 reviews the evidence on attitudes to work and how they are changing. Attitudes to the sexual division of labour in the home are examined in a cross-national perspective to show how differential sex-roles are being remodelled rather than abandoned. One sex-role stereotype that seems most resistant to change is the idea that power and authority are in some way a male prerogative. Women are surprisingly unwilling to co-operate with women managers.

If women's labour force attachment has really been increasing in recent years, as is so often stated, we would expect to see increasing employment stability and continuity of employment among women. A review of the evidence in Chapter 5 shows on the contrary that the sex differential in labour turnover rates has not changed in 20 years and that women's employment histories display rising discontinuity.

The key explanation offered by patriarchy theory for women's disadvantaged position within the workforce is that occupational segregation is used to restrict women to a female job ghetto of low-paid work, so that women invariably earn less than men. Chapter 6 reviews the evidence to find that in this area there has been far more change, all of it to women's advantage, than feminist theory admits. More important, recent comparative studies show that occupational segregation is not the main cause of the pay gap between men and women, as was long believed. A review of the impact of legislation in Chapter 7 confirms the importance of equal opportunities policies, but shows the law to be a two-edged weapon. Overall, women made real gains in the 1980s and 1990s which cannot be explained solely by equal pay and opportunities legislation. We must thus reconsider the competing theories explaining women's social and economic position and assess how effective they are now in accounting for current developments.

Theoretical perspectives

Much recent theorising on women's position has been misinformed, resting on reviews of the evidence that are incomplete, mistaken or one-sided. Perhaps this is not surprising. A full assessment of the empirical evidence has to be grounded in economics as well as sociology, anthropology, demography and social psychology. Few of those who contribute to the expanding field of women's studies have a sufficiently broad disciplinary base, for example, to appreciate the contribution from economics and rational choice theory as well as social psychology. This has resulted in misunderstandings about theory and evidence, and even confusion about the basic concepts of work and employment, as shown in Chapter 2. In some cases the errors are less excusable, as illustrated in Chapter 5 by the problem of research results distorted by sample selection bias, which is more common (and hidden) in sociology than in economics.

There is no shortage of theories claiming to explain women's subordinate position in the labour market and in the family. All of them are plausible; have some element of truth in them. Very few of them have been subjected to rigorous testing in a wide range of cultures. In *Theorising Patriarchy*, Sylvia Walby reviews the enormous number of theories that have been offered in the last 20 years to explain women's relatively subordinate position in society and the workforce or, as she puts it, women's exploitation and oppression. However, her review, like so many others, discusses theories in terms of their intellectual merits and explanatory adequacy. At the end of the day the crucial test of theory is against reality. Theory that rests on inadequate or selective evidence is weak, no matter how coherent a world view it offers.

Following Einstein, theory is not right or wrong. Theory is either useful, or not useful, in making sense of the world, helping one to understand change processes and formulate further questions to address. On this basis, there are four main theories that are currently useful for understanding women's social and economic position. The most important competing theories today are Steven Goldberg's theory of the inevitability of male dominance and patriarchy based on psycho-physiological processes; Heidi Hartmann's theory of men's collective organisation to further their own interests against those of women through trade unions, the legal system and political organisations, as illustrated by a pattern of occupational segregation that is to men's advantage; Gary Becker's rational choice theory of the allocation of time and labour to domestic work and employment based on the role specialisation of husband and wife; and Catherine Hakim's preference theory showing that women (and men) choose between home-centred, work-centred and adaptive lifestyles after women gain genuine choices in modern liberal societies.

Between them these theories cover the full range of explanations so far offered: physiological, psychological, sociological and economic.

The standard sociological explanation for women's position in society, and in the workforce, is that social structural and institutional factors explain everything; women's lives are wholly determined by forces outside them: the particular country they live in, its social policies, and employers' policies. For example, Crompton (1997) and Padavic and Reskin (2002) discuss women's position in the workforce within a 'victim feminism' framework that allows women no room for active responsibility or decision – no 'agency' as social scientists put it. They are unable to explain *why* women have co-operated and colluded with social systems (and men) that exploit and oppress them, and *why* women rarely rebelled against sex discrimination. The four theories discussed here all provide, for different time periods, answers to these ultimate questions of *why* particular social structures and institutions have been created and maintained, by women as well as men, even though they appear to disadvantage women. The theories also identify what needs to change in order for women's position to improve.

The pattern of women's employment, and non-work, remains central to any theory. Women's position in society as a whole is jointly determined by their access to, and role and status in paid employment and the status accorded to their reproductive and domestic activities. In industrial societies women's economic position in the workforce is gaining importance relative to non-market domestic and childcare functions. Various theories link the segregation of men and women in paid employment to the domestic division of labour between husband and wife. An adequate theory must be able to explain patterns of sex-based occupational segregation, in particular the *vertical* job segregation that finds men concentrated in the higher status and higher-paid positions. It must also be able to account for the domestic division of labour, and women's choice between the full-time domestic role and some combination of paid employment and non-market work.

Patriarchy and male dominance: Goldberg

Goldberg's theory of *The Inevitability of Patriarchy* and male dominance based on psycho-physiological processes was originally published in 1973 and has been the subject of intensely critical debate since then. A much more precise, developed and persuasive (though repetitive) version of his theory was published in 1993 under the new title *Why Men Rule*. Goldberg focuses on the impact of physiology on social attitudes and behaviour, in particular the effect of male hormones such as testosterone as a source of sex differences in motivation, ambition and behaviour. He argues that testosterone and other differences in male physiological development make men generally more self-assertive, aggressive, dominant and competitive. In consequence, they invariably seek to obtain the top positions in any hierarchy, such as the top positions in political or other public leadership hierarchies, the highest status jobs or roles in the workforce, sport, the arts, crime or any other area of social activity with a hierarchy of status and power that prompts competitive behaviour.

A second element of his theory points to the effect of hormonal and other physiological differences in shaping the character of private heterosexual relationships, and the mutually reinforcing *congruence* between personal styles in public and private spheres. Sex differences have their roots in physiology, and are developed further by the socialisation process, to create an emotional expectation or preference for *male dominance* in personal and sexual relationships. Private heterosexual relationships set a pattern for relationships between men and women in the workplace. At the minimum, this creates an invisible barrier to establishing egalitarian and relaxed work roles and relationships that are not 'coloured' by patterns in the sexual arena. At worst, sex-roles and styles of behaviour established in heterosexual relationships carry over into role expectations and behaviour patterns in the workplace, consciously or subconsciously.

Goldberg is sometimes wrongly classified as an evolutionist sociobiologist, castigated for evolutionary theories he does not address and for exaggerations of his own theory that he does not offer. His approach is similar to that of Rossi (1977), who sought to incorporate the influence of physiological factors in interaction with social and cultural factors to explain why women actively seek greater involvement in childcare than do men, especially in the first six years of a child's life, although she refers to evolutionary theory, which Goldberg eschews completely. Goldberg set out to explain why men invariably get almost all the top jobs and top positions in *all* societies, past and present. In his first book, the emphasis was on anthropological research evidence showing that no society had ever existed in which women ruled. In his more recent book the emphasis shifts to contemporary societies and the evidence that within the workforce vertical job segregation is pronounced. All other hierarchies are also dominated by men. Goldberg points out that exceptional women sometimes reach the top, Golda Meir and Margaret Thatcher being two examples. However, the exceptions will remain exceptions unless social and cultural factors start to overcome the influence of hormonal differences in the development of children and adolescents. He accepts that determined social engineering might achieve this, but it remains to be seen. The Israeli *kibbutzim* failed in their efforts to alter sex-role differentiation; socialist Russia and China failed to eliminate vertical job segregation; egalitarian and family-friendly policies in Sweden reduced sex differences in earnings, but again failed to reduce vertical job segregation. Physiological differences between males and females do not fully determine behaviour: they only create dispositions which may be valued or belittled, encouraged or discouraged by a society. Similarly, Goldberg is not saying that men are necessarily more able, competent or effective in using positions of power and authority, only that they are motivated to seek such positions with greater determination and persistence than women, and are more prepared to make sacrifices to get there, in terms of effort and foregoing other activities or benefits.

As a result, patriarchy is universal in that authority and leadership are, and always have been, associated with the male in every society. He defines *patriarchy* as any system of organisation (political, economic, industrial, financial, religious or social) in which the overwhelming number of upper positions in hierarchies are occupied by males. Patriarchy refers only to suprafamilial levels of organisation. Authority in familial and dyadic relationships is a manifestation of the psychophysiological reality he labels *male dominance.*

The attraction of Goldberg's theory is that it is simple, specific and provides a sufficient explanation of vertical job segregation in the workforce and of male domination in politics and other public hierarchies. It is the only theory that can explain some of the more inconvenient facts about women as well as men, such as the apparently universal preference for a male leader or boss, as noted in Chapter 4. His theory is also consistent with Chodorow's (1978) and Gilligan's (1982, 1993) theories of qualitative personality differences between men and women. Gilligan describes men as being more individualistic, achievement-oriented, detached from others, and oriented more towards power, distinctive activity and success. She argues that women define themselves in terms of personal relationships, are unselfish, concerned about fulfilling the needs of others and feel powerless. Along with Miller (1976) she describes women as accepting subordinate relationships with men (1993: 168). Gilligan insists that women's greater interest in social relationships is invariably benign, consisting of a concern to *care* for others rather than a detached curiosity or a desire to manipulate and control others emotionally. The empirical validity of her work has been questioned (Treadwell, 1987: 280–81; Beutel and Marini, 1995: 438). Despite this, Gilligan's thesis has been accepted with positive acclaim, rather than rejected as 'sexist' in the same way as Goldberg's thesis and other theories that acknowledge important gender differences in personality and behaviour have been.

Goldberg also offers a novel explanation for the fact that the most highly-paid occupations tend to be male-dominated. The explanation usually offered is that male-dominated occupations are rewarded disproportionately well and female occupations are undervalued and less well-paid. This theory led to demands for equal pay for work of equal value policies (Treiman and Hartmann, 1981) as noted in Chapter 7. Another explanation is that workers queue for jobs and, as (male) employers invariably prefer men over women if men are available, men get the cream of the jobs and women end up in the worst paid jobs (Reskin and Roos, 1990). Goldberg points out that if these theories were true, there would be no male-dominated occupations that paid substantially less than women's occupations. In fact, there are many male jobs that are low status and low-paid. Male roles are not high status because they are male, Goldberg argues. It is simply that any role that acquires high status (as indicated by high earnings) will attract more men than women, so will become male-dominated as a result of its position in the hierarchy (Goldberg, 1993: 108). Men never need to be encouraged to apply for promotion, whereas women do. The example is often quoted of the job advertisement that failed to attract any women applicants at all until the salary was reduced by half in a re-advertisement (Hakim, 1979: 50).

Goldberg points out (1993: 106) that sexual differentiation in motivation to attain high status positions is statistical and probabilistic, like other attitudes and behaviour differences, rather than an absolute difference. Socialisation in childhood and adolescence magnifies and enhances psychological and personality differences to create the discrete qualitative differences observed between adult men and women. Physiology does not determine, but predisposes, towards ambitious competitiveness in males far more than in females, but there is variation around the two averages. Other writers have also criticised the misleading use of averages to describe and differentiate male and female behaviour and attitudes, as averages hide the large overlap between the two groups in terms of behavioral styles; however, they have also emphasised the striking differences between men's and women's testosterone levels and the much larger variation in male levels (Treadwell, 1987: 269, 278; see also Hakim, 2000: 259). Within-group variation for men is almost as large as the sex differential. More important, the sex differential in testosterone levels is substantial enough to contribute some part of the explanation for sex differences in everyday behaviour.

Goldberg's thesis is supported by more recent research on the effects of testosterone, and on mate selection. Dabbs (2000) had the clever idea of testing testosterone levels using samples of saliva instead of blood, because people are more disposed to spit for science than to give blood. He was thus able to test for the effect of testosterone on men and women in a wide variety of occupations and social situations. He found some degree of sorting by testosterone levels both within and between occupations, which helps to explain the low proportion of women in publicly competitive jobs. He found that high testosterone had the same impact on men and women, making them more sexually attractive, competitive, interested in sex, power and success. A similar review of the impact of testosterone and other hormones on sex differences in behaviour is presented by Pinker (2002: 337–71).

Research on marriage markets, though rare, again supports Goldberg. For example, a national survey in France found an ideal age gap of three to four years between spouses in all social groups (Bozon and Héran, 1990a, b). Women were more insistent than men on a husband who was taller and older. Bozon and Héran eventually concluded that it was women, not men, who most eagerly sought male dominance in marriage; this was most pronounced among less-educated and younger women, and those in lower-grade occupations. Similar results were obtained by Buss (1989; 1995) from a much larger study covering 37 countries and cultures in five continents. This showed that even the most educated modern women prefer male partners who are economically strong, while men seek physical attractiveness instead. Wealth and power are the principal sources of status for men, while physical attractiveness is the principal source of status for women in marriage markets. A national longitudinal study of the 1958 NCDS birth cohort found that attractive women are more likely to marry, and also that attractive people have higher earnings (Harper, 2000), so physical attractiveness also has benefits for men. However, male dominance in physique, age, and financial status seems to be a continuing advantage in mate selection, because women want it that way.

Goldberg's theory of patriarchy and male dominance is proven in that there has never yet been a society in which women normally held all the most senior posts or filled most high status non-maternal roles. He sees only one avenue of change, through intensive socialisation to eliminate sex differentiation. But this has achieved limited results in Sweden, for example, which has the highest level of occupational segregation among modern societies. Two other theories that focus on fundamental sex-role differences are more historically time-specific than Goldberg's thesis. Lerner's (1986) historical study of the development of patriarchy concluded that it resulted from men's desire to control women's sexuality and reproductive work, in order to safeguard (male) inheritance of private property. Male control of women's employment and other public activities was only a side-effect of the sexual control of women, not a central aim in itself. In this case, the introduction of reliable genetic tests of a child's paternity overcomes the need for patriarchal control of women's activities, so patriarchy should eventually fade away, in relation to employment as well as sexual activities.

Firestone's (1974) theory argues that women's reproductive functions make them physically and socially vulnerable while they are bearing or rearing children, at the minimum restricting their activities and potentially allowing men to take advantage to dominate and subordinate them. In this case, childlessness offers one obvious avenue of escape. Another is for women to organise collectively to ensure that childbearing is rewarded at an appropriately high level, in social and/or economic terms. (Swedish pro-natalist policies are a direct response to declining fertility, for example.) The fact that women generally do not do this, and produce babies without adequate compensation is itself informative. Women who provide a commercial baby production service, selling the child for substantial sums of money are criticised, never praised, by women as well as men; women who fail to honour these deals and decide they cannot bear to give the child away are even admired. Women actively collude with men in labelling venal sexual activity and reproduction as deviant. Even feminists accept the labelling of prostitutes as deviant and exploited rather than liberated from the yoke of marriage, and focus instead on the sexual double standard that fails to treat male customers as equally deviant (Smart, 1976; Downes and Rock, 1988: 273–92). Indeed, rape, which is rare, and largely confined to Western industrial society, attracts far more attention than prostitution (Smart and Smart, 1978; Walby, 1990), a universal occupation providing regular employment for thousands of women. It appears that women's sex-role attitudes and behaviour are resistant to change.

The reasons for women's failure to organise as effectively as men to promote their interests has been developed further by Hartmann.

Patriarchy, male organisation and job segregation: Hartmann

A classic short paper by Hartmann first published in 1976 provides the essential framework for theories that place patriarchy centrestage as the key explanatory factor. Hartmann defined *patriarchy* as men's domination of women, specifically men's control over women's labour as illustrated by historical developments in trade union policies in Britain and the USA. Subsequently, she extended her concept of patriarchy to include heterosexual marriage, women's economic dependence on men, male-dominated social institutions, the domestic division of labour, women's disproportionate share of housework and childcare, all creating the potential for conflicting rather than harmonious interests between spouses or between men and women (Hartmann, 1979; 1981).

Hartmann's theory was developed by Walby, initially in a historical analysis of British trade union policies to exclude women from paid employment and restrict them to the less well-paid areas of work through occupational segregation (Walby, 1986), then later in a broader theoretical statement (Walby, 1990). Walby defines patriarchy as a system of inter-related social structures and practices through which men dominate, oppress and exploit women (1990: 20). She sets out how patriarchy operates through the private household, the labour market, heterosexuality, culture, male violence towards women as illustrated by rape, and through state support for the ideology of patriarchy, as illustrated by laws that restrict women's employment and control divorce, through welfare state regulations that impose traditional sex-roles.

Social class and social stratification have been the main concepts used in sociological theory on social inequality, whereas economists focus on earnings or income inequality. A voluminous literature struggled to reconcile explanations of gender inequality with Marxist theories of social stratification, exploitation and the value of labour power (Walby, 1990; Fine, 1992). Fine (1992) insists that the oppression of women can be adequately incorporated into class analysis, but the general consensus is that it is more useful to treat capitalism and patriarchy as theoretically separate but interacting. Hartmann views capitalism and patriarchy as broadly in harmony much of the time, while Walby sees them as being in conflict more often.

Hartmann's theory of patriarchy emphasises occupational segregation as the central mechanism used by men to restrict and constrain women's access to income and earnings, thus rendering them financially dependent on men, forcing them to become domestic servants for their husbands. Hartmann recognises that this is not the only mechanism, just the main one. The separation of the workplace from the home brought about by the development of modern industry also meant that many women ceased to be gainfully employed in the family enterprise. However, the ideology of the sexual division of labour became a force in its own right, leading women and men to prefer feminine and masculine jobs, and leading men to refuse to be formally subordinate to a woman in the workplace (Hartmann, 1976: 151, 154, 164, 168–69). These processes are demonstrated by studies of women's employment in male jobs during World War Two (Milkman, 1987: 9, 157–59) and other historical studies of the USA and Britain (Matthaei, 1982: 187–232; Bradley, 1989: 225–30; Strom, 1989). Walby differentiates the two mechanisms used by men to limit women's access to earnings: total *exclusion* from the market economy and wage labour; and the *segregation* of male and female workers within the workforce, restricting women to the lower-paid jobs. Both policies are seen as ensuring that men have more financial power in the home and in the labour market.

Walby claims that the exclusion strategy was dominant in 19th century Britain, while the segregation strategy is most influential today, as illustrated by the segregation of full-time and part-time work. This is the basis of her thesis that patriarchy has changed and developed from the *private patriarchy* which characterised the 19th century, with women excluded from paid work, devoting their time instead to domestic work and rearing children for the benefit of an individual patriarch (that is, their husband), to the *public patriarchy* of the 20th century and today in which large numbers of women are now in employment but collectively exploited by employers who pay women workers wages below the level that would be expected in terms of women's human capital (in essence, their qualifications and work experience).

Our analysis of the evidence on the feminisation of the workforce in Chapter 3 shows that Walby's theory of the historical development of patriarchy is simply not supported by the facts on trends in female employment. A fuller critique by Fine (1992: 52–66) questions the power of trade unions to impose their will on employers who wanted to hire cheaper female labour. Fine also argues that protective labour legislation that excluded women from working in the mines and at night was motivated by a wider range of social concerns than a patriarchal desire to restrict women to the homemaking role alone. Trade union policies were also irrelevant to women employed in domestic service and exclusively female occupations such as dressmaking and sewing, which remained the most important occupations for women well into the 20th century. Finally, the exclusionary strategy of the marriage bar lasted until well into the 20th century: in Britain, Holland and other European countries the exclusion of married women from employment was only made unlawful by the sex discrimination and equal opportunities legislation of the 1960s and beyond. More puzzling, trade union policy on unequal pay for women is downplayed by Walby (1986: 214–17; 1990: 51, 162). Milkman (1987: 77–83, 158) shows that pay equity is the more important issue in industries where the work cannot easily be stereotyped as male or female. Grint (1988) shows that job segregation strategies were not necessary as long as trade unions maintained unequal pay for women doing the same jobs as men. Lower wage rates for women had been traditional in agriculture and were carried over into manufacturing industry and white-collar work, with female wages being 50–60% of male wages. Even when formally in favour, British trade unions generally remained opposed to equal pay for women, overtly or covertly, right up to the Equal Pay Act 1970, which was pushed through by a woman minister, Barbara Castle, in a Labour government (Grint, 1988: 101–05; Castle, 1993: 409–12, 427). In sum, the key changes in policy all occurred after 1950, with simultaneous legislation on unequal pay, exclusion and segregation in Britain and other industrial societies. Walby's attempt to develop a dynamic theory of patriarchy fails on the evidence.

We thus return to Hartmann's original simple and elegant account of patriarchy as male organisation to further their interests against those of women, especially to control women's wage work, which remains the basis for most formulations today. Exclusion, segregation and unequal pay all achieve the same purpose of limiting women's access to earnings and the independence of spirit that comes with an independent income. The key element of Hartmann's theory which no-one challenges is the idea that men organise collectively to further their own interests against those of women through the labour market, laws, political organisations, culture and ideology. Male solidarity and male organisation are the key factors, which Walby (1986) and Milkman (1987) illuminated further in their research on trade union strategies in Britain and the USA. It is less important whether trade unions used exclusion, segregation or unequal pay strategies, and less important that their strategies sometimes failed, than it is to underline that male solidarity is high, that men organise collectively to advance their own interests, and that men perceive a conflict of interests between men and women much of the time. Walby added to this the point that women also organise collectively to advance their own interests against those of men, at least occasionally, that women are not purely passive actors in their own lives (Walby, 1990: 58, 87–88, 93, 125–26). However, Grint (1988) concludes that this was never the most important factor in achieving the equal opportunities revolution, which was largely forced by the changing industrial composition of the economy.

The idea that women make real choices is developed further by Becker and other human capital theorists.

Rational choices within families: Becker

Rational choice theory (sometimes termed rational action theory or exchange theory) is simply economics applied to social institutions which are more commonly studied by sociologists or political scientists, such as the family or voting in elections. The most well-known area of rational choice theory is the 'new home economics' and human capital theory which studies non-economic aspects of the family, including the sexual division of labour in households, the supply of wives' labour to the market economy, decisions about investments in children, and decisions about marriage and divorce. Most of the time, economics treats the family, or household, as a single undivided unit, a black box, that makes choices about work or leisure, production or consumption in order to maximise its utility (satisfaction or valued benefits, not only money). The novelty was to open up the black box of the family, to study and model how decisions are made within it to maximise collective and individual utility. It has to be remembered that economics relies on scarce resources as its starting point. It is not possible for everybody to have exactly what they want all of the time. If it were, we would be in paradise, the word choice would have no meaning and we would have no need for social science. Therefore, we study how people make decisions that get the best 'deal' possible out of the options and constraints that confront them. Rational choice theory focuses on the personal or mutual advantage individuals gain through co-operative exchange. It assumes people know what they value (have stable preferences) and act rationally to achieve their aims, to maximise or optimise their desires. The main problem is that the theory can veer towards tautology: whatever happens must have been desired and preferred, otherwise people would have done something else. But this is a general problem of economics rather than of rational choice theory.

The key text is Becker's *A Treatise on the Family*, originally published in 1981 and reprinted in 1991 with additions, in particular a paper on the sexual division of labour first published in 1985. The book was initially criticised by sociologists, who felt uncomfortable with the application of clear-headed logic to social institutions that are idealised in Western culture as structured around loving relationships, which are assumed to be incompatible with reason. The 1985 paper argued that if they work at all, most married women economise on the effort expended on paid employment by seeking less demanding jobs. It prompted an immediate rejection by some sociologists as having no empirical basis (England and McCreary, 1987; Bielby and Bielby, 1988), although others showed the thesis to be vindicated by research on the characteristics of part-time workers in Britain (Hakim, 1991; 1993b; 1997; see also Bradley, 1989: 226). Becker argues that even if a husband and wife are intrinsically identical, they gain from a division of labour between employment and household work, with one specialising more in employment and the other specialising more in domestic work. The sexual division of labour is mutually advantageous because it is efficient, and raises the productivity of the person who specialises in domestic work as well as the productivity of the person who specialises in employment. Even small initial differences between people, such as the fact that only women bear children and this gives them an advantage in subsequent childcare, would cause a sexual division of labour which, extended over the years, would produce an enormous gender gap in earnings, even in the absence of sex discrimination. Becker does not deny that discrimination exists in the labour market, and that husbands may exploit their wives. Indeed, he argues that, logically, the entire difference in average earnings between men and women could be classified as due to discrimination and other sex differences which cause the sexual division of labour, even though differences in human capital may be the immediate, visible explanation.

Becker argues that the sexual division of labour in the home leads women to invest less and men to invest more in their human capital: education, training, career development and work experience. It leads wives to choose jobs that are less effort-intensive and are generally compatible with domestic responsibilities. It causes occupational segregation, since wives will seek jobs that are less demanding even if they work full-time. These processes affect single men and women, as well as married couples, if they anticipate marriage and parenthood, as most people do.

There are two obvious sources of change in this theory. First, Becker assumes that childcare is a major element of household work, because any decline in fertility rates is offset by parents investing extra time and effort to produce higher quality children. On the other hand, raising a single child does not generally require the same investment of time and effort as raising four children, and single children are now quite common, even outside China. Further, intentionally childless couples could potentially have a qualitatively different bargain, with far less incentive to adopt differentiated sex-roles if both have decided to invest in careers. If their careers are sufficiently rewarding, this may compensate for a loss of efficiency in their domestic work, due to both partners being amateur cooks and so forth. Secondly, Becker is obliged to assume that individuals have stable preferences. In fact, some people's preferences change markedly over the life cycle. Women who have children early in life can become bored with motherhood, at a young enough age to initiate a late-start career. Women who invest in a career may become disenchanted with the 'rat race', and retire to the haven of domestic life and motherhood and learn to cook. Generational changes in the attractiveness of the homemaker role and in the relative returns to paid employment and homemaking can also alter the precise balance in the sexual division of labour. Chapter 4 explores the evidence on changing attitudes to the division of labour in the family.

Finally, Becker himself notes that the family is becoming a less and less important institution as functions are transferred out of it. Education and training, social insurance against unemployment or sickness, healthcare, entertainment and social activities in clubs and other organisations – all are provided by public sector or commercial organisations, reducing reliance on families for these services. Commercial goods and services are usually available, at least in large cities, to replace many domestic goods and services. The volume of work done in the home is increasingly a matter of choice, and the outcome of negotiations over who does it becomes less predictable.

Becker's thesis is the fullest development to date of human capital theory and models formulated originally by Mincer (1962) and extended by others seeking to explain the characteristics of female labour force participation with reference to the family division of labour (Mincer and Polachek, 1974; Mincer, 1985; Blau and Ferber, 1992: 34–71, 141–87; Jacobsen, 1994: 73–103, 258–84; Padavic and Reskin, 2002: 112–14). All treat women as a single homogeneous group with interrupted work histories due to their family role. Human capital theory is useful for analyses of female employment, especially for explaining earnings, and differences in earnings between men and women (Blau and Ferber, 1992: 34–71, 141–87). The earnings gap between men and women is due in large part to differences in work experience and employment-related investments, as noted in Chapters 5, 6 and 7.

Unfortunately, human capital theory became somewhat discredited, especially among sociologists, by one particular application. Polachek (1979) tried to explain the segregation of men and women in the workforce as being due to women choosing occupations with lower penalties for discontinuous employment histories, arguing in effect that job choices were rational and efficient, a thesis that has repeatedly been refuted, in somewhat different formulations, for the USA (England, 1982; 1984; Corcoran et al, 1984) and for Britain (Hakim, 1996a; 2000: 39; 2003a: 163–87), for reasons set out in Chapter 6. In addition, some sociologists reject it because the emphasis on explaining women's behaviour with reference to family roles is sometimes seen as sexist and linked to discredited Parsonian functionalism (Walby, 1990: 30–32). However, the theory is in fact very similar to the sociological idea of household work strategies with husband and wife making joint decisions about the allocation of time to employment, informal work, household production and domestic work (Pahl, 1984), the key difference being that Pahl shows how household work strategies vary across the life cycle and in response to events such as unemployment of the breadwinner. This seems to be another instance where the concepts and language used by economists and sociologists differ more than the substance of their ideas, so that a fruitful theoretical synthesis is feasible (England and McCreary, 1987).

Preference theory: Hakim

Preference theory is a new theory to explain women's choices between market work and family work. The theory is historically informed, empirically based, multi-disciplinary, prospective rather than retrospective in orientation, and applicable in all rich modern societies (Hakim, 2000). Three features distinguish it from other theories: first, it is historically specific; secondly, it recognises the diversity of women's lifestyle preferences instead of assuming that women can be treated as a single homogeneous group; and thirdly, Hakim carried out new surveys in Europe to test and develop the theory (Hakim, 2003a).

Preference theory argues that five historical changes collectively produce a qualitatively new scenario for women in rich modern societies in the 21st century, giving them options that were not previously available. Hakim notes that small elites of women born into wealthy families, or prosperous families with liberal ideas, did sometimes have real choices in the past, just as their brothers did. However, genuine choices are now open to women in the sense that the vast majority of women have choices, not only very particular subgroups in the population. The five conditions that create a new scenario are:

- the contraceptive revolution which, from about 1965 onwards, gave sexually active women reliable and independent control over their own fertility for the first time in history;

- the equal opportunities revolution, which ensured that for the first time in history women obtained equal rights to access all positions, occupations and careers in the labour market. Sometimes, this was extended to posts in the public sphere more generally. In some countries, legislation prohibiting sex discrimination goes much wider than just the labour market, giving women equal access to housing, financial services, and other public services;

- the expansion of white-collar occupations, which are far more attractive to women than most blue-collar occupations;

- the creation of jobs for secondary earners, people who do not want to give priority to paid work at the expense of other life interests; and

- the increasing importance of attitudes, values and personal preferences in the lifestyle choices of prosperous, liberal modern societies.

The five changes are historically-specific developments in any society, and the timing of the five changes varies greatly between countries. The two revolutions are the essential core of the social revolution for women. The five changes collectively are necessary to create a new scenario in which women have genuine choices and female heterogeneity is revealed to its full extent.

Hakim (2000) also argues that once genuine choices are open to them, women choose between three different lifestyles: adaptive, work-centred or home-centred. These divergent preferences are found at all levels of education, and in all social classes.

Adaptive women prefer to combine employment and family work within their lives without giving a fixed priority to either. They want to enjoy the best of both worlds. Hakim has shown that adaptive women are generally the largest group among women, up to two-thirds of all women in any country, and are found in substantial numbers in most occupations. Certain occupations, such as schoolteaching, are attractive to women because they facilitate a good work-life balance. The majority of women who transfer to part-time work after they have children are adaptive women, who seek to devote as much time and effort to their family work as to their jobs. In countries and occupations where part-time jobs are rare, other types of job are chosen. For example, seasonal jobs, temporary work, or term-time jobs all offer a better work-life balance than the typical full-time job, especially if commuting is also involved.

Work-centred women are a minority, despite the massive influx of women into higher education and into higher grades of work in recent decades. Work-centred people (men and women) are focused on competitive activities in the public sphere – in careers, sport, politics, or the arts. Family life is fitted around their work, and many of these women remain childless, even when married. Qualifications and training are obtained as a career investment rather than as an insurance policy, as with the adaptive group. Hakim has shown that about half of men are work-centred, compared to around one-fifth of women. Preference theory predicts that men will retain their dominance in the labour market, politics and other competitive activities, because only a minority of women are prepared to prioritise their jobs (or other activities in the public sphere) in the same way as men. This has made the theory unpopular among feminists, who believe that women are just as likely as men to be work-centred once opportunities are opened to them, and that sex discrimination alone holds women back from the top jobs in any society.

The third group, *home-centred women*, is also a minority (about one-fifth), and a relatively invisible one, given media focus on working women and high achievers. Home-centred women prefer to give priority to home and family life after they marry. They are most inclined to have larger families, and these women prefer to avoid paid work after marriage except in times of financial stress. They do not necessarily invest less in qualifications, because the educational system functions as a marriage market as well as a training institution, and the likelihood of marrying a graduate is hugely increased if the woman herself has a university education (Hakim, 2000: 193–222). However, home-centred women are less likely to choose vocational courses with a direct economic value (such as accountancy or law), and are more likely to take courses in the arts, humanities or languages, which provide cultural capital but have lower earnings potential.

The three lifestyle preference groups are not merely qualitatively different. They constitute interest groups that sometimes bring women into conflict with each other – for example, on whether public childcare services are necessary or not, whether positive discrimination in favour of women for promotion to top jobs is a good thing or not. In the USA, for example, the conflict between work-centred and home-centred women has been expressed through the two women's movements: the feminist 'women's liberation' movement and the maternalist movement, with conflict often focused on the issues of abortion and the proposed Equal Rights Amendment.

Hakim argues that social scientists and the EC are wrong to expect convergence in women's workrates and attitudes in modern societies. Women's heterogeneity will be enhanced by women's differential response to social policies affecting women. She points out that institutions, laws, customs, national policies and cultural constraints continue to shape and structure behaviour. Choices are not made in a vacuum. Social and economic factors still matter, and will produce national variations in employment patterns and lifestyle choices. So there will always be differences between countries in women's patterns of employment, and scope for change as the social and economic context alters. The fact that almost half of men are adaptive (rather than work-centred) also offers scope for substantial change in work-life balance among men as well as women.

Preference theory states that in prosperous modern societies, preferences become a much more important determinant, sometimes even the primary determinant of women's employment patterns. Lifestyle preferences do not predict outcomes with complete certainty, even when women have genuine choices, partly because of variations in individual abilities, chance events in individual lives, and variations in the social and economic environment. However, Hakim claims that lifestyle preferences broadly determine women's fertility (both childlessness and, for the majority who do have children, family sizes); women's employment pattern over the life cycle (choices between careers and jobs, full-time and part-time work, and associated job values); and women's differential responsiveness to family policy, other social policies, employer policies, economic and social circumstances.

These claims are supported to some degree by her own tests of preference theory using two national surveys carried out in Britain and Spain (Hakim, 2002; 2003a, b, c; 2004). For example, she has shown that lifestyle preferences determine *which* social and economic contextual factors women respond to: childcare responsibilities affect the employment decisions of home-centred and adaptive women, but not the behaviour of work-centred women, who have aspirational motivations.

Some scholars regard preference theory as an extension of rational choice theory, but preference theory was developed in a quite different manner. Rational choice theory was developed by top-down theorising from first principles, using deductive logic. Preference theory was developed bottom-up, as grounded theory (Glaser and Strauss, 1967), based on a wide-ranging review of the research evidence on women's choices and preferences after the contraceptive revolution and the equal opportunities revolution, using inductive logic. It is also historically situated, unlike rational choice theory, and specifies the particular social and economic changes that are required to give women genuine choices for the first time in history. In a sense, preference theory explains what happens *after* patriarchy ceases to be the dominant factor in women's lives. The other important difference is that preference theory identifies no less than *three* qualitatively different 'rational' solutions to the career-family conflict, whereas rational choice theory assumes one optimal solution.

Other scholars regard preference theory as having an affinity with Goldberg's socio-biological explanations for women's lesser achievements in public life, because of the emphasis on the work-family conflict. However, Hakim rejects evolutionary theory in favour of chaos theory as a model (Hakim, 2000: 26, 40–41, 189, 198, 222, 287; 2003a: 239–40). She points out that the new pattern of about 20% of women remaining voluntarily childless disproves the notion of there being a biological imperative for women to have children and raise them. Preference theory focuses on the different value systems of home-centred, adaptive and work-centred people, and it is in practice a unisex theory, arguing that the only cleavages that will matter within the workforce of the 21st century will be the continuing differences between primary and secondary earners and the widening differences between lifestyle preference groups (Hakim, 2003a: 261). Home-centred (or family-centred) people have what can be loosely called 'family values' that emphasise the sharing, caring and non-competitive values of private life. Work-centred people have marketplace values, with an emphasis on competitive rivalry, achievement orientation and individualism rather than collectivism (Hakim, 2003a: 259–60). These are similar to the two value systems of masculinity (instrumentality and goal directness) and femininity (affectivity, expressiveness, supportiveness) identified by Talcott Parsons and, as he recognised long ago, they are often incompatible, and potentially in conflict (Parsons and Bales, 1955). Hakim argues that Parsons' mistake was in assuming these were essentially and intrinsically male and female value systems, rather than characteristics of particular social settings and activities in them (Hakim, 2003a: 264).

Preference theory is an example of person-centred analysis: it recognises the heterogeneity of individuals and their responses to the social and economic context; and it takes account of extreme cases, which can amount to 20% of cases at either end of a distribution (Magnusson and Bergman, 1988; Cairns *et al*, 1998; Magnusson, 1998; Hakim, 2003a: 139–40).

Feminist debates

The four theories provide different explanations for sex differences in employment patterns and earnings in the past, and different predictions on whether these differences might eventually disappear in the future. These are two of the central questions addressed by the research reviewed in later chapters. The feminist position on these questions has been that sex discrimination is the primary reason, perhaps even the sole reason, for differences between men and women in the labour market. There are no 'natural' differences between men and women; all such differences are socially created, hence artificial, and would vanish in a society with equality between men and women. The feminist position has been adopted by the EC as a basis for policy-making, leading it to expect, even demand, symmetrical roles in the workforce and the family for men and women in the EU.

One consequence, unfortunately, is that political correctness now impedes rigorous research on the extent of any sex differences in social attitudes and behaviour, and whether they are shrinking or not. The distortion of scientific research by political advocacy, and political correctness, is illustrated by two recent debates, in the USA and Britain.

In March 1995, *American Psychologist* carried a debate between Eagly and others on the feminist and political constraints on research that seeks to establish which sex differences in personality, ability and social behaviour are vanishing, and which are still important. Eagly pointed out that some social scientists argue that research comparing men and women should be discouraged, in case the results support stereotypes. Her own synthesis of recent research concluded, however, that there was no sign of sex differences in social behaviour and personality eroding over time. Quoting Swim (1994), she also noted that stereotypes of male and female personality and behaviour are, in practice, well-informed: they correspond closely to research findings, and tend to *under*estimate rather than overestimate sex differences. Eagly's article was followed by comments from Hyde, Plant and Marecek, who challenged her conclusion that feminism created a political climate that led researchers to minimise psychological gender differences; they then proceeded to reiterate that sex differences are tiny, unimportant, or socially constructed. Another comment by Buss offered an explanation for stable psychological sex differences in domains connected to sexuality and mate selection, but not in other domains.

A similar debate appeared in the September 1995 and March 1996 issues of the *British Journal of Sociology*. An article on 'Five feminist myths about women's employment' by Hakim (1995a) prompted responses by no less than 11 sociologists and economists (Ginn et al, 1996) to which Hakim (1996b) responded in turn. Here again, the issue was how feminist ideology distorted research reporting, so that incorrect conclusions about the disappearance of sex differences in work orientations and employment patterns were widely disseminated, and repeated, to become received wisdom. Hakim noted that studies of women often shaded into advocacy research, demanding a better deal for women, rather than normal social scientific studies, and she worried that this could diminish the public status of sociology. She also argued that it was pointless ignoring substantial sex differences in the workforce, because employers would still be aware of them, and act on them. This debate was later extended in articles by Crompton and Harris (1998) and McRae (2003), with further responses by Hakim (1998b; 2003b).

In summary, the question of whether there are any important differences in the personalities, work attitudes, and workforce behaviour of men and women excites vigorous debate. This debate is frequently framed in political and feminist contexts.

A cross-national comparative review

In the following chapters we assess the usefulness of the four theories in accounting for the empirical evidence on developments in female employment in modern societies in recent decades. Just as methodological triangulation produces more reliable research results than studies based on a single method, theoretical triangulation gives us a firmer grasp of the influences on women's choices and changes in behaviour (Sayer, 1984: 219–28; Hakim, 1987a: 144–45). The four theories are complementary rather than mutually exclusive choices in a zero-sum game. They identify areas where change is unlikely, such as vertical job segregation, and areas where change is most possible, such as the precise nature of the sexual division of labour. They point to women's failure to organise collectively as problematic. Taken together, they warn us against automatically equating differences between men and women with inequality or subordination, and against automatically labelling different outcomes as reflecting sex discrimination. In a civilised society, differences are valued rather than just tolerated. Social equality does not require clone-like similarities across all actors and social groups. Our review of the research evidence on women's work in the following chapters draws on reports from a wide range of countries in addition to Europe and North America. Inevitably, there is a particular focus on the USA and Britain, simply because there is the greatest volume of research evidence for these countries. However, there are also some advantages to this emphasis.

Britain and the USA are both liberal societies, *laissez-faire* economies, and relatively unregulated labour markets, which provide the least restrictive environments for the emergence of new social patterns and innovations in the organisation of employment, and family life. Despite their differences, the two countries are often classified together in typologies of welfare state systems, gender regimes or labour market regimes as the 'liberal' model (Esping-Andersen, 1990; Bosch et al, 1994; Mósesdóttir, 1995; Hakim, 1996a: 17–18; Sainsbury, 1996: 9–32; Blanpain and Rojot, 1997: 10–12; Cousins, 1998). But they can equally well be described as having social, fiscal and labour policies that are chaotic, confused and contradictory when compared with hegemonic modern societies. In contrast, many

European societies impose more coherent, consistent and unidirectional social, fiscal and labour market policies based on well-defined models of family life, sex-roles and the standard job, thus creating an environment in which spontaneous change and innovation are less likely.

It is no accident that the pattern of weekly working hours in Britain is completely different from the pattern of working hours in all other EU countries: both for men and women there is a fairly flat distribution across all hours, whereas people typically work standard full-time hours in other EU countries (Hakim, 1997: 26–29; 1998a: 106–09), and any deviation from convention provokes strong reactions (Hörning et al, 1995). Similarly, there is relatively greater acceptance of 'eccentric' behaviour and cultural differences in private and family lifestyles, and often in public behaviour, especially in the big cities of the USA and Britain. The multi-cultural, multi-ethnic, 'melting pot' character of the USA is well-known, but Britain also has always been a multi-cultural and multi-ethnic society, with the same advantages of a higher potential for social innovation and change. Theory attempts to formulate what happens, *all other things being equal*. One approximation to this condition is to study societies and situations where there are no major constraints limiting choice or forcing choice in particular directions. The USA and Britain thus provide theoretically important social contexts for the study of women's involvement in paid and unpaid work, and the values that inform their choices.

The relatively unregulated labour markets of the USA and Britain are immensely valuable for *research purposes*, even though they are often decried by trade unionists. To the astonishment of most Europeans there were no laws in Britain specifying annual holiday entitlement, maximum daily hours of work or part-time work hours, until the EC insisted there should be such rules for all EU Member States. Even today, neither a carpenter nor a hairdresser requires qualifications or a license before starting work. With their heavy reliance on statute law, European labour markets can seem over-regulated to British and American eyes. Britain appears to be a case of unregulated chaos and anarchy in the eyes of the EC. In reality, common law, collective bargaining, custom and practice combine to produce much the same regulation of the labour market as statute law achieves in other European countries (Hepple and Hakim, 1997), but on a much more flexible basis than with statute law – as illustrated by the decades required to delete sexist laws in countries which introduced them during the Great Depression. Change and development can happen more easily in the USA and Britain, unconstrained by regulations that impede innovation, whether good or bad. These two countries can almost be regarded as a kind of ongoing natural experiment. One example is the early development of part-time jobs, which could not be created in the Netherlands, for example, until the law was changed to allow this innovation. The advantage to the Netherlands was that they then designed and shaped the direction of policy on part-time work very carefully indeed (European Commission, 1994: 117; Visser and Hemerijck, 1997), whereas policy in Britain has been piecemeal, often reacting to developments rather than shaping them. In the USA, individual States develop innovative social and employment policies which, if the experiment proves successful, then become the model for federal policy.

Both Britain and the USA are also multi-cultural and multi-ethnic societies. Although formally Christian, Britain is one of the most secular societies in Europe and has substantial communities of Jews, Moslems, Buddhists, Hindus, Jains, Sikhs, Ismailis, Rastafarians and Shintoists. The full diversity of cultures and communities is illustrated by the fact that in London one can sample the cuisines of almost every country in the world in some 1,400 restaurants with a distinctively non-English character. Over 300 languages are spoken in London (Baker and Eversley, 2000). Britain retains richly diverse regional and social class cultures that confuse and mystify newcomers (Mikes, 1966) as well as a large Asian community and a black community with distinctive roots in the Indian subcontinent and the West Indies. It is indicative that for the 1991 and 2001 UK Population Censuses the self-completion forms for private households were printed and issued in no fewer than 12 languages in addition to English and Welsh: Arabic, Bengali, Chinese, Greek, Gujerati, Hindi, Italian, Punjabi, Somali, Turkish, Urdu, and Vietnamese. Few countries can match this public demonstration of recognition and acceptance of ethnic minority groups. This cultural diversity makes Britain interesting to study, but it also leads us to expect diversity and difference in choices rather than homogeneity in preferences and responses to social and economic change. There is no such thing as a representative Englishman or woman, or family, and no single set of norms to which everyone conforms. Similarly, New York illustrates the enormous ethnic diversity of a country founded almost entirely on immigrants from elsewhere. The 2000 Census showed the New York population to consist of 25% blacks, 27% Latinos, 35% non-Hispanic whites, and 10% Asians and Pacific Islanders. One in seven people are recent immigrants. There are substantial immigrant communities from Japan, China (including Hong Kong), Taiwan, India, Mexico, Puerto Rico, Dominica, Ireland, Poland, Russia and Greece, among others.

In summary, the two melting pots of the USA and Britain provide a picture of the modern world in microcosm, and illustrate the diversity of perspectives on women's roles, and women's labour force participation more succinctly than many cross-national comparative studies. Such large and culturally diverse societies provide far more reliable information on social behaviour, values, and responses to public policy than the small Scandinavian societies, which are often held up as models for women, yet are too homogeneous in race, religion, culture, and even political opinion, to provide lessons for other countries.

Chapter 2
Marginal Employment, Voluntary Work, Unpaid Household Work

In all industrialised societies, except for the Scandinavian countries, fewer women than men participate in the labour market. It is widely believed that women's employment has been increasing throughout the 20th century, especially in recent decades, so that this difference in participation rates may soon be eliminated. Chapter 3 examines this idea in some detail. An alternative thesis, addressed in this chapter, is that national statistics are faulty and ideologically biased: women's work has been systematically undervalued and undercounted, giving the false impression that workrates are now higher than in the recent past. Women have always worked, it is argued, often longer hours than men. Due to the undervaluation of women's work, national statistics provide an incomplete picture of women's full contribution to the economy and of their role in society.

This idea occurs repeatedly in historical research, with historians and sociologists claiming that the true volume of female employment was higher, in their case study areas and industries, than was shown in contemporary population census statistics (Roberts, 1984: 230; Bose, 1987: 96–97, 103–07, 115; 2001: 22–54; Higgs, 1987; Nyberg, 1994; Horrell and Humphries, 1995: 95). The thesis became a central feature of discussions of women's role in the development process, on the need for more comprehensive statistical information on household production, as well as work in the market economy, in order to monitor the changing location of productive work and its impact on women as well as men (Boserup, 1970: 160–67; Benería, 1981; Benería and Sen, 1981; Redclift, 1985). The thesis was also a feature of the domestic labour debate in the 1970s, a lengthy exploration of the social and economic significance and value of women's domestic labour in capitalist society (Fine, 1992: 169–91), a debate that was restricted to theoretical analysis and speculation by the limited empirical data on domestic work, apart from case studies (Oakley, 1974, 1985). Restricted may be the wrong word here; theoretical speculation is often freer and wilder when it is not informed by reality.

A seminal article by Benería (1981, 1988) provides the most detailed and persuasive presentation of the thesis. Unlike many others, Benería is fully cognisant of the economic conceptual framework underlying labour market statistics, the practical difficulties involved in operationalising new conceptual frameworks, and the continuous efforts of bodies like the International Labour Office (ILO) to improve labour force statistics. Her informed discussion concludes that censuses and surveys should be redesigned to collect information on all productive labour, for two reasons: first, to counteract the ideological undervaluation of women's work and to give recognition to the long hours of labour in which women are engaged; and secondly, to inform development strategies and programmes in the Third World (Benería, 1981, 1988: 384–85, 388–89). Waring (1988) offers a more passionate and extensive presentation of the thesis, incorporating a critique of economic concepts and theory, of statisticians' practices, and of the United Nations System of National Accounts (SNA) which institutionalises all these errors and imposes them, imperialistically, on developing countries.

In this chapter we assess this thesis in the light of the available empirical evidence. The focus is limited to modern industrialised countries, so we do not address the issues relating to the development process. There are two logically separate elements in the thesis, which are often conflated in debates. First, we address the thesis that women's paid work in the *market economy* is under-counted, due to under-reporting and relative invisibility. Secondly, we address the thesis that women's unpaid *non-market work* is undervalued and hence not counted. For completeness, we also look at voluntary work, a type of work that falls between unpaid household work and paid work, and is institutionalised in industrial society.

There is no suggestion that national censuses and surveys undercount women's full-time year-round employment. All the debates focus on what we can broadly describe as women's marginal work, work that is relatively less visible, or more difficult to count because it is part-time, seasonal, irregular or combined with domestic work – types of work that differ from the standard male profile of full-time year-round gainful work. Because of this, we first need a clear understanding of definitions of work, and the practical rules applied at the boundary line to separate work and non-work. The next section reviews the basic conceptual framework on which national labour statistics rest, and which is so often the source of misunderstandings and confusion. Following this, we examine the available evidence on *marginal paid work*: first, general studies of marginal work, then data on types of marginal work that are most likely to be hidden, invisible and under-counted, such as family helpers, home-based work and the informal economy. Voluntary work is treated as a separate category, as it is highly public and visible, yet always excluded from labour force statistics. We then examine the evidence on *unpaid household work*: domestic work, reproductive and other caring work. Finally, research on the social status of the housewife, treated as an occupation like any other, sheds new light on the whole debate. We show that, overall, any undercount in modern societies is small. More important, marginal employment and household work are not exclusive to women; the sex differential is smaller than feminists claim. Overall, when all forms of work are added together, men and women do equal amounts, on average.

It is worth noting that the questions addressed in this chapter can be answered more easily today than 10 years ago. Female scholars' insistence that more data was needed has paid off: new research has been done, and new surveys have been created to cover unpaid work in the household. For example, on the historical front, historians have compared census employment rates for certain towns with statistics on women's work derived from local interview surveys that were concerned to identify *all* sources of household earnings, however small, including part-time and home-based work. These careful and detailed comparisons, for different towns, reveal that census statistics may have *over*counted women's employment, by including wives who no longer exercised their profession. Thus, Hatton and Bailey (2001: 87) conclude that the under-enumeration of women's work in the early 20th century is a myth. Another study by Horrell and Humphries (1995) also employs a newly assembled household survey dataset, this time for the pre-census period 1790–1865. They conclude that wives' employment rates genuinely did decline in the 19th century, due to mounting institutional and ideological obstacles to women working. However, the decline in workrates was neither continuous nor uniform across occupations and industries, which explains the discrepant findings from studies of particular trades and areas. Overall, wives became increasingly financially dependent on their husbands, as the census statistics record (Hakim, 1980). Thus, the thesis that wives' home-based paid work is undercounted in the early censuses seems to be plausible, but not validated. The thesis that women's unpaid work in the household is undercounted in the 21st century can also be answered with new time budget survey data.

Work and employment: the conceptual framework

Labour market statistics are collected within the theoretical framework of economics. Sociologists have never even tried to produce an alternative framework, the closest being the idea of national social and economic indicator systems that were developed in the 1960s and 1970s. More specifically, the concept of economic activity is based on the SNA to ensure that employment statistics and production statistics are consistent and can be analysed jointly (Dupre *et al*, 1987; Hussmanns, 1989). Sociologists, historians, social geographers and others regularly overlook this fact; assume that 'official' statistics are shaped solely by political ideology and public administration needs; offer critiques that are wide of the mark and draw inappropriate conclusions because they have not bothered to acquaint themselves with the basic economic concepts that are operationalised in employment statistics. For example, Oakley (1974, 1985) thought it necessary to demonstrate that housework is work. Nyberg (1994: 153) suggests that statisticians collect data on any 'interesting' topic, in line with personal prejudices. In Britain, there is a long tradition of challenging the perceived political bias of national statistics produced by the state apparatus and exposing their role in maintaining cultural hegemony (Irvine *et al*, 1979).

Work is any productive activity, any activity that produces goods or services. *Employment* is any work done for pay or profit, any work producing goods or services that are traded in the market economy. The key distinction is between *market* work and *non-market* work. Economists are fully aware that domestic work and work in the subsistence economy are productive work, and ideally would like to measure the value of all types of work. Market work can be assigned a monetary value with reference to earnings or profits from traded goods or services. It is a great deal easier to collect data on market work than on the work that produces goods and services consumed immediately within the household or bartered with neighbours, for example. No theoretical distinction is made between formal and informal economic activity: casual childminding for a neighbour is market work if it is paid for, just like any commercial supply of childcare services. Informal economic activity is still market work, even if its casual nature makes it difficult or impossible to measure reliably, even if its value in GNP is too trivial for the effort and cost of data collection to be justified, so that it is allowed to slip through the net. The economic character of the conceptual framework is reflected in the modern terms 'economically active' and 'economically inactive', usually shortened to 'active' and 'inactive', in the same way as 'gainful work' and 'employment' are regularly replaced by the simpler term 'work'. The term 'inactive' is misunderstood by non-economists to mean 'idle' when it is applied to full-time housewives, but students in full-time education are also classified as 'inactive' and no-one suggests that they are idle. It is immediately obvious that some of the misunderstandings and arguments are due to sensitivity and doubts about exactly how much necessary work housewives do in industrial societies. No-one doubts the massive workloads of women in Third World countries, especially in the agricultural sector and in rural areas (Boserup, 1970; United Nations, 1995). Like all work, housework expands to fill the time available (Friedan, 1963: 233–57), and full-time housewives devote more time to housework irrespective, even at weekends, to prove how useful they are (Vanek, 1974).

Most household activities are not work but personal activities, such as eating, sleeping, personal grooming, studying, taking part in sport and leisure activities, watching TV, maintaining social relations within the family and with neighbours. These activities take up 70% of each 24 hour day, on average, for adults aged 16 and over in Britain, for example. Work of all kinds takes up the other 30% of the average 24 hour day (Short, 2000: Table 1). The substitution rule, or third person criterion, is used to distinguish between work and personal activities, between production and consumption. If an activity would lose its value (utility) if a substitute performed the task, it is not work. An activity is deemed productive if it can be performed by a third person, someone other than the one benefiting from it (Hawrylyshyn, 1977; Goldschmidt-Clermont, 1990: 280; Mogensen, 1990: 14–19; Thomas, 1992: 17). Studying is not work, because the value of it would be lost if the task was done by a substitute. Playing with one's child, gardening or cooking a special dish would all be personal activities, rather than work, if their performance by a third person would spoil the pleasure of them. Routine cleaning is more likely to be work, if the same purpose would be achieved by having a substitute do it. The dividing line between productive non-market activity and personal activities can be a fine one within the household, and can depend on personal taste. One person buys a power tool to use in household tasks (such as putting up shelves) to enjoy the exercise of skill it demands, particularly if the activity differs from their normal day job. Another person does the same thing purely to save on the labour costs of getting these tasks performed commercially. For many people, both objectives are combined, to varying degrees. Childcare can be regarded as a chore (hence work) by one woman, or as an enjoyable and creative activity by another mother. Successful professionals and entertainers can enjoy such high job satisfaction that they work long hours and prefer not to retire. Some people enjoy their work as much as leisure activities, thus clouding the difference between them. There is no simple operational definition to divide productive work from leisure activities. This provides fertile ground for sociologists to explore the theoretical problems of defining the meaning of work, employment and leisure (Pahl, 1984; 1988; Harding and Jenkins, 1989; Erikson and Vallas, 1990; Mogensen, 1990: 371–418). In the past, household work included a lot of market-oriented production work, on the family farm, or in the family business, shop or other enterprise. In industrial society, most domestic work is consumption work, with goods and services produced for immediate consumption within the household, so that productive work in the household context is less easily identified.

The two key features of any operational definition of employment are the time reference period and the hours threshold applied. At present, the most common reference period is one week, but in some surveys one year is used. Obviously, the number of people identified as being in employment is higher the longer the reference period. Questions that ask about 'usual' occupation or activity are in practice using a reference period of a year or longer. Similarly, the lower the threshold of hours worked, the higher the number of people identified as having paid work. At present, the ILO recommendation, followed in almost all European labour force surveys, is to use a minimal threshold of just one hour's work in the last week. This means that large numbers of marginal workers are counted into the workforce – if they remember to mention the one hour's gainful work in response to an interviewer's enquiry. In recent decades, and in other countries, much higher thresholds have been used – such as a minimum of 13 hours' work a week, a minimum of 15 hours in the last two weeks or, for unpaid family workers, at least a third of usual weekly hours in the job (Benería, 1981, 1988: 375; Hussmanns, 1989: xiv; ILO, 1990a, b). Surveys that collect information about 'usual' or 'main' occupation or activity are generally referring to the activity which takes up most hours in the week, thus ignoring any secondary jobs or activities. This approach generally increases the numbers of women classified as homemakers. In contrast, the one hour a week threshold for paid work classifies everyone with marginal jobs as being in the workforce, rather than inactive, following the rule that economic activity always takes precedence over inactivity.

The utility of the one hour a week minimalist definition of employment is now being questioned by statisticians, sociologists, economists and international bodies. In a chaotically unfruitful discussion of labour statistics with the House of Commons Select Committee on Employment in May 1995, two representatives of the British Royal Statistical Society (RSS), Professors Bartholomew and Moore, explained that they would campaign for changes to the ILO recommendations for national Labour Force Surveys. In particular, the RSS felt that one hour a week was too low a threshold to meaningfully classify someone as being in employment (Employment Committee, 1995: para 124). Hakim has argued that for sociological analysis, the appropriate focus is on someone's *main* activity, which locates them within the social structure, reflects and shapes their ideas and values, provides the basis for personal identity and for other people's perceptions of them and their social status. Thus, marginal workers, who work very few annual hours, due to working part-time and/or part-year, might be counted in national surveys, for monitoring purposes, but would be excluded from analyses of the employed workforce. Marginal workers would be classified by their principal activity as students or homemakers (Hakim, 1993a: 112–13). Attempts to create a consistent time series on female employment 1951–1981, especially for part-time work, led Joshi and Owen (1987) to question the value of a headcount measure, given variable coverage of women's part-time and marginal work. Following a detailed analysis of working hours across Europe, the EC concluded that people working less than 10 hours a week should be treated as a somewhat different, marginal category; that the label of part-time work should be reserved for people working 10–29 hours a week; the label full-time work being reserved for people working average weekly hours of

30 and over (European Commission, 1994: 116). This classification ensured that people working slightly reduced hours, such as the so-called 'part-time' workers in Sweden who work a six hour day and 30 hour week, would be correctly grouped with full-time workers, thus ending a long-standing misunderstanding in cross-national economic comparisons. Variation in the incidence (or reporting) of marginal work had distorted international comparisons, it was found (European Commission, 1994: 116–18). In sum, the one hour a week minimum limit to define a worker is questioned on economic, sociological and statistical grounds.

As most censuses (and some labour force surveys) are carried out in the spring, harvest work and other seasonal jobs are not covered at all. This does not mean there is an undercount. Since the primary aim of these data collections is to monitor trends over time, this does not matter: by comparing the size of the workforce in spring each year, you are comparing like with like, and any upward or downward trend is reliable. Obviously, a spring census tells you nothing about the numbers of people doing harvest work; a separate survey would be needed for that. For this reason *continuous surveys*, with interviews carried out throughout the year, are becoming popular, as they can yield averages across the year, or data for particular quarters of the year (Hakim, 1987a: 77–81). Most national labour force surveys and multi-purpose household surveys are now continuous surveys. In the long term, there is increasing interest in the year instead of the week as the reference point for data on employment and working time, as well as in data on lifelong working hours (Bosch *et al*, 1994: 5–15), and alternative measures to the conventional economic activity rate are often proposed (Hakim, 1993a: 108–14). But even in the USA, where annual work profiles have been collected for many decades, the data are rarely used except to show the discrepancy between single-time and year-round employment profiles (Mellor and Parks, 1988; Clogg *et al*, 1990; see also Table 3.6).

These definitions, and the economic conceptual framework, have been developed over more than a century. Early population censuses applied a quite different *social* classification of main activity which included full-time domestic work and full-time studying alongside gainful work. In Britain, for example, full-time unpaid domestic work was listed as an occupation in the census classification up to 1871; however, 42% of women were counted as having another occupation in the relevant professional, commercial, agricultural or industrial class up to 1871 (Hakim, 1980: 556–57; Hakim, 1993a: 98–101). The classification of family workers varied between censuses, but they were generally included as gainfully occupied. By 1911, wives engaged full-time and exclusively in domestic work were classified as outside the workforce. These and other changes reflected the move away from the 19th century concern with documenting and understanding the changing social structure towards the 20th century focus on the cash economy and market work (Hakim, 1980: 571). The focus on the market economy emerged earlier in the USA census (Davies, 1980: 594).

The relatively unregulated British labour market allows many forms of marginal work to emerge and flourish, then disappear, in line with the economic cycle, to a far greater extent than is possible in the heavily regulated labour markets of other

European countries, such as Germany. Studies of the informal economy, the black economy and clandestine employment regularly find that there is less of it in Britain than, say, Italy, because the relative absence of regulation allows marginal employment to come and go in the formal economy, instead of pushing it into the shadows (De Grazia, 1980; 1984). In some EU countries part-time work and temporary jobs were not legal options until the law was changed, prompting a massive increase (Hakim, 1990a, b). Thus, the national regulation of employment contracts can alter the relative importance of the different types of work.

Time budget surveys are a new alternative to labour force surveys for measuring all forms of work and activity, not just employment. Time budget surveys ask people to record their activities every hour (or every quarter-hour) of the day, for one day or one week, using a time diary. Early time budget surveys were conducted by the BBC in Britain, to monitor how much time people spent watching television, at which times of the day. Szalai (1972) organised the first 12-nation comparative time use survey in the 1960s. Time budget surveys are now used to study occupations with non-standard work hours, consumer behaviour, urban planning issues, the household division of labour and household production of services, *inter alia* (Andorka, 1987; Gershuny and Sullivan, 1998; Williams, 2004). The 1993 SNA continued to exclude unpaid production of services in the household from the accounts, but it recommended the use of Satellite Accounts to cover such activity, as a complement to traditional economic accounts. In the 1990s, Eurostat (the statistical office of the EC) developed proposals for a Satellite Account of household production which relies on time budget survey data on unpaid, non-market work done in households. The first round of the Harmonised European Time Use Surveys was carried out in 2000 in over 20 countries. Australia and Canada have also been running a series of time budget surveys from 1971 onwards. These and all other extant national surveys are collected together in the Multinational Time Budget Archive (MTBA) initiated by Gershuny at the University of Essex in Britain. The Multinational Time Use Study (MTUS) is producing harmonised datasets and documentation, to facilitate comparative research (Gershuny, 2000: 270–88; see also MTUS website www.iser.essex.ac.uk/mtus). This new type of data, and new field of research, is already greatly enhancing our knowledge of household production, and how paid and unpaid work are shared within households. In the meantime, we have a series of comparative and historical analyses by Gershuny (1983a, b; 1988; 1992; 1993; 2000), and occasional survey reports on couples' division of labour and time management (Young and Willmott, 1973; Hochschild, 1990; Gershuny et al, 1994; Moen, 2003). In addition, there are early reports from the new series of comparative European Time Use Surveys (Murgatroyd and Neuburger, 1997; Short, 2000; Holloway et al, 2002; ONS, 2003a; Williams, 2004).

Marginal market work

There is no doubt that women's market work is undercounted, to some extent. However, the size of the undercount is small; the volume of excluded work, measured in hours or earnings, is tiny; and the main reason for the undercount is the unwillingness of women themselves, or their husbands, to report small amounts of gainful work, since it does not constitute their *main* activity and social identity. The problem has been exaggerated by social scientists who did not have the skills to measure its impact, which is small.

It is well known that particular national surveys exclude people with small earnings, due to the way the data are collected. In Britain for example, the New Earnings Survey (NES) only collects earnings data for people who pay income tax, thus excluding people with earnings below the tax threshold. As part-time work has expanded, the number of people thus excluded has increased since the NES was initiated in 1968. By April 1992, there were 2.75 million women employees in Britain with earnings below the level where income tax becomes payable; of these, 2.25 million earned less than the lower threshold at which social insurance taxes (termed National Insurance contributions in Britain) became payable. Independent estimates from the Family Expenditure Survey (FES) showed about 75% of these women were married women; 20% were single women and 5% were lone parents. In spring 1994, it was estimated that one-fifth of all part-timers were excluded from the NES due to the tax threshold. Various other estimates have been produced from these two sources at different times, most of them too broad-brush to give a picture of numbers, trends and whether more women than men are excluded from the surveys. The most detailed and reliable estimates so far available are provided by Hakim (1989b), based on special analyses of FES merged data for 1985 and 1986 (Tables 2.1 and 2.2); earnings and tax allowances were also uprated to provide estimates for the 1987/88 tax year (Table 2.3).

Women constitute the great majority of people with small earnings, and this is due almost invariably to working part-time hours rather than to small hourly earnings in full-time jobs. Unexpectedly, the results also show that about one-quarter of people with small earnings are self-employed rather than employees, many of them full-time workers (Table 2.3). The self-employed are a small minority of the workforce but, contrary to stereotype, they have a disproportionate share of low earners (Tables 2.1 and 2.3).

Table 2.1 People with earnings below the National Insurance (and tax) thresholds, Great Britain, 1985–86

	The proportion (%) of workers in each category with earnings below the thresholds		
	Employees	**Self-employed**	**Total**
Full-time workers	0.3	6.8	1.0
Part-time workers	24.1	52.3	26.3
All in employment	6.4	16.1	7.3
Men	1.7	6.5	2.3
Women	12.1	48.8	14.0
All in employment	6.4	16.1	7.3

Source: Family Expenditure Survey merged data for 1985 and 1986. See notes at Table 2.2.

Table 2.2 Characteristics of people with earnings below the National Insurance (and tax) thresholds, Great Britain, 1985–86

	Employees	Self-employed	Total
Men	11	7	18
Women	67	15	82
All in employment	79	21	100
Full-time workers	3	7	10
Part-time workers	76	14	90
All in employment	79	21	100
Aged under 19 years	9	1	9
19–24 years	4	1	5
25–59 years	66	20	86
60 and over	*	*	*
All in employment	79	21	100

* Less than 0.5%.

Source: Family Expenditure Survey merged data for 1985 and 1986. Data for persons aged 16 or more with gross earnings below the lower personal tax threshold (£42.50 per week for 1985 and £45 per week for 1986) and with zero National Insurance contributions ($N = 1146$). Information on usual earnings was used for employees, and information on earnings as reported for people who are self-employed in their main job. But note that part-time self-employed people with tiny earnings (less than £5.00 per week in 1985 and 1986) and with no other employment are classified as unoccupied rather than as self-employed from 1982 onwards in the FES, and are hence excluded from this table. Part-time work is defined as normally occupying 30 hours a week or less including overtime regularly worked.

Some people have other tax deductions in addition to the basic 'personal allowance' tax deduction which is treated as the income tax threshold. So the total numbers not paying any income tax at all are slightly larger than those below the basic tax threshold: 3 million rather than 2.9 million (Table 2.3). It is notable that about half of all part-time workers, both employees and self-employed, pay no income tax at all and would pay only a tiny amount of social insurance taxes. This is consistent with the repeated research finding that many wives, whose earnings are supplementary to their husband's earnings, intentionally keep their earnings below the taxable level. The easiest way of doing this is to work less than full-time hours, or to vary the hours worked so that annual earnings remain tax-free. Comparing these results for 1987/88 with the more recent data quoted earlier for 1992 shows that there was an increase of about 0.4 million women with earnings below the tax threshold over this four year period.

The FES is a continuous survey that goes to some trouble to obtain comprehensive income and expenditure data for households, which is why the FES data on workers with small earnings is more complete than in most other surveys (Hakim, 1982a: 108–14). Consistent results were also obtained from a special survey, the 1980 Women and Employment Survey (WES), which went to great lengths to identify all types of paid work done by women, including the relatively invisible

Table 2.3 National estimates for workers who earn less than the National Insurance and/or income tax thresholds

	People with earnings below the 1987/88 National Insurance threshold			People earning less than 1987/88 basic tax thresholds			People who are working but are non-taxpayers			Base No (thousands)
	No (thousands)	%	% of total	No (thousands)	%	% of total	No (thousands)	%	% of total	
All working	**2,154**	**100**	**8.9**	**2,913**	**100**	**12.1**	**3,095**	**100**	**12.9**	**24,062**
Full-time employees	71	3	0.4	199	7	1.2	276	19	1.6	16,984
Part-time employees	1,598	74	34.6	2,067	71	44.7	2,084	67	45.1	4,633
Full-time self-employed	223	11	11.8	348	12	18.4	436	14	23.2	1,882
Part-time self-employed	262	12	45.6	299	10	52.1	299	10	52.1	573
All employees	1,669	77	7.7	2,266	78	10.5	2,360	76	10.9	21,617
All self-employed	485	23	19.7	647	22	26.3	735	24	29.9	2,455
All full-time	294	14	1.6	547	19	2.9	712	23	3.8	18,866
All part-time	1,860	86	35.8	2,348	81	45.4	2,383	77	45.9	5,206
All men	329	15	2.4	540	19	3.9	697	23	5.0	13,846
All women	1,825	85	17.9	2,373	81	23.2	2,398	77	23.5	10,219

Source: National estimates based on 1985 Family Expenditure Survey data for workers aged 16 to 64 years, but with earnings uprated to 1987 levels (using the average rise in earnings in the intervening period) and applying 1987/88 tax and National Insurance thresholds and tax allowances. The 1987/88 National Insurance threshold was £2,030 pa for employees and the same figure was used for the self-employed for convenience. The 1987/88 basic tax threshold was £2,425 for all persons except the minority of married men (who constituted only 38.5% of the labour force in 1987) for whom it was £3,795. Other tax allowances may be claimed in addition to the basic tax allowance (for example for mortgages), so that the number of working non-taxpayers will always be higher than the number of people with earnings below the basic tax thresholds. In this analysis, mortgage tax allowances have been attributed to husbands rather than to wives in the case of married persons. As the analysis is based on FES data, large numbers of part-time self-employed people with tiny earnings (less than £5.00 a week in 1985 and 1986) and working less than 30 hours a week are automatically excluded from the results.

jobs women do at home as childminders, mail order agents, outwork and seasonal work. The 1980 WES survey found that 14% of *non-working* women between the ages of 16 to 59 years said they did such work – that is, about one in eight women who had already said they did not have a job, and would be classified as 'inactive' on the conventional definition admitted later, in response to specific prompts, that they were doing occasional paid work of this nature (Martin and Roberts, 1984: 8–10, 31–32; see also Kay, 1984). Applying the figure of 14% to the total of 11.3 million economically inactive women aged 16 and over shows that 1.6 million women who would not report themselves as working were in practice earning small sums of money from marginal jobs. On average, these jobs involved only five hours work a week, and earnings of £4.10 a week or on average just over £200 a year in 1980, placing them far below the thresholds at which income tax and social insurance tax would be applied. Most important of all, these women were classified as non-working throughout the 1980 WES survey, rather than being reclassified as part-time workers. Pilot work confirmed that they could not meaningfully be asked the questions put to women with paid jobs. More significantly, the vast majority (90%) of these women did not think of themselves as 'working' – their work was too irregular or insignificant in its effects on their lives. Martin and Roberts concluded that marginal work was of too limited importance, both in terms of the numbers of women who do such work, and the hours of work and earnings involved, to merit further research attention, or to justify changes to the conventional classification of economic activity. If all the women doing marginal work were to be included in the workforce, this would have raised the female economic activity rate by 4 percentage points. The average of 5 hours' work a week meant that these 1.6 million women contributed the equivalent of 200,000 extra full-time workers to a 1989 workforce of 24 million in Britain, an almost negligible addition.

Similar results are obtained from other surveys. The British General Household Survey (GHS) and the British Social Attitudes Survey (BSAS) have both found it necessary to adopt a lower limit of at least 10 hours' work a week for some or all of their questions on labour market experiences, as the questions make little sense to marginal workers. Since its initiation in 1983, the BSAS has classified everyone working less than 10 hours a week as economically inactive rather than in employment. Some 15% of women classified as 'looking after the home' are marginal workers; their exclusion depresses economic activity rates for women aged 18–59 years by 4% overall (Witherspoon, 1988: 180–81). Around one-fifth of people who report themselves as part-time workers are working less than 11 hours a week (Hakim, 1998a: 125).

One advantage of the 10 hours a week minimum definition of employment is that it automatically excludes schoolchildren and students with part-time jobs from the workforce. Some students have Saturday-only jobs, which can consist of an eight hour day, while others have jobs delivering newspapers to private households, or a variety of other jobs involving a few hours a week. The proportion of students with such jobs rose sharply from one-fifth to over one-third in the 1980s (Hutson and Cheung, 1991). By 1991, students and schoolchildren aged over 16 years accounted for some 600,000 part-time jobs, 10% of the total (Naylor and

Purdie, 1992: 158). By 1994, 40% of schoolchildren aged 16–19 and 32% of higher education students aged 20–24 had a summer vacation job. Confusingly, the Labour Force Survey (LFS) count of people in employment is in fact a count of *jobs*, including jobs held by students in full-time education, who are not strictly part of the workforce. By 1997, there were 1 million students in full-time education who had a part-time job, or 15% of the 6.4 million part-time workforce in Britain. White students are more likely to have a part-time job than ethnic minority students (Hakim, 1998a: 145–77). Student jobs have a longer history in the USA, and over half of 17-year-olds have a job of some sort, normally part-time. It is estimated that two-thirds of all American students work at some time while they are in college. Organisation for Economic Co-operation and Development (OECD) studies show a continuous rise in the fraction of students with jobs of some sort, throughout modern economies, as mass education systems expand (Hakim, 1998a: 176). However, the key finding is that there is little or no sex difference in employment rates for students. Any undercount of employment applies equally to men and women.

In summary, people doing very small amounts of market work are knowingly excluded from some surveys, such as the NES, with regular estimates produced of the numbers excluded by the design of the survey. Other surveys include them, and fill the information gap. Regular surveys, like the FES and BSAS, and special surveys, like the 1980 WES, have all measured the size of the undercount and found it to be tiny in terms of the hours and earnings involved. Large numbers of people do tiny amounts of work for pay or profit, thus allowing commentators the option of claiming a large undercount on a headcount basis, but this applies equally to men and women outside the labour market. Finally, the LFS routinely identifies large numbers of people working less than 10 hours a week, in Britain and other EU countries (Watson, 1992). It appears that these are mainly employee jobs done on a *regular* basis, in contrast with the more *intermittent* nature of the jobs that do not get included in the labour force count.

International comparisons show that marginal work, defined as working for no more than 10 hours a week, is concentrated in countries with large and increasing numbers of part-time workers: the Netherlands, Denmark and the UK, with 15%, 6% and 8% of female employees respectively being marginal workers. In Germany, only 4% of female employees are marginal workers, and in all other EU Member States the percentage is under 3%. Marginal workers account for a large part of cross-national differences in rates of part-time working; when they are excluded, part-time work varies much less across Europe (European Commission, 1994: 115–18). In most industrial countries, the majority of part-time employees work half-time hours: 20–29 hours a week. However, the second most important type is the marginal job of under 10 hours a week, which is clearly a qualitatively different category (OECD, 1994: 77–86). Within Europe, Denmark has the second highest rate of part-time work among men, consisting typically of marginal jobs (OECD, 1994: 80), which explains why they have exceptionally high turnover rates (Hakim, 1996c: Table 8). The exclusion of marginal workers from labour market statistics would thus greatly improve cross-national comparisons. The Netherlands has already done this in its own national employment statistics.

The diversity of part-time work is concealed by the practice of reporting average weekly hours for each type of worker (Table 2.4). The long term decline in usual

Table 2.4 Average actual weekly hours worked 1979–1994

	1979	1983	1988	1994
Full-time employees	39	38	39	38
Part-time employees	17	16	15	16
Full-time self-employed	..	50	43	39
Part-time self-employed	..	14	14	13
Unpaid family workers	..	..	..	15
Employees: second jobs	10	9	9	9
Self-employed: second jobs	12	10	9	9

Source: Derived from Table 2 in Butcher and Hart (1995: 216) reporting LFS data for Britain, Spring 1979–1994.

work hours is not necessarily reflected in *actual* weekly hours worked, as overtime working rises and falls in line with the economic cycle. The averages give the impression that part-timers work a fairly constant 15–17 hours a week in employee jobs, 13–14 hours a week in self-employment jobs, and 8–10 hours a week in second jobs (Table 2.4). In reality, one-quarter of part-timers are marginal workers working 1–10 hours a week, while one-third work half-time hours that can approach those of full-time workers (Naylor, 1994: Table 5).

Marginal workers are an extreme example of secondary earners (as noted in Chapter 3), and their involvement in the workforce is too small, and fluctuating, to justify detailed statistics (Hakim, 1997; 1998a: 102–77). Most of them are women, purely because more women report themselves as economically inactive. However, men and women are equally likely to do marginal jobs (as is demonstrated by students) so there is no sex bias in excluding them from employment statistics.

Family workers

The thesis that women's market work is undercounted is sometimes argued on the basis of female family workers not being counted in national censuses and surveys. The most well-documented example is Nyberg's (1994) study of female family helpers on Swedish farms in the 20th century, for which there is only a brief summary in English of the full research report in Swedish. Bose (1987; 2001: 22–54) also rests her case for an undercount in USA censuses primarily on female part-time family labour on farms not being counted in the 1900 Census whereas it was counted from 1940 onwards. However, Nyberg's study is unique in providing concrete data on the hours worked by Swedish farmers' wives taken from surveys carried out at regular intervals by the Swedish farmers' association. The surveys sought to document the total volume of hours worked on Swedish farms for input-output accounts which were used to lobby the government for subsidies and other assistance to farmers. Thus, Nyberg is able to present trend data on the proportion of farmers' wives who participated in agricultural work (which varied from 50% to 95%) and on the average annual work hours they contributed, by size of farm. The work was almost invariably part-time work, typically milking, and it declined rapidly over time with mechanisation. In general, wives contributed a larger volume of work on small farms and a smaller volume of hours on large farms where mechanisation was more common and hired labour more often employed. Nyberg shows that trends in female family labour cannot be studied through census data in Sweden, due to the census practice of recording only full-time regular work in main occupations, a practice that was retained up to 1950. From 1960 onwards, part-time work in family farms and family businesses was counted, so that the labour supplied by wives and other family helpers began to be documented.

Nyberg recalculates labour force participation rates for married women including family workers and shows that the rates were as high in 1880 and 1900 as in 1980 at about 50%, but they declined to a low point of around 25% in the 1950s. The sexual division of labour which created the full-time housewife is shown to be a transitory phenomenon in Sweden. Like Bose (1987: 108), Nyberg goes on to note that survey definitions have now swung too far towards inclusiveness in Sweden, as large numbers of women are counted among the employed, even though they are at home full-time, on extended parental leave, thus giving a misleading impression of equality between men and women in economic activity rates. Nyberg goes on to claim that censuses measure above all changing values and ideologies about women's market work, rather than real changes in women's participation in the labour force (Nyberg, 1994: 153–54).

Family workers were identified as a separate employment status in British censuses up to 1971 (Hakim, 1982a: 35) although they were not always separately identified in the published statistics (Hakim, 1980: 562). As the status became increasingly rare, the information ceased to be collected in the census from 1981 onwards. Family workers are also declining in the rest of the EU, but remain important in Greece (13% of all employment in 1990), Spain, Italy and Portugal (3% to 5%), Belgium, France and Ireland (2% to 3%). Thus, information is collected in the LFS in almost all EU Member States, and comparative analyses are published periodically (Meulders et al, 1994: 130–46). From spring 1992, the British LFS also began identifying family workers as a separate category and found some 180,000 in Britain, 50,000 men and 130,000 women; 30,000 were in agriculture; 63,000 in retail distribution, hotels and catering; 24,000 were in the construction industry, where wives often take responsibility for business accounts and correspondence; and 62,000 in other industries (Chamberlain and Purdie, 1992: 487; see also Watson, 1994: 241). Average hours are very similar to those of other part-time workers and are declining (Table 2.4). In Britain, about 70% of family workers are female. The proportion varies from half in Ireland, where many are unmarried sons or daughters working in a family farm or business, to 100% in Denmark where virtually all are wives (Meulders et al, 1994). Family workers constitute a small share of women's employment: less than 10% in all EU countries in 1990, except for Greece where they reached 28%. In the USA, time use surveys from the 1920s onwards show that women in rural areas spent an average of only 10 hours a week on farm work (gardening, dairy activity and the care of poultry), making it a fairly marginal activity (Vanek, 1974). By 1981, family workers accounted for less than 1%

of total employment, down from almost 3% in 1950, and fewer than half were in agriculture. Over 70% were female, many of them doing white-collar work for a family business (Daly, 1981). By 1991, family workers were less than half of 1% of the workforce, and they were greatly outnumbered by homeworkers (Hakim, 1998a: 180–82).

When Britain returned to collecting data on family workers in 1992, the Employment Department was forced to assess how they had been classified previously in the LFS, and what difference the new classification made. Just under a quarter would have been defined as employees or self-employed before 1992 and 11% would have been classified as unemployed; a two-thirds majority would previously have been counted among the economically inactive (Butcher and Hart, 1995: 213). This proves that identifying a separate category of family workers in surveys increases the number of people (most of them women) who are counted as employed rather than out of the labour force. However, it also proves that the omission was unimportant: the addition of 120,000 previously uncounted people to a workforce of 25 million is negligibly small, a bare 0.5% (1% for women and only 0.3% for men). Family workers do not account for any significant element of female employment in modern industrial society today. This seems unlikely to be reversed, despite the resurgence of home-based work, given women's preference for jobs which give them some degree of financial independence from their spouse.

Family labour is productive market work in that the goods and services produced by the family business are traded in the cash economy. The constant emphasis on it being *unpaid*, in the sense of not wage-earning, is irrelevant. Family labour is work for profit rather than for pay, as few are paid a regular wage. However, family labour has none of the other characteristics of market work. Workers cannot be dismissed if the quality of work is poor; they cannot be made redundant; their hours are not fixed. There is none of the competitiveness or discipline of wage labour; family workers are not selling their labour in the wider labour market. Because they are not wage-earners and pay no taxes, they are excluded from virtually all social welfare benefits, such as unemployment compensation or disability benefit (Meulders *et al*, 1994: 146). In many respects they resemble voluntary workers, or homemakers working for their own family, rather than wage-earners.

Home-based work

Family work may be in terminal decline but home-based work more generally is undergoing a regeneration and renewal. The separation of home and work imposed by the industrial revolution and the creation of large manufacturing establishments is slowly being reversed as the service sector replaces manufacturing as the main field of employment. Information technology allows white-collar jobs to be done at home, or almost anywhere. The internet and telecommunications begin to replace public transport systems as a means of getting the work and the worker together.

There is extensive literature on the manufacturing homework that was the focus of public concern and legislative controls in late 19th century Britain and survived in small numbers throughout the 20th century (see, for example, Allen and Wolkowitz, 1987; Boris and Daniels, 1989). From the 1970s onwards, but particularly after the 1980s, when personal computers, notebooks and the internet revolutionised home-based work, traditional manufacturing homework was supplemented, and overtaken by white-collar homework: professional, artistic, technical and clerical work carried out as a personal or family business, or undertaken for employers on variable contractual terms. A major research programme on home-based work in Britain carried out by the Employment Department documented these developments and their social, economic and policy implications (Cragg and Dawson, 1981; Hakim and Dennis, 1982; Leighton, 1983; Huws, 1984; Kay, 1984; Hakim, 1985; 1987b; 1988b). There is much speculation about future trends, some predicting a revival of cottage industry (Applebaum, 1987; Meulders et al, 1994: 147–59) and self-employment (Hakim, 1988a; 1998a: 178–220).

The invisibility of homework is said to contribute to an undercount of women's market work. Unlike family labour, this is work done directly for pay or profit, so there is no doubt it should be reported as employment in national censuses and surveys. The main reason for under-reporting is simply that the work is often irregular, and is regarded as too casual to constitute 'a proper job' (Hakim, 1988b: 619). There is no suggestion that home-based work that is regular and full-time is under-reported.

Surveys of home-based work invariably reveal large overlaps between home-based work, self-employment, work in a family business, second jobs, part-time and intermittent work, leading to some confusion in the literature over numbers in each category. Only a detailed personal interview survey can attempt to separate out all these overlapping aspects, and this has so far been too small a labour force minority to justify more than occasional studies. Population censuses (Felstead and Jewson, 1995; Hakim, 1998a) and the LFS (Meulders et al, 1994: 147–59) simply identify everyone who does gainful work in domestic premises or uses their home as a base for work carried out elsewhere. Self-employed plumbers, consultants or salesmen, for example, may do their accounts at home, but do most of their work elsewhere. In Britain there were 2.4 million people working at home or from home as a base in 1994 (Table 2.5), about 10% of the workforce, a substantial increase on the figure of 1.7 million or 7% of the 1981 England and Wales workforce (Hakim, 1988b: 613). Of these, 1.7 million were working from home as a base, most of them men; 53,000 were family workers, all of them women; and 664,000 were homeworkers, most of them women, with clerical work the largest single occupation (Table 2.5). Virtually identical figures have been obtained each year since the questions were introduced into the LFS in 1992. In the 1991 Census, 2.6 million people reported that their work was linked to their home, about 12% of the workforce: 1.1 million homeworkers and 1.5 million people working from home as a base (Hakim, 1998a: 183). There was no sex differential in the incidence of homeworking, but men were more likely than women to work from home as a base. The stability of the figures, and the steady increase, seems to invalidate the thesis of substantial under-reporting. Despite the large numbers, homework remains marginal work for women: two-thirds work less than 16 hours a week and have short job tenures. In contrast, most men work full-time and have long job tenures (Hakim, 1988b: 615–17; 1998a). The sex differentials that characterise the main workforce are simply duplicated among homeworkers (McOrmond, 2004).

Table 2.5 People working at home in their main job by occupation and industry

	Thousands		
	All	Men	Women
Managers and administrators	152	68	84
Professionals	76	44	32
Associate professional/technical	110	51	58
Clerical and secretarial	135	*	130
Craft and related	49	19	30
Plant and machine operatives	21	*	18
Other	118	20	98
Manufacturing industries	85	20	65
Non-manufacturing industries	577	191	368
Who they work for:			
an outside organisation	124	39	85
on their own account	330	127	203
a family business	185	38	148
Employees and self-employed working in own home – subtotal	664	212	452
Unpaid family workers working in their own home	53	*	44
People doing paid work in different places with home as a base	1,678	1,359	320
All others working in own home or using home as a base – subtotal	1,731	1,368	364
Total – All home-based work	2,395	1,580	816

Source: Labour Force Survey data for Britain, Autumn 1994 not seasonally adjusted, as reported in *Employment Gazette*.
Figures below 10,000 shown as *.

The expansion of second jobs in the 1980s in Britain and the USA is linked to the growth of home-based work, stimulated by recession and the growth of sub-contracting as well as new technology (Stinson, 1990). Between 1984 and 1995, the number of second jobs grew from 0.7 million to 1.2 million in Britain, although average hours remained constant at 9 hours a week (Table 2.4), making them marginal jobs. Men and women are equally likely to have second jobs, although women began to outnumber men in the 1980s (Naylor and Purdie, 1992: Table 11).

The informal economy

Definitions of the informal economy vary from country to country, but the term usually refers to small-scale enterprises producing goods and services that may be under-represented in national statistics on the economy and the workforce, because of the small scope and informal character of the activities involved (Thomas, 1992).

In developing countries, the term refers to small street traders, for example. In industrial societies, the concept embraces all types of marginal work, small family enterprise and home-based work that might be under-recorded in national statistics. As we have already demonstrated, data can be produced on all these groups, if wanted. Thomas (1992) draws a useful distinction between the *informal economy*, which produces legal goods and services, the *irregular sector*, which involves some illegality, such as tax evasion or the avoidance of minimum wage laws, and the *criminal sector*, where the output itself is illegal, such as the manufacture and sale of drugs. Others group all three types of activity together under the label of 'clandestine', 'secondary', 'hidden', 'black', 'informal', 'underground', 'parallel' or 'twilight' economy, meaning all economic activity that goes unrecorded in national accounts statistics (De Grazia, 1980; 1984).

There has been increased interest in the informal economy in recent years. In developing countries the informal sector is argued to be the engine of economic growth, which should be assisted, even if regulations are sometimes ignored. In industrial society, there is concern that if the picture presented by national economic statistics is seriously incomplete, attempts to manage the economy may have unintended consequences. Italy is invariably taken as the prime example in Europe of an economy with a large and growing informal sector with substantial evasion of tax and labour laws (De Grazia, 1984). In the relatively unregulated British labour market there are fewer laws for small enterprises to avoid (Hepple and Hakim, 1997). Employment contracts that would be classified as illegal in other EU countries can be perfectly legal in Britain. In a sense, Britain lacks a substantial irregular sector because it lacks the body of restrictive legislation that stimulates and defines it. For example, a homeworker whose earnings over the year remain below the basic personal tax-free allowance has no need to 'declare' or 'register' her activities, and no need to pay any income tax. Too often it is assumed that any 'unreported' work is necessarily unlawful, or that any marginal work or second job automatically involves substantial tax evasion, as did Pahl (1984: 247) in his survey of informal household work (Hakim, 1989b: 484–85) and as do many other sociologists (Harding and Jenkins, 1989). There seem to be more incorrect assumptions, and more unscientific research reports, on the informal or 'black' economy than on any other aspect of the labour market (Hakim, 1989b: 483–94).

As demonstrated earlier (Tables 2.1–2.3), there are large numbers of marginal workers in Britain, most of them women, whose short and irregular work hours and small earnings leave them outside the income tax and social insurance systems. All of these people can be labelled as working in the informal economy. All could be suspected of tax evasion and hence incorrectly labelled as being in the black economy (Hakim, 1989b). Adding together the 2 million workers with earnings low enough to leave them outside the tax and social security net (Table 2.3) who are excluded from some surveys but included in others and the 1.6 million non-working women with small earnings from occasional jobs gives a total of some 3.6 million people whose earnings are small enough to classify them as marginal workers, invisible to the income tax and social welfare systems. Making some allowance for non-employed men with similarly small earnings (such as students with part-time jobs) brings the total to over 4 million marginal workers who could be classified in the informal economy. Clearly there are huge numbers of *people* doing small amounts of paid work who may not appear in the LFS, or in other national surveys which do not have any special questions probing about marginal activities. However, the number of *hours worked* are too trivial to make a great difference to conventional measures of the size of the labour force and the *earnings* involved are too small to dramatically alter their financial dependence on others, or to seriously affect economic statistics.

A 1981 study that set out to display the size and importance of the informal economy in Britain in fact proved its insignificance. Informal work was defined very broadly as any work that had ever been done for the household by friends, relatives or neighbours, whether on the basis of reciprocal exchange or payment. Even on this definition, half of all households had *never* used this source of labour for any household task (including periodic tasks like car maintenance, house maintenance and repairs, decorating, gardening and window-cleaning) and another third had only used it once. Only 16% of all households had ever used informal labour sources (paid or unpaid) on two or more occasions, compared to one-third using commercial firms for the same household tasks (Pahl, 1984: 237–41). Virtually all household tasks are done by members of the household themselves, normally, which is hardly surprising.

Thomas (1992) reviews the methods used to measure the size of household production, the informal economy, the irregular sector, and the criminal sector, and summarises available research results. On the informal economy, much of the research he reviews concerns less developed countries in Latin America, Africa and Asia. In most developing countries, unemployment is a luxury that few can afford. People who lose a job in the formal economy resort to informal economic activities, typically self-employed. The informal sector is thus generally larger, more important economically, and more intensively researched. In Pakistan and Peru, there are even micro-banks that specialise in micro-loans to informal sector traders, some of whom are illiterate. In developing countries, the informal sector employs between 20% and 73% of the working population, so it can dominate the economy. In Europe, economic indicators suggest that the Italian informal sector forms a substantial part of the economy, but there are no estimates of participation rates. Italy seems to be a special case within Europe, and much of the activity seems to be full-time employment involving tax evasion etc, rather than small-scale, casual activity, as in Britain. In Europe, new immigrants, and illegal immigrants, are understood to be major participants in the informal economy, but again there are few figures (Thomas, 1992: 173–201). However, there is no suggestion that women are under-represented, nor that women's informal work is more likely to be under-reported than men's activities. Patterns of employment in the informal sector seem to mirror patterns of formal employment.

Seasonal and temporary work

The final category of marginal work is seasonal, casual and other temporary jobs. These jobs usually involve full-time work, in contrast with the short part-time hours involved in homework, family work and most other forms of marginal work. The argument is that they are undercounted because they are not year-round jobs, because they are short-term and intermittent, as illustrated by seasonal work in

Table 2.6 Trends in non-standard employment in Britain 1981–1993

		Thousands and percent		
		All	**Men**	**Women**
1981	Employed workforce	23,606	14,093	9,512
	Full-time regular employees	16,639	11,581	5,058
	as % of employed workforce	70%	82%	53%
	All other workers	6,967	2,512	4,454
	as % of employed workforce	30%	18%	47%
1987	Employed workforce	24,257	13,958	10,299
	Full-time permanent employees	15,560	10,616	4,944
	as % of employed workforce	64%	76%	48%
	All other workers	8,697	3,342	5,355
	as % of employed workforce	36%	24%	52%
1993	Employed workforce	25,381	13,934	11,446
	Full-time permanent employees	15,685	10,204	5,480
	as % of employed workforce	62%	73%	48%
	All other workers	9,693	3,729	5,964
	as % of employed workforce	38%	27%	52%

Sources: LFS data for Britain, Spring 1981 and 1987, reported in Hakim (1990: 165) Table 1 and Spring 1993 LFS for the UK, reported in Watson (1994: 240) Table 1.

harvesting or in summer holiday resorts. The argument seemed plausible before the advent of continuous year-round surveys such as the GHS and the LFS (Hakim, 1987a: 80–81). However, the continuous surveys do not yield significantly higher measures of female employment than the time-specific measures from the spring census and the LFS.

Women are more likely than men to take seasonal, temporary and casual jobs: from 1984 to 1994 about 4% to 6% of female employees had short-term jobs compared to 2% to 3% of male employees (Beatson, 1995: 10). Men and women had similar rates for fixed-term contract jobs, which rose from 1.5% of employees in 1984 to 3.5% by 1994. Adding these two categories of employment together, 6% of men and 7% of women had non-permanent jobs in 2002 (European Commission, 2003). There is a small undercount of women's seasonal and casual jobs in the spring LFS data, but the summer and autumn LFS results show the effect to be very small indeed. Even in the summer months the percentage of temporary jobs rises to only 7% to 8% of all employee jobs. The absolute increase is about 200,000 jobs divided fairly equally between men and women, a relatively small addition to the 1.4 million year-round total for all temporary workers, which is again split fairly evenly between men (600,000) and women (800,000). The key differences between men and women doing non-permanent jobs are that men are more likely to be working full-time, whereas many women take part-time jobs; men are more likely to say they are really seeking a permanent job, while women are more likely to welcome a non-permanent job. In short, temporary contracts of all types are a small and stable element of the British workforce, increasing minimally from 5% to 6% between 1984 and 2002. The failure to include part-year work in time-specific economic activity rates does not seriously under-represent women's employment. More important, the sex differential is tiny, so men and women are affected equally.

In the EU as a whole, 12% of men and 14% of women in employment had fixed-term contracts and temporary jobs in 2002 (European Commission, 2003). Levels are stable in most member countries, but are substantially higher in some countries, notably Portugal (20% and 24% of employed men and women respectively), and in Spain (29% and 34% of employed men and women respectively). In Spain, many young people take temporary jobs, to avoid unemployment, while looking for a permanent position. Although the much larger size of the workforce in non-permanent jobs increases the potential for some undercounting, the problem (if any) still affects men and women equally.

Non-standard employment

There is good evidence that women's work in developing countries is undercounted, because distinctions between household production and market work are less clear. It is hard to find any evidence of undercounting in modern economies. There seem to be two sources of the idea that women's market work is under-reported. First, the criminal and irregular sectors clearly involve substantial volumes of money, even if headcount employment in these sectors is small. Some authors conflate these sectors with the informal economy, which has a large headcount but is very small in terms of hours worked and earnings. Prostitution is the only business where women predominate, which may fall in the non-legal sector (in some countries), and is possibly undercounted. Secondly, the steady growth of non-standard jobs (that is, non-full-time, non-permanent jobs) creates the idea that there are large areas of activity that are not covered by official surveys. When data were collected through employer surveys, this would have been a problem, but modern labour force surveys are based on household surveys, so jobs are self-reported by workers.

There is no suggestion that censuses and surveys undercount regular full-time jobs. In previous decades, this was the only type of job counted, due to the emphasis on people's main activity or usual occupation. Now, however, definitions have been broadened so that even a single hour's work for pay or profit in a week allows someone to be classified as economically active, and employed, rather than inactive. A great deal of part-time, intermittent work is now pulled into the definition of employment. Given the overlaps between home-based work, family labour and other types of marginal work, the total potential undercount is probably tiny. In Britain, it is probably around the 4% obtained from national surveys, as noted above, with a similar figure for men. The two key points are, first, that the undercount is far more trivial than this headcount suggests if measured by hours and earnings and, secondly, that men's marginal work is also undercounted. Men's marginal work consists of part-time jobs done by students and the semi-retired, and the second jobs of those in employment. The problem is not exclusive to women and does not reflect an ideological bias against the types of marginal work done by women. It arises from the practical difficulties of measuring very marginal work, set against the low benefits of its inclusion. Surveys repeatedly show that the main impediment is people's natural unwillingness to treat a few hours' work done on an informal 'own account' basis as equivalent to the full-time permanent employee job which still provides the common idea of 'a proper job', what the OECD refers to as 'standard' employment and what the EC calls 'typical' employment. As standard employment declines, statistical surveys have become more adept at identifying and measuring all types of non-standard employment which replace it, which is why there is now good data on the diverse forms of marginal work identified above.

To overcome the substantial overlaps between varieties of non-standard and marginal employment, the analysis in Table 2.6 provides an overview, dividing the whole workforce into just two categories: full-time permanent employee jobs (standard employment) and all other types of paid work (non-standard employment). All the self-employed are allocated to the non-standard category. Most self-employed men are working very long full-time hours in permanent jobs; however, most self-employed women are working relatively short part-time hours (Table 2.4), so the self-employment category is very mixed, especially as it includes labour-only subcontractors (the solo self-employed) as well as people in business on their own account (Hakim, 1988a; 1998a). However, most non-standard jobs are part-time employee jobs; self-employment, non-permanent jobs and family workers contribute smaller numbers.

Throughout the 1980s, the female workforce in Britain was divided almost equally between standard and non-standard jobs. In 1981, standard jobs predominated (53%); by 1993 non-standard jobs dominated female employment (52%). Among men, the loss of full-time permanent jobs was more dramatic, as they declined from 82% to 73% of all jobs, with non-standard jobs rising from less than one-fifth (18%) to one-quarter (27%) by 1993. In the workforce as a whole, standard jobs outnumber non-standard jobs by two to one in Britain. In the EU as a whole the ratio is the same, varying from four to one in Luxembourg to one to two in Greece due to high levels of self-employment in family farms and businesses (Hakim, 1987c: 554; 1990a: 173–79; 1990b: 179).

The substitution of part-time for full-time jobs is examined more fully in Chapter 3. Here we simply note that, with all its limitations as a time-specific count, the spring LFS works well in identifying non-standard and atypical forms of employment, and in measuring trends over time in comparison with conventional jobs. In Britain, women's employment already consists *mainly* of non-standard jobs, and the expanding part-time workforce suggests this will be the pattern in other EU countries as well. Increasing this count to include more marginal types of non-standard employment would speed up this trend.

Voluntary work and civic participation

Voluntary work is a separate category of activity falling between market work and unpaid household work. The purpose of voluntary work is to provide a service to others, a public good provided below market cost, and it is typically defined as any work undertaken without coercion for an organisation, either in an unpaid capacity or for a token payment. As the label implies, voluntary work is definitely productive activity which easily passes the third person test. Yet it has never been counted in national labour force surveys, even though the voluntary and non-profit sector provides an important complement to public services. On the face of it, voluntary work provides the strongest example of women's contribution to society at large (not just to their own families and friends) being under-reported and under-valued. It also provides the strongest refutation of the argument, because there are no differences between the voluntary work contributions of men and women, either in Britain or in the USA. The undercount affects men as much as women, and sometimes more. The absence of any sex difference in voluntary work is consistent with the absence of any sex difference in altruism and helping behaviour; on some indicators, men are more altruistic than women (Eagly and Crowley, 1986).

Voluntary work is important in developing as well as industrial societies, but the ILO continued to exclude it from labour force statistics in its latest review, along with household work (Dupre *et al*, 1987: xiv). They noted that in most countries volunteer workers contribute to private non-profit organisations which supply various social services to their community, such as child and elderly welfare, education and medical related services. Sometimes emergency services, such as sea rescue and fire services, are also organised on a volunteer basis. Furthermore, in many developing countries, particularly in rural areas, household members often provide work on a volunteer basis for community development, such as filling ditches, cleaning tanks and flood prevention.

The Office of National Statistics (ONS) carried out surveys of voluntary work in Britain in 1981, 1987 and 1992 through the GHS (OPCS, 1983: 160–80; Matheson, 1990; Goddard, 1994). The 1992 GHS defined voluntary work as unpaid work, except for the refund of expenses, which is done through a group or on behalf of an organisation of some kind. It should be of service or benefit to other people or the community, and not only to one's family or personal friends. The definition was explicitly intended to exclude informal caring of family or friends, and help to neighbours, which is potentially reciprocal. The definition also excluded fostering children, contributing to collections for charity, attending fund-raising events, doing jury service in court, being a blood-donor, voluntary work organised by a school for a student to gain work experience, and work done for a trade union or political party. The three British surveys yield almost identical results. There is almost no change over time in voluntary work.

Once neighbourly activities, and services to friends and family, are excluded, voluntary work is relatively rare. In 1992, one-quarter (24%) of people aged 16 or over said they had done some kind of voluntary work through or on behalf of a group in the 12 months before interview. One in six (16%) had done so in the four weeks before interview. Men and women were fairly equally likely to do voluntary work: 21% and 27% respectively had done so in the year before interview; but men contributed an average of 17 hours' voluntary work within the preceding four weeks compared to women's average of 15 hours. It was not necessarily those who had most time to spare who were most likely to volunteer, as volunteering was strongly associated with higher educational qualifications and higher grade occupations. People who were in employment were more likely to do voluntary work than the economically inactive (27% versus 20%). Women working part-time were most likely to do voluntary work and full-time housewives were one of the groups least likely to volunteer (37% and 22% respectively). This means that voluntary work does not even out the differences between the working and non-working populations (Matheson, 1990: 9–11; Goddard, 1994: 4–6). On the contrary, it enhances the polarisation already manifested in paid work. If voluntary work for political parties, trade unions, employers' associations and professional associations is added into the picture, it is clear that men do more voluntary work than women, as men tend to dominate active membership of these organisations.

A 1980 survey of one community in Britain provides information on voluntary work for relatives, friends and neighbours of the sort which is potentially reciprocal and excluded from the GHS surveys, such as house repairs, babysitting, shopping and gardening. Men and women were equally likely to do such work (25% in each case); employed men and full-time housewives were most likely to do jobs for relatives, friends and neighbours; men most often helped with house repairs and women most often provided domestic services, or did sewing, but both did a wide range of voluntary work tasks (Pahl, 1984: 248–51).

The National Centre for Volunteering has also carried out national surveys in Britain, in 1981, 1991 and 1997 (Smith, 1998). They too found no change in levels of volunteering over the period, and higher levels of volunteer work among men than women. Their definition of volunteer work includes civic participation, so is broader than the ONS definition: any activity which involves spending time, unpaid, doing something which aims to benefit someone (individuals or groups) other than, or in addition to, close relatives, or to benefit the environment. On this basis, half of all adults did some voluntary work in the previous year; one-fifth did so in the last week; and about 30% are regular volunteers. They find that volunteering is more common in higher income groups, among people in professional occupations, in higher education groups, and among people in employment. There were no sex differences in patterns of volunteering, but men gave more hours than women. Smith (1998) found that there is almost no quality control of volunteer work; but quality control is most common among male volunteers, implying more responsible tasks and roles. The surveys also collected information on the type of informal help given to neighbours and friends that was excluded from the ONS surveys: three-quarters of people do this. Again, there was no sex difference in overall participation, but women were more likely to do this regularly. Finally, the 1997 survey found that women are more likely than men to *receive* voluntary help from others. Overall, over the previous 12 months, 11% of people had received formal voluntary help, and 24% had received informal voluntary help. It is notable that these figures are far below the figures for giving formal and informal voluntary help. It appears that people remember (or exaggerate) giving, but forget (or minimise) receiving help.

The pattern of voluntary work in the USA is almost identical to the results for Britain (Harman, 1982; Blau and Ferber, 1992: 56–59; Wilson, 2000). Surveys have been carried out in 1973 by a volunteer association, in 1989 through the USA equivalent to the European LFS, the Current Population Survey (CPS), and in the 1998 General Social Survey. However, the most important source of information is the series of biennial surveys conducted by the Gallup Organisation for the Independent Sector (Hodgkinson and Weitzman, 1996; Wilson, 2000). Statistics Canada has also carried out a national survey (Hall *et al*, 1998).

American studies tend to define voluntary work so as to include participation in interest groups, clubs and community activities that benefit the participant, directly or indirectly – such as Parent-Teacher Associations, trade unions, political groups, and professional associations. (The public good created by such organisations is generally restricted to fellow members, rather than society at large.) Despite the broader definition, participation levels are lower than in Britain, which has a strong civic culture. One of the earliest surveys of participation in voluntary organisations, in 1959–60, found identical levels of participation (two-thirds) among men in the USA, Britain and Germany, with systematically lower levels (less than half) among women in these countries, and also in Italy and Mexico (Almond and Verba, 1965: 247–48).

In the USA, in 1973, about one-quarter of women and men participated in volunteer activities. In 1989, only 20% did so. Using a broader definition of volunteering, which included neighbourly helping, a 1988 Gallup survey found 45% participated. By 1998, Gallup found 56% of adults volunteering at some point in the past 12 months – still well below levels found in Britain on this wider definition. Surveys find no important sex differences in participation rates; people in employment provide more hours than people not in employment, and this is especially true of women; and volunteering rises with occupational status, income, education, and religiosity (Wilson, 2000). The EC (2000: 86) reports that one in four Europeans does unpaid work for charitable causes, voluntary groups and community groups. In Europe, Stubbings and Humble (1984) found the highest rates of volunteering among part-time workers, and the lowest rates among people not in the labour force: the unemployed and homemakers. This is a consistent pattern, found in all modern societies. Wilson (2000: 227–28) is puzzled by the absence of a clear gender difference in favour of women, given women's tendency to attach more value to helping others. As noted in Chapter 4, social psychologists characterise men as agentic, and women as communal: caring, emotionally expressive, and responsive to others. Wilson concludes that men's volunteer work is raised by their higher levels of human capital (work skills, essentially, since educational levels are equalising). The lack of any sex difference in voluntary work may not be surprising, as it is consistent with the absence of any sex difference in altruism and helping behaviour; indeed, on some indicators, men are more altruistic (Eagly and Crowley, 1986).

The absence of any substantial sex differential in voluntary work is important, because the failure to measure women's voluntary work has been given special emphasis in critiques of labour force statistics and the SNA (Waring, 1988: 113–15), and is popularly believed to be important. What this tells us is that women are highly conscious of all their own activities, but largely oblivious of the equivalent activities of men. No doubt the reverse is also true. This means that virtually everyone feels their contributions are not fully highlighted and appreciated. It seems we are dealing here with a problem of human nature, not a problem specific to women or statistics. The idea that women are unique, in doing a substantial volume of voluntary work, has no basis in reality. Men do just as much voluntary work as women, whether formally organised or informal neighbourly work, and on some indicators men do more. In contrast, there is no doubt that women do the majority of household work, which is also not represented in national labour force statistics.

The Household Satellite Account attempts to value the contribution of voluntary work to the economy. The contributions of men and women might differ in value, even if they put in the same hours of voluntary work, because the voluntary activities of men and women differ just as much as their occupations in the workforce. Holloway *et al* (2002: 43–50) valued the hours of formal voluntary work as a separate category, and allocated informal neighbourly helping to the adult care or childcare categories of the Household Satellite Account. Synthesising the results of all available sources on voluntary work, plus a new module in the 2001 ONS Omnibus Survey, led to the conclusion that females contribute slightly more time to voluntary work than men: 53% of the total, with men contributing 47% (ONS, 2003b: Figure 9.6b). However, by the end of 2003, the value of voluntary work had not been estimated separately for men and women. The total formed a tiny fraction – less than 0.5% – of the total time spent on household production (ONS, 2003b: Figure 2.4).

Household work

Economists have always thought it desirable to include household production work in national accounts. The reason for not doing so has simply been the methodological difficulty of measuring the value of household work, or indeed any non-market non-traded work for which there are no prices (Goldschmidt-Clermont, 1982; 1987; 1990; Gronau, 1986). Transfers of production occur between the household sector and the market economy, causing GNP to rise and fall while the actual amount of goods and services available to the population does not change. For example, a sizeable share of laundering moved from the household to commercial laundries in the late 1920s and early 1930s; it then moved back to households as appropriate domestic equipment became available. In the past, clothing for women and children was usually made at home; today it is purchased ready-made from commercial establishments, despite the domestic electric sewing machine. In contrast, power tools for home use have created a new Do-It-Yourself (DIY) industry of house repairs and decorating dominated by men. These changes cannot be identified when GNP measures exclude household production. However, difficulties in measuring the value of household work are real. The number of hours of work can be misleading, given flexibility in the homemaker's use of time. Domestic work can be carried out with different degrees of intensity, efficiency and productivity, interspersing it with leisure time and other breaks. Domestic work carried out by hired labour invariably requires far fewer hours than are typically reported by full-time homemakers, and wives in employment spend half as much time on housework as do full-time housewives (Vanek, 1974). The measurement of domestic work must rely on the number of hours expended, and hence time use data, but there is no direct or constant relationship to output (Myrdal and Klein, 1956, 1968: 34–37; Vanek, 1974; Goldschmidt-Clermont, 1989).

As Hawrylyshyn (1977: 84–85) pointed out, it is only the *minimum required time* for an activity that constitutes the work element; additional time is only devoted to an activity if it provides satisfaction and pleasure (utility, in economic terms). In practice, an hour of household time may combine production and consumption, indirect and direct utility. In the same way that a car provides both transport and status, cooking may provide a meal to eat but also a relaxation. She concludes that the minimum necessary time for domestic work is most closely approximated by the hours allocated to it by women in full-time employment, who are obliged to be more efficient than full-time homemakers (1977: 91). However, Household Satellite Accounts are based on total time expended on household work, whether necessary or not. Thus, the production element in household work is overestimated relative to the consumption element. For example, if a mother drives her children to and from school every day, instead of letting them walk to school, the extra task is valued at a chauffeur's wage, or at the national average wage, even if it was arguably unnecessary. Thus, rising standards of living and consumption tend to increase the time and value of household work in industrial societies.

Studies of the activities of full-time homemakers reveal a remarkable lack of concern with efficiency; on the contrary, tasks are constantly expanded into huge amounts of unnecessary make-work (Friedan, 1963; Oakley, 1974, 1985: 85, 110, 121; Pahl, 1984: 112, 228–29, 256). One notable finding from Oakley's landmark study is that the extra work did not arise from housewives seeking to upgrade the skill content of their work, for example by cooking more complex or unusual dishes, but from endlessly repeating the same unskilled tasks. For example, full-time homemakers cleaned and shopped daily instead of weekly, washed and ironed sheets twice a week instead of once a month, insisted on giving all their children a fresh set of clothes every day, vastly increasing the volume of laundry and ironing (Oakley, 1974, 1985: 92–112). Variations in hours spent on domestic work are *not* explained by the number of children being cared for, access to labour-saving equipment and other amenities, or the purchase of more services in the market (Oakley, 1974, 1985: 94, 110–12; Blau and Ferber, 1992: 55). One explanation for the reluctance of husbands to help with domestic work is the suspicion that there might be no need for it, if efficient work methods were used. Despite the advances in household technology, women in the 1960s spent as much time on housework as did women in the 1920s (Moen, 1992: 71). Full-time homemakers often create a self-imposed domestic slavery which cannot be blamed on men (or patriarchy), especially as the majority of wives say they are satisfied with their husband's contribution to housework and childcare (Martin and Roberts, 1984: 101–02; Oakley, 1974, 1985: 159; Pahl, 1984: 112, 257, 269; Brannen, 1991: 65).

Studies of household work generally include childcare, along with domestic work (cleaning, cooking, laundry, etc), gardening, repairs and DIY. Some studies include pet care, but this is arguably a non-essential leisure activity. Childcare, which is discussed separately below, now constitutes a relatively small part of all household work across the whole life cycle. However, childcare is overwhelmingly dominant when children are very young. Oakley's (1974, 1985) study of housework is thus biased by focusing exclusively on mothers with at least one child under five years, almost all full-time homemakers, for whom childcare and domestic work were indistinguishable and time-consuming. Studies that use broader samples of the adult population include working women, and women with no dependent children, and thus give a different picture of housework and childcare.

A recent British study showed that full-time homemakers spend over three times as many hours on cleaning as do women with full-time jobs; they also spend almost twice as many hours on preparing meals. Overall, women with full-time jobs spend about half as much time on domestic work: 18 hours a week on average compared to 30 hours a week reported by full-time housewives. Domestic work is defined here as house cleaning and tidying, meal preparation, washing up after meals, repairs, gardening, shopping and laundry, but not time spent on childcare. Husbands typically contribute 10 hours a week of domestic work, an increase on earlier decades. Overall, couples who both work full-time spend 28 hours a week on domestic work compared to 40 hours a week in homes with a full-time homemaker, or 8% and 12% of total time (Horrell, 1994: 207–12). Averages reported for the USA are very similar: wives do 25 hours of housework per week and husbands do 7 hours a week (Brines, 1994: 670). Housework has stood at 10% of individuals' total time for the last 30 years in Denmark, despite substantial changes in paid work time (Mogensen, 1990, quoted in Horrell, 1994: 204). Up to half the full-time homemaker's hours could be attributable to inefficiency, unnecessary make-work, or to activities done for pleasure rather than necessity. Further evidence comes from comparisons of time spent on housework by single people. Unmarried women were found in one study to do twice as many hours of housework as unmarried men in 1975, a large reduction on 1965, when they did three times as many hours (Stafford, 1980: 58). Single women spend 50% more time on domestic work than single men, an average of three hours a day instead of just two (Mogensen, 1990: 110). This suggests that one-third or more of the time spent on housework by women consists of optional extras, in effect consumption.

All these results rely on time use surveys which require respondents to complete diaries reporting their activities for each 15 minute section of the day, often for one week. Anyone who has been obliged to complete such time use diaries for an employer knows that the description or classification of activities in time use accounts is open to just as much, perhaps more, manipulation and bias as responses to interview surveys; if the purpose of an enquiry is not clear, people apply their own assumptions. The validity of subsequent researcher coding of reported tasks and activities as 'work' or 'leisure' can also vary, given that the classification of an activity depends very much on why it is done and for whom. Finally, people do not naturally perceive activities in terms of blocks of time, as required by time use surveys, but in terms of tasks to be performed and responsibilities to be remembered (Pahl, 1984: 128, 256; 1988: 744–47). Time allocation is not a natural category of self-knowledge (Gershuny et al, 1994: 157). The 'objectivity' of time budget data is not all it is claimed to be (Anderson et al, 1994: 157–58, 205–07, 271–72; Robinson and Gershuny, 1994; Gershuny, 2000: 272–88). This invisible problem of data validity is just as important as the more frequently discussed problem of obtaining data for fully representative national samples (Mogensen, 1990: 31, 371–418). Most dubious of all is the practice of *imputing* data on unpaid household work hours from a single time use survey to earlier and later years, as Fuchs (1986) and Leete and Schor (1994) have done. Data from conventional interview surveys can in practice be as good as, or better than, time use survey data. For example, ordinary research methods have shown the contradiction, in many households, between a couple's stated ideal of a symmetrical division of labour, and the reality of the husband being the main breadwinner and the wife taking responsibility for domestic tasks and childcare or, alternatively, the fact that women with full-time jobs ideally prefer to work part-time or be full-time homemakers (Hochschild, 1990: 203; Brannen, 1991; Hakim, 1997, 2003a: 135, 153–56).

Thomas (1992: 13–47) provides an invaluable review of the economic theory, data collection problems and research results on household work and subsistence production. He sets out the current SNA rules which list many primary production activities that should be included in national income accounts, distinguishing these from what might be called consumption work in the household. He explains why this work is conventionally excluded from the GDP; reviews the arguments now offered for estimating its value within national accounts; sets out the methods used to do so; and the results obtained. For developed countries, the total value of household work ranges widely from 9% to 48% of the GDP, although most estimates cluster in the 20 to 40% range. For developing countries, estimates are in the range of 23% to 49% of the GDP. It is often noted that there is no tax on the imputed income from household work and that, if domestic work can be valued, it should be taxed in order to remove the fiscal bias in favour of couples with a full-time homemaker (Gronau, 1980: 411; Stafford, 1980: 59).

The high value of domestic work in industrial societies is explained by the growing importance of consumption work. As Galbraith (1975: 45–53) pointed out, the conversion of women into a crypto-servant class was an economic accomplishment of the first importance. Menially employed servants were available only to a minority of the preindustrial population. The servant-wife is available, democratically, to almost the entire male population. Women's labour to facilitate consumption facilitates indefinitely increasing consumption levels in capitalist society, legitimated by the notion that lifestyle expresses individual personality and cultural capital. The great achievement of Western capitalism has been to persuade women that housework and homemaking are an expression of their femininity

(Friedan, 1963; Oakley, 1974, 1985; 1976: 128; Matthaei, 1982), in sharp contrast with values and ideas in other cultures. This may explain why hours spent on housework peaked in the 1960s, before the second wave of feminism questioned the need for it, and prompted a slow decline (Hartmann, 1981; Gershuny, 1988: 587–88). However, domestic consumption is labour-intensive and time-consuming in Western industrial society, fuelled especially by the purchase of housing, cars and other vehicles, consumer durables and clothing, all requiring care and maintenance (Mogensen, 1990: 100, 111).

Gershuny (2000) has carried out the largest study of time use, using 44 surveys from 21 countries: Australia, Austria, Belgium, Britain, Bulgaria, Canada, Czechoslovakia, Denmark, East Germany, West Germany, Finland, France, Hungary, Israel, Italy, the Netherlands, Norway, Poland, Sweden, the USA and Yugoslavia. His comparative research has identified some major changes over time in patterns of paid and unpaid work, and how work is divided between men and women. Gershuny (1983a: 149–51; 1983b: 38; 1988: 587; 2000: 171–202, 219–21) has shown that time spent in household work (including childcare) shows opposing trends when analysed by social class. Over the last 50 years, working class women have come to do less domestic work, due to time-saving devices like the washer-dryer and drip-dry shirts. In contrast, middle and upper class women now do far more domestic work, since they no longer have servants to do it for them. Working class women also spend less time in employment too, due to part-time work options, and more educated women enter employment more often and work considerably longer hours. As the leisured class has become the overworked class, and the working class now does far less work of any kind, the working class has more leisure than the middle class (Gershuny, 1993: 581; 2000: 179). Up to 1980, men did roughly one-third as much domestic work (including childcare) as did women (Gershuny, 1983a: 145) and women did one-third to one-half as much paid work as did men (Joshi et al, 1985: S171), producing a certain balance. From the 1970s onwards, longitudinal data for a dozen industrial societies (including Britain) show that economic growth (as measured by GDP) produces contrasting trends among men and women: total hours of employment decline among men and rise among women while total hours of domestic work (broadly defined) rise for men and decline for women – leading to a long term convergence in total work hours of men and women (Gershuny, 1992: 15–20; 1993: 583; 2000: 219–21) as predicted over 30 years ago by Young and Willmott (1973).

Adding together market work, domestic and childcare work, the evidence for the 1970s onwards is that wives and women generally do fewer total work hours than husbands and men generally (Stafford, 1980: 58; Blau and Ferber, 1992: 53; Coleman and Pencavel, 1993), and that women's dual burden of paid work and family work is diminishing (Gershuny, 2000: 68–69, 182–84). From the 1970s onwards, wives without paid employment had the shortest total work hours, shorter than wives with market work, even though they spent more hours on domestic work than employed wives (Blau and Ferber, 1992: 53). By the start of the 21st century, even in families with a child under five years, spouses in employment contributed roughly equal total work hours (paid and unpaid) in most modern societies. On average, full-time mothers had a lower workload than fathers with full-time jobs (OECD, 2001: Table 4.5).

It appears that studies focusing on mothers with young children at home have given a misleading picture of the family division of labour across the whole life cycle. Mothers with children aged 0–2 years spend around 3 hours a day on housework and childcare, but this falls rapidly as children grow up. Older women without children at home do significantly less work than men. Adding together employment, study, voluntary work, housework and childcare, on average men and women in Britain spend exactly the same total amount of time working, just under 8 hours a day (ONS, 2003a). There is little evidence that wives generally, or full-time homemakers, are exploited in the sense of working longer hours in total than men. Paid and unpaid work balance out, overall. The most important determinant of spouses' sharing of housework and childcare are their relative employment hours and contributions to household income (Deutsch et al, 1993). The leisure time of men and women is exactly the same (Bittman and Wajcman, 2000). The conspicuous consumption of expensive goods has replaced the conspicuous consumption of leisure as a status marker (Gershuny, 2000).

The total value of household work, as an addition to GDP, depends very much on how labour and time are priced: at average market wages, at average wages for men and women respectively, or at average market wages for the particular type of domestic work in question: cleaning, laundry, etc. In each case, it may be appropriate to deduct relevant taxes, or taxes and work-related costs, to show net value. Depending on which pricing system they applied, Murgatroyd and Neuburger (1997: 68) valued unpaid household work (including childcare) in Britain at between 39% and 122% of GDP, very close to equivalent estimates for Germany. Short (2000: 54) produced estimates in the range 44% to 104%. Studies of other countries have produced estimates in the range 38% to 72% of the GDP, and between 6% and 72% of the GNP (Bruyn-Hundt, 1996: 50). In the USA, total housework has been valued from 17% to 48% of national income (Thomas, 1992: Table 2.3). The British Household Satellite Account for 2000 estimated the Net Value Added by unpaid household production (including voluntary work and civic participation) to be £628,366 million in total for 132,999 million hours' work. Females contributed 59% of the total and males contributed 41% (ONS, 2003b). A small proportion of the greater contribution of females is simply because there are more women in the population. The sex differential in household work is smaller than for paid employment.

Reproductive and caring work

A century ago, childbearing and childcare dominated married women's adult lives, except for those rich enough to afford numerous servants (Lewis, 1984), in part because few people lived beyond the age of 50. Today, families of 16, 12, eight and even four children are almost unheard of. Very few women will have more than two or three children; many will have only one child; and voluntarily childless couples are becoming a feature of modern society (see Chapter 5). Childbearing and childcare are no longer the dominant activities for women in prosperous modern societies. They occupy a small proportion of the life cycle, even if they become overwhelmingly full-time activities for a few years. The expansion of compulsory education up to age 16 in Britain, 18 in some European countries, means that childcare is a full-time activity for only the first four to six years of a child's life, about 10 years with two children. Discussions of domestic labour often emphasise women's reproductive work, overlooking the fact that this now forms a tiny element of household work over the whole life cycle, which is dominated by year-round housework and periodic house and car maintenance (Pahl, 1984: 223, 273–75; Oakley, 1974, 1985; Fine, 1992: 186–87).

A 1986 study found that childcare occupied on average 19 hours a week for full-time homemakers, 7 hours a week for women working part-time and 1 hour a week for women working full-time, compared to 6 hours a week for non-working men, 4 hours a week for men working part-time and 1 hour a week for men working full-time (Horrell, 1994: 209). So, on average, childcare accounted for 10% of weekly time for full-time homemakers, 4% and 1% of weekly time for women working part-time and full-time respectively, and for 3%, 2% and 1% respectively of men's weekly time. Given differentiated sex-roles, as shown in Chapter 4, women do the bulk of childcare, but even so, averaged across all women aged 20–60, childcare represents a tiny fraction of adult life. Producing children is still a major feature of women's lives, in terms of personal identity and attitudes, but it is no longer the dominant activity in terms of time and effort.

The decline in childcare work is being replaced to some extent by the care of elderly relatives, which is potentially more time-consuming and burdensome. A mother's care of her children is based on unreasoning love and affection, at least some of the time, in most cases. Care of the elderly is based on love and obligation. The dependency of children does not last long, but people caring for the elderly cannot look forward to a bright future. The elderly can only be expected to get more frail, more unreasonable and more dependent, and one never knows when the caring activity will end. Compared with childcare, care of the elderly is a heavier and less rewarding burden.

Nationally representative data on informal caring was collected in the 1985 and 1990/91 GHS and in the 1991 British Household Panel Survey. All three surveys yield almost identical results (Green, 1988; OPCS, 1992; Arber and Ginn, 1995; Corti and Dex, 1995). Men and women are equally likely to be caring for a sick, disabled or elderly person living with them (4%) or living in another household (10% to 15%) and they are equally likely to devote over 20 hours a week to caring (4%). Most commonly, the person cared for is a spouse living with the carer, or else parents or parents-in-law. Differences in caring between men and women are generally small and caring responsibilities are only weakly associated with employment patterns among men and women. However, caring responsibilities can have more dramatic consequences for men's employment than for women, who are more often full-time homemakers anyway and can more readily get part-time jobs. The popular stereotype of caring work being an almost exclusively female activity is unfounded: men are as likely to be carers as women. The number of male carers has been increasing rapidly (Weir, 2002: 586; Alcock et al, 2003). The reason why women dominate in terms of absolute numbers of carers is simply that women live longer than men.

Status of the housewife and househusband

In one sense, the entire debate on the undercounting of women's productive work is irrelevant. The main reason for the debate is that women feel the status of the housewife has fallen; therefore they seek a revaluation of their role and status by underlining the marginal market work done by women, and the productive character of household work. A more direct approach to the question is to assess the social status of the homemaker, and whether the role has in reality fallen in status in recent decades.

The conventional social stratification theory response to this question says that a wife, along with any children in the home, takes her social status from the male income-earner's occupation. The homemaker's Social Class (in Britain) or Socio-Economic Status (in the USA) is taken from the husband, and is thus independent of the quantity and value of any household work she does. Indeed, a housewife traditionally has higher status the less domestic work she does herself, and the more such work is given to servants, as this implies greater wealth from the husband's activity, whatever his occupation. As the workforce becomes more highly qualified, there is a long term drift upwards in the entire socio-economic structure, with an increasing proportion of professional, technical and managerial occupations and fewer unskilled occupations. Collectively, housewives must have risen in status too, in parallel with the upward drift in the class structure in recent decades. In this perspective, homemakers cannot have fallen in status.

The alternative view is that most people are aware that the homemaker's job as housekeeper and mother has shrunk in size in modern industrial society, leaving time free for other activities. Wives are now expected to do other things as well, instead of being 'just a housewife' in the sense of an exclusive life-long role. Wives who are full-time homemakers have thus lost status in some subtle way. True or false?

To answer this question we must resort to a study carried out in 1972 in the USA, the only large-scale study that included the housewife among the list of occupations to be ranked in prestige and status by respondents (Bose, 1985; Bose and Rossi, 1983). Studies of occupational status in Britain have been limited to male workers and occupations (Goldthorpe and Hope, 1972; 1974). The extrapolation of occupational status scores from data for male occupations to typically-female occupations has been accepted, *faute de mieux*, but creating a status score for the housewife has not been attempted. A study carried out in the USA offers somewhat indirect evidence on the status of the homemaker in Europe and other countries, as there may be subtle differences between cultures, but it is the best data available.

The main focus of Bose's study was the relationship between occupational segregation and occupational prestige, that is, whether female occupations tend to be ranked as lower in status than male occupations. The study combined experimental design with survey research, with randomly varying descriptions of 110 occupations presented to a sample of householders living in Baltimore who were asked to rate each occupation's prestige on a scale from 1 to 9. (The study included a survey of college students' occupational prestige ratings, but these results are ignored here as unrepresentative of anyone except this minority group.)

The innovation was that the list of occupations included 'housewife', 'househusband' and 'person living on state welfare', and a separate chapter of the report was devoted to the social status of these non-employed positions (Bose, 1985: 44–57).

The somewhat surprising result was that the housewife was accorded higher social status than any of the labour market occupations that corresponded roughly to domestic work (Table 2.7). Within a scale that ranged from a high of 90 for college professor to a low of 8 for parking lot attendant, the housewife had an average occupational prestige score of 51, well above the score of 25 for a paid housekeeper, 39 for a hairdresser, 15 for a laundry worker and 12 for a maid, but below the score of 63 for a social worker and 65 for a primary school teacher. This high status score applied only to the traditional female homemaker; the househusband was accorded very low status indeed: a score of 15 compared to 51 for the housewife, reflecting the fact that the non-employed male is not yet a legitimate role in society. However, there was little consensus on the housewife occupation, which had the largest variance in scores in the study (1,018), followed by the artist role (a variance of 876), followed by a dozen occupations with variances in the 600 range: coalminer, farmer, househusband, landscape gardener, social worker and sociologist. These occupations cover diverse grades of work, so it is clearly something about the occupations themselves that creates confusion or disagreement on where they should be placed on a prestige scale.

Lack of consensus on the housewife's status was also reflected in the marked divergence of opinion between men, who gave it a score of only 41, and women, who gave it an above average score of 61. No other occupation attracted such a marked sex difference in prestige rating. The male rating placed the housewife role much closer to equivalent jobs in the labour market, such as hairdresser or housekeeper. The female rating placed it closer to white-collar, typically female-held jobs in the labour market, such as secretary (Table 2.7). It seems that men evaluated

Table 2.7 Average status of housewife, househusband and related occupations

Occupation	Prestige score	Occupation	Prestige score
Secondary school teacher	70	Hairdresser	39
Administrative assistant	68	Housekeeper	25
Primary school teacher	65	Boardinghouse keeper	24
Hotel manager	64	Short order cook	22
Social worker	63	Waitress	22
Private secretary	61	Babysitter	18
Dental assistant	55	Laundry worker	15
Office secretary	51	Maid	12
Housewife	**51**	**Househusband**	**15**

Source: Derived from Tables 4.1 and 4.2 in Bose (1985: 48, 50) reporting average prestige scores awarded by householder sample for occupations without descriptions of the incumbents.

the housewife's prestige in terms of her domestic functions and activities. Women gave her a 50% average mark-up in prestige compared to men, which was stronger than their general tendency to give higher gradings to female occupations (Bose and Rossi, 1983: 329).

These results demonstrate the ambivalence that surrounds the homemaker role in modern industrial society, and confirm that women rate the role much higher than men do. They also explain why the full-time homemaker role is attractive to working class women, for whom it represents a higher status position than the manual jobs they have access to in the labour market, and is unattractive to middle class or professional women, for whom it represents a drop in status compared with their occupational prestige scores (Bose, 1985: 50–51).

One of the best known studies of the housewife is by Oakley (1976; 1974, 1985; see also Lopata, 1971). She interviewed 40 young mothers of young children in a London suburb in 1971, almost all of them full-time homemakers. Oakley concluded that three-quarters of these mothers were dissatisfied with domestic work, due to the long hours of work and perceived low status of the housewife role. Mothers who had previously been employed in high status jobs were most dissatisfied with domestic work. Middle class women perceived themselves as mothers and wives with interests beyond the home, rather than housewives, and enjoyed looking after their children; in contrast, working class women displayed positive attachment to and identification with the homemaker role but were at best ambivalent about looking after their children. Attachment to the homemaker role was associated with far longer hours devoted to domestic work and, paradoxically, with greater job satisfaction. Domesticity was seen as feminine, and the sexual division of labour in the home was seen as natural by these mothers. They valued the autonomy of the homemaker role, and being 'your own boss'. There was little evidence that these mothers longed to return to employment, and they had no sympathy with the women's liberation movement (Oakley, 1974, 1985: 42–43, 72, 106–12, 120–33, 166, 176, 182–92). This richly detailed study has been taken as representative of housewives generally, and dissatisfaction with domestic work has been interpreted as dissatisfaction with the housewife *role*. Both conclusions are incorrect.

Oakley's study of non-employed mothers of young children is not representative of housewives generally, neither for 1971 nor today. The GHS and LFS both show that across the two decades 1973–1993, among women aged 16–59 years who were economically inactive, only one-third had a child aged under 5 years; only half had a child aged under 10 years. Among non-working wives living with their spouse, less than half had a child under 5 years at home. If we add the 6 million wives aged 60 and over, virtually all of whom are full-time homemakers, to the 3 million inactive women of working age, the mothers of young children shrink to a small minority of the total. Over half of all wives have no dependent children at home; four-fifths of wives have no child aged under 5 years at home. Oakley's sample of housewives was biased towards domestically-oriented mothers, a subgroup of all homemakers. The dissatisfaction they expressed was due primarily to the long hours of childcare work at this stage of the life cycle (Pahl, 1984: 273–75; Hakim, 2000: 179–84).

Bonney and Reinach (1993) also point out that Oakley's study was not representative of housewives generally, most of whom do not have young children to care for, so that Oakley's portrayal of housewives as rebelliously dissatisfied was misleading. Using a large representative 1986 survey dataset, Bonney and Reinach showed that among 500 full-time homemakers aged 20–59 years only 16% said they planned to return to full-time employment at some point in the future. The vast majority (84%) of housewives saw homemaking as their principal activity in the long term: 37% intended never to return to employment and 47% were only interested in part-time jobs eventually. Only half the sample had any young children to care for; the rest simply regarded themselves as permanent homemakers. Attitudes towards the homemaker role, and the disadvantages of being without a paid job revealed that the majority did not regret the lack of a job and found being at home satisfying. There was no sign that the role was perceived to be of low prestige and social recognition as Oakley had concluded. The main disadvantages of the homemaker role were reported by everyone to be the social isolation and, for those who had children, the heavy workload entailed in caring for young children. The young mothers in the sample spent a median of 73 hours a week on childcare compared to only 28 hours a week on domestic work (a distinction that Oakley fails to make in her study). Even so, no more than one-quarter of any group of full-time homemakers expressed general dissatisfaction with their situation (Bonney and Reinach, 1993: 616, 619, 621–22, 626). The 1990 BSAS also found no evidence that women looking after their children at home full-time were dissatisfied, or that a majority wished to join the labour market instead (Witherspoon and Prior, 1991: 151). Oakley's study is revealed as seriously misleading in its conclusions due to sample selection bias (see Chapter 5) – in this case a focus on only one stage of the life cycle. The same problem arises with Hochschild's (1990) study of 50 North American couples both working full-time and with a child aged under 6 years, who experienced even greater workloads than did Oakley's full-time housewives.

Conclusions

Marginal work for pay or profit, some of it carried out in the informal economy, is fully measured in some national surveys but is undercounted in others, despite the one hour a week minimalist definition of employment. Almost all marginal work involves so few hours and such small earnings that it remains below the tax threshold, exempt from deductions. Its inclusion would add only 4 percentage points to female workrates in Britain. However, the utility of the one hour a week definition of employment is now widely questioned, as it reclassifies into the workforce students in full-time education, people retired on employer pensions as well as women whose principal activity, and main identity, is full-time homemaking.

Household work produces goods and services that are consumed immediately within the household, which represent a substantial addition to the GDP as measured by market work. However, there is still no single agreed method for valuing non-market work, and valuations of household work vary hugely. A substantial and growing proportion of domestic activity also consists of consumption which is not work as identified by the third person test, but cannot be excluded from Household Satellite Accounts. Women still do more than half of all household work; men contribute 40% on average. Both in household work, and in marginal work, the sex differential is smaller than popularly believed. However, domestic work and family labour, while productive, differ fundamentally from wage work in the competitive market economy. Whereas wage work is social and abstract, domestic labour is private and individual-specific. The absence of competition in the household work market means there are no norms to set reasonable labour time limits for tasks. There is no rigid distinction between work and leisure, between production and consumption. There is no pressure to increase productivity, or to reduce costs, and no external control over the production process (Fine, 1992: 169–91). Only market employment allows work to be separated from family relationships and ascribed roles, with increases in individual productivity (Goldin, 1990: 11, 119). The sex differential in household work mirrors the sex differential in market work, and the long term trend is towards convergence in the hours of paid and unpaid work done by men and women. When all forms of work are added together, men and women do exactly the same total hours of productive activity. In 1972, the full-time homemaker had a fairly average rank in occupational prestige scales. It is not clear whether the homemaker's status has declined since then, but it is notable that it is high achievers in public life who attract most media attention, and approbation.

Throughout this review of all forms of marginal and non-market work, differences between men and women have been small or non-existent. In some areas, such as home-based work, men dominate. Among family workers, women dominate. Voluntary work of all types is done equally by men and women. Caring work is done equally by men and women, although women do more childcare. Marginal and non-market work are visible, counted, done by men as well as women, and do not markedly alter the overall picture on workloads. Criticisms of the ideological bias of the economic conceptual framework for labour statistics have been ill-informed, and have often rested on a lack of familiarity with the basic concepts of labour economics and economic sociology.

The argument that women's work is undercounted can most fruitfully be reformulated as an argument in favour of a more informative classification of the main activities of people classified as economically inactive. At present, people in full-time education, the long term sick, and the retired are usually separately identified. Other working-age non-employed people are otherwise not differentiated, not even to distinguish those with young children at home from the rest. More information would obviously be useful on what full-time homemakers do with their time. This is now a genuine question. If feminists want to see proper valuations of women's household work, this will mean a lot more prying into private lives, to assess efficiency, quantity and quality of outputs, instead of guesstimates of time allocation at the end of each day. This seems an unlikely development in the near future.

Chapter 3
Feminisation of the Workforce

The most important change in the labour market in recent decades has been the steady rise in women's employment. This chapter examines the feminisation of the workforce, and its consequences. Has women's entry to the workforce driven men out, by taking their jobs? Has the feminisation of the workforce produced greater equality between men and women in the workplace, and at home? Has the nature of work itself been changed by women's increasing presence in a masculine work environment? The answers to these questions are sometimes surprising. Undoubtedly there have been massive changes in the economy and the labour force in the 20th century, but behind the highly visible rising economic activity rates for women, especially married women, there have been more complex changes in the composition and characteristics of the workforce that undermine expectations for social and economic changes resulting from women's increased presence in the workforce.

The creation of a part-time workforce

In 1985 the *Journal of Labor Economics* published an extensive comparative analysis of trends in female employment in seven European countries (Britain, France, Germany, the Netherlands, Sweden, Italy and Spain) plus the USSR, the USA, Japan, Australia and Israel. Summarising the results, Mincer (1985: 35) noted that, historically, the shrinkage of farm, family business and other household-based employment and its eventual replacement by employment outside the home, and independent of the spouse, creates a U-shaped trend in aggregate female workforce participation that can take a long time to materialise. In Sweden, the changeover from a heavily agrarian economy to an industrial economy continued until well into the 20th century, so that the low point of the U-shaped trend was in the 1950s, when female economic activity rates fell to about 25%, as shown in Nyberg's (1994) study (discussed in Chapter 2). In Britain, the low point was not very low, and it lasted from about 1881–1921, when employment rates fell to one-third of adult women compared with virtually all of adult men (Hakim, 1993a: 93–102). In the mid-19th century female employment rates were a constant 42% to 43% falling to 32% by 1881 and remaining at this level until World War Two (Table 3.1). The 10% reduction resulted primarily from a genuine fall in women's workrates, plus some under-reporting, as working class and middle class families all sought to conform to the ideal of the full-time housewife supported by a husband earning a 'family wage' (Horrell and Humphries, 1995; Hatton and Bailey, 2001).

From the 1950s onwards, economic activity rates rose rapidly, from 43% of women aged 15–59 in 1951 to a projected 75% of women aged 16–59 by 2006 (Table 3.1). Among ever-married women, the rise seems sharper: from 26% in 1951 to 49% in 1971 and to 71% in 1990–1994, whereas male economic activity rates fell from 91% in 1979 to 85% by 1994 (Hakim, 1979: 3; 1993a: 100; Sly, 1994: 405). Before equal

Table 3.1 Economic activity rates 1851–2006

	Men aged 20+	Women aged 20+		
1851	98	42		
1861	99	43		
1871	100	42		
1881	95	32		
1891	94	32		
	Adult men*	Adult women*	Men 16–64	Women 16–59
1901	84	32	96	38
1911	84	32	96	38
1921	87	32	94	38
1931	91	34	96	38
1941	..	..	..	..
1951	88	35	96	43
1961	86	38	95	47
1971	81	44	91	57
1981	77	48	89	64
1991	74	52	87	71
1996	71	54	84	87
2001	70	55	83	74
2006	69	56	82	75

* 1901–11 people aged 10 and over, 1921 people aged 12 and over, 1931 people aged 14 and over, 1951–71 people aged 15 and over, 1981–2006 people aged 16 and over.
Sources: Derived from Hakim (1979) Table 1 and Hakim (1980) Tables 1 and 2 based on analyses of Population Census reports for England and Wales or Great Britain 1801–1971, and Ellison (1994) Table 3 presenting mid-year estimates based on 1971 and 1981 Census results and Labour Force Survey (LFS) results up to 1993, and labour force projections to 2006 based on these sources. Figures for 1851–1961 relate to England and Wales; figures for 1971–2006 are for Great Britain. Figures are for the 'occupied' population 1801–1951 and for the 'economically active' population 1961–2006. Figures for 1851–1871 exclude people whose sole occupation was unpaid household work (listed as an occupation in these censuses) in order to achieve comparability with other censuses. Figures for the population of working age 1901–1971 are for people aged 15–59/64; figures for 1981–2006 are for people aged 16–59/64.

opportunities legislation, the *marriage bar* rule required female workers in many occupations to resign on marriage. Abolition of the marriage bar allowed women to remain in their jobs after marriage, typically until the first birth, although some returned to work later on. As marriage rates rose over the century, married female workers substituted for unmarried female workers, a process found in the USA as well as in Europe (Oppenheimer, 1970). The female workforce became representative of all women of working age. Female employment was redistributed across the life cycle, whereas before the 1950s it was concentrated among unmarried younger women (Hakim, 1979).

The rise in female employment rates is due primarily to the creation of a new part-time workforce (the USA being a rare exception). All modern industrial economies now have a substantial and growing female part-time workforce. In the

Table 3.2 Employment rates and part-time work in Europe, 2002

	Working age population 15–64 millions	Total employ- ment millions	Employment rates % of working age population			Part-time workers % of all employed		FTE employ- ment rate
			All	Men	Women	Women	Men	Women
Denmark	3.5	2.8	76	80	72	30	11	63
Sweden	5.8	4.4	74	75	72	33	11	63
Finland	3.5	2.3	68	70	66	18	8	62
Portugal	7.0	5.1	68	76	61	16	7	58
France	37.9	24.9	63	70	57	29	5	51
Austria	5.5	4.0	69	76	63	38	6	51
UK	39.0	29.5	72	78	65	44	9	51
Ireland	2.6	1.8	65	75	55	30	7	47
Luxembourg	0.3	0.3	64	76	52	25	2	46
Germany	54.9	38.9	65	72	59	36	5	46
Belgium	6.8	4.1	60	68	51	37	6	43
Netherlands	10.9	8.3	74	82	66	73	21	42
Greece	6.8	3.9	57	71	43	8	2	41
Spain	27.6	16.3	58	73	44	17	3	40
Italy	38.7	23.9	56	69	42	17	4	39
EU15	250.6	170.4	64	73	56	34	7	47
Slovenia	1.4	0.9	63	68	59	8	5	58
Lithuania	2.3	..	60	63	57	..	..	57
Latvia	1.6	1.0	60	64	57	..	..	57
Estonia	0.9	0.6	62	67	58	11	5	56
Czech Republic	7.2	4.8	66	74	57	8	2	56
Cyprus	0.5	..	69	79	59	..	..	56
Romania	15.3	7.7	58	64	52	13	11	52
Slovakia	3.7	2.1	57	62	51	3	1	50
Hungary	6.8	3.9	57	64	50	5	2	49
Bulgaria	5.4	3.0	51	54	48	3	2	48
Poland	26.2	13.8	52	57	46	13	9	45

Notes: The FTE (full-time equivalent) employment rate assumes that most part-timers work half-time hours, so that two part-time workers are equivalent to one full-time worker. Part-time work is self-defined in the EU LFS, with some variation between countries in the upper limit for what are regarded as a part-time hours.
Sources: LFS data for 2002 and other sources reported in European Commission, *Employment in Europe 2003*, 2003.

Table 3.3 Women and part-time work in OECD countries, 2000

	% part-time among those working		Female share (%) of total employment in each category		
	Men	Women	FT work	PT work	Total
Australia	13	45	33	74	44
Austria	2	24	38	89	44
Belgium	7	34	35	79	42
Canada	10	27	41	70	46
Czech Republic	1	5	43	77	44
Denmark	9	24	42	71	47
Finland	7	14	46	65	48
France	5	25	39	79	45
Germany	4	34	35	86	44
Greece	3	9	36	67	38
Hungary	2	5	53	80	52
Iceland	9	32	40	77	47
Ireland	8	33	34	76	41
Italy	6	23	32	71	37
Japan	12	39	20	70	41
Korea	5	9	40	59	41
Luxembourg	2	28	32	91	39
Mexico	7	26	22	65	34
Netherlands	13	57	27	77	43
New Zealand (2001)	11	35	38	74	46
Norway	10	43	36	79	47
Poland	9	18	32	62	45
Portugal	3	13	43	78	45
Slovak Republic	1	2	50	75	51
Spain	3	16	34	80	37
Sweden	8	23	44	73	48
Switzerland	8	46	32	81	44
United Kingdom	8	40	35	81	45
Unites States (1999)	7	19	43	70	47
OECD average (unweighted)	7	26	37	75	44

Source: OECD *Employment Outlook: 2002 edition*, Table 2.1, p 69. Copyright OECD. Data for people aged 15–64. All percentages have been rounded.

EU, between 8% (Greece) and 73% (the Netherlands) of working women are in part-time jobs, so that Full-Time Equivalent (FTE) workrates are identical in these two countries (Table 3.2). Portugal and Finland are the only EU countries with long-standing high female workrates despite low proportions in part-time jobs; for some reason, these two dissimilar countries have exceptionally high female full-time employment rates. Otherwise, high female workrates are due to a large proportion of part-time jobs (Table 3.2). Among Organisation for Economic Co-operation and Development (OECD) countries (Table 3.3), women's share of full-time jobs remains

Table 3.4   Full-time work rates among women 1951–2003

| Proportion (%) of women of working age who work full-time | | | |
women aged 20–64 years		women aged 16–59 years	
1951	30.3	1984	33.1
1961	29.8	1985	33.6
1971	29.0	1986	33.9
1981	31.6	1987	34.5
		1988	35.9
		1989	37.4
		1990	38.2
		1991	37.4
		1992	36.5
		1993	36.1
		1994	35.8
		2003	36.2

Sources: Population Census data for Great Britain 1951–1981 reported in Joshi *et al* (1985: S154), and LFS data for Great Britain 1984–1991 reported in Department of Employment (1992: 444), updated with annual LFS reports.

around one-third (30% to 40%), whereas women take three-quarters of all part-time jobs. Part-time work is rare among men, except in the Netherlands (Table 3.2). The growth of the part-time workforce is due in part to student jobs, and to part-time work among early retired older men, but mainly to married women's entry into the labour force (Hakim, 1997). In some countries, such as Britain, women switched from full-time jobs to part-time jobs as these became available, so there has been a *substitution* of part-time for full-time work. In some countries, such as the Netherlands, the part-time workforce has been a significant *addition* to the full-time workforce. Most countries have a combination of both processes, to varying degrees.

In Britain, full-time work rates changed very little after 1950, while part-time employment grew rapidly (Tables 3.4 and 3.5). Full-time work rates fluctuated around one-third of the age group from 1951 (30%) to 1994 (36%), and have risen a fraction since then. In effect, women's *full-time* employment rates have been virtually stable since 1851. From 1851–2002, women's full-time employment rate fluctuated only within a 30% to 40% range, very similar to the 34% to 43% workrates in France over the past century (Riboud, 1985). Pott-Buter (1993) also shows a remarkable stability in female workrates since 1850 across Europe. There is no evidence that women have been taking full-time jobs from men, or that changes in female workrates could account for the loss of men's jobs.

All the increase in employment in Britain since 1950, from 22 million jobs in 1951 to 26 million in 1997, consisted of growth in female part-time jobs (Table 3.5). By the early 1980s, two million full-time jobs were lost in the male workforce, most of them in manufacturing. Another one million jobs were lost in the female workforce, but then regained by the early 1990s. The only increase in female employment since the

Table 3.5 Trends in full-time and part-time work, Britain 1951–2003

	Total in employment thousands	Full-time employment thousands	Part-time employment thousands	% part-time
All workers				
1951	22,135	21,304	831	4
1961	23,339	21,272	2,066	9
1971	23,733	19,828	3,904	16
1981	22,881	18,977	3,905	17
1984	23,246	18,395	4,851	21
1988	24,664	19,264	5,400	22
1991	25,294	19,667	5,627	22
1995	25,402	19,256	6,146	24
2003	25,148	17,271	7,877	31
Women				
1951	6,826	6,041	784	11
1961	7,590	5,698	1,892	25
1971	8,701	5,413	3,288	38
1981	9,146	5,602	3,543	39
1984	9,638	5,346	4,292	45
1988	10,527	5,837	4,690	45
1991	11,072	6,230	4,842	44
1995	11,322	6,302	5,020	44
2003	12,520	6,502	6,018	48
Men				
1951	15,309	15,262	47	*
1961	15,748	15,574	174	1
1971	15,032	14,430	602	4
1981	13,736	13,374	362	3
1984	13,608	13,050	558	4
1988	14,139	13,429	710	5
1991	14,222	13,438	784	6
1995	14,080	12,954	1,126	8
2003	12,628	10,769	1,859	15

* less than 0.5%

Sources: Hakim (1996a) Table 3.3, updated with March 2003 LFS statistics. There are some discontinuities (in definitions of part-time work, etc) between population census results for 1951–1981, LFS data for the whole workforce for 1984–1995, and 2003 LFS seasonally adjusted data for employees only. No FT/PT split is given for the self-employed, people in the Armed Forces, and people on government work training schemes in 2003. With these groups added, the total in employment would be 28,882 in 2003.

1950s, and indeed since 1851 or before, is the massive expansion of part-time jobs, from 0.8 million in 1951 to 5.5 million by 1997, echoed by a much smaller growth of part-time jobs among men, reaching one million in the 1990s. The headcount increase in female employment conceals an almost unchanging contribution of total hours worked by women, which remained below 33% up to 1980 (Joshi et al, 1985: S171).

The relatively unregulated British labour market allowed part-time work to develop earlier, and grow faster, than elsewhere in Europe (Joshi et al, 1985), but similar trends are observed in other European countries (Hakim, 1993a: 431; Meulders et al, 1993; 1994; European Commission, 1995a: 9–18). Across the EU, the growth in part-time jobs is generally double the growth in full-time jobs (European Commission, 2003: 33). The dramatic increase in female employment in Sweden has also been exposed as largely illusory, due to including in the employment count women who are at home full-time with their children on long parental leave, as well as women working part-time (Jonung and Persson, 1993). In West Germany, the rising female employment rate, from 48% in 1960 to 59% in 1994, is explained mainly by rising part-time employment (Fitzenberger et al, 2004: 84).

Only the USA has had a steady and accelerating growth in women's employment (OECD, 1988: 129). However, there was little or no growth in married women's average work experience, measured in years (Goldin, 1989; 1990), and there was a 9% decline in women's annual market hours from 1940–1988 (Coleman and Pencavel, 1993). In sharp contrast to Britain, all the growth has been in women's full-time year-round employment in the USA, and not in part-time part-year employment rates, which have remained stable for men and women for decades (Table 3.6).

Table 3.6 Annual work experience profiles in the USA, 1966–1986

	Percentage of population of working age in each group								
	Full-time year-round employment			Part-time and/or part-year employment			No employment over the year		
	All	M	F	All	M	F	All	M	F
1966	39	60	20	28	25	30	33	15	50
1971	37	55	22	30	29	30	33	16	48
1976	36	52	22	31	29	32	33	19	46
1982	37	49	26	30	29	31	33	22	43
1986	41	53	30	28	26	30	31	21	40

Source: Derived from Table 1 in Mellor and Parks (1988). Full-time year-round workers are those who worked 50 weeks or more during the year and usually worked 35 hours a week or more. That is, they must work full-time hours for at least 25 weeks in the year. About 8% of this group have some weeks of part-time work (under 35 hours a week).

Part-time workers and secondary earners

Rising female employment has been seen as an indicator of greater equality between men and women. In reality, female full-time employment rates have remained fairly constant for over a century, and are still around half the male rate. In most countries, male full-time workers still outnumber women two to one (Table 3.3). The main innovation is the new part-time workforce, which has different characteristics from the full-time workforce (Hakim, 1998a; OECD, 2002). Most part-time workers are secondary earners rather than primary earners (Hakim, 1997). There is thus no reason to expect major social and economic change from recent changes in female employment, in effect, from a rise in secondary earners.

Secondary earners are not earning a living; they are financially dependent on another person, or on state income support, for the basic necessities of life such as housing, food and fuel. Earnings from employment are thus *supplementary* or *secondary* to this other, larger source of income. Primary earners must necessarily obtain a *regular* income to cover basic necessities; therefore they work full-time and continuously. Secondary earners may work on an intermittent basis as well as part-time, and they often work closer to home (Madden, 1981). Secondary earners may take full-time jobs which are relatively low-paid but provide compensating advantages such as convenient hours, an agreeable work environment and pleasant social relations. Secondary earners may even forego earnings completely in favour of voluntary work, educational courses or other activities. Their earnings may be an important contribution to the family budget, providing some flexibility, private schooling for children, birthday gifts or the holiday that gives a lift to life. However, the defining factor is not the level of earnings, nor their use. Primary earners are people who may decide to work more or fewer hours, or to vary their work effort in other ways, but for whom the question of whether or not they are in employment is not in doubt. Secondary earners are people who may choose to work, or not, according to a range of considerations, financial and non-financial, and thus have intermittent work histories. Primary earners respond to marginal tax rates, whereas secondary earners are affected by the average rate of tax on the whole of their earnings (Kay and King, 1978: 37). The work decision differs qualitatively between primary and secondary earners.

Married women are the most important group of secondary earners; in the past, they were the only group. Today, they are joined by rising numbers of students with jobs of some sort, and semi-retired older people who take (part-time) jobs (Hakim, 1998a: 134–77; O'Reilly and Fagan, 1998). Barron and Norris (1976) classified all women as secondary earners in the secondary labour force in the 1960s, noting their above-average turnover rates. The secondary earner label is also used more narrowly to refer to marginal workers and discouraged workers who move in and out of the labour market in response to the economic cycle, almost a 'reserve army of labour' classification (Joshi, 1981). The size, stability and separateness of the part-time workforce in countries like Britain and Denmark ensures it cannot just be a reserve army of labour (Bruegel, 1979; Beechey and Perkins, 1987). However, particular groups of women and men have markedly higher cyclical movements, notably young people, older people, and young mothers, and these are also the groups most likely to work part-time (Joshi, 1981; Owen and Joshi, 1987; Blossfeld and Hakim, 1997; Hakim, 1997: 60–61; O'Reilly and Fagan, 1998).

Although numerically important, part-time workers are the most mobile members of the workforce; their primary identity is as homemaker or student rather than worker; they are even more satisfied with their jobs than full-time workers; and their contribution to household finances is generally too small to change their role and power within the family. Almost all part-time workers are secondary earners. However, not all secondary earners work part-time; some have full-time jobs (Martin and Hanson, 1985). In the relatively unregulated British labour market, part-time work expanded quickly after 1950 to provide the majority of jobs taken by secondary earners. In countries where part-time jobs are less widely available, such as the USA or Spain, secondary earners often work full-time. In most countries, secondary earners also work full-time before they start childbearing.

On average, in Britain, it takes 2.4 part-time employees to provide the same number of work hours as one full-time employee (Table 3.7). Among the self-employed, the ratio is 3 to 1. People in second jobs work the equivalent of a bare one day a week (see Table 2.4). The real contribution of part-timers to the workforce is much smaller than the headcount suggests. By the mid-1990s, part-time employment accounted for 22% of all jobs in Britain, or closer to one-quarter if the part-time self-employed are included. But 5.4 million part-timers still only accounted for 10% of all hours worked (Table 3.7). The self-employed were more important, contributing 15% of hours worked despite a dramatic decline in their average work hours in the 1980s (see Table 2.4). Even though full-time employee jobs have been declining, they still account for three-quarters of total work hours, completely dwarfing part-timers' contribution (Table 3.7).

Table 3.7 The relative significance of part-time employees: jobs and hours

		1979	1983	1994
Total employment in thousands = 100%		24,210	22,589	24,481
Total hours worked in millions = 100%		863.0	782.1	816.3
Full-time employees	– Employment	18,411	16,298	15,872
	as % of total	76%	72%	65%
	Hours worked	708.1	616.3	606.4
	as % of total	82%	79%	74%
Part-time employees	– Employment	4,020	3,990	5,401
	as % of total	17%	18%	22%
	Hours worked	70.0	63.9	83.7
	as % of total	8%	8%	10%
Self-employed	– Employment	1,779	2,301	3,208
	as % of total	7%	10%	13%
	Hours worked	85.0	101.9	126.3
	as % of total	10%	13%	15%

Source: Derived from Table 2 in Butcher and Hart (1995: 216) reporting spring LFS results for Britain. Figures include unpaid overtime hours except in 1979 when the information was not collected.

The relative invisibility of part-timers within the workforce is reinforced by the vast majority of part-time jobs being concentrated within a narrow range of female-dominated occupations, which function as labour market entry and exit jobs for male students and pre-retirement older workers as well as women (Hakim, 1993b; 1995b: Table 5; 1998a: 102–77). Women's part-time jobs are concentrated in clerical work, retail sales, personal service occupations and other unskilled occupations; very few are in the professional and managerial occupations that employ over one-quarter of women full-time workers and male workers (Table 3.8). Part-time jobs are often low-skill jobs with few promotion prospects (Rubery et al, 1994: 210–14). Part-time employees have the lowest levels of trade union membership, one indication of a lesser involvement with the world of work. There is little difference in trade union membership rates among men and women working full-time. Trade union membership among part-timers is half that among full-timers: 21% versus 38%; only among the self-employed are rates lower than this (Beatson and Butcher, 1993: 676; Corcoran, 1995: 192).

In countries that already have a large part-time workforce, these jobs are just as permanent and secure as full-time jobs (Hakim, 1990a: 185–97; Rubery et al, 1994: 214). In any event, EU legislation now gives part-time workers the same legal rights and employment benefits as full-time workers. However, labour mobility remains consistently higher among part-timers than full-timers (Gregg and Wadsworth, 1995: 80; Hakim, 1996c; 1998a: 135–38). For example, annual job turnover among part-timers is twice as high as among full-timers, and very few part-timers stay in the same job for 10 years or longer (see Table 5.5). Secondary earners, and hence most part-time workers, have qualitatively different work orientations (as shown in Chapter 4). Sometimes, this leads to a lower investment in training and skills, or what economists term 'human capital'. They are then typically restricted to low-skill jobs with low earnings, which are also the jobs most readily organised as part-time jobs by employers (Beechey and Perkins, 1987; Rubery et al, 1994; O'Reilly and

Table 3.8 Occupations of part-time and full-time workers

	Men	Women working		
		All	Full time	Part time
Managers and administrators	19	11	16	5
Professional occupations	11	9	11	5
Associate professional and technical occupations	8	10	12	8
Clerical and secretarial occupations	7	26	30	21
Craft and related occupations	22	3	4	2
Personal and protective service	6	15	11	20
Sales occupations	5	12	6	18
Plant and machine operatives	14	4	6	3
Other occupations	9	10	3	18
Base: all in employment (thousands = 100%)	13,301	10,617	5,910	4,604

Source: Winter 1992–93 LFS data for Great Britain reported in Sly (1993: 489) Table E.

Fagan, 1998). Full-time work declines sharply from 65% among professional and managerial women to 6% among unskilled women. The incidence of part-time work rises from 16% to 57% as a woman's occupational grade declines and, to a lesser extent, so does economic inactivity, that is, full-time homemaking (Table 3.9). Most part-time jobs have similar or lower status than the housewife role (see Table 2.7), so that the opportunity cost of not working is low, in social and economic terms. This explains some contradictory research results on part-timers, who are found in some studies to place greater importance on social relations at work or on the intrinsic interest of a job, and yet found in others to be instrumental workers, working only at times of particular financial need. Either way, part-time work seems to have little or no value for long term careers (Corcoran *et al*, 1984: 184, 189).

People with part-time jobs may be just as attached to their jobs, for different reasons, as full-timers are attached to theirs (see Table 4.8). However, secondary earners do not have a central self-identity as workers in the same way as primary earners. Women working part-time often see their primary responsibility as keeping house, with employment fitted around family life (see Tables 4.1 and 4.3). Despite their short hours, women part-timers are far more likely than full-timers to take unpaid time off work for domestic reasons (Rubery *et al*, 1994: 219). The secondary earner's distinctive balancing of family life and employment explains the paradox of part-time workers being equally or more satisfied with their typically low status low-paid jobs than full-timers with their objectively superior and more attractive jobs. The disproportionate job satisfaction of part-timers has been observed in so many surveys, in so many countries, that the pattern is no longer disputed (Martin and Roberts, 1984: 41, 74; Hakim, 1991: 101–03; Curtice, 1993: 104–15; Fenton-

Table 3.9   Patterns of work and inactivity among women of working age by occupational grade

Socio-Economic Group (SEG)	Full time work	Part time work	Unem- ployed	Economically inactive	Total N = 100%
Professional and Managers/employers	68	14	3	15	2,342
Intermediate and Junior non-manual	41	32	5	22	9,146
Skilled manual and Own account	39	32	4	24	1,409
Semi-skilled and Personal service	27	31	6	34	3,941
Unskilled occupations	7	51	5	36	1,202
All occupations*	39	31	5	25	18,040

* includes women in the Armed Forces, in inadequately described occupations, and women who have never worked.
Source: OPCS, *Living in Britain 1996*, 1998, Table 5.5 presenting combined data for 1994, 1995 and 1996 for Britain. The nine SEGs are combined into just five occupational groups in this table. Data are for women of working age (16–59 years) reporting occupation of current or last job. Percentages have been rounded.

O'Creevy, 1995; Clark, 1997). Although some of the 'excess' satisfaction is attributable to the fact that part-time jobs offer more convenient hours, produce less stress and exhaustion at the end of the day, and generally offer pleasant social relations at work, there seems to be an additional factor over and above these, which must be due to the different perspective of the secondary earner (Martin and Hanson, 1985; Curtice, 1993: 115; Clark, 1997; Hakim, 1997). When secondary earners are forced to work full-time hours, they are far more dissatisfied than other full-time workers. Employed women who do not want to work express the lowest marital satisfaction (Moen, 1992: 67). Pringle (1988, 1989) and Hochschild (1990) describe secondary earners whose primary self-identity and commitment is the homemaker role, despite working full-time hours, usually in limited-career jobs such as secretarial and clerical work.

The dominant feminist view, now widely accepted, is that part-time work is an unwilling 'choice' forced on women by the need to reconcile employment with childcare responsibilities, and by the lack of childcare services (OECD, 2001; 2002: 69). The idea is plausible, but the evidence does not support the thesis, and even the EC now accepts that childcare problems are not the main factor (Hakim, 1997: 44–47). The vast majority of married women take a part-time job in preference to a full-time job; among unmarried men and women, many of the part-timers are still students. Virtually all part-time work is voluntary, in the sense of being preferred over a full-time job, in Britain, Germany, Ireland, Denmark and the Netherlands, all countries with high levels of part-time work, apart from Ireland (Hakim, 1990a). Although childbirth may be the initial stimulus to taking up part-time work, most part-timers feel their combination of employment and household work gives them 'the best of both worlds', and they continue with part-time work long after children have left home, or their husband has retired (Watson and Fothergill, 1993). Across Europe, part-time work is chosen by women without children as often as by mothers. This choice is simply not available to primary earners, who are obliged to work full-time throughout life. Part-time work is an option open only to people who have choices to make, such as secondary earners. Men only take part-time jobs during the transition from full-time education into the labour market, or during the transition out of employment into full-time retirement. Students take holiday jobs, or do seasonal part-time jobs, and they are the ones most likely to work less than 10 hours a week (Naylor, 1994: 480; Hakim, 1998a: 162–63). Men who have taken early retirement on an employer's pension sometimes take a part-time job in the years up to full retirement at normal pension age. Both these groups are secondary earners in that they have another main source of income: their occupational pension in the case of older men, their student grant or parental support in the case of young people.

Siltanen's case study of primary and secondary earners in the Post Office showed that married men were almost invariably primary earners, working unsocial and long overtime hours when necessary, in order to support a wife and children. The few men in sex-atypical secondary earner jobs were generally young single men still living with their parents. White women were typically secondary earners if they were married, and primary earners if they were not supported by a husband. In contrast, black women behaved like primary earners throughout the life cycle, choosing jobs that ensured their financial independence whether they were currently married or not, even when they had young children (Siltanen, 1994: 85–87). Black women demonstrate clearly that there is nothing inevitable about mothers becoming secondary earners, or financially dependent, as a result of childbirth; it is a choice white women feel they can safely make.

Siltanen's case study is especially valuable because many of the secondary earners were doing full-time jobs rather than part-time jobs. However, the secondary earner jobs were distinguished by not having the unsocial hours, in particular nightwork, and long hours of regular overtime that characterised the primary earner jobs. Overtime hours averaged a 33% addition to a basic 43 hour week, so the secondary earners were working much shorter weekly hours than the primary earners, even though both groups were classified as full-time workers. Primary and secondary earners also had quite different employment histories. None of the primary earners had ever worked part-time: either they worked continuously, or they had one short domestic break and returned to continuous full-time employment. None of the secondary earners had worked full-time continuously: the great majority worked intermittently, in a combination of part-time and full-time jobs (Siltanen, 1994: 33, 134).

It is because women part-time workers are secondary earners that their work roles and earnings do not produce significant changes in their primary role as homemaker, and have only a small impact, if any, on their relative power in family decision-making. Secondary earners often trivialise their earnings, emphasising that their earnings only pay for 'extras' or holidays, underlining that they are only 'helping out' and not usurping the primary earner's role as breadwinner (Zelizer, 1989). Some women do this even when they are working full-time, and their earnings constitute more than half the couple's income. They underline the fact that these earnings are temporary, and will cease when she stops work for childbearing. Or they emphasise that the wife's earnings are lower than the husband's after deducting all childcare costs from her salary. The point of these family 'myths' about economic and domestic roles is not that they are objectively untrue in the immediate present, but that they are true within the longer-term horizon of a permanent relationship in which a normative sexual division of labour is accepted, and in which short-term variations are unimportant. Jobs can be changed or lost in a day. Partnerships have longer time horizons. When men cease to believe in the sexual division of labour, or have a wife who overturns sex-role stereotypes by working continuously for years, they start to share more of the household work (Kiernan, 1992: 104; Gershuny et al, 1994: 170; Gershuny, 2000).

Household money management systems provide one indicator of relative power in family decision-making. Generally, research shows that financial equality depends on a wife's full-time employment. Part-time employment simply reduces the pressures on the husband's wage, without increasing wives' influence over finances (Kiernan, 1992: 103; Vogler, 1994b: 246). However, money management systems are more strongly related to normative views on sex-roles than to the actual division of labour within couples: male control over family finances is associated with a couple agreeing he should have ultimate responsibility for income-earning; couples who manage their finances jointly are more likely to agree that they should have joint responsibility for income-earning (Vogler, 1994b: 250–53).

Unlike women who work full-time, many part-timers retain primary responsibility for housework (see Tables 4.1 and 4.3). They do as many hours of domestic work as do full-time homemakers, almost twice as many hours as done by women working full-time (122 hours and 74 hours a week respectively). However, they spend far less time on childcare than full-time homemakers: 27 hours a week compared to 74 (Horrell, 1994: 208–09). The only indication that their part-time job alters their position within the family is a slight increase in their sharing of financial management with their husband (Kiernan, 1992: 101–03).

One might expect part-timers to fall half-way between full-time workers and non-working women in terms of attitudes and behaviour. On some work-related attitudes they do, but most often part-timers are closer to full-time housewives than to women working full-time. Homemakers and part-timers accept financial dependence on their spouse and differentiated sex-roles. Secondary earners often take jobs that are too small and too intermittent to significantly alter family roles, and earn too little for financial independence.

Some secondary earners are providing an important supplement to household income, others are making a lifestyle choice, and may pursue careers. Today, the second pattern is more common than the first (Eggebeen and Hawkins, 1990). However, the majority of dual-earner couples are not dual-career couples, who remain a minority of 10% to 20% of couples (Hakim, 2000: 111; 2003a: 80). Wives' financial dependence on their husbands has fallen, but husbands still remain the principal breadwinner in most households (Sorensen and McLanahan, 1987; Rubery et al, 1998: 197; Van Berkel and De Graaf, 1998; Hakim, 2000: 110–17). Sorensen and McLanahan (1987) estimate that the proportion of white wives who were 100% economically dependent on their spouse fell dramatically from 84% in 1940 to 31% in 1980 in the USA; however, the proportion with earnings equal to or greater than their husband's rose only from 6% to 15%. Substantial financial dependence remains the norm for wives in the USA as well as in Europe. Across the EU, three-quarters of men regard themselves as a primary earner, compared to only one-third of women (Hakim, 2003a: 4). In Britain, a working wife's earnings typically contribute one-third of household income among couples without dependent children, and one-quarter of household income among couples with dependent children. The picture in Nordic countries is not, in practice, very different from other European countries, despite higher employment rates. Among dual-earner couples, husbands earn on average about two-thirds of household income, twice as much as wives. Among all couples, husbands contribute two-thirds to three-quarters of household income (Table 3.10). A fuller analysis by Hobson (1990), using data for the mid-1980s, shows that the Nordic countries differ in having lower proportions of wives with no earnings at all, who are totally dependent on their husband: 11% in Sweden and 25% in Norway, compared to 68% in the Netherlands, 53% in Switzerland, 49% in West Germany, 40% in Australia, 36% in Canada, and about 30% in the USA and UK. However, the Nordic countries have not produced substantial numbers of couples where spouses have roughly equal earnings: 12% in Sweden and 8% in Norway, compared to 10% in the USA, 8% in Canada and Australia, 6% in Germany and the UK, 3% in Switzerland and the Netherlands (Hobson, 1990: Table 1; see also Sorensen, 1994: Table 5; Nock, 2001: 761). Even by

Table 3.10 Wives' financial dependence

Percentage of total earnings contributed by the husband, on average, in couples with a wife aged 20–60 in 1985

	All couples	Dual-earner couples
Finland	58	59
Sweden	61	63
Norway	66	67
USA	67	67
Canada	68	66
Australia	68	67
Belgium	74	59
West Germany	74	68
Netherlands	77	68

Source: Calculated from Figure 6.7, p 164 in D Spain and SM Bianchi, *Balancing Act*, Russell Sage Foundation, 1996, based on analyses of Luxembourg Income Study. Percentages have been rounded.

the 1990s, less than one-fifth of wives had equal earnings in Nordic countries, compared to 10% to 17% in the USA, Britain and Germany, and 7% in the Netherlands (Sorensen, 2004: 285). Wives' economic dependency is reduced, but certainly not eliminated in the Nordic countries. Nordic wives are typically secondary earners, just as they are in other advanced economies.

The main difference between dual-earner couples today, and in the past, is that spouses today have jobs that are independent of each other, and may present conflicting demands. In the past, spouses typically worked together on a family farm, or in a family business, so that work and family life were integrated for both spouses. The distinction between primary and secondary earners is a modern development.

The wife's secondary earner status and identity is observed within middle class and highly-educated dual-earner couples, even when the wife has a full-time job. As noted in Chapter 4, women generally prefer an older, more educated and higher-earning spouse. When the husband is older or more educated than the wife, spouses generally give priority to his career. Overall, in the USA, half of dual-earner middle class couples report that the husband's career takes priority, less than one-fifth say that her career takes priority, and one-third say they take turns (Moen, 2003: 183–200). Thus, over the life cycle, in at least half, and possibly two-thirds of dual-earner couples, the earnings gap between spouses will increase steadily over time, and the working wife will become an increasingly dependent secondary earner.

Globalisation and the demasculinisation of work

Most modern economies have seen a decline in manufacturing industry and a growth of service sector industries. Generally, there has been a net loss in male employment. Workforce projections predict further job losses in manufacturing, and greater growth in female employment than in jobs typically held by men, particularly in part-time jobs and self-employment (IER, 1995). The nature of work is changing. The question is, is it changing to the detriment of men, and to the advantage of women?

In Britain, the workforce now consists of almost equal numbers of men and women: men are only 55% to women's 45% when part-timers are included (see Table 3.3). This is one source of the fear that jobs are being demasculinised. Another is the all too visible decline of mining, agriculture and manufacturing industry, the location for huge numbers of male manual jobs, skilled and unskilled. Such fears are expressed in Campbell's *Goliath* (1993), which points out that young working class men, whose energies are not harnessed by unskilled jobs, will express their energies in more destructive ways, rioting and fighting the police. The globalisation of labour markets also raises fears about manufacturing jobs being exported to countries with cheaper labour costs. More recently, service sector jobs have also been exported, as illustrated by call centres transferred out of Europe to India and other Asian countries. However, it is more common for manual jobs and manufacturing plants to be relocated, speeding up the contraction of male-dominated occupations.

In practice, the feminisation of the workforce has usually been limited to the creation of a separate part-time workforce recruiting secondary earners who are not competing with primary earners for jobs. Chapter 6 demonstrates the segregation of the part-time and full-time workforces, and the polarisation of the workforce in recent decades (see Table 6.5). Given that over two part-time workers are needed to replace one full-time employee (see Table 2.4), the feminisation of the workforce looks more dramatic than it is in reality. In most cases, the full-time jobs lost, and the part-time jobs gained, are in different occupations and industries, so that quite different employers are involved. Sales assistant jobs in urban shops do not substitute directly for coalmining jobs. Most employers are traditionalists or opportunists in their use of part-time, temporary and self-employed workers (Hakim, 1990b), so they do not directly substitute part-time for full-time workers, women for men. The increased use of non-standard employment contracts is found in heavily regulated European countries as well as in Britain (Hakim, 1987; 1990a), partly due to the impact of recessions and economic uncertainty, and partly due to changing patterns of consumption. Finally, case studies of the clothing, textiles, food production and electronics industries in the Netherlands (which displays the most dramatic expansion of the part-time female workforce) find almost no cases of female workers substituting for male workers (Van Klaveren and Tijdens, 2003). Occupational segregation serves to protect male and female occupations from competition, as well as imposing rigidities (Rubery *et al*, 1998: 289).

The long term trend is for work to be demasculinised *and* defeminised. Occupations are becoming more skilled, technical and gender-neutral (Routh, 1987: 39, 67). Between 1911 and 1971, the proportion of the British workforce employed in professional, managerial and clerical occupations doubled from 19% to 37% (Routh, 1965, 1980: 5). Between 1971 and 2001, people in professional, technical, managerial and clerical occupations increased from 40% to 53% of the workforce (IER, 1995: 41). Over the 20th century, manual occupations shrank from 81% to 47% of the workforce in Britain. The stereotyping of jobs as 'male' or 'female' is more common for manual and lower-grade white-collar occupations (see Table 6.2). White-collar occupations that require special skills or knowledge, training and education, rarely have any obvious sex-stereotyping. Men and women can both be teachers, accountants, librarians, dentists, lawyers, doctors, musicians, economists, systems analysts and information engineers. Local, social, economic and historical factors determine the actual pattern of jobs taken up by men or women at any one time. As we show in Chapter 6, work cultures are far more heavily gendered than are occupations.

As the entire occupational structure shifts upwards over time, unskilled jobs are contracting and more qualified jobs are expanding; the occupational structure is gradually becoming gender-neutral (Hakim, 1998a). Since male jobs have always outnumbered female jobs in the past, the scope for the demasculinisation of work was always greater than for the defeminisation of jobs. The shrinkage of male manual jobs that were physically hard, dirty and dangerous is illustrated by the decline of the mining and ship-building industries. On the other hand, we have to remember that women and children were working in mining in Britain 150 years ago, so the masculinity of such work is socially determined.

Another source of the demasculinisation of work is the impact of technological change in reducing, even eliminating, the need for physical strength and risk-taking in many jobs, not just in the manufacturing industry. Jobs in construction require far less brute force as machines are now used to lift and place materials. Power steering on buses and other large vehicles allows slender young women to drive and control vehicles that previously required strong male drivers. Even war has become more high-tech, intellectual rather than physical in many areas.

Everyone feels personally threatened and discouraged by the discovery that one's skills are no longer in demand, are even redundant, that there is no demand for one's occupation and experience. Unskilled working class men are the largest group affected by the long term changes in the nature of work. Within the British working class culture, manual labour has been valorised as an expression of masculinity through movement, action and assertion. The physical domination of the world is valorised over the 'effeminate' intellectual domination of the world represented by educational attainment and white-collar jobs. Willis (1977) offers this inverted snobbery as an explanation for working class young men's acceptance of manual occupations at the lower end of the social class structure. (Willis mistakenly equates these attitudes with *machismo*, an entirely different gender ideology with no link to manual labour, valorising force of personality rather than physical strength.) Reliance on a masculine work identity was closely tied to the 'lads'' insistence on the sexual division of labour which restricted women to domesticity or to 'effeminate' white-collar work and office jobs. Thus, manual labour was associated with the social superiority of masculinity, and mental labour was associated with the social inferiority of femininity (Willis, 1977: 147–52). Unemployment for this group is thus doubly threatening: they are denied the psychological reassurance of doing masculine work in male work groups, and they are thrown into the feminine social environment of the domestic home, often on socially isolated housing estates, dominated by the quite different daily pursuits of mothers and children. Women exclude men from the domestic sphere just as effectively as men have tried to exclude women from the workforce. The disadvantage of the sexual division of labour is that it can make men strangers and trespassers in their own homes, so that they cannot function effectively there, forcing them out into the streets, bars and clubs when not at work.

While it is understandable that unemployed unskilled men might see women as the scapegoats for their loss, in fact both groups have experienced the effects of globalisation, and of structural and technological change at work. Men's loss of manual jobs and masculine work cultures has occurred in the same process as the defeminisation of women's jobs. In 1891, one-third of women were employed as indoor domestic servants and one-fifth worked in dressmaking and sewing; over half of all women worked in these feminine jobs, often in private households rather than in industry. By 1991, the most typically female occupation of secretaries, typists, personal assistants, and word processing operators provided jobs for no more than 7.5% of women, and childcare jobs provided work for only 3%. In 1991, the largest occupations employing women were simply low-skill jobs with no particular association with women's domestic skills, such as sales assistant, sales worker, check-out operator, clerk and cashier. As noted in Chapter 6, the most important occupations for women are today gender-neutral rather than typically feminine work. They are also jobs carried out in highly public locations, involving interaction with a large and diverse clientele. The social seclusion of employment in domestic service has given way to low-skill jobs that are very much in the public eye (Hakim, 1994: 445).

The aristocracy of labour used to be in highly skilled craft occupations, and trade unions used to express craft professional identities as well as class interests. Even less skilled men could take pride in work that was difficult and dangerous, as manual work generally required physical effort, skill and judgment. Today the aristocracy of labour is in professional and intellectual occupations; the most highly paid and risky occupations are in financial services; trade unions are in decline. Working class men have lost face and have lost courage. They cannot, like women, retreat into domestic life during recessions. Women had far less to lose in the decline of manufacturing, and they have far more to gain from the expansion of white-collar work, which has favoured women by being more gender-neutral, without the exclusively masculine character of manual jobs. White-collar jobs require skills and qualifications plus the social skills required for providing a service to others, as exemplified by the teacher, police officer and management consultant. Service sector jobs can involve manual work too, albeit combined with social skills, as illustrated by nurses, hairdressers, waiters and cooks. These jobs are clearly as open to men as they are to women. If women have any advantage in the service sector it is in their greater willingness to service and care for others, in contrast with men's more aggressive, self-centred or 'individualistic' achievement orientation. On the other hand, jobs as cooks, waiters, bartenders, sales and related work are held equally by men and women in Southern European countries, whereas they tend to be female-dominated in Northern European countries (Rubery and Fagan, 1993: 46–47); proof, once again, that it is work cultures that are gendered rather than occupations themselves. Social change is far more open-ended than institutional sociologists admit.

Childcare services and homecare allowances

Discussions of female employment almost invariably underline the need for good quality and affordable childcare services to help working women to reconcile family work with paid jobs. For example, the OECD (2001) argues that family-friendly policies help to raise employment rates among young women. The EC has always argued the case for improved public childcare services, and this has been a dominant demand among feminists.

The focus on childcare issues has led scholars to overlook the opposite problem: women who prefer to be at home full-time with their young children, if only they can afford it. The hugely successful homecare allowance in Finland and Norway, with similar schemes in France and Germany, has revealed the low work commitment of mothers. The schemes prove that almost all mothers prefer to look after their young children themselves, at home, instead of using public nurseries and returning to their jobs. The homecare allowance varies between countries, but is never large. In Finland, for example, the allowance amounts to 40% of the average monthly earnings of female employees (Ilmakunnas, 1997; Hakim, 2000: 232–35). Despite the popularity indicated by take-up rates close to 100%, these cash-for-care schemes are contentious in Scandinavia (Ellingsæter, 2003) and in France (Fagnani in Drew *et al*, 1998), because they reduce female employment rates.

Women's positive response to the homecare allowance schemes, and to childcare services, illustrates a general characteristic of secondary earners: the fact that they are easily persuaded to enter, or quit, the labour force. Other studies confirm that wives and mothers will quit the workforce for a relatively small independent income. For example, studies of the effects of a basic income in the Netherlands have shown that an income of 50% of legal minimum wages would lead to a 40% fall in female labour supply (Bruyn-Hundt, 1996: 168–69).

Do welfare states matter?

The EU's most important impact on social science has been to promote, even insist upon, cross-national comparisons of Member States – initially, as regards patterns of employment, especially among women; later on, of social and economic differences in the round. The central script for this new flood of comparative work became Esping-Andersen's *The Three Worlds of Welfare Capitalism* (1990), and variations of that typology. This approach has been adopted in several unsuccessful attempts to explain the very variable size of the female part-time workforce, and other differences in female employment (Rosenfeld and Birkelund, 1995; Fagan and Rubery, 1996; Blossfeld and Hakim, 1997; O'Reilly and Fagan, 1998; Cantillon *et al.* 2001; van der Lippe and van Dijk, 2002). Studies always find differences between nations. So the invariable conclusion of comparative studies is that welfare states make a difference, but this is not proven. Differences between countries could be due essentially to differences in history, national culture and politics, which produce differences in women's employment patterns and differences in the welfare state.

No study has yet proven that it is the welfare state *per se* that shapes female employment in each country. And there is plenty of contrary evidence that is routinely ignored. The EC has a vested interest in finding that welfare states do matter, because this strengthens its case for an active social policy role.

For example, women's involvement in the 1789 French Revolution produced a new climate of gender equality in France long before the feminist movements of the 20th century. The French Revolution also led to the secularisation of the educational system, to counteract the influence of Catholic teaching within the family, especially from mothers. Thus, nursery education from a young age was developed early in France, primarily as part of an aggressive secularisation policy, and within a republican ideology of universalism, not as a service to working mothers (Plaisance, 1986; Hakim, 2001). Today, social scientists routinely claim that good childcare services are the cause of high female workrates in France, without any recognition that this is a recent side-effect, not the original central aim. In fact, family policy in France has generally been pro-natalist, and encouraged full-time motherhood until quite late in the 20th century (Letablier, 2004).

Another difficult fact is that female employment rates, especially full-time equivalent rates, are close together in Germany, France and Britain (see Table 3.2; see also OECD, 2002: Table 2.2), despite large differences between these countries in childcare services, family policy, fiscal policy, employment flexibility, and national culture. The age-employment profiles for women in the three countries are almost identical (OECD, 2002: Chart 2.2). There is little difference between the three countries in employment rates for mothers with a partner and a child under 6 years: 51%, 57% and 61% in Britain (OECD, 2001: Table 4.1). There is no difference in employment rates for mothers with at least one child under 15 years (OECD, 2002: Table 2.4). The only difference is that French mothers with young children under 6 are more likely to work full-time than part-time: 31% compared to 21% in Germany and 20% in Britain (OECD, 2001: Table 4.2). This convergence in female employment belies the sharp differences between these welfare states.

Even more important is the abject failure of the welfare state thesis to explain why the two European countries with the highest female full-time employment rates, and relatively little part-time work, have little in common as regards welfare state services for mothers: Finland and Portugal. Attempts to explain female employment in Finland, as compared with West Germany and the Netherlands, or in comparison with Scandinavian countries, are no more successful (Pfau-Effinger, 1993; 1998; Melkas and Anker, 1998).

It seems doubtful that typologies of countries that focus on institutional factors could have real explanatory or predictive power, in practice, when tested properly. This does not exclude the possibility that particular policies can have a visible impact *within* a country, if adequately funded, as illustrated by the homecare allowance discussed above. This is especially likely in small and socially homogeneous countries.

Esping-Andersen's classification of welfare states is undoubtedly useful for comparative work on welfare states. It was not designed as a multi-purpose typology of European societies that could be used for analyses of women's employment, so it is not surprising that it is not ideal for this purpose. It seems doubtful that any useful typology of this kind could be devised for research on women's employment.

Conclusions

The feminisation of the workforce produced great expectations, which have not materialised. Reviews of recent developments repeatedly note the paradox of, on the one hand, an enormous growth of female labour force participation and, on the other hand, an intensified segregation of women into lower-grade, low-paid jobs. Women's rising employment has brought them few 'good jobs' (Jenson et al, 1988: 4–9, 44). The paradox is of course the result of superficial analyses that fail to distinguish trends in full-time and part-time work, continuous and intermittent work. As noted in Chapter 2, the one hour a week minimalist definition of employment has produced inflated employment rates which are ultimately misleading. The main growth has been in part-time jobs, most of them half-time jobs, but also many marginal jobs involving less than 10 hours a week, which some people think should be excluded from national employment statistics. The relatively unregulated British labour force represents an extreme case, but most European countries are discovering that the apparent rise in female employment in recent decades is due mostly to the creation of a part-time workforce for secondary earners, with a substitution of part-time for full-time women's jobs in some countries (de Neubourg, 1985; Hakim, 1993a; Meulders et al, 1994: 3; OECD, 1994: 77). Between the 1960s and the 1990s, in modern societies, there was a steady decline in the total volume of men's work hours, but the total for women remained constant (Gershuny, 2000: 173). In other words, in most countries, total employment hours were redistributed among women, but did not rise, contrary to the impression given by headcount statistics.

Full-time employment rates among women have not changed much for over 100 years in most European countries. The importance of this finding is difficult to overstate. It means that all the expectations of social and economic change, of greater equality between men and women in the workforce, and in the home, have rested, in practice, on the creation of a large part-time workforce. This is clearly nonsense. Even if part-time workers were identical to women working full-time in terms of qualifications, occupations and work experience, differing only in their shorter working hours, they would be poorly placed to provide the vanguard of change in the labour force, and the catalyst for wider social and political change resulting from women's greater economic independence. The example of Sweden is instructive.

So-called 'part-time' workers in Sweden are in fact working reduced hours of 30 hours a week, which classifies them as full-timers by European Commission standards (1994: 116). Most commonly they continue to work in the same job when they transfer temporarily to reduced hours work, so there is no reason for the 'part-time' workforce to develop as a separate, segregated sector. Despite this, and a vigorous policy of promoting equal opportunities, occupational segregation is higher in Scandinavia than in other OECD countries. Women are concentrated in the public sector, in jobs that replace unpaid household work: childcare, care of the elderly, healthcare and education services. Few women work in the private sector, and women are less likely to attain management positions than in the competitive hire-and-fire economies of North America. Rosenfeld and Kalleberg (1990) showed that women are less likely to achieve senior positions at work in Scandinavian countries than they are in North America: only 1.5% of women working full-time had management jobs in Sweden compared to 11% in the USA. Swedish women still fail to achieve the jobs with most power and authority in the workforce, even though they now hold 40% of political representative posts compared with an average for European parliaments of 11% (Statistics Sweden, 1995; Wright *et al*, 1995). As noted in Chapter 6, the pay gap is no lower in Sweden than in other modern economies. Sweden is widely viewed as a 'best practice' case for women's employment. It provides conclusive evidence that high female employment rates do not automatically produce gender equality, even when accompanied by good childcare services and egalitarian policies; indeed they have the opposite effect. It leads us to ask whether the two goals are mutually incompatible.

Our findings have important theoretical implications. As noted in Chapter 1, Walby's theory that there has been a change from private to public patriarchy, and a change from exclusionary to segregationist strategies for maintaining women's subordination rests heavily on the premise that more women are in employment (Walby, 1986; 1990: 48, 53–57). She also believes that women now work continuously apart from a five year break for having children (1990: 9), which is also untrue, as shown in Chapter 5. Walby's thesis collapses in the face of the evidence. True, the part-time workforce is a segregated workforce, but its development owes little to trade union segregationist strategies in Britain or other European countries. Until the 1990s, the British Trades Union Congress (TUC) and most trade unions simply ignored part-time workers as marginal workers who were not really part of the workforce. Employers do not care whether part-timers are male or female, which is why young men and older men also pass through part-time jobs at particular stages of the life cycle. Part-time jobs are only of interest to secondary earners, who are not in competition for jobs with primary earners, so there was no need for a trade union strategy towards them. Furthermore, male employers resisted trade union attempts to exclude female workers, from clerical work for example, right from the start, so that exclusionary and segregationist strategies were pursued *in parallel* over this period by different trade unions. Employer resistance to trade union attempts to control and restrict the supply of labour warns us against generalising from specific trade union policies to a broad theory of patriarchal policies pursued by men generally against women generally. Milkman's (1987) analysis of trade union strategies in the USA reveals a similar diversity, denying the idea of consistent and hegemonic patriarchal policies restricting women's employment and wages.

Trade union campaigns for a family wage and protective legislation restricted women's wage work, forcing wives into economic dependency and full-time domestic work – arguably to the benefit of the women themselves, as well as their families, in the working class (Humphries, 1981). Unpaid household work in one's own home was usually preferable to paid domestic work as a servant in someone else's home, the occupation of one-third to one-half of women in the late 19th century (Grossman, 1980; Matthaei, 1982: 197–203, 284; Hakim, 1994). The clearest evidence of policies to exclude women from employment was the marriage bar introduced in the late 19th century, maintained in some British trade unions up to the 1960s (and not formally eliminated until the Sex Discrimination Act 1975), with similar policies applied by many USA employers (Cohn, 1985; Grint, 1988; Goldin, 1990: 160–79). But most women accepted the marriage bar. As late as 1930, a ballot among women in government employment found only 3% in favour of abolishing the marriage bar (Grint, 1988: 101). Furthermore, occupational segregation on the basis of sex was already well-established by 1891 but then *declined* over the next century (Hakim, 1994). On closer examination, the trade union policy of maintaining unequal pay for women, even when doing the same jobs as men, was the most effective deterrent to women's employment and guarantee of their economic dependency. Hartmann and Walby are right to see male-dominated trade unions as the clearest illustration of patriarchy in the labour market. But the 20th century saw the demise of patriarchy as practised by the aristocracy of labour and the trade unions. By the 1990s the British system of industrial relations itself was in decline (Millward *et al*, 1992: 350; Purcell, 1993; Cully *et al*, 1998; 1999; Millward *et al*, 2000).

Not all working women are secondary earners, but most secondary earners are married women, who rely on their husband as main breadwinner, as shown in Chapter 4. Since the rise of female employment cannot be the catalyst for recent social and economic change, we must explain any change that did occur with reference to other factors, such as the impact of sex discrimination legislation (Zabalza and Tzannatos, 1985a, b; 1988; Manning, 1996), wars (Milkman, 1987: 152), changes in attitudes and values (Hakim, 2000) or even in the sex ratio (Britton and Edison, 1986) – a much wider range of explanations than a simple focus on male policies for subordinating women.

The domestication of women (Rogers, 1981) lasted less than a century. However, as we show in the next chapter, the sexual division of labour did not die but was simply regenerated in its modern form.

Chapter 4
Work Values, Work Plans and Social
Interaction in the Workplace

By the 1990s, it had become received opinion among social scientists that sex differentials in attitudes to employment had faded away. One after the other, research reports and literature reviews asserted confidently that any differences in work-related values that may have existed in the past had now disappeared. As Eagly (1995: 145) points out, some went further, to argue that all sex differences were disappearing, and that none should be studied or reported, in case they supported gender stereotypes. This view has been offered in Britain, in other European countries and in the USA. It was never challenged, and sometimes regarded as ideologically suspect to do so. Like many other myths about women's employment (Hakim, 1995a), the constant repetition of this claim has required selective and one-eyed presentation of the research evidence. Fortunately, social scientists are now beginning to recognise that sex differences still remain in social identity and aspirations that can be crucial to careers and work histories.

There is no doubt that in the 1950s most working women regarded their jobs in a substantially different light from men, attitudes that were reflected in rates of absenteeism that were two, three or four times higher than among men, even after disregarding absences due to pregnancies and childbirth (Myrdal and Klein, 1956, 1968: 94–106). After reviewing the evidence for Britain, Sweden and the USA, Myrdal and Klein concluded that women had 'a less serious attitude to their work', displaying 'a certain laxity' and 'immaturity' in their tendency to stay off work for any domestic reason. However, they pointed out that this behaviour occurred at a time when women were constantly reminded of their lower value and unequal position in the workforce by being paid at a lower rate than men for the same job (Myrdal and Klein, 1956, 1968: 98, 101, 105, 108). Equal pay and equal opportunities laws and policies removed this factor from the 1970s onwards, and absenteeism no longer displays any marked sex differential. It seems plausible that sex differences in work orientations have also disappeared, and studies often draw this conclusion.

Just one example is a report on a 1992 British survey concluding that the difference in the significance of employment to men's and women's lives would appear to have largely evaporated (Gallie and White, 1993: 18). The explanation for this finding is of course that the study only reports data for employees, leaving five million non-working women out of the picture altogether. The Netherlands has long had the lowest female workrate in Northern Europe (Pott-Buter, 1993: 28), and the Full-Time Equivalent (FTE) employment rate for women remains below the EU average (see Table 3.2), yet Tijdens still suggested that the work commitment and work orientations of men and women do not differ because one-fifth of *working* women and men in the Netherlands plan a career (Tijdens, 1993: 84). In the USA, Reskin and Padavic simply dismissed sex differentials in work commitment and work effort as implausible or out of date ideas (1994: 39–41, 86, 112–13). Their evidence was a study by Bielby and Bielby (1988) which purported to test and reject Becker's thesis about some married women giving priority to family responsibilities over market work, thus seeking less demanding jobs. They used the 1977 and 1973

USA Quality of Employment Surveys, which collected data only on permanent jobs involving at least 20 hours a week, with the emphasis therefore on the full-time workforce, despite the fact that currently non-working wives, wives in part-time jobs of under 20 hours a week, and wives in temporary jobs were all crucially relevant to the theory being tested. Bielby and Bielby acknowledged that the dataset was not appropriate, but went ahead anyway. Within their selective group of workers, work effort was significantly lower among part-time and part-year workers, women with young children and in the lower occupational grades. Greater work effort was associated with all the features typical of men rather than women: longer education, greater work continuity, self-employment and, paradoxically, with being female. The results seem to confirm that women have to work harder than men in the same job, but they do not even address, let alone refute, Becker's thesis. The majority of wives, who do no market work at all or work less than 20 hours a week, were excluded from the study, so that results are weakened by sample selection bias (see Chapter 5). By 2002, Reskin and Padavic admitted that women are less likely than men to be continuously employed, to gain work experience, and to have relevant education. However, they completely ignore research evidence on sex differences in workers' attitudes to focus exclusively on employers' gender stereotypes and discriminatory ideologies to explain the pay gap (Padavic and Reskin, 2002: 52, 114, 134, 137–38).

This chapter examines the evidence on sex differences in attitudes to work, and it also assesses whether attitudes are important determinants of achievements in the workforce.

Attitudes to the sexual division of labour

Studies which investigate attitudes to the sexual division of labour, that is, *qualitative* differences between the roles of men and women, are surprisingly rare, compared with innumerable public opinion surveys on whether mothers of young children should stay at home or go out to work, and whether women are as capable as men of doing a job well. Early studies identified four theoretically distinct components of sex-role attitudes, and showed that male and female views converged on some and diverged on other components (Osmond and Martin, 1975). Even among university students, men and women accepted a sharp sexual division of labour in the family, with wives retaining primary responsibility for the home and childcare, and husbands responsible for income-earning. Disagreement was centred on the character of women's labour force participation, their role in public life and politics – with men being more traditional than women in allocating political and other leadership roles and career commitment to men. Yet men were happy to accept a wife earning more money than they did, more than women believed they would be (Osmond and Martin, 1975: 755). The huge volume of research since then has been less sophisticated, addressing public attitude to women's employment, most of it showing women to be more 'modern' than men, much of it relying on multivariate analysis rather than on theory to identify components within sex-role attitudes (but see Scott and Duncombe, 1991). However, studies generally find little or no association between public attitude statements and respondents' own employment choices (Bielby and Bielby, 1984; Hakim, 1991: 105; 2003b; McRae, 2003).

The conventional explanation for these results has been that attitudes are poor predictors of actual behaviour: very low associations were typically found (Wicker, 1969; Bielby and Bielby, 1984). However, public opinion on the desirability of women working or not tells us little about women's personal preferences and aims. Too many surveys fail to make the distinction between approval and choice, between personal goals and general beliefs, between what is desired by the survey respondent for themself and what is desirable in society in general (Hofstede, 1980: 21; Hakim, 1991: 105; 2000: 73–82; 2003a: 47; 2003b; 2004). If we want to understand the choices women make, research must focus on women's plans for their own life. There is thus a gulf between attitude surveys revealing steadily increasing public approval (or tolerance) for working wives and mothers, and other research showing that only a minority of women plan long term careers, aim at higher grade occupations and invest accordingly in appropriate educational qualifications (Sutherland, 1978; Jacobs, 1989b: 77–84; Hakim, 1991; 2000). Even among college and university graduates, a minority of women have firm plans for employment careers; most expect to work while giving priority to marriage and motherhood (Bielby and Bielby, 1984; Gerson, 1985). Fiorentine points out that higher education functions as a marriage market as well as providing training for future occupations. Many female students (typically those who are academically weaker) drop out of career-track college courses because they have an alternative route to high social status, through marriage to a physician instead of becoming one themself. Occupational success is twice as important for men as for women. So men cannot drop out, although they may fail (Fiorentine, 1987; Fiorentine and Cole, 1988; 1992; Cole and Fiorentine, 1991; see also Hakim, 2000: 193–222).

There have been huge changes in sex-role attitudes in recent decades, with few now insisting that women are defined entirely by their family role. The speed of change in public opinion is shown by comparing results from a 1986 survey using the same attitude questions as shown in Table 4.1 for 1999. The 1986 survey showed that the majority of people in Britain (between 50% and 68%) still accepted a rigid sexual division of labour that made women ultimately responsible for housework and men ultimately responsible for income-earning. About half of adults agreed that men remain the main breadwinner in a family, even when wives have a job (Vogler, 1994a; Hakim, 1996a: Table 4.1). Data for 1999 are shown for people of working age, 20–59 years, excluding people of 60 and over who have the most traditional views (Scott, 1990: 54). By 1999, there was no change on the last question: about half of all adults of working age in Britain still believed that women's employment did not alter men's role and responsibility as main breadwinner for the family. However, rigid role differentiation had lost favour; three-quarters of adults now reject this idea. Similarly, three-quarters of people reject the idea that men take priority over women for jobs in times of high unemployment. Equal opportunities policies have clearly had a huge impact on public opinion. The pattern of responses was similar in Spain, although there is evidence of a political correctness bias in results, with replies that are even more 'modern' than in Britain, despite Spanish patriarchal attitudes (Hakim, 2003a: 62–68).

Table 4.1 Attitudes to the family division of labour

	Women working			Women without jobs	All men	All women
	FT	PT	All jobs			
Britain						
The female partner should be ultimately responsible for housework – % agreeing	14	30	21	32	24	21
The male partner should be ultimately responsible for breadwinning – % agreeing	11	22	16	25	19	23
Even when women work, the man should still be the main breadwinner in the family – % who agree/are indifferent	34	53	42	53	45	50
In times of high unemployment married women should stay at home – % who agree/are indifferent	16	24	20	35	24	27
Spain						
The female partner should be ultimately responsible for housework – % agreeing	5	3	5	22	14	21
The male partner should be ultimately responsible for breadwinning – % agreeing	7	10	8	23	16	21
Even when women work, the man should still be the main breadwinner in the family – % who agree/are indifferent	23	25	23	32	28	34
In times of high unemployment married women should stay at home – % who agree/are indifferent	14	8	13	31	23	27

Sources: Nationally representative surveys of Britain and Spain, 1999, reported in Hakim (2003a). Data for people aged 20–59 years who have completed their full-time education.

However, the main finding in Table 4.1 is the sharp polarisation of attitudes between women with full-time jobs (who are most likely to be careerist) and women who are either full-time homemakers or else have a part-time job. In Britain, where the female workforce is divided fairly evenly between full-time and part-time workers, there are sharp contrasts between the attitudes of the two workforces. Women with part-time jobs are almost identical to full-time homemakers in their perspective on the sexual division of labour. In Spain, where there is only a tiny part-time workforce, the key dividing line is between women with jobs and those without, and the same pattern is found in the USA, where women hold more traditional attitudes than in Britain (Scott and Duncombe, 1991).

By 2000, Germany also displayed a sharp polarisation of sex-role ideology between employed women and full-time homemakers, both in East and West Germany (Mayer, 2003). Between 1982 and 2000, West Germans became ambivalent about the household division of labour: three-quarters (1982) falling to half (2000) supported complete role segregation in marriage, thus moving closer to East German opinion. However, attitudes polarised between working and non-working women, between highly-educated and less-educated women, in both parts of the country (Mayer, 2003).

Two conflicting conclusions can be drawn from these results. On the one hand, the majority of men and women in Europe now reject a rigid sexual division of labour in the household. Family roles have become more flexible, overlapping, responsive to circumstances and family needs. On the other hand, there remains a substantial minority of European couples, between one-quarter and half, who still believe in the complete separation of roles in the family. The continuing force of the ideal of role differentiation is also indicated by the fact that around half of Europeans of working age still believe that men remain the principal income-earner in a family; women's earnings do not fundamentally alter family roles.

So where does the idea come from that women are challenging the traditional sexual division of labour? From the minority of women working full-time and continuously (see Tables 3.3, 5.2 and 5.3), it would appear, the group most likely to include the media reporters, social scientists and other opinion-leaders who claim to know the trends. Among women working full-time, and *only* in this minority group, a clear majority accepts that the equal opportunities revolution and women's access to an independent income fundamentally alters sex-roles so that men cease to be the main breadwinner (Table 4.1). Women working part-time emerge as a relatively conservative group, like non-working women. The polarisation of attitudes between women working full-time and other women is far greater than the contrast between men and women (Hakim, 1991: 105; 1993b: 308–10). The 1991 British Social Attitudes Survey (BSAS) shows that the sexual division of labour was accepted by twice as many women working part-time and full-time housewives as by women working full-time: 55% and 60% compared to only 28% of full-time workers accepted the statement 'A husband's job is to earn the money; a wife's job is to look after the home and family', and in each case husbands held similar views (Kiernan, 1992: 99). So the views of women full-time workers are seriously unrepresentative of the views of the majority of adult women. Women currently working full-time divide into two groups: the minority who work full-time throughout adult life, with or without breaks, and those who change to part-time work and, often, intermittent work after having children (see Chapter 5). It appears that the views of women working full-time and continuously are the least representative of women as a group: hardly surprising, since they constitute only one-tenth of adult women (see Table 5.3). This analysis also shows that the BSAS practice of reporting attitudes among all adult women is misleading, creating the profile of an 'average' British woman who does not exist. For example, Table 4.2 shows that in 1988 about half (42%) of all British women accepted sex-role differentiation, but this result combines full-timers who rejected the idea with part-timers and non-working women who accepted the idea.

In the 1980s, Vogler (1994b) found that actual practice reflected views on the appropriate division of labour. Half of all married couples aged 20–60 years agreed between them that the husband was in practice the main income-earner and 42% agreed that he *should be* ultimately responsible for income-earning. Three-quarters of married couples agreed between them that the wife was in practice the principal

Table 4.2 European views on the roles of men and women

Percentage disagreeing with these two statements:
A A husband's job is to earn the money; a wife's job is to look after the home and family
B Being a housewife is just as fulfilling as working for pay

	Separate roles		Housewife job	
	Men	Women	Men	Women
Britain	47	58	33	36
USA	47	52	22	21
Irish Republic	40	50	17	24
West Germany	33	35	29	32

Source: 1988 ISSP data reported in Scott *et al* (1993: 30–31).

housekeeper, and 54% agreed she *should be* ultimately responsible for housework. Hardly any couples agreed they should both be responsible equally for the housework. Only one-quarter of couples agreed that in practice and in principle they were both equally responsible for income-earning (Vogler, 1994b: 251–53). Thus, among couples of working age the majority still adhered to and agreed on differentiated sex-roles, with only a minority choosing a more egalitarian approach.

The degree of consistency between stated ideals and reality seems to be much lower in other studies. For example, Brannen (1991) found profound contradictions in the views of young mothers with children under 3 years who had returned to work, typically full-time. They regarded their husband as the main breadwinner for the family, and their own earnings as secondary or peripheral. The husband's job was treated as more important, while children were the main concern of the mothers. If necessary, they would give up their jobs to be full-time mothers. Despite this, in response to a direct normative question, the majority of mothers supported the idea of spouses doing equal shares of domestic work and childcare work. The symmetrical roles model of the family was treated as the ideal to aim for, even though reality was organised on different principles that were agreed between spouses. Most of these mothers took responsibility for childcare and domestic work, and the great majority were content with their partner's limited contribution. Similarly, Väisänen and Nätti (2002) found that across Western Europe, the preferred household division of labour is exactly the same as the actual division of labour, on average, in each country.

Men are notably more open to sharing the income-earning role than are women, a finding that does not accord with the theory that a key patriarchal strategy for keeping women under male control is to exclude them from wage work. Women are usually more open to sharing domestic work than childcare. For example, men's use of paternity leave is very low compared to women, even in Scandinavia, and surveys show that mothers do not want to share parental leave with spouses (Hakim, 2000: 242; OECD, 2001: 145–46). Since arranged marriages are rare in modern societies, we can assume that people choose partners with compatible views on the sexual division of labour and family life. Married couples usually hold consistent views on their roles within the relationship (Kiernan, 1992: 99). Wives generally have a clear idea of their husband's views; inaccurate perceptions are rare (Martin and Roberts, 1984: 107–08). So there is little reason to expect major disagreement between spouses. However, there is some evidence that divorce rates are higher among people (especially women) who claim to prefer the symmetrical roles model of the family (Hakim, 2003a: 115–16).

Commentaries on women's rising workrates tend to assume that dual-earner couples espouse the symmetrical roles model of the family and aim for an equal division of domestic and family work in the home, and then express surprise that men in dual-earner couples still do not do their fair share of housework and childcare. Blossfeld and Drobnic (2001) is just one example. Table 4.3 demonstrates that we cannot deduce the sex-role ideology of husbands and wives from the mere fact of them both having jobs, or even from the fact of them both having full-time jobs. The majority of working wives still regard themselves as secondary earners, and employment does not provide their central identity. They do not aim for the symmetrical roles model of the family, they are not work-centred, and they do not reject patriarchal values. Wives with full-time jobs are more likely to aim for symmetrical roles, yet the majority are not work-centred, so they still fail to accept equal responsibility for family finances (Table 4.3). In sum, there is plenty of evidence of inconsistencies between stated ideals and reality in spouses' roles in the family today, possibly due to the influence of political correctness on stated ideals (Hakim, 2003a: 62–66, 134–36, 153–56). Men's 'good provider' role remains important, and is never optional, as is a wife's financial contribution (Christiansen and Palkovitz, 2001). Indeed, there is evidence that women become less committed to a marriage, and are much more likely to divorce, if they work full-time and are equal financial contributors (Han and Moen, 2001; Nock, 2001; McRae, 2003).

It is often argued that women's role in childbearing and childcare is central to the sexual division of labour. Case studies of voluntarily childless couples contradict this assumption. The traditional division of labour is often maintained even among

Table 4.3 Do dual-earner couples aim for symmetrical roles?

	Dual-earner couples		Full-time workers		Wives in PT work	Wives not in work
	M	F	M	F		
Ideal family model: % choosing symmetrical roles model	44	41	44	56	26	31
Work orientations: % who are work-centred	55	21	55	33	10	7
Attitude to patriarchy: % who accept or are ambivalent	53	50	53	42	59	63
Base = 100%	699	673	674	334	339	256

Source: Extracted from Table 5.6 in Hakim (2003a), reporting nationally representative data for Britain for married and cohabiting couples aged 20–59 who have completed their full-time education. Dual-earner couples are those where either spouse reports being in employment; some of the men may not in fact have a working wife.

couples rejecting parenthood, with the wife's job treated as secondary to the husband's because he retains the primary income-earning role (Campbell, 1985: 68–79). Some feminists argue that the ideology of motherhood is part of patriarchal ideology, serving to keep women subordinate to and dependent on men (Badinter, 1981). Women who reject motherhood are belittled as unwomanly (Morell, 1994). However, all the evidence is that in modern industrial society the social pressures towards parenthood are equal for men and women, and that it is typically women who are the prime movers in seeking or rejecting childbearing within couples (Campbell, 1985; Marshall, 1993). Childlessness is acceptable to a higher proportion of men than women. Many women welcome motherhood as a confirmation of their sexual and social identities. Some gain an irreversible sense of achievement from childbearing, reducing the motivation to seek achievements in the labour market. But homemaking activities are also treated as an expression of femininity, so that the homemaking role can be actively retained, even in the absence of children, in competition with a paid job, as Matthaei (1982: 301–07) has most eloquently described.

Work-life balance

Work-life balance is often presented as an issue for trade union bargaining with employers, but in reality it is primarily an issue for negotiation between spouses. Most men and women live in partnerships, or aspire to do so, and they need to agree how they will organise domestic and childcare work in combination with paid jobs outside the home. The Scandinavian model of the family requires all adults to do both paid work and unpaid family work, and the EC champions this model as appropriate for all European citizens (Hakim, 1999).

Most surveys measure attitudes somewhat crudely in terms of acceptance or rejection of statements proposing a complete division of labour between wives and husbands, in the sense that income-earning is presented as an exclusively male function and home-making as an exclusively female function. This approach is illustrated in the International Social Survey Programme's (ISSP) item 'A husband's job is to earn the money; a wife's job is to look after the home and family' which is often treated as a measure of 'modernity' in attitudes. Throughout the 1980s and into the 1990s this statement (or equivalents) attracted roughly 50% of men and women disagreeing and 50% agreeing or indifferent, in Britain, in other European countries, and in the USA, with attitudes fluctuating over time but broadly balanced (Matthaei, 1982: 317; Witherspoon, 1988: 189; Scott, 1990: 57; Kiernan, 1992: 97–99; Scott et al, 1993: 34; Haller and Hoellinger, 1994: 102). In Germany, Italy, Austria and Hungary, support for the statement is stronger than disagreement. For example, only one-third of German men and women reject the complete sexual division of labour compared to half in Britain (Table 4.2). Attitudes to the housewife role are less ambivalent and more positive, with a majority agreeing that it can be just as fulfilling as working for pay; only one-third in Britain and Germany and even fewer in the USA reject the idea (Table 4.2). However, sex-roles have been updated to accept wives going out to work as a secondary activity. The domestic division of labour is now *relative* rather than absolute, and attitudes to income-earning are changing at a faster pace than attitudes to the homemaker role.

The EU Eurobarometer survey is unique in measuring support, across Europe, for the *modern* sexual division of labour, which falls half-way between complete role segregation and symmetrical roles with equal sharing of income-earning and domestic functions (Table 4.4). In the early 1980s, roughly one-third of the EU

Table 4.4 The diversity of family models in Europe
Percentage of adults supporting each of three models of the family division of labour

	Symmetrical		Compromise		Separate roles		Total
	1987	1983	1987	1983	1987	1983	
Denmark	58	50	29	33	13	17	100
Spain	50	..	20	..	30	..	100
United Kingdom	49	39	32	37	19	24	100
Portugal	47	..	26	..	27	..	100
Netherlands	46	41	30	27	24	32	100
France	46	42	30	27	24	31	100
Greece	46	53	30	23	24	25	100
Italy	43	42	32	28	26	30	100
Belgium	38	35	33	25	28	40	100
Ireland	37	32	22	26	42	42	100
West Germany	28	29	37	38	35	33	100
Luxembourg	22	27	34	23	44	50	100
Men – all	41	35	31	34	28	31	100
15–24 years	59	49	28	33	13	18	100
25–39	50	40	31	38	19	22	100
40–54	36	28	34	36	30	36	100
55 and over	27	26	30	28	43	46	100
Women – all	44	41	31	31	25	28	100
15–24 years	62	60	26	25	12	15	100
25–39	52	45	29	32	19	23	100
40–54	39	36	33	34	28	30	100
55 and over	28	31	34	29	38	40	100
Total for EU of 12	43	..	31	..	26	..	100
Total for EU of 10	42	38	32	32	26	30	100

Notes: The question asked: 'People talk about the changing roles of husband and wife in the family. Here are three kinds of family. Which of them corresponds most with your ideas about the family?'
- A family where the two partners each have an equally absorbing job and where housework and the care of the children are shared equally between them.
- A family where the wife has a less demanding job than her husband and where she does the larger share of housework and caring for the children.
- A family where only the husband has a job and the wife runs the home.
- None of these three cases.
Percentages have been adjusted to exclude the 3% not responding to the question and the 2% choosing the last response.
Source: Derived from *Eurobarometer* report No 27, June 1987. Data for people aged 15 and over, interviewed at home.

population supported each family model. By the late 1980s, there was a small shift from the total segregation model to the symmetrical roles model, with the middle compromise model unchanged. The symmetrical roles model attracted most support in Denmark, Spain and Britain. The complete separation of roles attracted most support in Luxembourg, West Germany and Ireland. But in all EU countries there was a wide spread of support for all three models of the family, none receiving majority support, with the single exception of Denmark's majority support for the symmetrical roles model, followed by Spain. This suggests that the 'modern' symmetrical roles family is really a reversion to a pre-industrial model, although research (Hakim 2003a: 62) suggests that political correctness may also be a factor. Overall, a three-quarters majority of European men and women favour the idea of the working wife, but a two-thirds majority also favour the wife retaining all or the major part of the domestic role. Within countries, differences by sex are negligible except in Greece, Italy and France where men are distinctly less favourable than women towards the symmetrical family (European Commission, 1984: 9). The key advantage of this survey is that it shows, for all European countries, that people who reject completely separate roles for men and women do not necessarily accept symmetrical roles: about half only go as far as supporting a secondary earner role for the wife, who retains the larger share of domestic and childcare work. Many attitude surveys have presented people with a false dichotomy which failed to recognise the *modern* version of the sexual division of labour, a compromise that stops a long way short of truly symmetrical roles.

Age has a strong influence on attitudes (Table 4.4). These results reflect the ageing process rather than generational differences. Hakim (2003a: 106–08) found that the ageing process in 1999 was identical to the picture in 1987, despite the 12 year gap. In Britain, there was also evidence of a swing back to the compromise model of the family division of labour in the youngest age groups rather than a swing towards the symmetrical roles model. However, younger Spaniards strongly endorse the symmetrical roles model (Table 4.5), despite the fact that it differs from the reality in most Spanish families (Hakim, 2003a).

There have been three important attempts to eliminate the sexual division of labour and create symmetrical sex-roles: in the Israeli *kibbutzim*, in Sweden and in China. All three have been only partially successful, revealing that social engineering cannot entirely eradicate sex-role differentiation. Tables 4.6 and 4.7 display the relative success of Sweden compared with other European societies and of China compared with other Far Eastern societies. The attitude statement in Table 4.6 proposes the complete separation of roles; the statement in Table 4.7 does not completely exclude wage work for wives.

In 1993, one-quarter of women aged 20 and over in Britain, France, Germany and the USA agreed with the rigid separation of roles in the statement 'The husband should be the breadwinner, and the wife should stay at home' (Table 4.6). In Japan and the Philippines two-thirds accepted the complete sexual division of labour. A decade earlier, in 1982, acceptance of the idea was invariably higher, except in the Philippines, even though the earlier survey was limited to women aged 20–59, excluding older women who are usually more conservative in outlook. Sweden demonstrates that energetically 'egalitarian' policies, which in this context means

Table 4.5 The diversity of family models in Britain and Spain
Percentage of adults supporting each of three models of the family division of labour

	Symmetrical roles	Compromise	Separate roles	Base = 100%
Britain				
men <40	54	35	11	654
men 40+	41	36	23	974
women <40	51	36	13	762
women 40+	36	45	19	1,128
Spain				
men <40	79	15	6	220
men 40+	52	25	23	299
women <40	79	15	6	212
women 40+	58	23	19	354

Source: Extracted from Table 4.6 in Hakim (2003a). Data for 1999 for people aged 16 and over in Britain, and people aged 18 and over in Spain.

policies promoting symmetrical roles for men and women and supported by vigorous fiscal policy and social welfare rules to prevent backsliding, can substantially change social attitudes: the vast majority (around 85%) of women reject the complete separation of roles. However, there remains a stubborn minority of women (16% in 1982 and 13% in 1993) who still accept this design for family life, albeit a lower proportion than in the rest of Europe (Table 4.6). While these results show how malleable attitudes are at the aggregate level, they also point to small minorities of women across Europe whose perspective has not changed, for whom the complete separation of domestic roles remains entirely satisfactory. China demonstrates both these points even more sharply.

China implemented the most determined social engineering policy aimed at eradicating the sexual division of labour and associated attitudes. The Marriage Law of 1950 laid down the principles of equality between the sexes, monogamy, freedom to choose marital partners and the right to sue for divorce, marking a break away from Confucian patriarchal values which supported an essentialist conception of the difference between the sexes and sharply segregated roles for men and women (Stockman et al, 1995: 141–54). The successes and failures of this largest-ever real-world social experiment are immensely valuable to social scientists. Success was greatest in eradicating centuries-old perceptions of sex differences in ability and in the practice of male dominance in the household. There was also substantial success in eradicating the sexual division of labour: a low-wage full-employment policy made it necessary for all adults to work and hence for couples to share domestic work as well. However, in 1988, after the economic reform programme begun at the end of the 1970s had introduced a new climate of opinion, there was a major public debate over a new trend for women to withdraw from wage work and their reasons for doing so. A survey carried out in Beijing in November 1993 showed that one-

Table 4.6 The sexual division of labour: cross-national comparisons
Percentage of women agreeing with or indifferent to the statement: 'The
husband should be the breadwinner, and the wife should stay at home'

	1993	1982
Sweden	13	16
UK	21	28
France	24	..
Germany	29	38
USA	27	35
Korea	33	..
Japan	62	76
Philippines	67	56

Notes: Results from nationally representative random samples of 1,000
or more women aged 20 and over in 1993 for all countries except Japan
where results are based on a nationally representative random sample of
2,000 women aged 20 and over interviewed in November 1992. Data for
1982 relates to women aged 20–59 years. The survey covered West
Germany only in 1982 but the whole of unified Germany (including East
Germany) in 1993.
Source: Calculated from Figure I-35 in Tokyo Metropolitan Government
(1994: 78).

quarter of all women, one-third of wives and two-fifths of men accepted the sexual
division of labour as the ideal to aim for (Table 4.7).

The attitude statement here was worded sufficiently vaguely as not to completely
exclude wage work (social labour in China), but the relatively large minorities of
women (especially wives) agreeing with the sexual division of labour is still
remarkable. Respondents to the survey were aged 20–69 years (typically 30–50
years) and resident in Beijing, thus including the most educated and most
cosmopolitan groups in Chinese society, 40% of them professionals and senior
administrators, who had lived in a communist society for virtually all their adult
lives. Half the wives had earnings similar to or higher than their husbands. The
policy of one child per family meant that in 1993, and for the foreseeable future, the
great majority of couples had only one child to raise, and they had access to good
socialised childcare facilities staffed by professionals. Yet even in these most
favourable circumstances, a consistent one-third of wives in all age groups (varying
slightly between 27% and 40%) preferred to stay at home as a housewife if their
husband earned enough money to permit it. Similarly, acceptance of the sexual
division of labour as the ideal was found in all age groups, varying only from 20%
for people in their 60s to 38% among people in their 30s.

It might be argued in this case that people were simply reverting to traditional
patriarchal values which had been suppressed but not abandoned. This might have
been so in rural areas, but not in urban areas, let alone Beijing. The 1993 survey
found strongly egalitarian attitudes on all other aspects of family roles and
relationships. For example, over three-quarters of husbands and wives in all age
groups stated that family decisions were made jointly (whereas the husband

Table 4.7 Far Eastern views on the roles of men and women

Percentage agreeing with each statement	Beijing		Seoul		Bangkok		Fukuoka	
	Men	Women	Men	Women	Men	Women	Men	Women
There are no significant differences of abilities between men and women	70	77	62	67	87	90	55	54
The ideal is for men to have a job and for women to take care of the family	40	24	69	51	68	71	72	60
If my husband earned enough money I would rather stay at home as a housewife (asked only of married women)	..	35	..	..	..	..	..	..

Source: Calculated from Figures II-5–1, II-5–20, III-6–1 and III-6–2 in Ma *et al* (1994: 122, 154, 344).
The surveys were carried out in 1989 (Fukuoka), 1991 (Seoul), 1992 (Bangkok) and 1993 (Beijing), with representative samples of N = 1736, N = 1608, N = 1570 and N = 1920 respectively.

dominated decision-making in Bangkok, Seoul and Fukuoka, the three other cities surveyed). Acceptance of the traditional family division of labour was lowest among people in their 20s, but also among people in their 50s and 60s. It was only among people aged 30–50 that acceptance rose to two-fifths, clearly linked to childcare concerns. Four-fifths of men and women in all age groups thought women should stay at home when a child is young (Ma *et al*, 1994: 122–33, 344–63). This is strong evidence to support Becker's argument that the sexual division of labour in the household can be accepted voluntarily as efficient and mutually advantageous rather than as something imposed on people by custom and patriarchy. The other side of the coin is that only one-third of wives (one-quarter of all women aged 20–69 years) would prefer this option; two-thirds of Chinese women rejected it firmly, despite the burden of combining wage work and domestic work, with consistent views on related topics (Ma *et al*, 1994; Stockman *et al*, 1995: 141–54). Townsend and Jankowiak (1986) report that party rules on the criteria for mate selection also broke down to revert to women's preference for high status men and men's preference for attractive women.

The impact of social engineering in China is highlighted by comparisons with almost identical surveys in Bangkok, Seoul and Fukuoka (a large town in central Japan with attitudes closer to the national average than to those of Tokyo residents) carried out in 1989–1992 (Table 4.7). Acceptance of separate sex-roles is much higher in Bangkok, Fukuoka and Seoul than in Beijing. The Thai case shows that this is not necessarily related to beliefs about sex differences in abilities, as the Thais do not believe there are any significant differences of ability between men and women, whereas in China this belief had to be eradicated. It appears that the complete separation of roles between men and women will continue to attract support, even if minority support, because it does, as Becker argues, offer certain concrete benefits to couples. The modern version of the sexual division of labour attracts even greater support.

Most reports on work-life balance focus exclusively on women. Hakim's national surveys of Britain and Spain are unusual in providing data on both men's and women's work-life priorities. She shows that sex differences are small or non-existent on many sex-role attitudes. However, men and women still differ strongly in their lifestyle preferences, as men are two to three times more likely to be work-centred. She predicts that sex and gender will cease to be important factors in the labour market, and are already replaced by lifestyle preferences as the main factor differentiating between workers (Hakim, 2000: 279–80; 2003a: 261). Among Europeans of working age (16–64 years), over two-thirds of women and about half of men favour a relatively even balance between employment and family life across the life cycle; roughly half of men and one in seven women are work-centred careerists who give priority to careers over family life (Hakim, 2003a: 84–87). The myth that *all* men are totally work-centred is unfounded; almost half of men also want a better balance between home and work life. At present, this option is discussed in relation to women only. It appears that there is much greater scope than so far recognised for gender-neutral work-life balance policies within government and employer policies (Hakim, 2000: 223–53).

However, such policies will probably have only a small impact, at the margin. An OECD (2001) review of family-friendly policies that raise employment levels among mothers of young children reveals some unexpected findings. For example, Portugal, Greece and Poland have the highest percentages of couples with a child under 6 years with both partners in full-time work: 61%, 41% and 36% respectively. The proportions are much lower, and closer, in France, Britain and Germany (31%, 20% and 21%), despite great variation in their family policies (OECD, 2001: 135; Gauthier, 1996a, b). Clearly, family enterprises can provide much greater flexibility than public policy. However, the crucial finding of the OECD review is the polarisation of mothers' employment in all OECD countries: well-educated mothers stay in employment while mothers with low education drop out of the workforce (OECD, 2001: 153). This pattern is found in all European countries, and the type of welfare state makes no difference (Cantillon et al, 2001). Individual cost-benefit analyses are ultimately more important than national policies and social structures.

Inglehart's research on long term changes in attitudes, values and beliefs helps to explain why individual values, including the relative emphasis on careers versus other life goals, are becoming more important in modern societies. Economic development produces a swing away from values emphasising survival towards values emphasising self-realisation, personal autonomy and individualism (Inglehart, 1990; 1997; Inglehart and Baker, 2000). In societies where basic survival is generally taken for granted, the emphasis switches to choice of lifestyle and personal goals instead. In the past, wives and mothers only worked in cases of economic necessity. Today, wives' employment is a lifestyle choice (Nock, 2001).

Work orientations

There is a huge volume of research contributed by social psychologists as well as sociologists on what is variously called work orientations, work attitudes or work values (Hofstede, 1980, 1994; Macarov, 1982a; MOW, 1987; Furnham, 1990). Concern about the declining work ethic or concern to increase work effort and productivity has prompted much of this research, and the focus has generally been on the work orientations of men rather than on those of women and any sex differential in work attitudes. For example, Kalleberg (1977) did not explore sex differences in work orientations although his dataset included women working full-time, and Furnham (1990: 124–25) is more interested in the impact of age (misread as generational change) than sex on work attitudes.

Results have generally been inconclusive, contradictory or ethnocentric, if interesting (Macarov, 1982b: 178). The failure to deliver conclusive results is illustrated by a series of cross-national comparative studies carried out in the 1980s to see if there were important cultural differences between societies in the strength of the work ethic and in work attitudes more generally (Hofstede, 1980; Fogarty, 1985; Yankelovich, 1985; Harding et al, 1986; MOW, 1987). Research on labour market behaviour is affected by the particular definitions, classifications and concepts applied, as noted in Chapter 3. However, in the volatile area of attitudes and opinions, research results are hugely determined by the questions asked, or not asked, the wording used and the methods of analysis. Studies variously address attachment to the current employer or job, to the occupation, or to paid employment generally (Kalleberg, 1977; Warr, 1982; Mueller et al, 1992). Some studies focus on the *relative* importance of work as against family, leisure, community and religion as central life concerns (Dubin, 1956; Bielby and Bielby, 1984; MOW, 1987). Here again, researchers often rely on multivariate analysis to identify components within work orientations, with theory playing a limited role in focusing attention on particular aspects or themes. Even when research topics and questions are carefully focused, cross-national comparisons reveal the problem of non-equivalent meanings of apparently simple words like 'achievement'. Cross-national comparisons also reveal the ethnocentric and male-centred character of theory in this field (Hofstede, 1980; 1991: 159–74). Furthermore, studies in this field vary hugely in design and scope. Large nationally representative sample surveys are rare. Samples are typically small, restricted to particular groups even when 'national' in aim, and frequently restricted to highly selective social, industrial, occupational or age groups. It is sometimes difficult to ascertain whether studies of 'workers' or 'employees' included women and, if they did, how large and representative a subgroup they formed. The consequence is a range of contradictory findings. Comparative studies have found that the centrality of work as a life interest increases with age (MOW, 1987: 86–87) while work commitment declines with age (Warr, 1982) or else rises with age (Harding et al, 1986: 167). They have found no sex differences in work orientations (Harding et al, 1986: 158), significant sex differences (Fogarty, 1985: 192–99; MOW, 1987: 87, 240) and even that women score higher than men on the work ethic (Yankelovich, 1985: 344–45). The volatility of research results is further illustrated by attempts to identify societies where the work ethic is strong or weak. If included in a study, Japan regularly emerges as having such a strong work ethic that it belongs in a category of its own, with a large sex differential in work orientations. However, studies regularly show Germany to have the lowest levels of work commitment and work ethic (Fogarty, 1985: 175; Yankelovich, 1985: 398–99; Harding *et al*, 1986: 169; MOW, 1987: 275, 283; Furnham, 1990: 130–39), although one analysis classifies it in a category of its own with the strongest work ethic in Europe (de Vaus and McAllister, 1991: 84). Within a single study, the UK is shown to have the lowest work ethic and a high level of work commitment when compared with the USA, Sweden, West Germany and Israel (Yankelovich, 1985: 398–99; see also Harding *et al*, 1986: 169). It should be clear that judgments about the theoretical and methodological adequacy of any study will determine whether its findings and conclusions are regarded as admissible, useful or relevant. In the field of work orientations, virtually any result can be manufactured, by accident or by design, and survey results can be implausible or perplexing.

Given widespread acceptance of the sexual division of labour, to varying degrees, with only gradual change across generations, we would expect men and women to differ in work orientations. Indeed, we would have to question research results that denied this. The most complete theory predicting a sex differential in work orientations and behaviour is Becker's thesis that married women economise on the effort expended on market work by seeking less demanding jobs, if they work at all (see Chapter 1). The evidence presented above on attitudes to sex-role differentiation indicates that Becker's thesis remains valid for the majority of couples of working age in Europe in the 1990s.

It is therefore surprising that studies of work orientations generally show small sex differentials. There are three reasons for this. First, there is the usual problem of a weak link between public opinion attitude statements and behaviour (Wicker, 1969; Yankelovich, 1985: 16–17, 263) so that people can endorse ideas that bear no relation to the work choices they personally make. Similarly, statements about what is valued in a job do not predict how hard people work, or their productivity. Secondly, more often than not there is the problem of sample selection bias (see Chapter 5), a common problem in studies of women's employment. Thirdly, most studies adopt a high-tech quantitative approach focused on the male work perspective which is unlikely to reveal *qualitative* differences between men and women, and between different groups of women, in the meaning and value of work. For example, quantitative studies ask about *intrinsic* job rewards (such as interesting work and the opportunity to use one's abilities) versus *extrinsic* job rewards (such as good pay and job security) and conclude that sex differentials in work orientations are small or non-existent (de Vaus and McAllister, 1991). Yet other studies reveal that paid work is rarely a central life interest for women and for most women takes second place to family concerns; that what women value in a job are convenient or flexible hours, the option of part-time work, pleasant colleagues and a friendly atmosphere – aspects of a job that are *qualitatively* different from the criteria relevant to men such as opportunities for promotion (Martin and Roberts, 1984: 71–74, 183, 191; Fogarty, 1985: 194–97; Hakim, 1991). Wives working part-time can regard work almost as a kind of social club, a place to meet people, to get out of the house while earning additional income (Rose, 1994).

Kalleberg used multivariate analysis of 1973 USA Quality of Employment Survey data for people working full-time (20 hours a week or more) to identify six dimensions in work orientations, that is, features of the work situation that can be of greater or lesser importance to individuals and can be the source of greater or lesser satisfaction with a particular job or type of work. The *intrinsic* dimension refers to the work task itself, whether it is interesting, challenging, develops and utilises skills. The *convenience* dimension refers to practical characteristics that make a job 'comfortable' for a worker: convenient hours, convenient journey to work, pleasant workplace and so forth. The *financial* dimension combines rates of pay, fringe benefits offered by the employer and job security – the monetary value of a job. *Relations with co-workers* emerged as a separate dimension and refers to the social character of the work situation, whether it provides opportunities for friendly interactions. The *career* dimension refers to opportunities for promotion and advancement in a career. The sixth dimension, labelled *resource adequacy*, refers to practical factors facilitating work performance, such as adequate equipment, authority and information required to do the job, helpful colleagues and supervision. The six dimensions combine features of paid work that may influence decisions to work, or not, with features affecting satisfaction with a particular job – the meaning that someone attaches to the work role as well as sources of satisfaction with the work role (Kalleberg, 1977: 129). While this classification is entirely reasonable within a Western cultural context, a very different classification was developed at the same time by Hofstede from a much larger cross-national dataset.

The most successful of the comparative studies was that by Hofstede (1980; 1991). Surveys of some 120,000 IBM employees around the world provided, in effect, carefully matched samples of occupations across 66 countries. This landmark study was the largest of its kind, and the analysis by far the most detailed and careful. In particular, Hofstede seeks cross-national validity in the dimensions of work orientations identified by the analysis; makes the crucial distinction between choice and approval, personal goals and beliefs; deals with the problem of acquiescence, the tendency to agree with everything, which is always greater among people with less education or in lower-grade occupations; and offers a theoretically-informed analysis instead of relying exclusively on multivariate analysis to shape the results. Furthermore, Hofstede's multi-level analysis of differences between countries, occupations and individuals enables him to show, for example, how masculine cultures enlarge gender differences in work orientations while feminine cultures reduce them to insignificance (Hofstede, 1991: 83).

Hofstede's analyses identified four dimensions of work orientations across national cultures: the relationship with authority (sometimes termed authoritarianism); the relationship between the individual and the group (often labelled individualism); ways of dealing with uncertainty, relating to the control of aggression and the expression of emotions, which he labels uncertainty-avoidance; and a social-ego dimension which contrasted dominance, reward and challenge against good social relations and job comfort factors, and which he finally labelled the masculinity-femininity dimension because it reflected gender differences in work orientations. In addition to analyses focused on national cultural differences,

Hofstede analysed work orientations at the occupational level, and then looked for any sex differences within occupations. At this level, only two of the four dimensions emerged as important. Authoritarianism emerged even more strongly than at the national level, but with no sex differential within occupations; education was the dominant correlate. The social-ego dimension was also most salient at occupational level and displayed sex differences so large that they provided the masculinity-femininity label. This dimension reflects apparently universal differences in the work orientations of men and women that echo Gilligan's account of personality differences between men and women (see Chapter 1) or else derive from sex-role differentiation: the 'masculine' goals of high earnings, promotion opportunities, up-to-dateness and opportunities for training and updating contrast with the 'social' goals of greater importance to women: good relations with colleagues and managers, a friendly atmosphere and a pleasant workplace. As secondary earners, women can afford to discount the financial and career features of a job in favour of social and convenience factors. On the other hand, in countries where more women hold jobs and more households have two earners, men too can afford to place less emphasis on the aggressive achievement-oriented features of work. The multi-level research design adopted by Hofstede, plus his huge research database, allowed him to reveal the variations across time, countries and occupational grades that cause so many contradictory findings across smaller and less sophisticated studies. For example, Hofstede shows that sex differences are largest among the less-educated in lower-grade occupations and smallest among the more highly-educated in higher-grade jobs. Sex differentials can be eliminated or even reversed in professional and managerial grades, in part due to selection effects (1980: 276–81). He shows that work is more central in life within countries with high masculinity scores, such as Japan, Germany and Britain while work has a less central position in life in countries with high femininity scores such as Sweden, Norway, the Netherlands and Denmark (1980: 285; 1991: 81–86). These results tie in with the MOW International Research Team's finding that higher educational qualifications are associated among women *only* with higher work centrality and greater work commitment (1987: 191–92; see also Bielby and Bielby, 1988: 1047), and with the sex differences found in the European Value Systems study (Fogarty, 1985: 194–97). Men are usually the main income-earners and their work orientations (and behaviour) show less variation than those of women, for whom work is a matter of choice and may be either central or secondary. Hofstede's study is unique in identifying the sex differential in work orientations, the personal and cultural/social factors that increase or eliminate sex differences, and the sources of the polarisation in work orientations emerging within the female population.

A longitudinal study in the USA provides another perspective on the qualitative differences in the work values of men and women. Halaby (2003) also rejects the simple dichotomy of intrinsic versus extrinsic job values to identify two distinct career strategies: a high-reward, high-risk 'entrepreneurial' strategy and a low-reward, low-risk 'bureaucratic' career strategy. Halaby analyses a longitudinal study of people born in 1939 who graduated from high school in 1957 at age 18 who were followed up until 1992, at age 53. The two most powerful determinants of work values and job preferences were sex and cognitive ability. People with higher intellectual ability, and men, have a stronger preference for the entrepreneurial strategy, while women and people of lower ability prefer the bureaucratic career strategy. People who prefer the entrepreneurial strategy value high earnings and the esteem conferred by a job, but they also value autonomy, variety and the opportunity to exercise judgment and discretion. People who prefer the bureaucratic strategy value job security, a good pension, on the job training, and a clean and pleasant work environment. Both groups value a combination of intrinsic and extrinsic job rewards, but different ones. As Halaby (2003: 277) points out, the two career strategies offer different perspectives on what 'achievement' means for men and women.

Work commitment and work centrality

One of the most popular indicators of work values is the 'lottery win' question on what people would do if they won or inherited a lot of money, thus removing the purely financial incentive to do paid work. This question has been asked in many surveys in Western countries with slightly different wordings (Morse and Weiss, 1955; Warr, 1982; MOW, 1987: 202; Rose, 1994; Hakim, 2003a). The question provides a simple measure of paid work as a key life interest without exploring exactly what it is about a job that makes it worth having, but is often regarded as a measure of the 'work ethic'. The measure has always shown a marked sex differential within the workforce in the USA and in Europe which has been falling gradually in recent decades (Hakim, 1991: 106–07) and appears to have been eliminated, in Britain at least, by the end of the 20th century.

Table 4.8 presents comparative information on work commitment from several nationally representative British surveys. Questions on work commitment are often addressed only to people in work, so we have less information on work values in the non-working population. Results indicate that the sex differential in work commitment has now been eliminated within the workforce, a group that is always more strongly self-selective for women than for men. The reduced sex differential is due partly to men becoming less committed to work and partly to women becoming more committed. One reason for the decline in the male work ethic might be the fact that the financial provider role is now more likely to be shared with a wife, at least in part, rather than because the welfare state reduces the will to work.

Work commitment is highest among young people, who have yet to prove themselves, and declines sharply with age, despite the fact that voluntary early retirement, sickness and redundancy take many people with low work commitment out of the workforce (Alcock et al, 2003). Work commitment is always highest in higher-grade occupations which require longer years of education and training so that people with low work commitment drop out long before they start work, and also because these jobs offer greater rewards which reinforce and sustain work commitment over the years (Warr, 1982; Fiorentine, 1987). As shown in Chapter 6, women have been taking an increasing share of the top jobs in Britain and other European countries, and this trend implies some increase in work commitment in the female workforce. It appears also that the expansion of a segregated part-time workforce noted in Chapters 3 and 6 has not had the opposite effect.

The commitment of a part-time worker to their part-time job is not the same as the commitment of a full-time worker to their full-time job, and the difference is

Table 4.8 Trends in non-financial work commitment, Britain, 1981–1999

Proportion (%) saying they would continue to work in the absence of financial need	1981	1984	1989	1992	1999
All workers	66	70	74	68	63
Women – all working	58	66	76	67	67
full-time	65	71	77	69	68
part-time	54	56	74	64	66
Men – all working	69	74	72	68	60
full-time	69	75	72	69	60
part-time	55	45	80	58	73

Notes: Question wordings vary between surveys, as follows. 1981: 'Considering both kinds of work, that is not only being employed by someone else but also being self-employed, if you were to get enough money to live as comfortably as you would like for the rest of your life, would you continue to work (not necessarily in your present job) or would you stop working?' For non-working people the end of the question was modified to ask 'would you want to work somewhere or would you want to remain without a job?'.
1984 and 1989: 'If without having to work you had what you would regard as a reasonable living income, would you still prefer to have a paid job, or wouldn't you bother?' Data for employees working 10+ hours a week.
1992: 'If you were to get enough money to live as comfortably as you would like for the rest of your life, would you continue to work, not necessarily in your present job, or would you stop working?' Data for people aged 20–59 years.
1999: 'If without having to work you had what you would regard as a reasonable living income, would you still prefer to have a paid job, or wouldn't you bother?' Data for people aged 20–59 excluding full-time students.
Source: Table 3.4 in Hakim (2003a)

more than one of degree. Qualitative differences between the work orientations of full-time and part-time workers are not reflected in the simple measure of non-financial work commitment in Table 4.8. As shown earlier, there are fundamental differences between women full-time and part-time workers in their self-identity as primary earners or as secondary earners. Part-time workers are most likely to value the 'feminine' job characteristics identified by Hofstede (Hakim, 1991: 107–09). Few women regard themselves as following a career, but the proportion is consistently higher among full-timers than among part-timers: 24% and 7% respectively gave this as a reason for working in 1980, 7% and 2% respectively gave this as the main reason (Martin and Roberts, 1984: 68). A less representative 1986 survey found equally large differences: 68% of the self-employed, 61% of men working full-time, 56% of women working full-time and only 22% of women part-timers saw themselves as having a career (Rose, 1994: 324). Further analysis revealed two qualitatively different work orientations in the full-time workforce and in the female part-time workforce. Full-time workers (men and women) were most likely to endorse what Rose labels the *work ethic*, a normative commitment to work as a central life interest, with employment seen as a long term career rather than as a short term job. In contrast, female part-time workers (and working class groups generally) viewed employment in instrumental terms which Rose notes can be regarded as the *inverse* of the work ethic: work was not seen in terms of a career, nor as a primary breadwinning activity, nor as a means of exercising skill and ability, but rather as a social activity and secondary source of income. This group had very low commitment to paid work in the absence of financial need and endorsed the view that the welfare state erodes the will to work. Finally, the work orientations of housewives who intended to return to paid work at some point in the future were very similar to those of part-timers (Rose, 1994: 290–96, 308–13, 333–34). We can safely assume that housewives who did *not* intend ever returning to paid work would have even less positive views on employment than the anti-work ethic of the part-timers.

A 1983 NOP national attitude survey in Britain found that half of all non-working women with children preferred not to work, even if they could make proper childcare arrangements. Part-timers were similar to non-working women in giving priority to their role as wife and mother over any job, and in refusing to believe that a full-time job could be compatible with running a family (Table 4.9).

Table 4.9 Contrasts between working and non-working women

% endorsing each opinion	Women working		No job in last 5 years	Stopped work 5+ years ago	All women 25–54 years
	FT	PT			
Would not work if not financially necessary	21	27	..	..	24
Would not work, even if had proper childcare	..	..	51	52	51
Married woman's first duty is to her marriage (rather than to her job or both equally)	52	72	63	68	62
A mother's first duty is to her children (rather than to her job or both equally)	83	92	91	93	89
A woman can successfully combine a FT job with running a family – % agreeing	77	52	59	55	62
Men make better bosses than women % disagreeing	66	70	68	61	67
Prefers a male boss (of those expressing a preference, having had both)	83	81	76	90	82
Base = 100%	309	261	237	176	983

Source: September 1983 NOP survey on women's issues. Representative sample of women aged 18–54 years in Britain. All % adjusted to exclude Don't Know and Undecided responses.

This survey did not find any difference in work commitment between part-timers and full-timers, but it showed that, in the absence of financial need, virtually all part-timers would work part-time, while roughly half of full-timers would continue to work full-time with the other half switching to part-time work. The preference to stop working, or stop working full-time, was determined by age more than childcare responsibilities. Similar results are found in the BSAS: the majority of full-time housewives and of part-time workers would only work part-time, or not at all, even if they had the childcare of their choice. There is no evidence that women looking after their children at home full-time are dissatisfied or that a majority would prefer to be working full-time (Witherspoon and Prior, 1991: 143, 148, 151; Hakim, 2000: 149).

Interest in promotion is another indicator of women's interest in their work as part of a career or as just a job. Surveys consistently reveal women to be less interested in promotion than men, with part-timers least interested of all. A 1980 British survey showed only half of all female employees aged 16–59 years to be interested in promotion, 60% of full-timers and 34% of part-timers. Family responsibilities and an unwillingness to take on more responsibility were the main reasons for not wanting promotion (Martin and Roberts, 1984: 53). Cross-national studies have also found a significant association between hours worked and work centrality (MOW, 1987: 90) and that women express less interest in promotion, partly due to competing family interests (Matthaei, 1982: 298; Fogarty, 1985: 196; Davidson and Cooper, 1993: 74, 142, 155, 193–95). Even in the highly selective group of working professional women, mothers of children work shorter hours and feel less job involvement (Carrier, 1995). The evidence is unanimous that part-timers invest less interest in their work, even if they work just as hard on the job. These qualitative differences cannot be picked up by the standard work commitment question in Table 4.8.

Overall, we conclude that the sex differential in work commitment (as measured by the lottery win question) had disappeared from the workforce by the 1990s. The conclusion is corroborated by a variety of behavioural indicators. There is no evidence that women work less hard than men; if anything they work harder. Part-time workers and homeworkers, for example, often have higher productivity because they are less likely to get tired than full-time workers who work much longer hours. The sex differential in absenteeism that concerned Myrdal and Klein in the 1950s has disappeared. Sickness absence rates stand at around 5% for all workers in Britain. International comparisons of absenteeism also find few differences between men and women, with the exception of countries like Sweden where long periods of state-funded parental leave are taken by women and seriously distort all labour force statistics (OECD, 1991; Jonung and Persson, 1993; Nyberg, 1994). So working women's work orientations and behaviour have grown closer to men's. However, women still regard themselves as secondary earners, typically, and so employment is less central in their lives as a whole.

As the EC has discovered through the Eurobarometer surveys, the great majority of European men regard themselves as the principal earner (or co-earner) within their household, whereas the majority of European women regard themselves as secondary earners, even in countries with relatively high female employment rates such as Denmark and France (Hakim, 2003a: 4).

Table 4.10 provides a more detailed analysis for Britain and Spain, based on nationally representative surveys for 1999.

Three-quarters of women adopt the identity of a secondary earner as soon as they become part of a couple. In contrast, over 90% of men with a partner regard themself as the primary earner (Table 4.10). Husbands accept this responsibility irrespective of employment status and income level. Wives with a job are much more likely to regard themself as a primary (co-)earner than wives with no job: 32% versus 13% in Britain, 46% versus 9% in Spain. The much smaller female workforce in Spain is more self-selected than the larger female workforce in Britain. But in both countries, the majority of women regard their partner as the principal earner, so their financial contribution is a secondary supplement to household income. The primary source of women's discontinuous work histories lies in family identities and family roles rather than lack of commitment to jobs once they have them.

The sharp difference between male and female work orientations is revealed most clearly by the indicator of work centrality in Table 4.10. People who are work-centred have adopted the identity of a primary earner, and they are also committed

Table 4.10 Primary earner role and job centrality among couples, Britain and Spain

	Husbands			Wives		
	in work	not working	all	in work	not working	all
Britain						
% regarding themselves as main (co-)earner						
20–39 years	94	78	93	27	9	22
40–59 years	92	73	89	36	16	30
All ages	93	74	91	32	13	26
% who are work-centred						
20–39 years	60	59	60	19	6	15
40–59 years	50	51	50	23	8	19
All ages	55	53	55	21	7	17
Spain						
% regarding themselves as main (co-)earner						
20–39 years	94	..	91	44	8	24
40–59 years	95	96	95	49	10	21
All ages	94	86	93	46	9	22
% who are work-centred						
20–39 years	47	..	44	28	4	15
40–59 years	44	44	44	29	4	11
All ages	45	36	44	28	4	13

Source: Table 3.11 in Hakim (2003a). Data for couples aged 20–59 years who have completed their full-time education.

to their paid work over and beyond the purely financial motivation – their job is central to their social identity and aspirations on *both* indicators. This index increases the similarity between women in Britain and Spain, showing around one-quarter of employed women, and less than one-fifth of all women with partners to be work-centred. It also shows that only around half of men are work-centred, disproving the stereotype of all men being totally work-centred. Clearly many men work because they feel responsible for family income, more than from choice.

In summary, there is no longer any difference between men and women in work commitment, using the standard 'work ethic' question. However, few women have as yet adopted the identity and responsibilities of a principal earner (or co-earner) in their household; women still view men as breadwinners. Jobs thus remain less central for women than for men. The loss of a job is still regarded as far more serious for men than for women, even today (Charles and James, 2003: 548).

Workplans

Do work values really matter? Do they predict behaviour? One problem for studies on the links between work orientations and labour market behaviour is that, even when they find a connection, cross-sectional surveys cannot resolve the problem of causality: which comes first, strong career aspirations or the stable career? The only adequate way of resolving the question of causal processes is the true prospective longitudinal study (Hakim, 1987a). There have so far been only a few longitudinal studies providing rigorous tests of the long term influence of work orientations, aspirations and work plans. The National Longitudinal Surveys (NLS) project initiated in the mid-1960s in the USA has provided a great wealth of longitudinal data on five age cohorts of young and mature women, young and older men. Of particular interest is the cohort of young women aged 14–24 in 1968 who were interviewed almost every year up to 1983 when aged 29–39 years. This cohort was asked in 1968, and at each interview over the next decade, what they would like to be doing when they were 35 years old, whether they planned to be working at age 35 or whether they planned to be keeping house or raising a family at age 35. This age was chosen as the peak age for competing work and family roles. Because it asked about personal preferences and choices, rather than general attitudes, the question turned out to have astonishing analytical and predictive power, and was used again in the second youth cohort study initiated in 1979.

Career planners constituted one-quarter of the 1968 young women cohort; another quarter consistently planned a homemaker career; the majority of the cohort were drifters with no fixed plans or had 'unplanned careers' (Table 4.11), as did women in the NLS mature women cohort aged 30–44 years at the start of the study in the late 1960s (Mott, 1978; 1982; Shaw, 1983). There are a number of independent analyses of the extent to which early workplans were fulfilled by age 35. They all show that women achieved their employment objectives for the most part, resulting in dramatic 'mark-ups' to career planners in terms of occupational grade and earnings (Mott, 1982; Rexroat and Shehan, 1984; Shaw and Shapiro, 1987). Furthermore, career planners were more likely to choose typically-male jobs and adapted their fertility behaviour to their workplans (Waite and Stolzenberg, 1976; Stolzenberg and Waite, 1977; Spitze and Waite, 1980). Workplans were a significant independent predictor of actual work behaviour. After controlling for other factors affecting labour force participation, a woman who consistently planned to work had a probability of working that was over 30 percentage points higher than did a woman who consistently planned not to work. Of the women who held consistently to their work plans, four-fifths were actually working in 1980, at age 35, compared to only half of the women who consistently intended to devote themselves exclusively to homemaker activities. Women who planned to work at age 35 were likely to do so unless they had large families or a pre-school child. Women who planned a homemaker career nevertheless were obliged to work by economic factors in half the cases: their husband's low income, divorce, or the opportunity cost of not working led half to be in work at times. On balance, the homemaker career emerged as less predictable. However, most young women in this cohort were drifters with no fixed plans.

Planning to work yielded a significant wage advantage. Women who had consistently planned to work had wages 30% higher than those of women who never planned to work. Those women who had aimed for the occupation they actually held at age 35 had even higher wages than women whose occupational plans were not realised. Women who make realistic plans and acquire necessary skills fare best in the labour market. Those who fare worst are women who aim for an exclusive homemaking career but end up working for economic reasons.

Perhaps most important of all, the NLS longitudinal analyses have finally disproven conclusions drawn from cross-sectional studies that women's work behaviour is heavily determined by the number and ages of any children, showing that the reverse process operates. Women who work only when their childcare responsibilities leave them free are in effect fulfilling a prior choice of emphasis on the homemaker career. Fertility expectations have only a small negative effect on

Table 4.11 Long term workplans and outcomes among women in the USA

	Distribution of sample	% working at age 35
Homemaker career:		
consistently indicate no plans for work: aim is marriage, family and homemaking activities	28%	49%
Drifters and unplanned careers:		
(a) highly variable responses over time, no clear pattern in plans for age 35	35%	
(b) switch to having future work expectations at some point in their twenties	12%	47% 64%
Career planners:		
consistently anticipate working at age 35 throughout their twenties	25%	82%

Source: Derived from Tables 2 and 3 in Shaw and Shapiro (1987: 8–9) reporting NLS data for the cohort of young women aged 14–24 years in 1968.

young women's workplans, whereas workplans exert a powerful negative effect on young women's childbearing plans (Waite and Stolzenberg, 1976; Stolzenberg and Waite, 1977). Factors which have long been held to determine women's labour force participation, such as other family income, educational qualifications, marital status, and age of youngest child are revealed as being most important in relation to women with no commitment to employment careers, who have so far been in the majority. Women with definite career plans manifest a rather inelastic labour supply, similar to that of men (Shaw and Shapiro, 1987). An even bigger USA study, the National Longitudinal Study of the High School Class of 1972, has produced results that corroborate those of the NLS. It showed, for example, that young women who became mothers early, before the age of 25, differed significantly from those who remained childless: they were less work-oriented, more likely to plan to be homemakers at age 30, less likely to plan a professional career, and held more traditional sex-role attitudes and aspirations *before* they gave birth. Parenthood strengthens pre-existing traditional attitudes in both young white men and women (Waite *et al*, 1986; Morgan and Waite, 1987). European studies have also found that personal workplans are more strongly correlated with employment choices than general statements of work commitment as measured in Table 4.8 (Haller and Rosenmayr, 1971: 503).

The NLS surveys also suggest a faster pace of change in the USA than in Europe in recent decades. About one-third of the first NLS cohort of young women, aged 14–24 in 1968, planned to be working at age 35, in the 1980s (Rexroat and Shehan, 1984: 352). In contrast, about two-thirds of the second NLS cohort of young women, aged 14–21 in 1979, planned to be working at age 35, in the 1990s, and barely one-third planned to be full-time homemakers (Desai and Waite, 1991: 553). Not all will hold to these plans consistently, but these single-time responses indicate a sea change in women's workplans during the 1980s. Similar findings are reported for Britain and other countries. One British study indicates that one-quarter of working women, compared to two-thirds of working men, had career-oriented employment in the primary sector (Burchell and Rubery, 1994), suggesting that sex differences in planned careers are much larger in Britain than the USA. Schoon and Parsons (2002) analysed two major longitudinal cohort studies in Britain, the 1958 National Child Development Study (NCDS) cohort and the 1970 British Cohort Study (BCS) to show that teenage aspirations, and parents' aspirations for their child's future career, were crucial determinants of career attainment in adult life.

Vella (1994) analysed the 1985 Australian Longitudinal Survey to look at the impact of sex-role attitudes on women's achievements in adult life. This cohort study covers young Australians whose education and employment decisions were made well after the equal pay laws of 1969 and 1972. He found that a simple seven item measure of sex-role attitudes was a strong predictor of young women's subsequent investment in education, occupational choice, extent of employment, and returns to education. Sex-role attitudes had no impact on young men's subsequent choice of occupation, education or employment decisions. Although he does not indicate what the distribution of attitudes is in this young cohort, Vella concludes that the diversity of women's sex-role attitudes is a major cause of wage variation among women, and therefore a source of the pay gap.

Surveys routinely collect information on educational qualifications, and human capital theorists pretend that career plans can be deduced from qualifications held. Separate information on career plans is rarely collected. It is as well to remember that even in the post-War period a minority of female college graduates in the USA and university graduates in Europe started work with plans for long-term employment careers (Goldin, 1990: 206–08). As noted in Chapter 5, qualifications can serve another purpose, achieving social status and economic rewards through the marriage career rather than through a personal career. In addition, we should distinguish between dual earner and dual career partnerships (Bonney, 1988). The majority of women in dual-earner couples regard themselves as a secondary earner (Hakim, 2003a: 134–36), as noted in Tables 4.3 and 4.10.

Attitudes to authority and male dominance

Due to concern at increasing social welfare expenditure and welfare dependency in Western democracies, researchers and policy-makers have paid close attention to the declining work ethic among men. Less attention is paid to attitudes to authority and male dominance, or to work-life balance issues, that impact on women's employment. The evidence suggests that attitudes to male dominance are just as important for understanding women's achievements *within* the workforce as 'work ethic' attitudes were for understanding decisions to *enter* the labour market or not.

Sex-role stereotypes are closely intertwined with occupational segregation and social relations in the workplace (Hunt, 1975: 173–90; Hakim, 1979: 50–53; Witherspoon, 1988; Vogler, 1994a). This interdependence of ideology and practice is exposed most clearly when people take jobs considered sex-atypical in the society in question, such as female Marines in the USA, forcing colleagues to rethink and renegotiate self-concepts, occupational identities and social relations in the workplace (Williams, 1989). There is much variation between societies and across time in what jobs are considered suitable for men or women. But at any point in time in a particular society, certain job choices will be *felt* to be inappropriate for persons of one gender, prompting floods of arguments to justify the *status quo*. Female priests and members of the clergy and male homosexual members of the Armed Forces are just two hotly debated examples. But female office clerks also provoked strong reactions when first introduced in the 20th century (Cohn, 1985), and many people still dislike the idea of female miners, for example. Occupations confer public social identities as well as income, and many people find it more comfortable when these roles are congruent with, or at least not markedly incongruent with, sexual identities (Matthaei, 1982: 187–203, 281–85). As noted in Chapter 1, Goldberg's male dominance theory goes further, to argue that men are more likely to do what is necessary to obtain the lion's share of top jobs in any society, and that women favour male dominance in public social relations, because it is congruent with private heterosexual relationships. In effect, sex-roles enter the workplace to support vertical occupational segregation more strongly than horizontal segregation, as noted in Chapter 6.

It is often claimed that women are by nature 'non-hierarchical' or egalitarian, and more inclined towards democratic processes, co-operation and consultation in the workplace and other social settings (for example, Tijdens, 1993: 88–89; Babcock and

Laschever, 2003: 164–79). First, when political scientists study core beliefs and values, they find that women are more egalitarian and less individualistic than men (Feldman, 1988: 427). Secondly, research on social interaction (reviewed below) shows that submissive-co-operative roles and identities characterise women's participation in small groups, and that women perceive themselves as essentially similar, as a homogeneous and subordinate group. Thirdly, and probably linked to this pattern of social interaction and identity, feminist theorists regularly insist on the democratic character and goals of women's groups and feminist practice, in contrast to patriarchal, capitalist and colonial social structures (for example, Alexander and Mohanty, 1997).

However, real-world research shows that the thesis of female egalitarianism, while attractive, is without foundation in reality (Kanter, 1977: 299–303). Social psychologists have shown that most women express and define themselves in terms of social relationships, whereas most men focus on personal achievement within hierarchies (Chodorow, 1978; Gilligan, 1982, 1993; see also Beutel and Marini, 1995), but they do not deny that women recognise and accept social hierarchies – on the contrary they are clear that women routinely accept male dominance (Miller, 1976; Gilligan, 1993: 168). Women accept hierarchy so long as it is men who are in positions of power and authority. Male dominance is accepted, as Goldberg argued; female dominance goes contrary to sex-role stereotypes and is unwelcome, uncomfortable and frequently rejected (Fogarty et al, 1971: 15, 191–207; Kanter, 1977: 69–126, 197–205, 230–37; Hennig and Jardim, 1978: 115; O'Leary, 1988: 203; Deaux and LaFrance, 1998: 804).

Women systematically reject the idea that men make better bosses than women (Table 4.9). Two-thirds (67%) of women aged 25–54 years reject the idea, with relatively little variation across subgroups. Age is the main correlate. Rejection is highest among women aged 18–24 but declines steadily with age so that opinion is evenly balanced among women aged 45–54 years. At first sight, it seems that women accept male and female bosses equally. Not so. Women consistently prefer a *male* boss. They only reject the idea that men make *better* bosses. It appears that women prefer men as bosses even though they know that men do not perform better than women, the implication being that mediocre male managers are more acceptable than competent female managers.

The question on preferences in Table 4.9 was only put to women who had experience of both male and female superiors: three-quarters of the sample said they did. After excluding 'Don't know' responses, roughly half said they had no preference and half had a preference. Among those expressing a preference, preferences for a male boss outnumbered preferences for a female boss by 4 to 1 across all groups of women, working and non-working (Table 4.9). Reasons given for preferring a male boss were numerous, but all reflect common stereotypes of male superiors as being easier to deal with, more fair, less emotional, less fault-finding than women and less inclined to have favourites. Reasons were consistent across subgroups, implying that these are fixed stereotypes, common to all women, working or not.

Consistent results are obtained from all surveys questioning women on the topic – whether in junior grades or in professional grades. Surveys of this sort have been carried out by employment agencies, who have been forced to confront this reverse sex discrimination among job *seekers* rather than recruiters. A 1991 survey of some 400 secretaries working for Alfred Marks, one of the biggest employment agencies in Britain, asked about preferences among women who had worked for both male and female bosses. Few were indifferent on the question. If the job was identical, two-thirds of secretaries preferred to work for a male boss and only 18% preferred a female boss. One-fifth (18%) of secretaries who had worked for a female boss would not do so again. Exploration of the reasons for preferences did not reveal any important perceived differences in working style that could account for these marked preferences. However, secretaries were significantly more likely to undertake additional duties, above and beyond everyday work tasks, for male bosses. Social sex-roles become integrated with work roles, and relations between male bosses and female subordinates reflect familial and sexual relations outside the workplace. Pringle (1988, 1989) argues that this enables men to exercise authority in the workplace with less coercion and more mutual pleasure in relations with female subordinates than is possible for female bosses. Far from wanting to remove sexuality and 'private' sexual identities from the workplace, secretaries regard these as positive features of an otherwise monotonous job.

Similar results were obtained from a 1994 survey of some 600 people in accountancy, law and other professions who were registered with Hays, a specialist recruitment agency in Britain. Among those who expressed a preference, most women preferred to work with men rather than with other women. Men were less choosy than women about the sex of colleagues, but only 4% wanted to work for a female boss. Professional women were equally unenthusiastic about having a female boss, and one-quarter actively preferred to work for a man. The indications are that preference for a male boss is stronger among women than men, even among professionals.

Similar results are found across the world. Numerous studies in the USA and around the world show that almost no-one wants to work for a female boss, partly due to a pervasive belief that men make better leaders than women (Kanter, 1977: 197; O'Leary, 1988; Deaux and LaFrance, 1998: 804; Mavin, 2004). In a review of women in management in France, Laufer (1993: 115) noted that there is much evidence that both men and women prefer to work for a male boss. In 1970 one-third of Dutch adults of working age agreed it would be unnatural for women to manage male subordinates; by 1987 the proportion had fallen to only 12% (Tijdens, 1993: 88). Blanket rejection of the woman manager had disappeared, but the social difficulties of the position had not been resolved. When asked who had the most difficult job, male and female workers agreed on the following ranking: male superior with male subordinates (easiest); male superior with female subordinates; female superior with male subordinates; and, most difficult of all, female superior with female subordinates (Tijdens, 1993: 89). Hofstede's cross-national study found that women, especially those in low-grade occupations, had *less* preference for a consultative managerial style than did their male colleagues (1980: 108–09). However, he held back from concluding that women were more authoritarian than men, after controlling for occupation, although other studies had drawn this conclusion. What he does admit is that there were marked differences in authoritarianism between occupations, largely due to the correlation with education. And of course women are concentrated disproportionately in lower-grade jobs.

A complex experiment used by Molm (1986) to study sex differentials in the use of power can also be interpreted as showing degrees of co-operation between a boss and subordinate, as measured by the total amount of exchange between such dyads in different situations. Co-operation was at its lowest with a legitimated female superior and at its highest with a male superior, with or without legitimation. Males and females were equally good, or poor, power users. However, the response of subordinates was crucial, and females responded differently to male and female superiors. Female subordinates were twice as co-operative with a non-legitimated male boss as with a legitimated female boss. Overall, the highest levels of co-operation were observed in male dyads and the lowest levels of co-operation were in female dyads, with cross-sex dyads in between, in line with the ranking of situations reported by Tijdens. Women are even more reluctant to acknowledge and co-operate with a female superior than are men, a conclusion confirmed most recently by Mavin (2004).

It is commonplace to focus on the problems caused by a male work culture and by male colleagues being unhelpful and unco-operative towards women in management and supervisory posts (Fogarty *et al*, 1971; Hunt, 1975: 183–84; Kanter, 1977; Hennig and Jardim, 1978; Matthaei, 1982: 293–300; Davidson and Cooper, 1993; Reskin and Padavic, 1994: 91–99; Padavic and Reskin, 2002: 100–19), with sexual harassment the most extreme mechanism for putting women in their place and excluding them from a male work culture (Crull, 1987; Husbands, 1992). This one-eyed view of the problem overlooks the equally important *active* contribution of women to maintaining a *status quo* that excludes women from the senior posts and management positions that give women authority. Women who succeed in getting top jobs create social and psychological problems for women in lower-grade posts and non-working women as well as for male colleagues. Male resentment is understandable, as competent women increase competition for top jobs in what is seen as a zero-sum game. Women ought to be delighted, as successful women open doors for female successors. Yet women are more likely than men to question the abilities of female managers and refuse to co-operate with them (Molm, 1986; Swim and Sanna, 1996). Goldberg's theory of male dominance is the only theory that can make sense of women's active role in maintaining women's exclusion from top jobs by refusing to co-operate with female managers as readily as they do with male managers.

Studies repeatedly find no evidence of sex differences in leadership aptitude or style (Kanter, 1977; Deaux and LaFrance, 1998: 805). For example, Wajcman's (1996; 1998) study of senior managers in high tech firms explicitly addressed the myth of women's feminine style of management, and found no evidence for it, even though some women managers supported the myth because they hoped it might give them an advantage. The study did find some differences between men and women in senior management: two-thirds of the women were childless, whereas two-thirds of the men had children and a full-time homemaker wife. The female managers divided into two groups: the work-centred women, who were childless or else employed nannies to care for their children, and who competed on an equal level with men, and the women who tried to retain a serious role as a homemaker and mother, which thus constrained their career. In contrast, all the men were work-centred (Wajcman, 1996; 1998: 163–64). Sex differences in work values appear even among managers.

Kanter explains the negative stereotype of the female manager in terms of the more restricted power and promotion opportunities of women in organisations. But she has no adequate explanation for *women's* resentment of women who get promoted out of the female job ghetto (Kanter, 1977: 142–59, 199–205; Mavin, 2004). Pringle explores the social and psychological problems that women experience in working for a female boss, noting that this situation provokes far more hostility than among men working for female superiors. Male authority is accepted as natural by women and male bosses are deferred to, even if disliked, because gender and sexuality are central to all workplace power relations, so that a streak of sexual excitement enlivens what is otherwise a master-slave relationship. The authority of female bosses is less 'natural' and more fragile, and women who have reached senior positions expose the subordination of secretarial and other lower-grade jobs as chosen rather than inevitable or natural (Pringle, 1988, 1989: 28–85, 108, 130, 240). Women in senior positions provoke hostility among female subordinates because they expose female heterogeneity most acutely, whereas for men they represent women joining their game, choosing the same values and criteria of success.

The difficulties of women managers can sometimes be mitigated by social processes that institutionalise and legitimate female leadership. In laboratory studies, Lucas (2003) found that female leaders encountered far more resistance than male leaders. For example, co-operation (male and female) with a woman leader appointed on the basis of ability was on the same level as co-operation with a randomly-chosen male leader. Women accepted a male leader far more readily than a female leader. However, social processes that institutionalised and legitimated female leadership as more appropriate than male leadership greatly improved co-operation levels. At present, it appears that female managers need additional props to overcome prejudice among female subordinates even more than among male subordinates.

Social interaction

Research by social psychologists has identified important sex differences in the way people relate to the world around them and to other people, and in social interaction. These differences help to maintain male dominance in public social settings, including the workplace. Laboratory experiments also demonstrate how sex discrimination (along with race discrimination and other types of inter-group discrimination) can emerge from ordinary social interaction between groups.

Rotter (1966) developed a 'locus of control' scale, which measures the extent to which individuals believe that their own behaviour shapes and determines events in their lives. People with high scores on the scale have an *external* locus of control, and feel that life happens to them. Their perspective tends towards the fatalistic. People with low scores on the scale have an *internal* locus of control, and believe they manage their lives. Such people are assertive, less vulnerable to negative feedback, and more likely to initiate activities that advance their interests. Locus of control can be taken as an 'agentic' trait. Even in the modern societies of Western

Europe and North America, adult women are more likely than adult men to have an external locus of control, and the same pattern is found in many other countries as well. The difference between men and women on locus of control has been confirmed using adult (as well as student) samples for Australia, the USA, Britain, Belgium, the Netherlands, Sweden, Poland, Hungary, former Czechoslovakia, Bulgaria, Romania, the former USSR, Israel, India, China, Taiwan, Mexico and Brazil (Strickland and Haley, 1980; Wade, 1996; Kunhikrishnan and Manikandan, 1995; Smith *et al*, 1997: 59). This finding is not due to the fact that women often occupy lower status and less powerful jobs than men. Even among senior managers, who have more control over their lives, women still score higher than men on the locus of control scale and they are more communal in values than men (Smith *et al*, 1997). In addition, there is no evidence of any change in attitudes among younger cohorts of men and women (Ferri *et al*, 2003: 277–79). This difference of perspective between men and women would lead to greater passivity among women and greater self-assertiveness among men.

Of course, this may change in the future. For example, Hakim argues that the contraceptive revolution, which started in the 1960s, gives women *personal* and *independent* control of their fertility, which can be the catalyst for a fundamental change of perspective among women, even a psychological change, creating not only contraceptive confidence, but also a sense of autonomy and personal freedom (Hakim, 2000: 45). Thus, changes in the objective conditions of women's lives can be expected to lead to changes in women's outlook on life.

On the other hand, family socialisation processes change relatively slowly. Mothers tend to give boys more independence, and boys' activities more often involve control of the physical world and social interaction outside the home, for example in team sports. Mothers control their daughters more, and women generally feel they have less freedom of movement in the world outside the home. Females tend to define themselves in terms of relationships whereas males define themselves in terms of achievements in the public sphere (Chodorow, 1978).

Social psychologists have demonstrated the normality of (gender) stereotyping, prejudice, and discrimination (Brewer and Brown, 1998; Fiske, 1998; Howard, 2000). To avoid the need for constant, daily re-assessment of all other people, individuals operate with good-enough stereotypes that shape their day-to-day feelings and behaviour towards others. Belonging is a, if not the, core social motive. Prejudice results from the need for a positive social identity with an ingroup one belongs to, so that other social groups are treated as outgroups that provide a relatively devalued contrast. Two decades of experimental research inspired by Tajfel's minimal intergroup situation have supported the general idea that *any* salient and situationally meaningful ingroup-outgroup, we-they distinction is sufficient to activate differential responses to other people, depending on their membership of the ingroup or outgroup. Discriminatory treatment of the ingroup one belongs to, in preference to outgroup members, has been demonstrated on evaluative, affective and behavioural measures (Tajfel, 1970; 1978; 1982; Tajfel *et al*, 1971; Brewer and Brown, 1998; Fiske, 1998). However, the evidence for ingroup favouritism is much stronger than for discrimination against outgroups (Howard, 2000: 370). This differential perception of and behaviour towards others can be triggered by the most trivial and nominal differences between two groups, such as calling them the 'red group' and the 'blue group'. Given that there will always be *some* differences between men and women, in attitudes, behaviour, or styles of dress and so forth that are visible in public social settings, including the workplace, these small differences can trigger ingroup-outgroup discrimination, purely as a structural feature of normal social interaction. Some social scientists argue that sex differences in personality and behaviour are in fact important in their consequences, and consistent with gender stereotypes (Swim, 1994; Eagly, 1995), so will readily prompt differential reactions. Similarly, age and race are primary categories in social interaction, and stimulate spontaneous response patterns.

Over a period of two years, in Sydney, Australia, Hargreaves-Heap and Varoufakis (2002) carried out a series of experiments with the Hawk-Dove game. The game is played on a computer terminal, with an unseen and constantly changing opponent, and requires participants to engage in negotiation and to predict their opponent's choices. Laboratory experiments of this nature provide highly controlled measures of behaviour towards an opponent. Repetitions of the game allow researchers to see how behaviour evolves over time, in response to particular signals within the game. Such experiments tend to produce more extreme behaviour than is normally seen in everyday life, where there are a lot of extraneous factors. They enable us to see more clearly the consequences of social interaction that are relatively invisible in daily social life. This study tested for the effect of randomly assigning players with a blue or a red label.

The study showed that players quickly adopted an aggressive or submissive strategy purely as a result of being classified as a red or blue player. The submissive 'doves' also tended to co-operate with each other, which the aggressive 'hawks' never did, but doves also colluded with hawks. The study shows that competitive-aggressive and submissive-co-operative roles and identities emerge very quickly in social interaction, on the basis of the flimsiest signals, and discrimination between the two groups is quickly established.

Experimental research in Geneva, Switzerland, by Lorenzi-Cioldi (1988; 1991) shows that, in practice, there is a large degree of overlap between male/female identities, dominant/submissive identities, and individualism/collectivism. He found that male groups regard themselves as a collection of individuals, while female groups regard themselves as an aggregation of essentially similar people. Thus, singularity and nonconformism is an accepted feature of male groups, in contrast with the imitative, conformist, inclusive universalism of female groups. These contrasting dispositions are consistent with research showing a greater tendency towards competitive rivalry in male groups and male behaviour, and a tendency towards co-operation and investment in relationships in female behaviour (Chodorow, 1978; Fiske, 1998; Babcock and Laschever, 2003), and consistent also with cross-national comparative studies on locus of control and affectivity (Smith *et al*, 1997). They could also help to explain why women have more difficulty than men in accepting female managers and leaders, as noted earlier.

In summary, there are distinctive features of male and female average styles of social interaction that underlie social stereotypes, and that readily trigger differentiating behaviour that can become discrimination in some cases. As Reskin (2003) points out, sociologists and economists who study the labour market have yet to incorporate this research knowledge into their theories and explanations.

Do attitudes determine behaviour?

Do attitudes and values really matter? There is a long-standing thesis in sociology that attitudes and values are either irrelevant, or else just *post hoc* rationalisations of choices already made. Indeed, this is one of the objections to preference theory, which states that lifestyle preferences are now a key determinant of women's choices in modern societies. For example, McRae (2003) challenged preference theory by showing only a weak link between mothers' employment decisions and their attitudes towards children, family life, and mothers' employment generally. However, the most recent research pointed out that the most recent research does show a clear causal impact on behaviour. Studies based on longitudinal datasets (such as that in Table 4.11) have been particularly important, because they avoid the criticism of *post hoc* rationalisation, showing that the long term impact of life goals and values is stronger than the short term impact (Hakim, 2002; 2003a; 2004).

In addition, it is important to distinguish between public opinion attitudes (such as patriarchal attitudes) which are generally non-causal, and more deeply held personal values and life goals, which are causal (Hakim, 2003a, b; 2004). The distinction between the two types of attitude helps to make sense of the contradictory research results noted earlier. Unfortunately, social attitude surveys collect public opinion data almost exclusively, and the same questions are then re-used in specialised surveys, such as McRae's longitudinal study of new mothers (McRae, 1991; 1996; 2003), leading to the idea of *all* attitudes and values being non-causal. When surveys ask questions about personal preferences and personal values, there can be a tight fit with behaviour. This was demonstrated by national surveys in Britain and Spain which found that lifestyle preferences strongly determined fertility and employment decisions, but only among women. Men had high full-time employment rates irrespective of their lifestyle preferences (Hakim, 2003a, c). In contrast, other public opinion attitudes had no impact at all on women's behaviour. For example, patriarchal attitudes (a popular topic in social attitude surveys) did not affect women's employment choices in any way at all (Hakim, 2003a, b; 2004).

There is a widespread expectation that problems affecting older cohorts of women will disappear among younger women, who are better educated, and have genuine choices regarding careers and lifestyle, as preference theory argues. In practice, the impact of attitudes and values (or personality traits, as psychologists see it) seems to be increasing in younger cohorts. Schoon and Parsons (2002) analysed data for 17,000 men and women born 12 years apart, in 1958 and 1970 (the NCDS and BCS cohort studies), and living in Britain. They found that teenage occupational aspirations (at age 16) are a stronger predictor of adult occupational attainment at ages 26 and 33 than academic achievement. Material conditions in childhood were also important, but they did not over-ride the influence of parental and teenage aspirations on men and women. On the basis of in-depth interviews with cohort members who escaped from disadvantage, against all the odds, to become high achievers, Pilling (1990) drew the same conclusion about the over-riding importance of motivation and aspirations, independently of academic ability.

Further analysis of the data for the cohort born in 1970 confirms the importance of 'psychological capital' (Feinstein, 2000). Locus of control and self-esteem measured at age 10 both determine earnings and (un)employment at age 26, but locus of control is more important among girls, while self-esteem is more important among boys. As Feinstein (2000) points out, these characteristics remain unmeasured and invisible in most studies of wage determination.

Using a unique USA dataset covering adults in employment, Filer (1981; 1983) also found that personality traits and IQ are strong predictors of high earnings, especially among college graduates. Drive and determination, high aspirations, achievement motivation, friendliness and tolerance for opposition were all strongly associated with higher earnings. There were no sex differences in returns to these factors, and their inclusion in analyses eliminated the sex differences in the returns to higher education. However, sociability (a liking for social activities, conversation, and having many friends) was *negatively* related to earnings (Filer, 1981; 1983).

In some cases, the impact of attitudes and values is diffuse, rather than specific. Babcock and Laschever (2003) noted that women are much less likely than men to ask for a salary increase, promotion, or a bonus. Men are far more disposed to ask for what they want, and to actively negotiate to achieve their goals. They report experimental studies which reveal an enormous 50% sex differential in the propensity to see the potential for negotiation to further one's interests, and to engage in negotiation. They present evidence to show how the entire sex differential in pay might potentially be explained by women's systematic failure to negotiate higher pay and salary raises across an entire career. But how can we explain this apparently perverse behaviour?

Babcock and Laschever point to the full array of social-psychological research showing sex differences in attitudes, values, personality, dispositions towards other people and the world in general. They argue that women's external locus of control means they fail to take responsibility for negotiating higher salaries; that women's tendency to focus on relationships rather than instrumental goals and achievements leads them to accept lower-paid jobs; that women's predisposition towards co-operation rather than competitiveness made them less assertive and ambitious; that women's desire to conform to stereotypical feminine behaviour, and to be liked, led them to avoid self-promotion in favour of modesty, selflessness, and even submissiveness. In short, Babcock and Laschever (2003) believe that the sex differences in personality, work values and life goals reviewed in this chapter collectively explain women's greater reluctance to ask for better wages (as compared with men) and hence their lower earnings. Moreover, they report this pattern among highly-educated young women just as often as among older and poorly-educated women, so it is not eliminated by women's improved education and the careers it opens up.

It appears that attitudes and values do matter, even if their influence is sometimes diffuse rather than direct, and can be as invisible as water in sand.

Conclusions

Ideas about male and female abilities and social roles have changed in recent decades. Male intellectual superiority is no longer asserted, as sex differences in educational attainment evaporate once the educational system is opened up to women (Hyde, 1996: 112; Hakim, 2000: 60). Public opinion has become more favourable to working wives and mothers following the equal opportunities revolution. Patriarchal attitudes are gradually disappearing; for example, only a minority of people now regard men as taking priority over women for access to jobs in recession. Complete sex-role segregation in marriage is now rejected by the majority of people. However, men and women still accept the *modern* sexual division of labour that allocates the main income-earning role to men and the main homemaking role to women. Work orientations and work commitment, workplans and interest in promotion are all informed by, or consistent with, acceptance of fundamental sex-role differentiation in private life (Hakim, 2003a).

Sex-role differentiation is also consistent with gender stereotypes. Men are characterised as *agentic*: independent, assertive, and initiating, while women are viewed as *communal*: caring, emotionally expressive and responsive to others. Few people now believe the 'essentialist' idea that men are different from women in every respect, due to biology. However, most people are aware that the overlap in their characters and personality is not perfect, that there are still some important differences between the male and female averages. Numerous studies confirm the broad validity of gender stereotypes, and that people have fairly accurate perceptions of average differences between men and women; underestimation of differences is more common than overestimation (Swim, 1994; Eagly, 1995: 154; Deaux and LaFrance, 1998: 795). As Eagly (1995: 152) points out, even small sex differences can be of enormous practical importance in particular contexts.

One consequence is that men and women differ, on average, in the characteristics of a job that they regard as most important, and in their satisfaction with jobs (Table 4.12). Women's satisfaction is higher on characteristics that are more important to men (pay, promotion, security and scope for initiative) as well as on characteristics that are more important to women (good relations at work, the work itself, and hours). One of the most puzzling findings of research on work values is the fact that women report consistently higher overall satisfaction with their jobs than men, and higher satisfaction with every characteristic of their jobs, despite the fact that, looked at objectively, women's jobs tend to be poorer than men's, in terms of earnings and promotion prospects, etc. Sociologists and economists who have attempted to explain this paradox (Hakim, 1991; Clark, 1997) have concluded that women have a distinctively different perspective on paid work, perhaps because it has a different place in their lives than it does for men. (Sousa-Poza and Sousa-Poza (2000) suggest that the paradox is most pronounced in Anglo-Saxon countries, and is seen there more clearly than in other countries.) This is now changing, but only among the minority of careerist women.

The only group seriously challenging the *status quo* are career women working full-time, who seem also to provide the vanguard of change within the workforce. This minority group is not representative of all working women, let alone all adult

Table 4.12 Characteristics of a job that are valued and satisfying

	% saying feature is most important		% saying they are highly satisfied	
	M	F	M	F
Total pay	19	13	31	39
Promotion prospects	4	2	30	33
Job security	36	25	50	59
Scope for initiative	9	8	69	71
Relations at work	5	10	61	70
Work itself	24	35	61	67
Hours	1	6	48	60
Something else	2	1	–	–
Total	100	100		
Overall job satisfaction			53	65

Source: Extracted from Tables 1 and 4 in Clark (1997). Data for employees from the 1991 British Household Panel Study.

women, yet its voice is the one most often heard. Once again, we find a polarisation among women that has not been recognised or addressed, a polarisation that reflects more fundamental conflicts of interest between career-oriented women and housewives or secondary earners, than between men and women working full-time.

Women are under-represented in senior-grade jobs. Undoubtedly, sex discrimination is one factor restricting women's access to well-paid top jobs. Men prefer to reserve the best jobs for themselves as long as they can, claiming that women do not have the necessary skills or do not fit in (Smith, 2002). But this review points up two additional factors which are sometimes overlooked. First, women (as well as men) prefer to work for male bosses, even when they recognise that men are not especially competent. Women in positions of authority and power present a serious challenge to sexual identities and sex roles for everyone, not only for male colleagues. This response is consistent with, and supports Goldberg's theory of male dominance. No other theory has been offered which can explain women's rejection of females in positions of authority. Secondly, employment careers are centrally important for only a minority of women, even today, even among university graduates. More than half of adult women still accept the sexual division of labour and treat market work as an additional, secondary activity, to be fitted in with the demands of domestic life. Significantly, many childless couples maintain differentiated roles in private life. Acceptance of sex role differentiation is independent of childbearing and childcare responsibilities and independent of views on women's abilities. Work-life balance typically means quite different things for men and women. These findings can be interpreted as supporting both Goldberg's and Becker's theories. Role specialisation can be a rational maximisation of efficiency, given socialisation processes in childhood and adolescence which create domesticated women and achievement-oriented men long before either spouse decides to reject parenthood as a major life activity. On the other hand, Becker's theory of comparative advantage predicts only specialisation, not which spouse will specialise in domestic work, and it is consistent with complete role reversal. If women specialise in homekeeping and men in competitive market work even in households that have intentionally avoided the constraints imposed by children, it is likely that some fundamental psychological factors are operating, as Goldberg and others argue.

Most research on the labour market deals exclusively with behaviour, which is more easily reported in regular national surveys and censuses. Research on attitudes, motivations, preferences and plans is more difficult to do well, but is absolutely crucial if we are to obtain a complete understanding not only of *what* people are doing, but also *why*. Similarly, sociological theory and labour economics must recognise and incorporate the central role of core values and life goals in explanations of labour market processes. At present, preference theory is the only theory to do this, and to recognise the diversity of women's work orientations.

Some social scientists (especially feminists) and some policy-makers argue that pointing to the impact of individual characteristics on achievement in the workforce constitutes 'blaming the victim'. Thus, micro-level theories and explanations are ruled out as inadmissible evidence, and only macro-level structural theories and explanations are considered acceptable. This argument excludes the valuable contribution of social psychological research to understanding women's position in the workforce. Evidence cannot be discarded simply because it is inconvenient, at least not in the academic community, although this sometimes happens in politics.

In summary, sex differences in work values and work orientations have vanished as regards commitment to jobs, but they remain in other areas, such as the type of job preferred. Sex-role ideology is changing much more slowly, so that most adults in modern societies still prefer some differentiation of roles in the family. It is these private life social identities that maintain continuing differences between the centrality of employment in men's and women's lives. The most recent research shows that 'psychological capital' does play an important part in shaping achievements in the workforce and public life, although it is far less studied than factors such as social class of origin or education.

Chapter 5
Labour Mobility and Women's
Employment Profiles

Is it true that women's attachment to work is increasing in leaps and bounds? This is certainly the impression given by contemporary research reports on women's employment, and by the European Commission (2002). Work attachment refers to continuity of employment over a period of years, or across the life cycle, and is measured at the individual level and longitudinally. It is thus quite different, and separate, from economic activity rates which are measured in aggregate data, usually at the national level and at a single point in time, using cross-sectional data (see Chapters 2 and 3). Studies of individual work histories routinely conclude that women's continuity of employment, or attachment to work, has been increasing in recent decades (Martin and Roberts, 1984: 187; Main, 1988a). Unfortunately, this is a one-sided and misleading reading of the evidence (Hakim, 1996c). The pattern of women's employment across the life cycle has certainly been changing, but not as yet in the direction of greater work attachment in Britain, although this is certainly a trend in the USA, and among the minority of childless women in modern societies. Within Europe, the British pattern of change is more common than the USA model.

Changing perspectives

Post-war writers on women's employment had no illusions about women's casual approach to market work. A comparative review of women's employment in the USA, Britain and other European countries by Myrdal and Klein (1956, 1968) acknowledged that women were less stable workers, with substantially higher rates of absenteeism and turnover. Like others writing on what was then labelled the 'controversial phenomenon' of women's employment, they sought to defend women's right to work, demonstrating their physical and mental abilities for wage work, and suggesting novel arrangements (such as part-time work) which could ease women's double burden of domestic duties and employment. Nonetheless, their espousal of this cause did not prevent a dispassionate data-based analysis of the question. Under the heading of 'employers' problems' they addressed sex differences in work attitudes, behaviour and performance that were claimed by employers to justify their preference for male workers over female workers, and to justify lower rates of pay for women doing the same job as men (Myrdal and Klein 1956, 1968: 91–115). Of these, the most important behavioural differences were women's higher rates of absenteeism, higher labour turnover and lower employment stability with an employer, all giving rise to additional costs. Employers' investment in on-the-job training offered a lower return in the case of female workers, who were less likely to stay with the company, due to more job-hopping or to leaving the workforce for family reasons; there were also the extra recruitment costs of replacing workers who left. From the employer's view, the specific reason for a woman worker leaving a job is irrelevant. Whether she leaves to marry, have a baby, to take another job because her husband's job has been moved to another city, or to take another job because it is closer to home does not alter the employer's need to hire and retrain a replacement worker, with the associated costs (Chiplin and Sloane, 1974).

As late as 1971, a government report stated that the most widely accepted 'law' of absence behaviour was that women were absent more frequently, and more in total, than men. The evidence was absence rates twice as high among women working full-time, and two to three times higher among part-time women, than among men in the period 1947–1949 (Jones, 1971: 18). Myrdal and Klein found that absenteeism was two to four times higher among women, even when absences associated with pregnancy were excluded. One study found that women lost about twice as much time as men, with married women losing up to three times as much as single women. They concluded that 'one of the major objections against the employment of women is based not merely on prejudice but on actual experience. The statistical data are undeniable evidence that, with all due variations as from one type of employment to another, the rate of absenteeism is higher among women than men in each occupational group' and they attributed this to a casual attitude to market work among women. Similarly, they found labour turnover to be very much larger among women than among men, on average 50% to 60% higher, but reaching 100% per year in the textile industries despite their long tradition of female employment. Even here, they noted that most women lacked a sense of career, and adopted a casual attitude towards continuity of employment, changing jobs for casual reasons (Myrdal and Klein, 1956, 1968: 94–107). A somewhat lower average annual turnover rate of 32% is quoted for women in the USA in 1957 (Blau and Ferber, 1992: 79).

Twenty years later, Hunt's report on a 1973 national survey of management attitudes towards women at work was necessarily factual in its presentation of the survey results, but her interpretation was already excusing and downplaying sex differentials as unimportant, glossing over the inconvenient results on labour turnover and absenteeism to underline those showing women in a positive light, notably employers' view that women scored higher than men in patience with dull work! (Hunt, 1975: 101, 105, 107, 109.) Nonetheless, the sex differentials remained in evidence. Only a minority of employers thought there was no difference between men and women in their propensity to take days off for sickness or for other reasons, or in the likelihood of their working continuously for one firm. The dominant view was that men were preferable for their lower absenteeism and turnover rates. The perceived sex difference in behaviour was corroborated by analyses of actual absenteeism, job tenure and job mobility. The same pattern was found in management perceptions of full-time and part-time workers: the majority view was that full-time workers were markedly better than part-timers on low absenteeism, continuity with the firm and working hard. Again, employers' 'prejudices' were found to be supported by, and clearly based on, actual experience within the company, with personal and family reasons dominating turnover rates among women (Hunt, 1975: 94–96, 105–06). It is notable that absenteeism remained higher among part-time workers, who already had more time for domestic activities, indicating that the casual attitude to employment as an optional extra continued into the 1970s.

Twenty years later, the issues of labour turnover and employment instability have disappeared from the social science research agenda. Studies routinely draw the conclusion that there is no evidence that women in general, and women working part-time in particular, show a lesser degree of attachment to work in terms of loyalty to a particular employer (Marsh, 1991: 57), that the employment stability of women part-time workers is no lower than among women full-time workers (Dex, 1987: 115), and that the evidence that part-time jobs are high-turnover jobs should not be taken at face value (Elias and White, 1991: 32–36, 58). When differences are found, they are attributed to the occupations in question rather than to the incumbents, to labour market segmentation (Blossfeld and Mayer, 1988: 129; Elias and White, 1991: 5) or to age effects (Elias and White, 1991). Studies that reveal dramatic sex differentials in work orientations and employment patterns nonetheless emphasise the similarities between men and women (Pollert, 1981: 79–115; Elias and Main, 1982: 3–11; Dex, 1985: 20–46) or, *in extremis*, reject the differences as implausible, even when national surveys yield the same result year after year (European Commission, 1994: 87). Sensitive to the climate of public opinion, economists often ignore persistent sex differentials in turnover and tenure as unworthy of emphasis in research reports (Burgess and Rees, 1994; Gregg and Wadsworth, 1995).

Turnover rates appear to have been lower in the USA throughout the 20th century because of the marked heterogeneity of the female population: those wives who worked did so continuously, while other women stopped work at marriage and never worked again (Goldin, 1990: 28–41). The entry of women with lower work commitment and less work experience to the labour market after 1950 may even have raised female turnover rates slightly. Even so, there is a sex difference in labour turnover in the USA as well, and a similar unwillingness to admit the differential runs through the USA social science literature (Reskin and Padavic, 1994: 39–41, 86, 112–13; Hakim, 1996c). A popular USA textbook on labour economics and female employment (Blau and Ferber, 1992) does not include a chapter on patterns of labour mobility and women's work histories across the life cycle, even though other chapters contain passing references to this topic, noting inadequacies in data on work histories and work experience. By the end of the 20th century, economists as well as sociologists were suggesting that sex differentials in employment patterns were disappearing or had disappeared (Blau and Ferber, 1992: 80, 162). Rhetoric had completely replaced dispassionate analysis of the evidence, even among social scientists (Hakim, 1996c).

The sources of change

There are three reasons for expecting fundamental change in this area in most modern industrial societies. First, there was the abolition of the marriage bar (the prohibition on married women's employment), through legislation making direct and indirect discrimination on grounds of sex or marital status unlawful. Secondly, equal opportunities legislation gave women the right to retain their jobs during pregnancy and to return to work after childbirth, supported by EU policy. Thirdly, the introduction of the contraceptive pill in the 1960s gave women the means to control and plan their fertility behaviour independently of men, leading to the new phenomenon of sexually active but voluntarily childless women who were able to devote their lives to a career. These developments, especially the last, broke the historical link between women's household and reproductive work and the pattern of women's employment (Tilly and Scott, 1990: 7).

In the USA and Europe, the marriage bar took the form of strong social norms against wives going out to work, especially in the middle classes; these norms were sometimes institutionalised in company rules and policies, especially for white-collar jobs such as teaching and clerical work (ILO, 1962; Oppenheimer, 1970: 39–55; Cohn, 1985: 99; Walby, 1986: 171–72, 180, 247; Grint, 1988: 96; Bradley, 1989: 211–13; Goldin, 1990: 160–79; Hakim, 2000: 59–60). Throughout history, the non-working wife, and concubine, has been a status symbol, proof of affluence, and often essential to achieving high levels of consumption. In the second half of the 19th century, formal policies were invented to exclude wives from wage work. Historians and sociologists have shown how the 'bourgeois' ideal of marriage, with the wife devoted full-time to creating a haven of comfort and relaxation for the family, was aspired to more often than achieved by working class families, as it relied on the husband having adequate and regular earnings (Holcombe, 1973; Roberts, 1984; Pollert, 1981). Marriage bars were often strengthened during the Depression of the 1920s and 1930s (Walby, 1986: 180), with social norms sometimes reinforced by law. In the Netherlands, for example, a law introduced in 1935 prohibited wives from holding jobs in the civil service, thus reserving jobs for men during the 1930s recession. However, the law was not repealed until 1957, long after the recession, and it encouraged private sector firms to apply similar rules, which lasted until 1979 (Pott-Buter, 1993: 246–51; Tijdens, 1993: 79, 87). In Britain, the marriage bar was a legally enforceable rule, jointly imposed and policed by employers and trade unions in certain industries, mainly for white-collar occupations, that women left employment upon marriage. Resignation from work was 'sweetened' by giving the bride a lump sum payment which some have construed as a 'dowry' or bribe to promote turnover (Cohn, 1985: 102), but was often a refund of pension contributions paid so far, as wives were expected to rely on their husband's earnings and pension rights. There is some debate over the social impact of the marriage bar, its economic efficiency and profitability in the period 1870–1950 in the USA and Britain (Cohn, 1985; Walby, 1986: 247; Grint, 1988; Goldin, 1990: 160–79). It seems clear that its main effect was to support the sexual division of labour, and power, within marriage. The key motive was patriarchy rather than profit, benefiting all men rather than a few employers (Grint, 1988: 97). Marriage bars institutionalised the marriage career for women, and discouraged young women from investing in qualifications and careers. After World War Two, the marriage bar was outlawed through equal opportunities and sex discrimination legislation, from 1971 onwards in Britain, from the 1960s in the USA and other European countries, but not until 1985 in Japan, for example. Direct and overt discrimination against women, or married women, became unlawful throughout modern industrial societies, and in many other countries as well. Women immediately started to invest in educational qualifications (Moen, 1992: 25–26; Shavit and Blossfeld, 1993).

A less visible, but profoundly important change is that reliable methods of birth control became readily available to the cohorts of women born after 1945 and entering the labour force in the 1960s. Having children ceased to be an uncontrollable hazard of women's lives, and became voluntary. Many women now sidestep childcare problems simply by not having children. In Britain, Germany, Australia and the USA about 20% of post-war cohorts of women are already, or are predicted to remain childless. The rising trend of voluntary childlessness, reaching 20% of women born after 1955 in Britain, is strongly associated with increasing levels of educational qualifications, that is, with an investment in their human capital and the employment career instead of the marriage career (Werner, 1986; Werner and Chalk, 1986). In the past, large proportions of certain cohorts of women have not had any children; for example, 20% of those born in 1920 in Britain remained childless. But childlessness in the past has typically been associated with poverty and poor nutrition, low marriage rates and shortages of men due to wars. Only in the case of women entering convents and other religious careers can we assume that celibacy and childlessness were voluntary, in most cases at least. The current trend emerges among women who are sexually active from a young age, expect to marry at least once during their reproductive years, and do not have to rely on a partner for reliable contraception. The World Fertility Survey shows that primary infertility affects only 2–3% of women aged 25–50 (Vaessen, 1984), so the new rising trend of childlessness is clearly socially determined and voluntary. Childlessness can emerge gradually from repeated postponement of childbearing, due to other activities taking priority, but some people make a firm choice early in life (Veevers, 1973; Campbell, 1985; Hakim, 2000: 50–56). Contrary to popular stereotype, childlessness is acceptable to half of men and women in Britain, other European countries and the USA, although most people routinely confirm the joys of raising children. The acceptability of childlessness doubled in the second half of the 20th century (Scott et al, 1993: 30–31; Hakim, 2000: 53).

Women in the lower social classes hold marriage and childbearing as their principal life objectives, and reach these goals earlier in life than women in the higher social classes, who are more likely to plan employment as well as marriage; social class thus remains the strongest and most enduring predictor of fertility patterns (Dunnell, 1979: 19–27; Campbell, 1985: 9). Women who choose to centre their lives on children and family life, with or without marriage, do not need to plan ahead in the same way as women choosing employment careers: they can rely on 'just letting things happen', which typically results in a greater number of children being born (Dunnell, 1979: 24–26). Today, most mothers have just one, two or three children, a huge reduction on the numbers common at the beginning of the 20th century. Feminist debates on the value of domestic labour, women's reproductive role and the need for childcare services, failed to take account of the dramatic decline in the childcare element within domestic labour, due to falling family size (Fine, 1992: 169–91). Declining fertility across Europe, and in other modern societies, is slowly becoming a policy issue (European Commission, 1995b: 59; Hakim, 2003c).

In summary, abolition of the marriage bar, equal opportunities and anti-discrimination legislation, and the contraceptive revolution of the 1960s, all give women new freedoms and new choices as to how to live their lives. In this new social context, women gain genuine choices regarding careers, or combining a career with marriage and motherhood. So there are good reasons for expecting fundamental change in women's employment profiles by the end of the 20th century.

The impact of childbirth on employment

Researchers devote special attention to women's employment decisions around the time of childbirth (Martin and Roberts, 1984; Desai and Waite, 1991; Glass and Camarigg, 1992; Rexroat, 1992; McRae, 2003). The arrival of a new baby provides a strategic case study of the factors that influence women's choices, how these are weighed up, and how they have changed over time. In the 1950s, most women would drop out of the labour market around marriage or the first birth, although many resumed work, at least briefly, many years later. In the 1980s, many women returned to work within a year of a birth and worked between births, so that the bimodal pattern of employment flattened into what looked like more continuous employment in many European societies (Meulders et al, 1993: 6–12; European Commission, 1994: 50–58; OECD, 1994: 55–61, 2002: 72–73). Maternity rights legislation is widely believed to be a key factor in this process, giving women new rights not to be dismissed for pregnancy, and to be reinstated in their job after a period of maternity absence. However, in practice, maternity rights have not altered women's work profiles to any major degree.

There have been three national studies of the impact of the maternity rights legislation introduced in Britain in the mid-1970s; in each case both employers and new mothers were invited to report their experiences, in 1979, 1988 and 1996. These surveys show that the statutory right to retain one's job is not a significant determinant of a woman's return to work soon after the birth. The 1988 survey is often quoted as showing an 'association' between the two, but it was not statistically significant (McRae, 1991: 183–84, 230–35). Having the legal right to keep one's job makes it easier to plan ahead for women who have already invested in training, qualifications and a career, but it does not become a motivating factor in its own right for other women. The determinants of a mother's return to work are the usual ones: better qualifications, higher earnings potential and higher occupational grade, all increasing the opportunity cost of not working.

Nonetheless, the maternity rights survey reports give the impression that women's attachment to work is increasing. For example, McRae emphasises her finding that the proportion of employees who gave formal notice to their employer of their intention of returning to work after the birth almost doubled between 1979 and 1988, from 26% to 47%. Almost three-quarters of women who qualified for the right to return gave formal notification during pregnancy of their intention to return compared with less than half in 1979 (1991: 170–74). These are indeed huge changes in just a decade, and testify to the impact of the maternity rights legislation on pregnant women's public statements. What she does not emphasise is the fact that the mothers' private attitudes and actual behaviour changed very little.

The right to reinstatement gives an employed pregnant woman the right to return to work with her former employer at any time between the birth of her baby and the end of her maternity leave. On returning, a woman has the right to be employed on terms and conditions in line with those which would have been applicable if she had not been absent. In 1988, reinstatement rights generally required two years' service with an employer, and women had 29 weeks' maternity leave. With certain employers, the qualifying period was shorter. In 1994, all pregnant women became entitled to 14 weeks' maternity leave, irrespective of their length of service with their employer. Women with at least two years' service were entitled to a longer maternity leave of 40 weeks in total. Periods of absence can be longer in some countries and shorter in others, and maternity benefits (as a proportion of lost earnings) vary from 0% to 100% (OECD, 1990; 1994: 182–85; 2001: Table 4.7). The law requires women to signal an intention to return in order to retain the option of doing so. It does not penalise women who do not fulfil their commitment to return to work, although it would penalise an employer who refused to reinstate a woman in her job. Pregnant women thus have every incentive to notify an intention to return to work, and nothing to lose by doing so. Even today, the successful outcome of a pregnancy cannot be guaranteed. The level of notifications has understandably shot up as a result of the new laws, but this says little about women's intentions of actually *using* their right to reinstatement. Among women who gave their employer notice of return, one-fifth (1988) and one-third (1979) of women had no intention or expectation of returning to work; another fifth (1979 and 1988) had hoped or planned to return but did not. Small numbers went back to work in a new job, typically part-time and closer to home, with a different employer. In the 1996 survey, employment rates after the birth were again boosted by women who took different jobs one year after the birth: generally these were part-time jobs, with less responsibility, closer to home, and with an easier journey to work. Clearly, these mothers' priorities changed substantially after the birth, and they did not return to the particular job held open for them by the employer (Callender *et al*, 1997: 81). Altogether two-thirds (1979) and half (1988 and 1996) of the women giving notice did not return to the job held open for them by their employer (McRae, 1991: 178; Callender *et al*, 1997); from the employers' point of view, notifications are not statements of real plans, as the likelihood of a woman returning to their job was no better than chance by the end of the 1990s.

Understandably, maternity rights legislation does not affect women's private intentions: about two-thirds (60% in 1988 and 66% in 1979) of all women working during pregnancy had no intention of going back to work within nine months of childbirth, typically because they wanted to care for their child(ren) themselves. Many of those who intended to return to work still did not wish to return to their previous employer, preferring part-time jobs closer to home instead. This was especially common in relation to first births, which often prompt a switch from full-time to part-time work and to a less demanding occupation. Overall, women's private intentions predicted their actual behaviour more strongly than their formal notifications to employers (McRae, 1991). Four-fifths of those planning to stay at home after the birth did so. Two-thirds of the women planning to return to work did so. McRae correctly underlines a striking increase in the 1980s in the rate of return to work after childbirth: rising from one-quarter in 1979 to almost half by 1988, even though women often returned to part-time rather than full-time work. It does indeed appear that women's attachment to work is increasing, even if (a sore point with employers) they do not necessarily fulfil their notification of a return to work in the same job and with the same employer within nine months of childbirth. Similar trends are observed in other European countries (Meulders *et al*, 1993: 14), the USA (Desai and Waite, 1991; Rexroat, 1992), and in Australia (Glezer, 1988), even where there is no maternity rights legislation. One might conclude that women's employment continuity is thus driven by personal motivations, social and economic factors quite independent of employment rights.

Sample selection bias

The key weakness in all these research results is sample selection bias, perhaps the most common error made in studies of women's work orientations and labour market behaviour. Sample selection bias, sometimes labelled *selection effects*, arises when research is based on a nonrandom subset of a wider population, typically because information is only available for cases that exceed a certain threshold. The systematic exclusion of cases with particular characteristics means that both the internal and external validity of research findings are in doubt (Berk, 1983). In the economics literature, the best known example is studies of wages earned by women. One can only observe wages for women who are employed, and employed women are a nonrandom subgroup of all women: they have stronger non-financial work commitment, a larger investment in qualifications and a career, and have higher potential earnings than non-working women (see Table 3.9). Similarly, one can only ask employed women about their interest in promotion, but working women are not representative of all women, whereas working men are (Cassirer and Reskin, 2000). Although there are techniques for the diagnosis of sample selection bias in quantitative studies (Berk, 1983), no techniques currently exist to eliminate or overcome the problem. The popular two-step estimator developed by Heckman (1976; 1979) can actually exacerbate the problem instead of removing the bias (Stolzenberg and Relles, 1997). Preference theory suggests that unobserved heterogeneity in values and life goals will inevitably and invisibly differentiate groups included and excluded from studies (Hakim, 2000: 284–86), especially as lifestyle preferences cut across income, social class and education groups (Hakim, 2003a).

Economists are more sensitive than sociologists to the heterogeneity of the female (working) population, are aware of the ensuing problems of sample selection bias, and of the misleading notion of the 'representative' or 'average' woman, as illustrated by the contributors to Scott (1994) and by examples reviewed in Hakim (1996c). American sociologists are more aware of the problem than are European sociologists, but they are also more likely to think that it is a purely technical problem with a statistical solution, thus ignoring the substantive and theoretically important heterogeneity of the adult female and male populations (Hakim, 2000; 2003a). Studies of the relationship between fertility and employment using event history analysis (such as Desai and Waite, 1991) are often assumed to overcome selection bias. However, they routinely exclude the substantively important minority of women who remain childless and work continuously, as well as women who were not working before the birth. In the maternity rights studies described above, only *half* the women surveyed in 1988, and 1996, were in employment when they became pregnant. The other half comprised 17% who had *never* worked, most of them with no qualifications at all, some of them women from Moslem ethnic minority groups and immigrants; 27% who had some work experience but were not working a year before the birth, most of whom already had at least one young child;

and 3% who had been in work 12 months before the birth but stopped working before or soon after becoming pregnant, many of whom had been in temporary and part-time jobs. As McRae herself notes, these three groups differed significantly in personal, family and employment history characteristics from the working women who were the focus of the maternity rights study, a group strongly biased towards the first births of younger, better educated women in full-time employment during pregnancy (McRae, 1991: 28–36). Taking the broader view, half of the women giving birth were in work during pregnancy, and only one-quarter were in work nine months after the birth (McRae, 1991: 196) – an entirely predictable sharp fall in work rates resulting from a birth. In 1996, one-third of all new mothers were in a job of some sort one year after the birth (Callender et al, 1997), yet the report invited readers to believe that two-thirds were working after a birth, and this figure has since been widely quoted (Hibbett and Meager, 2003: 506).

Findings on the rising work attachment of women who remained in employment throughout pregnancy cannot be extrapolated to conclusions about all new mothers, let alone all women. Yet the inevitable process of simplifying and summarising research results in literature reviews, and in media reports, means that this sort of misleading generalisation often emerges. Genuine facts about unrepresentative minorities of working women become generalisations about all women of working age, including those who have never held a job!

Finally, McRae's most recent 1999 survey of the new mothers first interviewed in 1988 shows that the return to work is often short-lived. Some women return to their employer, as promised, and then drop out of the workforce shortly afterwards, especially if they have a second child. More than 10 years after the birth of the first baby, there are fewer mothers employed full-time than there had been within 12 months of that birth: 28% versus 32% (McRae, 2003: 321). Most mothers who did work had switched to part-time jobs instead. Overall, the results of the final survey of mothers were in line with preference theory: a minority (9%) of these mothers had never worked since their first birth; another minority (10%) had remained in continuous full-time work since the first birth; and the four-fifths majority of mothers pursued a flexible mixture of full-time motherhood, part-time and full-time jobs that is typical of adaptive women. Most important, the majority of mothers did what they wanted to do after the birth. Only a minority were unable to implement their preferences (Hakim, 2003b: 342; McRae, 2003).

Movement in and out of the labour force

Women who have never worked are a rarity in most modern societies. Only 2% of a nationally representative sample of women aged 16–59 years in 1980 in Britain claimed never to have had a paid job (Martin and Roberts, 1984: 122). Partly due to Moslem and other ethnic minority groups in Britain who prefer to keep women at home, this percentage had not changed by 2001 (Weir, 2002: 585). Thus, the vast majority of women have some work experience, but women's patterns of work nonetheless differ greatly from those of men, because most women leave and re-enter the workforce repeatedly across the life cycle.

Among prime age workers (aged 25–50) in the USA, women are two to five times more likely than men to enter or leave the workforce (Table 5.1). Sex differences are smallest among people retiring and among young workers aged under 25 years. In the 35–39 year age group, women are five times more likely than men to leave the labour force (11% versus 2%) and they are four times more likely to (re-)enter the workforce (8% compared to 2%). Similarly in Britain, labour mobility differs little between men and women aged 16–25 during the labour market entry phase and in the retirement phase starting from age 50 onwards. But women are two to four times more likely than men to enter and leave the workforce during the prime age years, irrespective of the type of occupation they are in (Hakim, 1996c; 1998a: 54).

Statisticians have devoted most of their efforts to developing single-time (cross-sectional) measures of employment, because this was adequate for studying male employment. Very different measures are needed to capture the dynamic character of female employment, with constant movement in and out of the workforce, and to measure the accumulation of work experience over the life cycle. An OECD analysis of employment continuity relied on the European Community Household Panel (ECHP), and equivalent panel studies in other countries, instead of the Labour Force Surveys (LFS) (OECD, 2002: 81–85). However, there are as yet no standardised measures of employment continuity; they are still being invented. What we really need are measures of lifetime accumulated work experience, which are very rarely available in datasets.

Table 5.1 Rates of labour force entry and exit over the life cycle in the USA

Age	Entries to labour force as % of population		Exits from labour force as % of population		Exits from labour force as % of labour force	
	M	F	M	F	M	F
16–19	21	21	12	13	25	29
20–24	14	16	9	14	13	23
25–29	5	11	4	12	4	18
30–34	2	9	2	8	2	13
35–39	2	8	2	7	2	11
40–44	2	7	2	7	2	11
45–49	2	6	3	7	3	11
50–54	2	5	4	6	4	11
55–59	2	4	6	7	7	14
60–64	3	3	11	8	21	25
65–69	4	3	9	5	38	37

Source: Derived from Smith (1982: 18–19) Tables 5 and 6 presenting mobility rates from worklife estimates. All percentages have been rounded.

The OECD study confirmed that the part-time workforce is more volatile than the full-time workforce, with much higher levels of labour turnover, and frequent switches to non-employment or full-time work. However, this is not true of Dutch women working part-time, who are more stable in their jobs than are full-time workers. In contrast, in France and Spain, more than one-third of women with part-time jobs had stopped working four years later. In Portugal, half of women working part-time in 1994 had switched to full-time work by 1998.

The OECD study also confirmed that women continue to have significantly lower rates of employment continuity than men. Over a 5 year period (1994–98), virtually all men in full-time jobs in Belgium, Denmark, France, Greece, Ireland, Italy, the Netherlands, Portugal, Spain, Germany and Britain remained in full-time work. On average, only 78% of women in full-time jobs in these countries remained in full-time work over the 5 year period; in the Netherlands, the proportion fell to two-thirds. On average, only half of women in part-time jobs in these countries remained in part-time work for 5 years, but the percentage was around two-thirds or more in the Netherlands, Belgium, Ireland and Germany. Looking at continuity over a 6–8 year period, in Canada and the USA, only three-quarters of women in full-time jobs remained in them for 6 and 8 years respectively. In Germany and Britain, only 62% and 58% respectively remained in full-time jobs over an 8 year period (1991–98).

As a general rule, low-educated women are less likely than highly-educated women to be in continuous full-time employment, with the notable exception of Italy. The impact of children on employment continuity is greater for low-educated women, and varies between countries for highly-educated women. The measure in Table 5.2 is continuity of employment (or full-time employment) over a 5–8 year period. Among men with children, between 80% and 92% are continuously employed, virtually all in full-time jobs. Among childless women with higher education, only around half are in continuous full-time employment. The proportion drops as low as 33% in the USA, 41% in Canada, and 26% in Germany. Although France claims that its childcare services and family policy facilitate greater employment continuity among women than in Britain and Germany, it has fewer highly-educated mothers in continuous full-time employment than in Portugal, Denmark, Spain and Belgium. France also has fewer highly-educated childless women in continuous full-time employment than in Britain, Portugal, Belgium and Denmark (Table 5.2). Employment continuity is invariably lowest among low-educated women with children, with the notable exception of Portugal, a long-standing outlier that has never been properly explained.

These results concern employment continuity over a short period of just 5–8 years. It is clear that over a lifetime, most women accumulate far less work experience than men, and far less full-time work experience, due to greater movement in and out of the labour market. However, most studies still do not measure actual lifetime work experience, even though this is a crucial factor, which explains around half the pay gap between men and women (Swaffield, 2000).

Table 5.2 Employment continuity by sex, presence of children and education

Persons in each category, as a percentage of persons age 20–50 years in the starting year, who have been employed at least one year during the period

	Women						Men	
	Without children			With children			Without children	With children
	Continuously employed	Continuously full-time	Continuously part-time	Continuously employed	Continuously full-time	Continuously part-time	Continuously employed	Continuously employed
A. Less than upper secondary education								
5 year period (1994–98)								
Belgium	63	38	14	51	30	9	86	89
Denmark	62	47	6	39	31	1	79	77
France	63	48	7	47	35	5	75	74
Germany	72	50	6	52	19	20	67	86
Greece	47	35	1	37	27	0	77	86
Ireland	38	16	9	16	6	5	67	72
Italy	62	52	3	55	36	4	71	82
Netherlands	73	35	25	43	3	28	65	84
Portugal	65	54	1	60	54	1	77	92
Spain	38	32	2	26	16	3	62	66
United Kingdom	76	43	14	54	15	20	82	80
Unweighted average	**60**	**41**	**8**	**44**	**25**	**9**	**73**	**81**
6–8 year period[a]								
Canada (1993–98)	56	26	7	42	11	6	74	82
Germany (1991–98)	61	25	10	31	5	12	65	84
United States (1990–97)	51	22	3	38	12	0	58	66
B. University/tertiary education								
5 year period (1994–98)[a]								
Belgium	87	64	9	88	51	13	89	96
Denmark	78	64	4	83	64	5	85	89
France	79	60	8	70	49	6	79	87
Germany	89	60	9	61	28	16	87	98
Greece	67	44	4	69	37	6	77	91
Ireland	81	49	8	78	32	7	87	98
Italy	67	33	11	83	35	22	79	98
Netherlands	85	48	14	77	8	31	90	94
Portugal	90	64	10	94	67	3	81	84
Spain	55	43	2	70	53	3	64	89
United Kingdom	81	66	4	70	27	13	85	86
Unweighted average	**78**	**54**	**8**	**77**	**41**	**12**	**82**	**92**
6 or 8 year period[a]								
Canada (1993–98)	80	41	4	70	21	9	85	90
Germany (1991–98)	66	26	8	37	1	12	82	95
United States (1990–97)	73	33	2	60	15	6	78	83

a) An individual is classified as 'employed full-time' in a given year if he/she has worked at least 1,560 hours (30 hours per week on average), 'employed part-time' if he/she has worked between 52 and 1,560 hours (between 1 and 30 hours per week). **Source:** OECD *Employment Outlook: 2002 edition*, Table 2.8, page 84. Copyright OECD

Continuity of employment over the life cycle: three employment profiles

If work attachment was really increasing among women, their work histories should resemble those of men more and more across generations. Analysis of work history data (Table 5.3) shows, on the contrary, a declining proportion of women in continuous work and a sharp increase in intermittent employment.

Continuous employment is the stereotypical male employment profile, consisting of continuous full-time employment throughout adult life, from the time of leaving full-time education to retirement. Strictly speaking, this should be labelled continuous economic activity, to allow for spells of unemployment. Given the practical difficulties of differentiating between unemployment and other non-working statuses among women (Cragg and Dawson, 1984; Martin and Roberts, 1984: 79–95; Hill, 2002), researchers usually measure periods of continuous employment (Elias and Main, 1982: 8; Main, 1988a: 24). On this basis, 80% of British men have had only one period of continuous employment in their life, albeit in different jobs. If periods of unemployment are ignored, virtually all men are economically active throughout their working age lives (Elias and Main, 1982: 10). The stereotype of the male employment profile is based on reality. Whether they choose it or not, this profile is imposed on men. A minority of women, about one-quarter, plan a career in market work irrespective of developments in their private life (see Table 4.11) and an exploratory analysis by Burchell and Rubery (1994: 96–97) found one-quarter of working women in continuous career employment in the primary sector. Long term workplans over-ride marital status as a determinant of continuous employment (Rexroat, 1992). However, there has been a systematic decline in continuous employment within successive cohorts of women (Table 5.3).

The *homemaker career* is the stereotypical female employment profile, consisting of a single period of continuous employment (if any) after leaving full-time education, which ends in early adult life and is never resumed. Permanent cessation of employment may be prompted by marriage or by childbirth, but it is anticipated long before the event, and involves a qualitatively different perspective on investment in educational qualifications, not necessarily a lower investment, as some human capital theorists assume. Higher educational qualifications may be acquired to ensure a girl marries a partner of at least equal status, rather than to acquire marketable skills for long-term employment. The returns to education in this group consist of the husband's earning potential rather than personal earnings potential. Women in Europe can still achieve greater social mobility through marriage than through their own employment (Goldthorpe, 1987: 282–87). The majority of women who attend university marry a graduate, professional spouse, which is better than male social mobility (Bozon and Héran, 1988: 139). The proportion of graduate women who marry a graduate spouse has increased steadily over the 20th century to 60%, 10 times more than the 6% national average (Hakim, 2000: 207–09, 216). The popularity of apparently non-vocational degrees in the humanities among young women in Western societies is attributable to these subjects being appropriate for the homemaker career. In developing countries, a wider range of subjects serve the same 'intellectual dowry' purpose.

Table 5.3 The decline in continuous employment and the marriage career

Year of labour market entry	Proportion (%) of each cohort in each category 15 or 20 years after entering workforce:						Base = 100%	
	continuous employment		discontinuous employment		homemaker career			
	15	20	15	20	15	20	15	20
1941–1945	20	13	36	51	44	36	511	502
1946–1950	18	13	39	56	43	31	449	433
1951–1955	15	10	47	67	38	23	523	510
1956–1960	11	8	53	73	36	19	609	574
1961–1965	13	..	61	..	26	..	655	..
Total	15	11	48	62	37	27	2,747	2,019

Note: .. sample too young for results at 20 years stage in 1980 survey
Source: 1980 Women and Employment Survey (WES), Great Britain, data for women aged 16–59 in 1980. Continuous employment consists of continuous spells of paid work (whether full-time or part-time) without any breaks. The homemaker career is defined as a single employment spell early in adult life that ended in permanent non-work. Discontinuous employment consists of all other work histories combining spells of work and spells of non-work.

For some women, termination of market work acknowledges an efficient household division of labour along lines theorised by Becker (1981, 1991). For others, it also signifies their incorporation into their spouse's two-person career, a pattern especially common among the wives of politicians, professionals and managers (Pahl and Pahl, 1971; Papanek, 1973; Finch, 1983; Maret, 1983: 112, 115), at least up to the 1960s (Bonney, 1988: 100). The homemaker career is open to men, in principle, although it remains a rarity even among 'postmodern' men in a liberal society such as the Netherlands. The homemaker career has long been the ideal held by the majority of girls, especially working class girls, in Britain and for a substantial proportion of one-third to two-thirds of women generally in modern societies (Matthaei, 1982; Pollert, 1981: 91–115; Hakim, 1991: 112) as shown in Chapter 4. Studies of mate selection criteria show that, unlike men, women tend to focus on income, social status, ambition, and resources (Feingold, 1992; Buss, 1995; Townsend, 1998; Hakim, 2000: 196–201), with a view to acquiring a 'good provider' mate. In some European societies, such as West Germany, this model of the family division of labour provided the basis for social welfare and labour legislation; in other countries, such as Finland, this is not the case (Pfau-Effinger, 1993). Fiscal and social policies can sharply reduce the numbers adopting this career choice, as illustrated by Sweden (OECD, 1994: 61), but even here about 10% of women are permanent full-time homemakers. This profile has been declining rapidly in recent decades (Table 5.3).

Discontinuous or intermittent employment is the third category and consists of work histories with periods of employment broken by domestic breaks or other periods of non-work other than involuntary unemployment. This group includes the simplest M-shaped work profile of two long spells of continuous employment broken by a single long domestic break, as well as 'marginal' and 'sporadic' workers whose employment is interrupted by several periods out of the labour market (Elias and Main, 1982: 11; Maret, 1983: 51). This group includes the drifters with no fixed objectives and unplanned employment careers identified in Chapter 4 (Table 4.11; see also Maret, 1983). Fragmented work histories are typical of secondary earners, so this group is increasing in size (Table 5.3). Deregulation of the labour market and the expansion of 'flexibility' in the workforce in the 1980s has also helped this category to increase in size in recent years in Europe, among men and women (Rodgers and Rodgers, 1989; Hakim, 1990a, b).

It is notable that there is in practice only one 'choice' of work history for men, compared to three for women. Feminists who emphasise that women's choices are constrained, and not completely free, overlook the fact that women have more choices than men, who have none at all.

Contrary to feminist assumptions, there has been no increase in continuous employment among British women in recent decades. The dominant trend is a massive increase in intermittent employment. In particular, the simple three-phase broken work profile has declined in importance, replaced by an expanding marginal workforce of women with increasingly numerous breaks in employment, shorter periods of employment and more numerous job changes, often associated with part-time work. These results have been largely hidden in research reports which choose to emphasise women's increasing 'attachment' to the labour force across the life cycle (as reflected in rising employment rates), rather than the fact that participation in market work has become fragmented and is now even more likely to be contingent on, and subordinate to, non-market activities than in the past (Elias and Main, 1982; Stewart and Greenhalgh, 1984; Dex, 1987; Main, 1988a).

The relative importance of the three work profiles is best identified at age 40–49 when we obtain a picture close to completed work profiles and before the picture is clouded by early retirement after age 50. Figures 1 and 2 separate cohort effects from life cycle effects to show women's employment profiles at about age 40 years. Figure 1 shows that only 3% of women aged 40 had been continuously employed up to 1980, a smaller proportion than in previous cohorts. As Main (1988a: 51) notes, Martin and Roberts (1984) confounded cohort effects and life cycle effects when they reported that 25% of the 1980 WES sample were 'always economically active' in Table 9.6 of their report on the 1980 survey. Main also showed that the frequency of breaks in employment has been increasing across age cohorts (Figure 2), so that the proportion of potential working life spent out of the labour force is also increasing across age cohorts (Main, 1988a: 28–41). He concluded that the typical employed woman now has a less intensive record of employment than she did a few decades ago (Main, 1988a: 42), a finding consistent with the results of earlier studies (Hunt, 1968b: 121; Elias and Main, 1982: 30–31; Stewart and Greenhalgh 1984: 495–99), and with Goldin's (1990; 1997) research on the USA. For example, 15% of women aged 45–59 in 1965 had always worked (calculated from Table D4c in Hunt, 1968b: 121) compared to less than 10% in 1980 (Table 5.3). Both Main (1988b:

117–18) and Elias (1988) note an association between women's discontinuous employment patterns and part-time work in Britain, despite the fact that most part-time jobs are permanent. Dex (1987: 84) notes an association between women holding traditional sex-role attitudes and downward occupational mobility, typically into part-time jobs.

As noted in Chapter 4, the *modern* version of the homemaker career permits employment after marriage if it is restricted to part-time and other jobs chosen to fit in with the domestic role, so that market work remains secondary to, and contingent on, a primary responsibility for home and family. Table 5.4 identifies the modern homemaker career by grouping together those who stop work early in adult life with women who return to part-time work after breaks in employment. This classification shows that there has been no change at all in the proportion of each cohort following the homemaker career broadly defined, about 60% of all cohorts entering the workforce after 1945. In effect, the decline in the homemaker career narrowly defined in Table 5.3 is balanced out by women adopting the modern profile with intermittent part-time work after a domestic break. Another 40% of each cohort work full-time in the 20 years following labour market entry, either continuously or, increasingly, with breaks in employment. This alternative classification of employment profiles indicates that there are essentially just two polarised employment profiles among women: the working woman and the homemaker (who may also be a secondary earner), with both profiles changing over time to include more employment discontinuity than before, so that the boundary between them appears blurred. Whereas the classification in Table 5.3 suggested qualitative changes in patterns of employment, the classification in Table 5.4 shows continuity and stability. The homemaker career is still followed by some two-thirds of adult women, consonant with about two-thirds of adult women accepting the family division of labour, as noted in Chapter 4.

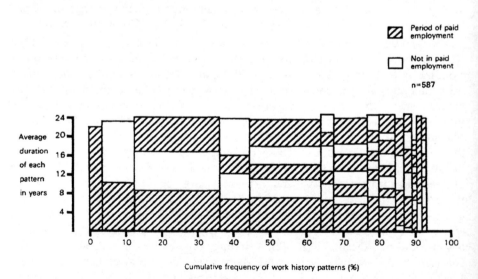

Figure 1 Distribution of work history patterns at age 40, women aged 40–44 years in 1980
Source: Main (1988a). Figures 1 and 2 based on analyses of the 1980 WES, data for women aged 16–59 in 1980 in Great Britain.

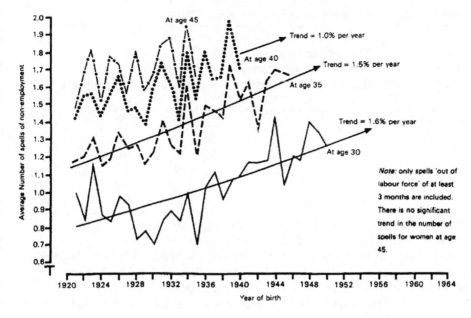

Figure 2 Average number of spells 'out of the labour force' for respondents who are in employment at a given age, by year of birth

The usual feminist response to disappointing research findings like these is to argue that things are different among younger generations of women, that there are significant changes across age cohorts. Unfortunately, the evidence from cohort studies does not support such wishful thinking (Hakim, 2000: 128–56). The general pattern is of increasing polarisation of women's employment profiles over time, and this is repeated in cohort study results: an increasing minority of women pursue full-time careers, and another growing minority become full-time homemakers (Hakim, 2000: Table 5.5). Within the 1958 NCDS cohort only 10%, and within the 1970 cohort only 14% of women had been continuously employed (not necessarily full-time) by the age of 30. There were no important differences in employment patterns at age 42 between the cohorts of women born in 1946 and 1958. If anything, the 1946 cohort had higher full-time workrates, and lower rates of non-employment than the 1958 cohort. Comparisons of women born in 1970 with the 1958 cohort show no increase in the average time spent in full-time jobs. A small reduction in the fraction of time spent out of the labour force is due to an increase in years in full-time education and in part-time jobs (Ferri *et al*, 2003: 54–57, 75–95, 168, 297).

Employment patterns in the USA are similar, but seem to be changing faster. Longitudinal studies show that the percentage of a married woman's life spent in employment is U-shaped, with high concentrations in the lowest and highest deciles, that is, in continuous employment and continuous non-work (Goldin, 1989: 25). In 1975, only one-quarter of *working* women aged 30–44 years had worked continuously since leaving full-time education; three-quarters had worked intermittently (Corcoran, 1979: 241). Discontinuous employment accounts for the

Table 5.4 The rise of the new homemaker career

| Year of labour market entry | Proportion (%) of each cohort in each category 15 or 20 years after entering workforce: | | | | | | | |
| | continuous employment | | discontinuous FT employment | | new homemaker career | | Base = 100% | |
	15	20	15	20	15	20	15	20
1941–1945	20	13	23	28	57	59	511	502
1946–1950	18	12	22	27	60	61	449	433
1951–1955	15	10	25	28	60	62	523	510
1956–1960	11	8	26	31	63	61	609	574
1961–1965	13	..	24	..	63	..	655	..
Total	15	11	24	28	61	61	2,747	2,019

Note: .. sample too young for results at 20 years stage in 1980 survey
Source: 1980 WES, Great Britain, data for women aged 16–59 in 1980.
Continuous employment consists of continuous spells of paid work (whether full-time or part-time) without any breaks. The new homemaker career is defined as a single employment spell early in adult life that ended in permanent non-work or in a transfer to part-time work. Discontinuous full-time employment consists of a career with breaks but continued with full-time work.

majority of women: around half of American women aged 30–44 years in 1967 (Stephan and Schroeder, 1979: 130; Maret, 1983: 54). The rise in full-time year-round employment among women in the USA (see Table 3.6) indicates a trend towards continuous employment among women, especially as women's work orientations seem to be changing at the same time, as noted in Chapter 4. Nonetheless, discontinuous employment is clearly important, as illustrated by the fact that, on average, twice as many women have some work experience in a year as work full-time year-round: two-thirds versus one-third. Over a lifetime, American women work in only half of all their adult years after leaving school (Hill, 2002: 43). Women's work histories thus differ from men's. Han and Moen (2001) identify five work histories in the USA. The male career (full-time continuous employment) is the most common, and has two versions: one with, and one without, frequent changes of employer. One-third of people in these two groups are women. The three other work histories are relatively rare (20% of the workforce altogether), and involve combinations of full-time and part-time jobs and not working. Two are exclusive to women, and one is shared by women and men. On this analysis, about half of American women pursue continuous lifelong full-time employment.

The implications of intermittent employment

Does employment continuity matter? It does, in two ways. First, higher labour turnover rates mean that women build up shorter job tenures than men. Secondly, women accumulate less total work experience than men, due to spells out of the labour force. There is a wealth of evidence that continuing sex differentials in job tenure and in cumulative work experience explain a large part of the pay gap between men and women, and that women's relative earnings increase when their work experience and job tenure increase (Sandell and Shapiro, 1980; O'Neill, 1985; Zabalza and Arrufat, 1985; Goldin and Polachek, 1987; Main, 1988b: 118; Goldin, 1989; 1990: 73; Sorensen, 1989; Sloane, 1990: 150–55; O'Neill and Polachek, 1993; Wood *et al*, 1993; Kilbourne *et al*, 1994; Rubery and Fagan, 1994: 127–31; Wellington, 1994). Many employers offer workers small but regular annual increments on fixed pay scales, rewarding people who stay with them for many years and gain firm-specific experience. In other sectors, it is total years of work experience with different employers that attract the highest salaries. Tenure in the current job and total work experience are important for achieving promotion up career ladders, with the same employer or with a change of job. The increasing number of spells out of the labour force shown in Figure 2 is important. A single long spell out of the labour force, in the traditional three-spell employment profile, is less detrimental to careers, given continuous full-time employment on return to the workforce. In sum, job tenure, continuity of employment and cumulative work experience are important determinants of earnings, and they contribute to women's lower representation in higher-grade posts, the vertical occupational segregation discussed further in Chapter 6.

Job tenure, or enterprise tenure, is a worker's length of service with an employer or enterprise, disregarding any change of occupation. Job tenure is theoretically important, as it provides a measure of the firm-specific skills and 'tacit knowledge' in the job that is accumulated over time but has no formal recognition in educational qualifications or certificates. Job tenure is important also in a policy context as it corresponds to the length of service criterion in labour law, which determines eligibility for important employment rights and benefits across Europe (Hakim, 1989a; Hepple and Hakim, 1997).

A sex difference in labour turnover and job tenure of about 50% has been the norm in Britain for the workforce as a whole for at least two decades (Elias and Gregory, 1994: 6–9; Burgess and Rees, 1994; Hakim, 1996c). Sickness absence is also 50% more common among women than men, on average, but is higher in the higher-grade occupations (Warr and Yearta, 1995). Britain's 50% sex differential in labour mobility is typical of the EU as a whole, even though labour mobility in Britain is above the EU average, along with Spain, Denmark, the Netherlands, Ireland and France, in contrast with the lowest mobility rates found in Germany (European Commission, 1994: 86–87, 97–99). Periodic OECD reports on employment stability and job tenure (OECD, 1984; 1989; 1993; 2002) show substantial sex differentials in job tenure in all modern economies, with the exception of France, where the differential had almost disappeared by 1991. Women's high job turnover, and hence lower job tenure, is not limited to those with children (Table 5.5). Women without any children are more likely to have relatively long tenures of 10 years or more with their employer: one-quarter compared to one in ten for women with children. But they still do not match the longer tenures of men: one-third have 10 years' service or longer with their employer, and it is these

Table 5.5 The sex differential in job tenure

% with stated length of time in present employment	all	Women youngest child aged <15	no dependent children	Men
under 1 year	27	30	25	19
over 2 years	59	54	62	70
over 5 years	37	27	42	52
over 10 years	20	11	25	35

Source: Derived from Department of Employment (1990) Table 8, reporting Spring 1989 LFS for Britain, people of working age (16–59/64 years) in employment.

long tenures that count most for promotion to management grades in the internal labour market of the organisation (Table 5.7).

These differences are associated with and extended by women taking up part-time work in preference to the full-time employment typical of the male employment profile. In 1992 one-third of full-time employees had 10 years' tenure or more compared to only 16% of part-time employees (Table 5.6). A comparison with 1986 shows that the gap between full-timers and part-timers is increasing. As the female-dominated part-time workforce grows in size, it is becoming more differentiated and distinctive in its labour market behaviour rather than more integrated into the mainstream workforce. A study by Gregg and Wadsworth (1995: 80) confirms that turnover levels are always higher for women than men, even in permanent jobs, whether full-time or part-time.

In general, higher-grade occupations have low turnover rates and long job tenures, and lower-grade occupations have high turnover and low average job tenures. Clearly these differences are features of the occupations themselves, and the industries where they are concentrated (European Commission, 1994: 87–90). However, the sex differential continues across all occupations, including managerial and professional occupations, so continuity of employment is also a characteristic brought to occupations by the people who self-select themselves into particular types of work (Hakim, 1998a: 54). Careers in highly qualified fields have the lowest turnover and longest tenures because the long periods of education and training required automatically ensure that people with low work commitment drop out long before they enter formal employment (Fiorentine, 1987). However, women have consistently lower average tenures and higher turnover, even in this group. The only exception is jobs in personal services, which recruit few men, where the sex differential is reversed (Table 5.7). Controlling for occupation tends to reduce the sex differential slightly below the average (Table 5.7), but it remains substantial in all occupational groups except for the female-dominated personal services group.

The implications of sex differences in employment continuity are illustrated by case studies of pharmacists and lawyers, two professions that recruited men and

Table 5.6   The decline in job tenure among full-time and part-time employees, 1986–1992

Proportion (%) with each length of service with the same employer	Full-time workers		Part-time workers	
	1986	1992	1986	1992
under 1 year	..	13	..	25
over 2 years	75	77	63	59
over 5 years	55	52	42	33
over 10 years	38	32	22	16

Sources: Spring 1986 and Spring 1992 LFS data for Britain. The 1986 data are for employees only (excluding family workers, students and people on government employment schemes for the unemployed), and part-time jobs are those involving less than 30 hours a week. The 1992 data are for employees and the self-employed (excluding family workers and people on government employment schemes for the unemployed), and part-time jobs are self-defined by survey respondents.

women in roughly equal numbers by the start of the 21st century. Men use pharmacy as a route into self-employment, ownership of an independent pharmacy, or management jobs in large retail chains, all jobs that demand long hours of work and continuous employment, but deliver higher earnings. Women use the profession as a source of well-paid mother-friendly, flexible and part-time employee jobs, with limited responsibilities that do not spill over into family time, and that permit intermittent employment. As a result, there is a substantial sex differential in the earnings of pharmacists – almost 30% in Britain, for example (Reskin and Roos, 1990: 111–27; Bottero, 1992; Hakim, 1998a: 221–34, 2000: 39).

Wood *et al* (1993) estimate a 40% pay gap among lawyers in the USA, due to different employment patterns among men and women. Men were more likely to work in large firms and private practice, which are more remunerative but demand long hours of overtime and continuous employment. Women were more likely to be in low-paying jobs in government, where hours are fixed and overtime not demanded. Half the pay gap was due simply to sex differences in hours worked and work experience; children *per se* made no difference at all, although 40% of the female lawyers were still childless 15 years after graduation. Baker (2002) found that the sex differential in earnings among lawyers had fallen to around 27% by 1993, but employment profiles still differed strongly between men and women. Compared with many other professions, legal work is mother-friendly, offering part-time work and career breaks that are still rare in many professions. Male lawyers had roughly double the full-time professional experience of female lawyers, and this pattern was repeated in other professions, including physicians and MBA-graduate managers.

Conclusions

Intermittent employment has expanded in absolute and relative terms, at the expense of continuous employment and the homemaking career. The result is a

Table 5.7 Mean elapsed job tenure in months by occupation 1975–1991

Occupations	Men			Women			Average sex differential M/F
	1983	1990	1975–91 average	1983	1990	1975–91 average	
Managerial and Professional	151	137	144	106	97	102	1.41
Other white collar	118	108	113	81	75	78	1.45
Personal service	81	47	64	78	73	76	0.84
Skilled manual	124	116	120	84	75	80	1.50
Other manual	105	94	100	79	65	72	1.39
Total	127	119	123	80	77	80	1.54

Source: Derived from Burgess and Rees (1994) Table 4, plus unpublished tables, based on analysis of General Household Survey data for all years 1975 to 1991. Data for all in employment.

large substitution of fragmented employment for continuous employment in the female workforce in recent decades, in parallel with the massive substitution of part-time jobs for full-time jobs documented by Hakim (1993a) for Britain, and by Jonung and Persson (1993) for Sweden. This finding for Britain is consistent with Goldin's (1989; 1990; 1997) conclusion that the large post-war influx of women into the USA labour force resulted in a *lowering* of average years of work experience among working women, thus explaining the lack of change in women's relative earnings and the continuing sex differential in pay. We conclude that increasingly fragmented employment profiles explain continuing sex differences in labour mobility and job tenure, and can contribute an important part of the explanation for the slow decline in vertical occupational segregation and the pay gap between men and women (Polachek, 1979; Zabalza and Arrufat, 1985; Main, 1988b: 118; Hakim, 1992) – a topic discussed further in Chapter 6.

Some USA studies claim that women's work experience averages three-quarters of men's work experience, measured in years (Reskin and Padavic, 1994: 41). However, this average conceals significant differences between working and non-working women, and overlooks the fact that women are far less likely than men to work full-time throughout the year in any given year of employment (Smith, 1982; Maret, 1983: 54; Goldin, 1990: 31), as shown in Table 3.6. Estimates of annual hours in the USA reveal that women's average annual work hours are only *half* those of men despite the fact that women appear to contribute equally to the workforce on a headcount basis (calculated from Table 4 in Smith, 1983: 17). The sex differential is substantially larger in Britain, even ignoring the greater importance of years with only part-time and/or part-year employment.

In conclusion, the picture commonly painted of women's increasing attachment to the labour force across the life cycle could more accurately be described as a picture of increasingly fragmented, discontinuous, intermittent employment, much of it in part-time jobs. The total volume of market work done by women has been redistributed across the life cycle, and between women, so that more women than before are now doing some market work, at different points in their lives. It is not obvious that employment has become a more salient priority in women's lives, rather than a more frequent interruption of their family work, which clearly dominates choices and takes precedence for most women. The male profile of continuous lifelong employment has become less, rather than more, common among women. This increasingly fragmented involvement in market work, along with the substitution of part-time for full-time employment noted in Chapter 3, undermines the story of women's rising employment and expectations of social and economic change following from it. Employment stability is a key characteristic of the primary labour market (Chiplin and Sloane, 1974: 375), so women's increasingly fragmented employment patterns must increase the chances of their segregation in the secondary labour market, a topic to which we turn in the next chapter.

Chapter 6
Occupational Segregation and the Pay Gap

There are few women in the top jobs, those with the highest status, authority and earnings. The gloomy view says this is a permanent situation that equal opportunities legislation has not changed to any significant degree. Pessimists point out that the majority of low-paid workers are women, that the earnings gap between men and women has not been eliminated, that there is a glass ceiling excluding women from the top jobs. This chapter looks at trends in the occupational segregation of men and women, in particular vertical job segregation, and in the sex differential in earnings, commonly called the pay gap. It shows that important changes started in the 1980s. These developments can only be identified if we take account of historical data showing the long term trend, thus revealing a sharp increase in the pace of change after equal opportunities policies were introduced in the 1970s.

The EC has targeted occupational segregation as a fundamental source of gender inequality in the labour market, and the main cause of the pay gap between men and women (European Commission, 2002: 3). This is also the general position of feminist texts on women's employment, and they more or less explicitly state that occupational segregation and the pay gap are imposed by employers (for example, see Padavic and Reskin, 2002). Our analysis suggests that the contemporary situation in modern societies is fundamentally different from the picture before the equal opportunities revolution, and that much current theorising looks backward to a previous era. On the other hand, the development process does not necessarily improve women's position. Rwanda, in Africa, has more female parliamentary representatives than any country in Europe or North America. Sri Lanka was the first country in the world to elect a female Prime Minister and head of state.

Job segregation and labour market segmentation

Segmentation and segregation are often confused and conflated, understandably, given that they are inter-related.

Segregation refers to social processes which ensure that certain social groups are kept apart with little interaction between them. The factors used to differentiate groups are normally personal, such as age, sex, race or religion, or they may be work-related factors such as occupational grade, as illustrated by separate canteens and trade unions for different grades of staff in an organisation. Occupational segregation on the basis of sex exists when men and women do different kinds of work, so that one can speak of two separate labour forces, one male and one female, which are not in competition with each other for the same jobs (Blaxall and Reagan, 1976; Hakim, 1979; 1998a; Reskin, 1984; Reskin and Hartmann, 1986; Rubery and Fagan, 1993). To a much smaller extent, race is an additional factor of occupational segregation, such that white and black women and men do not compete for the same types of job, although this is more pronounced in the USA than in Britain, where racial intermarriage is common (Mayhew and Rosewell, 1978; Tomaskovic-Devey, 1993; Bhavnani, 1994; Owen, 1994). In some societies, jobs in government administration and all senior positions are reserved for members of the largest or dominant religious or ethnic group. For example, Catholics were debarred from the professions and senior posts in Ireland until 1829, and substantially separate labour markets for Catholics and Protestants persist in Northern Ireland (O'Leary and McGarry, 1993: 81, 206, 262).

In the past, occupational segregation resulted from a combination of de jure or direct discrimination and de facto or indirect discrimination. For example, before 1970, professional schools in the USA admitted few women. Before 1975, a relatively low quota of places in British medical schools (about 10%) were open to women applicants; this ensured that membership of the medical professions was reserved largely for men. Since 1975, when equal opportunities laws took effect, de jure occupational segregation has disappeared, although entry to certain religious occupations is still reserved for men in Britain and in many other countries and cultures. However, people with a common culture and interests tend to congregate together in social and geographical space, in neighbourhoods, occupations or clubs, producing varying degrees of natural, voluntary de facto segregation in areas of residence, the labour market or leisure activities. The problem for the social scientist is to distinguish between natural, voluntary occupational segregation and that which occurs because people of one sex, race or religion are prevented from entering a particular occupation by a variety of subtle indirect exclusionary social processes, some of which will be lawful, some of which will be unlawful. The requirement that officers are transferable from one posting to another in the Diplomatic Service produces a preponderance of men in this area of work. This mobility rule is not challenged, whereas mobility rules in other employment contracts have been challenged and judged to be discriminatory, as shown in Chapter 7. A person who is 'frozen out' of a work group by colleagues' silently hostile behaviour at present has no legal redress, whereas hostile behaviour which takes the form of sexual comment is now covered by sexual harassment regulations in most companies, and the victim may have redress under sex discrimination laws. What counts as indirect discrimination and indirectly exclusionary practices is being continuously re-assessed in each society, as this is socially defined rather than specified by an abstract logical principle.

Segmentation is the differentiation of the labour market into distinct firm-specific labour markets, each offering quite different conditions of employment, career patterns and rewards, as shown in Figure 3. The fourfold classification here was developed by Loveridge (1983: 159; 1987) from an earlier version by Mok and is often used in European research (Loveridge, 1983; 1987; Blossfeld and Mayer, 1988; Hakim, 1990a, b; Crompton and Sanderson, 1990: 39; see also Althauser and Kalleberg, 1981). It is obtained by cross-cutting internal and external labour markets with primary and secondary labour markets. An organisation's core workforce is in the primary internal sector offering full-time permanent jobs with career ladders, combining flexible but firm-specific skills with a high span of discretion and long term stable earnings. Part-time jobs typically fall in the secondary sector, either the internal market for permanent jobs, or the external market for temporary jobs. The self-employed and sub-contractors are in the external labour market, which

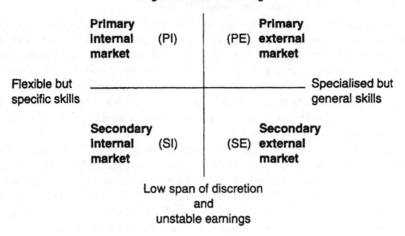

High span of discretion
and
long term stable earnings

Primary Internal (PI) market	Primary (PE) external market

Flexible but   Specialised but
specific skills   general skills

Secondary Internal (SI) market	Secondary (SE) external market

Low span of discretion
and
unstable earnings

Figure 3 Labour market segmentation.
Source: Loveridge (1983: 159)

generally has higher rates of labour mobility. Professional and skilled craft work requiring occupation-specific skills rather than company-specific skills may be supplied on a fixed-term contract or self-employed basis in the primary external market. Seasonal and casual jobs, homework and unskilled labouring jobs are typical of the secondary external sector. At the minimum, the segmentation perspective provides a useful description of qualitatively different sectors within the labour market. Some regard it as the basis for labour market theory which argues, for example, that there is little or no mobility between the four sectors: workers enter one sector, by design or by accident, and remain there permanently, unless there is a marked change in their qualifications or other characteristics. For example, people may move up to the primary labour market as a result of obtaining a university degree, or they may move down to the secondary labour market as a result of physical injury which limits the work they can do, or because their priorities change after they have children.

Barron and Norris (1976) argued that women are generally confined to the secondary labour market because employers perceive them to have little interest in training and careers, above-average turnover and little solidarity as reflected in low rates of trade union membership, features which equally well describe secondary earners, as they themselves recognise (see Chapter 3). Their analysis was possibly valid for the 1960s and early 1970s, but is now dated. The proportion of women in full-time permanent employee jobs is about one-half compared to two-thirds of men (see Table 2.6). The winter 1994/95 Labour Force Survey (LFS) showed that 89% of all men in employment were in full-time permanent jobs compared to only 53% of women in employment in Britain. A full 39% of working women were in *permanent* part-time jobs and a further 8% were in a variety of temporary jobs. Thus, by the mid-1990s, about half of all working women were in the primary labour market, and only half were in the secondary labour market.

There is no fixed relationship between occupational segregation and labour market segmentation. In societies which insist on the physical segregation of men and women, there are good job opportunities for women in women-only schools, universities and hospitals; it can be easier for a woman to become the director of a girls' school in a Moslem country than of a mixed school in Western society where women have to compete directly with men for senior posts (Boserup, 1970: 119–38; Lewin-Epstein and Semyonov, 1992). Educational systems are universally perceived as non-discriminatory today, whereas labour markets are seen as discriminating against women, with the political arena seen as the most sexist and discriminatory of all (Sorensen, 1990: 158; Tokyo Metropolitan Government, 1994: 17–32). In most modern societies, similar proportions of men and women now achieve tertiary-level qualifications (around 20% and rising), although men are more likely to get university degrees and women are more likely to get nursing and teaching qualifications below degree level. The qualifications gap between men and women is disappearing, although sex differences remain in subjects studied (Shavit and Blossfeld, 1993; Hakim, 1998a: 34–37). Discrimination is limited to the labour market, and to politics.

Vertical job segregation and the pay gap

Segregation can be both horizontal and vertical and no single measure can capture both these aspects. Most measures, in particular the popular Dissimilarity Index (DI), measure horizontal segregation, but vertical job segregation is far more important. Cross-national comparisons of the UK, USA, Canada, Sweden, Norway, Australia and Japan suggest that vertical job segregation is largely independent of horizontal occupational segregation (Wright *et al*, 1995).

Horizontal job segregation exists when men and women are most commonly working in different types of occupation – for example, women are dressmakers and men are tailors, women are cooks and men are carpenters. *Vertical job segregation* exists when men dominate the higher-grade and higher-paid occupations and jobs, or when men are promoted further up career ladders within occupations – for example, men are heads of schools while women are teachers. Other labels for this are the *authority gap* (Wright *et al*, 1995), and the glass ceiling. Occupational classifications vary from 10 broad occupational groups to 400–600 specific occupations, and they generally identify some combination of vertical and horizontal segregation. For example, teachers are usually identified as a separate occupation group, which is staffed by a mixture of men and women, so it is integrated rather than segregated. More detailed classifications distinguish between primary school teachers (usually dominated by women), secondary school teachers (with a mixture of men and women) and tertiary level teachers (generally dominated by men). Even more detailed occupational classifications might distinguish between ordinary teachers and head teachers or directors of educational establishments at each level (who are typically male). The more detailed the occupational classification, the greater the degree of occupational segregation identified, a point which is important for comparisons across time and across countries.

The degree of detail in the occupational classification is even more important for studies of earnings differentials. There is invariably a large difference in pay between primary school teachers and university teachers, between heads of educational establishments and ordinary teachers. If most primary school teachers are women and most university teachers are men, there will be a large sex differential in pay *within* the teaching profession that is attributable entirely to vertical occupational segregation which is hidden if all teachers are grouped together. Similar problems occur with occupational classifications that do not separate school managers from teachers, a grading difference that has a large impact on earnings. These points may seem obvious, yet they are regularly overlooked in reports that claim to be surprised, even outraged, at the size of the difference in average earnings between men and women. Perhaps university teachers should be paid the same as primary school teachers. However, this is a totally different argument from the idea that, within current salary structures, the lower earnings of women reflect sex discrimination. Scandinavian countries have reduced earnings differences between men and women without changing the high level of horizontal and vertical occupational segregation (Jenson, Hagen and Reddy, 1988: 181–85; Rosenfeld and Kalleberg, 1990; Wright et al, 1995), but in Britain and the USA periods of pay equalisation have always been followed by periods when differentials were re-established and the earnings dispersion increased.

Studies of the pay gap between men and women within particular occupations indicate that vertical job segregation accounts for virtually all the difference, and national studies confirm this finding. The impact of vertical segregation can be assessed easily in school teaching because of the formalised job grading absent from many other occupations. An analysis of data for 1973, some 12 years after equal pay was introduced in teaching in Britain, found that one-third of the earnings differential was explained by women being concentrated in the lower-paying primary sector and the remaining two-thirds by women being concentrated in posts with lower responsibility and grading (Employment Department, 1976: 965). Analyses of the New Earnings Survey (NES) invariably conclude that vertical job segregation *within* occupations explains more of the pay gap than horizontal occupational segregation. Chiplin and Sloane (1974; 1976) analysed NES data for 1974 while Sloane (1990) analysed NES panel data for 1970–1982, a period when average earnings of female full-time employees rose from 67% to 75% of male pay. Astonishingly, both studies gave the same result: vertical job segregation within occupations explained three-quarters of the difference in earnings and horizontal occupational segregation explained only 20% to 27%. Sloane concluded that it is not the particular occupations that women enter that depress their pay, so much as their failure to advance up the occupational ladder, to gain promotion to better-paid posts after entry to the occupational group (1990: 135–46). In the USA, horizontal occupational segregation only explains one-quarter of the difference in earnings (Sorensen, 1989: 74) with vertical job segregation the main cause of the pay gap (Goldin, 1987). Sieling (1984) found the pay gap was virtually eliminated when comparisons were drawn between men and women in the same grade of specific white-collar occupations. For example, the earnings of female chemists rose from 75% to 96% of male earnings after job grade was controlled. In virtually all the white-collar occupations studied, women were concentrated in the lowest grades. In general, white-collar occupations and jobs are more likely to have a variety of pay rates and grades, and a larger wage spread, than manual occupations which very often have only a single rate of pay in any establishment (Buckley, 1985). As a result, the earnings spread, and the sex differential in earnings are larger in white-collar occupations and jobs than in manual occupations and jobs (Buckley, 1985; Sloane, 1990: 134; Payne, 1995). More recently, Hakim (1998a: 76–79) found that the pay gap is largest in integrated occupations that employ highly-qualified men and women (rather than in segregated occupations), and in managerial occupations.

Studies at establishment level invariably identify far more segregation of *jobs* in individual workplaces than is found in national studies of segregation in the *occupational structure*: teachers may be all-male or all-female in particular schools while the teaching profession as a whole is mixed. Due to sex discrimination legislation, there are now virtually no occupations which are 100% male or 100% female at the national level. Exclusively male or female jobs are still common at establishment level, however, and many establishments have no mixed occupations (Hunt, 1975: 173–79; Hakim, 1981: 527–28; Bielby and Baron, 1984: 35, 51). About half of all men and women report that they work with members of their own sex only in their workplace (Kiernan, 1992: 94). This limits the impact of equal pay laws to jobs that are integrated, or mixed, at company level, unless equal pay for work of equal value (comparable worth) laws are introduced to allow pay comparisons between men and women doing different jobs of similar value to their employer. Generally, statistical analyses of the level and pattern of job segregation at company or workplace level are mainly of interest for internal practical purposes, and rarely have theoretical value. From a social science perspective we are much more interested in knowing whether women have access to the teaching profession, than in knowing whether women are employed in every school across the country, large and small. It is useful to know that many people, men and women, work in single-sex work groups at their workplace, so that the workforce can appear to be totally segregated at the individual level. However, this is not a public policy issue even if it is interesting. Most adults are aware of the world beyond their own workplace; they know that there are male as well as female teachers, that the occupation is mixed even if it is not part of their immediate experience. Case studies of particular industries or occupations that try to identify causal processes are of course useful, as illustrated by Reskin and Roos (1990), Rubery and Fagan (1993), Hakim (1998a: 221–34), and Hinze (2000), but these are rare, and involve quite different research designs (Hakim, 1987a: 61–75).

In sum, vertical occupational segregation is most important, because it reflects women's access to jobs with status, power, and authority, and it explains sex differences in income. However, it is more difficult to study, so most research looks at horizontal occupational segregation, especially studies that examine trends over time, or draw comparisons between countries.

The impact of equal opportunities laws

The sex discrimination legislation that took effect in 1975 proved to be a turning point for patterns of occupational segregation and the pay gap in Britain. A study of occupational segregation over 1901–1971, the 70 years prior to the equal opportunities legislation, showed that at the national level there was little overall change: the decline in horizontal segregation was balanced by a marked increase in vertical segregation (Hakim, 1979: 23, 27–29; 1981: 521). The most notable change was that 'exclusive' occupations disappeared completely for women and were almost eliminated among men. Occupations that were 100% female employed 11% of all working women in 1901; by 1961 they had disappeared. In 1901 half (47%) of the male workforce was employed in 100% male occupations; by 1971 the proportion had fallen to only 14% (Hakim, 1979: 24). Trends in the 1970s suggested that legislation had a dramatic and immediate impact in lowering the overall level of occupational segregation, but that these gains were partially reversed in the deepening recession at the end of the decade (Hakim, 1981). Since 1979, there has been a small but steady decline in horizontal occupational segregation (Hakim, 1992: 137–38; 1998a: 8–17). More important, the marked long term increase in vertical segregation in both white-collar and manual occupations was dramatically reversed after 1971 (Table 6.1).

In the 1980s, women's dominance in lower-grade and lower-paid occupations was reduced and their representation in all grades of professional and managerial occupations increased. The smallest increase, from the lowest starting point, was in professional and related occupations in science, engineering and technology, but here too there was an improvement, as also in literary, artistic and sports jobs. Women with the very highest earnings in Britain are writers (especially fiction writers), actresses and sportswomen, although earnings in these fields are also the most variable. Some types of work remained almost exclusively male throughout the decade: construction, mining, materials moving, transport operating, and production work involving metal and electrical goods remained virtually unaltered, with negligible or tiny female representation even by 1990 (Hakim, 1992: Table 3). As noted in Chapter 3, there is no evidence of feminisation of the most stereotypically masculine occupations.

Women's share of top jobs increased sharply after 1971 in all industrial societies (Rubery and Fagan, 1993). Table 6.1 shows trends in vertical segregation over the two decades 1971–1990 by examining women's share of the most senior occupations which play the major part in running a country. The occupational classification does not identify parliamentary representatives. Equally invisible are the 'captains of industry', the managing directors and chief executives of the largest companies in the private sector, who are men almost without exception. Women's exclusion from these upper echelons of the top jobs was underlined in a 1990 Hansard Society report showing women to be 6.3% of parliamentary representatives (the lowest figure in Europe at the time), 1% of High Court judges, 3% of university professors, and 0.5% of directors of the Confederation of British Industry's top 140 firms. Managers of large and small establishments in the various sectors of industry are grouped together in Table 6.1. At this aggregate level, women's share was relatively high at one-fifth in 1971 rising to over one-quarter by 1990. Other professional and managerial grades also experienced sharp increases in women's share of these jobs,

Table 6.1 Women in top jobs 1971–1990

Percentage of women in each of the following occupations	1971	1981	1990
Judges, barristers, advocates, solicitors	4	14	27
General administrators – national government	12	19	29
Local government officers – administrative and executive functions	20	31	51
Statutory and other inspectors	2	10	18
Senior officers – police, prison, fire services	2	2	*
Officers – UK Armed Forces	5	4	3
Accountants, valuers, finance specialists, underwriters, brokers	4	10	19
Personnel and industrial relations managers, O&M, work study offers	12	29	46
Economists, statisticians, systems analysts, computer programmers	15	19	19
Marketing, sales, advertising, public relations, purchasing managers	11	16	24
Other professional and related supporting management	34	43	52
Teachers in higher education – university, further and higher education	25	27	37
Medical and dental practitioners	18	23	30
Biologists, chemists, physicists, mathematicians, other scientists	7	20	26
Engineers – civil, municipal, structural, mining, quarrying	*	*	2
Engineers – mechanical, aeronautical	1	1	2
Engineers – electrical, electronic	1	2	7
Architects, town planners, quantity building and land surveyors	1	4	6
Managers – large and small establishments	21	23	28
Women's share of total employment	36	39	43
Women's share of full-time employment	27	30	32
Women's share of full-time permanent employment	..	30	35

* less than 0.5%

Sources: 1981 Census *Economic Activity*, Table A, 10% sample data for England & Wales 1981 and 1% sample data for 1971 recoded to 1980 classification; Spring 1990 LFS results for Britain. Figures for all persons in employment.

with a few exceptions. Women are barely visible with less than 5% of senior posts in engineering professions, the Armed Forces, the police and the prison and fire services. Despite the fact that the expanding 'new' computing professions have no established 'traditional' entry barriers and sex stereotypes, there was virtually no change over the two decades in women's share of economist, statistician, systems analyst and computer programmer jobs. Apart from these areas of stability, women made significant gains in the decades after the equal opportunities revolution. Perhaps appropriately, the legal professions were among the first to open up, with women's share of jobs rising from a meagre 4% in 1971 to 27% by 1990, followed closely by national government management, with an increase from 12% to 29%. By 1990, women's share of top jobs in certain sectors was broadly level with their share of total employment: local government administration and management, personnel and industrial relations managers, organisation and management and work study professionals, and the miscellaneous category of other professionals supporting management which includes company secretaries, management consultants, librarians, information officers, trade union officials, property and estate managers, officers of trade and professional associations, and officers of charities.

The vast majority of professional and managerial jobs are full-time permanent posts. Arguably, the more appropriate comparison is with women's share of full-time permanent jobs, or at least their share of full-time jobs, rather than their share of total employment (Table 6.1). The percentages are lower, and increase more slowly than the more commonly quoted share of total employment, reaching one-third by 1990. Using these alternative comparisons, and accepting that there will be some variation around the mean, the *majority* of top jobs listed in Table 6.1 had already achieved a fair share of women by the 1990s. The exceptions were those with hardly any women, which would be outliers whatever measure was used: the engineering professions and security services. Using the new comparison points, two occupational groups are now identified as having disproportionately *high* female shares: local government officers (51%) and professional and related supporting management (52%). Apart from women's exclusion from the upper echelons of the top jobs, as noted earlier, vertical job segregation was effectively eliminated in the short period of two decades after the introduction of equal opportunities legislation.

This analysis also demonstrates how inadequate the standard occupational classifications are, even at the most detailed level, for identifying the extent of vertical segregation *within* occupational groups, especially in the expanding white-collar sector. Within the legal profession, judges rank higher than lawyers in status and earnings, yet all grades are grouped together in the occupational classification used for Table 6.1, even though it is a relatively detailed one with 162 occupational groups which are further subdivided into 550 occupations. It is often remarked that occupational classifications identify male occupations in more detail than female occupations. The more general point is that occupational classifications excel at differentiating types of manual work, which may not attract very different earnings, but classify white-collar occupations into broad groups, even though these merge grades with substantial skill and earnings differences. This is why many studies fail to explain earnings differences between men and women: they use only broad classifications of white-collar jobs.

Measures of occupational segregation

The most widely used measure of occupational segregation is the Duncan and Duncan (1955) Dissimilarity Index (DI). Originally developed in the USA for studies of racial segregation in cities, neighbourhoods and schools, its use was extended to trend analyses of the sex segregation of occupations as well (Williams, 1976; England, 1981; Reskin, 1984; James and Taeuber, 1985; Reskin and Hartmann, 1986; Jacobs, 1989a; Charles and Grusky, 1995). The DI is used in European research on social mobility, where it is well suited to measuring the dissimilarity of social classes of origin and destination (Goldthorpe, 1987; Erikson and Goldthorpe, 1993: 231–77) as well as in research on occupational segregation (Blossfeld, 1987; Rubery, 1988; OECD, 1988; Hakim, 1993b, 1998a; Rubery and Fagan, 1993). However, as soon as research moves beyond the analysis of long term trends in one country, the limitations of the DI (and similar single number indices) become serious (Hakim,

1993b, c; 1995c), especially for cross-national comparisons (OECD, 1988; Jacobs and Lim, 1992; Wright *et al*, 1995: 429; Anker, 1998). Perhaps the most important practical limitation is that the DI requires comparisons of pairs, and only permits comparisons of pairs. This becomes an impossible constraint as soon as one moves beyond analyses of national trends to comparisons of subgroups within the workforce. The point is illustrated by King's (1992) attempt to compare occupational segregation on the basis of both sex and race in the USA workforce, which required no less than six sets of paired comparisons, and by Hakim's (1993b) attempt to compare the degree of occupational segregation within the full-time and part-time workforces in Britain. As Goldthorpe has argued in relation to studies of social mobility, the single number index cannot adequately describe the pattern of change and movement within the occupational structure (Goldthorpe, 1990: 416; see also James and Taeuber, 1985: 26).

One alternative is an analytical framework which distinguishes integrated and segregated occupations and measures their relative importance across groups and across time. This approach allows some variation in the definition of integrated occupations; can be adapted to cross-national comparisons; allows comparisons between any number of labour market subgroups; is not excessively sensitive to the degree of detail in the occupational classification available in the data source; and is useful in policy research as well as theoretical research. Perhaps most important of all, it facilitates theoretical linkages between macro-level studies and case studies of changes within particular industries, occupations, regions or labour market subgroups (Hakim, 1993b; 1998a). This approach is applied in Tables 6.2 to 6.6. In each case mixed or integrated occupations are identified as those falling in a narrow band (±15% or ±20%) around the average female share of total employment for the period in question.

The new pattern of occupational segregation

One approach to analysing vertical segregation is to use the social class classification. As Goldthorpe (1987) pointed out, occupational segregation and social stratification are theoretically distinct facets of the distribution of occupations, status and rewards, so that research on the two topics has legitimately proceeded separately and in parallel. More recently, Erikson and Goldthorpe (1993: 277) concluded from a cross-national comparative study of women's class mobility in Europe that an explanation of the gender inequalities that are a common feature of modern industrial societies needed to be developed outside the scope of class analysis. Our analysis of the relationship between occupational segregation and social stratification (Table 6.2) points in the same direction. The classification of occupations into segregated and integrated categories is based on 10% sample data from the 1991 Census, that is, on data for 2.5 million workers who are coded to 371 occupations (OPCS, 1994: Table 4) and we use the standard Social Class classification (OPCS, 1991). The dataset is the 1% Sample of Anonymised Records (SAR) from the 1991 Census of Population for Great Britain which has opened up new avenues of labour market analysis (Hakim, 1982a: 54; 1995b; 1998a).

Integrated occupations are the smallest group, and they are the most highly qualified as well, with no jobs in the lowest unskilled Class V and almost three-

Table 6.2 Social Class composition of integrated and segregated occupations

	Distribution of workforce in 1991 in each type of occupation			
	Male	Mixed	Female	Total
I Professional	8	8	*	5
II Managerial and Technical	20	65	18	27
IIIN Skilled white-collar	5	7	48	24
IIIM Skilled blue-collar	42	7	7	21
IV Semi-skilled	18	13	18	17
V Unskilled	7	0	9	6
Base thousands = 100%	114	48	128	289

Mixed occupations are those 25% to 55% female (40% ±15%) using an occupational classification with 371 occupational groups. The classification of occupational groups is based on 10% sample data from the 1991 Population Census.
Source: 1991 Census 1% Household SAR for Britain, which is Crown Copyright. Data for current and last jobs of people aged 16–64 years, excluding people in the Armed Forces and those with occupation not stated or inadequately described.

quarters of all workers in Classes I and II, as Scott and Burchell (1994) also found with a much smaller dataset. Male-dominated occupations include some professional occupations, which are virtually non-existent within the female-intensive sector (Table 6.2). Otherwise, male-dominated and female-dominated occupations are almost identical in their Social Class composition, apart from the well-known tendency for men to be concentrated in skilled blue-collar work while women are concentrated in skilled white-collar work – Social Classes III Manual and III Non-Manual respectively. Contrary to expectation, it is not male occupations which have the highest proportion of higher status and higher-paid occupations, but the small category of mixed occupations, which constitute one-fifth of 371 separately identified occupations and one-fifth of the total workforce (Hakim, 1998a: 26–85). Integrated occupations are the most highly qualified and, partly associated with this, have the highest proportion of self-employed people, which suggests that they fall in the primary internal and primary external segments of the labour market. Table 6.2 shows that the middle group of desegregated, or mixed, occupations separating the male-dominated and female-dominated sectors is not a random category with no distinguishing features, but a qualitatively different sector of the labour market. In the integrated sector, certificated skills seem to create a uniquely egalitarian and open labour market, avoiding the need to rely on sex stereotyping and statistical discrimination to allocate people to jobs (Phelps, 1972; Cain, 1986: 724–29; Hakim, 1998a: 39). Looking at it another way, there is less sex segregation in the higher-grade occupations than in lower-grade occupations. The two groups of segregated occupations, male and female, are characterised by horizontal segregation rather than vertical segregation. However, in terms of absolute numbers, there are more men than women in Social Class I and II occupations. Table 6.2 provides an explanation for contradictory results from studies that dichotomise occupations into male and female, or that use a single continuous variable of % female to characterise occupations (Rosenfeld, 1983; England, 1984; Kilbourne *et al*, 1994). Two-thirds of male occupations are skilled and unskilled manual work, and two-thirds of female occupations are skilled and unskilled white-collar work, so there is no strong variation in occupational sex ratios, status and earnings except in the top two classes, where integrated occupations are dominant. The occupational structure is dominated by horizontal occupational segregation except in the top grades of highly-paid professional, technical and managerial occupations.

A unique analysis by Blossfeld (1987) studied the pattern of occupational segregation across the life cycle using the richly detailed 1981–83 West German Life History Study. His analysis took account of the qualitatively different employment profiles of men and women to show that women with discontinuous employment were more likely to be in typically-female occupations than those who worked continuously. In addition, Blossfeld found a surprising cross-sectional rising trend in occupational segregation across age cohorts, a result that was confirmed after separating cohort and life cycle effects. He concluded that occupational segregation rides at successively higher levels within each younger age cohort in Germany, despite an impressive equalisation of educational attainment, albeit with increasing segregation of educational subjects. The puzzle he was unable to solve is why declining segregation in educational attainment was not matched by declining segregation in occupational attainment. One explanation is explored below: a tendency for people to prefer sex-typical occupations and work cultures, which seems to apply equally to men and women, and has to be regarded as benign rather than noxious. However, there is no reason to expect this preference to intensify in younger age cohorts; indeed quite the obverse. A second explanation may be that, as noted in Chapter 5, an increasing proportion of women use their educational qualifications to improve their prospects in the marriage market as well as the labour market (Hakim, 2000: 193–222). Only a minority of graduate women have careers. The total returns to college education for women are the same as for men when the indirect returns (through marriage to a graduate husband) are included (Goldin, 1997: 39–42). The third possible explanation, which is consistent with the second, is that the creation of a segmented part-time workforce tends to increase occupational segregation, given that most of the increase in female employment is due to the expansion of part-time work in successive cohorts (OECD, 1988: 139). The impact of part-time work on occupational segregation is explored below with reference to the British labour market, which has one of the largest part-time workforces in Europe. The fourth explanation, suggested by the cross-national comparisons reviewed below, is that rising female workrates increase occupational segregation in each successive age cohort in a country. Finally, the subject of educational qualifications may be just as important as the qualifications level, but studies of the returns to education have focused only on the level attained.

In the USA and across Europe as a whole, female employment is polarising, with women increasing their share of professional, technical and managerial occupations at the same time as they increase their share of lower level service and clerical work

(Power, 1988: 145; Hakim, 2000: 84–127). As Rubery and Fagan point out (1993: xxi; 1995a), trends over the 1970s and 1980s have been pulling in opposite directions, so that overall measures of occupational segregation at the national level generally reveal little or no change; any change that is found may be upward or downward (OECD, 1988; Rubery and Fagan, 1993; 1995). Cross-national comparisons (Anker, 1998) reveal a large degree of convergence in the occupations in which women are concentrated, but also puzzling diversity. Women's share of computer professionals varies from just 13% in the Netherlands to 31% in Greece, with Denmark, Portugal and Ireland following closely at 27% to 28% (Rubery and Fagan, 1995a: 224). As this is a new profession, historical and institutional factors have little force here. In Spain, women's share of economists and legal professionals jumped from 9% to 16% in 1980 to 33% to 36% by 1991 in the private sector. In Germany, women's share of lawyers, judges and scientists increased by 50% in the period 1977–90, whereas there was relatively little change over the decade in France (Rubery and Fagan, 1993: 19; 1995a). There is a haphazard element in the allocation of jobs to men and women which emerges most clearly in cross-national comparisons (Hakim, 1979: 37–43).

In summary, occupational segregation is gradually falling at the national level in most modern countries. However, it is not necessarily lower in successive younger age cohorts. These contradictory trends may be due to the polarisation of women's employment patterns, but there are also several other possible explanations for new trends.

Masculine and feminine work cultures

Women are now entering previously male-dominated professional and managerial occupations in substantial numbers. On the face of it, this trend is inconsistent with Jacobs' 'revolving doors' thesis. Jacobs' social exclusion (or social control) thesis was that male colleagues refuse to provide the informal job induction process, the camaraderie and co-operative teamwork that new female entrants need to succeed, that male colleagues regularly ignore, harass and undermine female colleagues, forcing them to leave male occupations (1989b: 181–82). In effect, he described the informal and invisible 'freezing out' mechanisms that complement the formal exclusionary policies of patriarchal trade unions described in Chapter 1. The thesis was plausible, resting as it did on patriarchy theory without ever using the term. However, by restricting his analysis to women, Jacobs fell into the sample selection trap noted in Chapter 5.

Fuller analyses comparing men and women, full-timers and part-timers, reveal that there is a *general* tendency for people to leave sex-atypical occupations and move towards sex-typical occupations across the life cycle (Table 6.3). This process occurs among men and women to a similar extent, so any explanation must apply equally to men and women. It is notable that men and women who leave mixed occupations usually move to sex-typical occupations. The most likely explanation is simply that working life is more psychologically and socially comfortable, or unproblematic, for many people when work colleagues are of the same sex, so that there is a natural tendency to drift back towards sex-typical occupations. The reversal to sex-typical occupations is 'natural' in the sense of being voluntary rather than forced on people by social institutions and work colleagues. Alternatively, men and women are equally hostile or unwelcoming to people of the opposite sex who 'invade' predominantly single-sex occupations. The 'revolving doors' process is not an exclusive feature of male occupations, as Jacobs argued, nor even stronger there. Among full-time workers, women are more likely to remain in male jobs than men to remain in female jobs. Waite and Berryman (1986) review reasons for women leaving male-dominated jobs in the military, an unsupportive social environment being only one of many.

Occupational stability outweighs the tendency to revert to sex-typical occupations. Table 6.3 uses the same definition of integrated occupations as in Jacobs' analyses for the USA, namely occupations that are 30% to 70% female (50% ±20%). The correlation coefficient between occupation type in 1971 and 1981 is around .40 for all subgroups shown in Table 6.3, varying only slightly or not at all between men and women, consistent with the results of other studies (Rosenfeld and Spenner, 1992: 429). Another replication by S Jacobs (1995) also found that occupational changes over 15 years and 25 years, for men and for women, were largely stable within the three categories of male-dominated, female-dominated and integrated occupations. So exclusionary processes, if any, are weak.

Research is documenting the way that jobs are constructed by employers as female or male jobs, even in times of labour shortage during wars (Milkman, 1987; Bradley, 1989; Strom, 1989). But one reason for this is that women often prefer to work with women, men with men, partly as a demonstration of and confirmation of sexual identities (Matthaei, 1982: 194; Bradley, 1989: 229). Workers play a more important role in gendering jobs than employers do. Workplace cultures are often heavily coloured by job incumbents: women regularly celebrate their private relationships and private lives at work; men celebrate their sexual exploits and sports interests (Pringle, 1988, 1989: 95, 120, 225, 243; Reskin and Padavic, 1994: 134–41). Both feminine and masculine work cultures and associated institutions, such as clubs, can be experienced as exclusionary by men and women. For example, women can ostracise a female colleague who refuses to discuss private relationships at work, while men can look down on a man who has no interest in cars or football. As yet we have little solid evidence on the informal 'freezing out' exclusionary processes, conscious or unconscious, applied by men and women to people in sex-atypical jobs, and more generally to people who do not conform to gender stereotypes. As noted in Chapter 4, this can include female colleagues, even secretaries, as well as men, refusing to co-operate with a female manager. Most of the time, masculine and feminine workplace cultures are unrelated to the nature of the work task; they are a gratuitous add-on. Quite often, it is the work culture that defines an occupation as male or female, not the work task itself.

All this is demonstrated in Cockburn's (1983) case study of male newspaper printers in Britain which complements the broader, more analytical case study of printing in the USA by Reskin and Roos (1990: 275–98). Printers were the quintessential craft workers, the aristocracy of the manual workforce, democratic within their elite organisations (Lipset et al, 1956). Between 1970 and 1990, printing feminised. In Britain, the percentage of compositors who were female rose from 3% in 1971 to 24% in 1991 (13% for printers by 1991). In the USA, the percentage of typesetters and compositors who were female increased from 17% in 1970 to 74% in 1988, as electronic composition and 'desktop publishing' computer programs

Table 6.3 Occupational change 1971–1981 among people in continuous employment

	Type of occupation in 1971	Proportion (%) in each type of occupation in 1981				Distribution of occupations in 1981 + Base
		Male	Mixed	Female	Total	
All persons	Male	84	11	4	100	57
	Mixed	30	55	15	100	26
	Female	13	21	66	100	17
	Total	58	24	18	100	100
	Base for this group					131,600
All women	Male	37	29	34	100	11
	Mixed	10	61	29	100	39
	Female	7	21	72	100	50
	Total	12	38	51	100	100
	Base for this group					39,200
All men	Male	87	10	2	100	76
	Mixed	47	49	4	100	20
	Female	44	22	34	100	4
	Total	78	18	4	100	100
	Base for this group					92,400
Women working full-time only	Male	48	31	21	100	14
	Mixed	13	67	20	100	44
	Female	9	26	65	100	42
	Total	16	45	39	100	100
	Base for this group					17,700
Men working full-time only	Male	88	10	2	100	76
	Mixed	48	48	4	100	20
	Female	46	22	32	100	4
	Total	79	18	3	100	100
	Base for this group					88,500
All working full-time only	Male	86	11	3	100	66
	Mixed	37	54	9	100	24
	Female	20	25	55	100	10
	Total	68	22	9	100	100
	Base for this group					106,200
All with any part-time work	Male	49	22	29	100	17
	Mixed	10	56	34	100	34
	Female	6	18	76	100	49
	Total	15	32	53	100	100
	Base for this group					25,400

Mixed occupations are those 30–70% female (50% ±20%) using occupational classifications with 223 groups (1971) and 350 groups (1981). The classification of occupational groups is based on 10% sample data from the 1971 and 1981 Population Censuses.
Source: Analyses of the Office of National Statistics (ONS) 1% Longitudinal Study. Data for people working in 1971 and 1981 aged 16 and over in England and Wales.

changed the labour process, so that relatively dirty, noisy skilled blue-collar jobs were transformed into clean, quiet, skilled white-collar jobs – to the dismay of the male-dominated trade unions, who had long opposed women's entry to this well-paid work, and did their best to resist the changes. Cockburn's case study of the masculine workplace culture in printing reviews the trade unions' long-standing policy of excluding women from the skilled grades of printing work; the links between regular wage work, skill, status, physical strength, endurance, masculinity and patriarchal attitudes; and men's need to create supportive all-male work groups to bolster fragile sexual egos and to hide from women's gaze their regular failures in the rat race for success and power. Cockburn describes the many arguments developed by working class men to justify the exclusion of women from skilled work, ranging from natural, physical, intellectual and temperamental inadequacies, which meant women could not do the work, to economic and social reasons why women should not compete with men for skilled work (1983: 132–40, 151–90). Virtually all the arguments and concepts had to do with men's ideology of sexual difference; preserving the sexual division of labour at home and at work; and avoiding competition between men and women in the workplace, because this would affect the way they related to women in their private lives. If women have been kept out of printing far more successfully in Britain than in the USA, it is due to trade union organisation and exclusionary male solidarity rather than anything to do with the nature of the work tasks. Explaining the much faster pace of feminisation in the USA, Reskin and Roos (1990: 279, 295) point out that technological change is the most visible factor, but is not in itself the main cause of social and economic change, as proven by contrasting developments in the USA and Britain.

In summary, Hartmann's and Walby's thesis of male exclusionary practices is becoming out-dated. Such practices undoubtedly existed in the past, and reserved well-paid occupations for men. They still operate successfully in some developing societies. But the globalisation of markets and new technology are breaking up male monopolies and undermining old systems. Women can convert male-dominated occupations into female-dominated occupations. However, the general pattern seems to be for men and women to prefer same-sex occupations and work groups, just as people mostly choose same-sex friends.

A segregated part-time workforce

One reason for the conflicting pictures emerging from recent studies is that the workforce is splitting into distinct full-time and part-time sectors, as noted in Chapter 3. The overall level of occupational segregation is thus the sum of two opposite trends which largely cancel out: declining segregation in the full-time workforce is hidden by higher and rising segregation in the expanding part-time workforce (Hakim, 1993b; 1998a). Up to 1961, part-time workers were a tiny and almost invisible element of the workforce, just 9% nationally (see Table 3.5). In 1971, part-time work had no substantial effect on the overall level of occupational segregation at that time (Hakim, 1979: 29–31). The emergence of a segregated part-time workforce is a new development, occurring only after the part-time workforce became large enough to become a separate and distinct sector of the workforce, consistent with labour market segmentation theory described earlier; consistent with the distinctive secondary earner characteristics of most part-time workers, as noted in Chapters 3 and 4; and consistent with the fact that part-time work is a key feature of the *modern* homemaker career and sexual division of labour, as noted in Chapters 4 and 5.

Using the DI to compare the full-time workforce as a whole with the part-time workforce as a whole yields a score of 49 for 1971 rising to 54 in 1991, within the possible range of 0–100. The two workforces differ markedly. More important, they are diverging rather than converging: as the part-time workforce grows in size it is becoming more differentiated rather than integrated into the mainstream; the peculiarities of a minority sector are becoming more extreme. The occupational structure of the part-time workforce is in sharp contrast to that of the full-time workforce (Table 6.4; see also Table 3.6).

The decline in horizontal occupational segregation 1971–91 is reflected in the increasing importance of mixed occupations, rising from 18% to 25% of occupations, and from 15% to 19% of the workforce, while male occupations shrank in size (Table 6.4). In 1971 and 1991 the occupational structures of the male and female full-time workforces are virtual mirror images of each other. In 1971, three-quarters of men and women were in occupations dominated by their own sex, with a bare 10% in what can be termed sex-atypical occupations dominated by the opposite sex. By 1991, despite changes, the mirror image pattern remained: two-thirds of full-time male and female workers were in occupations dominated by their own sex, and a good fifth were working in mixed occupations. In contrast, the part-time workforce is completely dominated by female occupations, which contribute three-quarters or more of the sector, and it became more segregated after 1971. As the part-time workforce grew over the period, from 16% to 22% of the workforce, it had an increasing impact on the national pattern of occupational segregation. The trend towards integration in the full-time workforce is thus concealed and cancelled by the trend towards a more segregated part-time workforce (Table 6.4).

These conclusions are reinforced by the contrasting trends of feminisation and polarisation shown in Table 6.5. Over the two decades up to 1991, the workforce feminised, and this trend was observed in all three types of occupation. In contrast, the expansion of part-time jobs was concentrated in female occupations, which changed from being one-third part-time in 1971 to half part-time by the 1990s. The workforce has polarised into a female-dominated secondary labour market with part-time jobs and high turnover rates, while the primary labour market consists of male-dominated and mixed occupations, full-time jobs and low turnover rates, confirming Barron and Norris' (1976) earlier analysis.

The location of part-time work on the periphery of the workforce is further demonstrated by the jobs taken by students in full-time education and by the last jobs of the retired (Hakim, 1995b: Table 5; 1998a: 102–77). The current and last jobs of students are concentrated in female occupations, even for male students. When the current or last job was part-time, the overwhelming majority of such jobs were in the female sector. The last jobs of the retired were also concentrated in female-dominated occupations if they were part-time jobs, even for men. In contrast, the majority of men who moved from their last (probably usual) full-time job to full-time retirement had been in typically-male work in their last employment. Female

Table 6.4 Divergent trends in a polarised workforce 1971–1991

Type of occupation		% of all occupa-tions	Complete workforce			Full-time workforce			Part-time workforce		
			% of all	% of men	% of women	% of all	% of men	% of women	% of all	% of men	% of women
1971 Census	Male	66	49	72	9	54	72	10	15	61	8
	Mixed	18	15	16	15	16	16	17	12	17	11
	Female	16	36	12	76	30	12	73	73	22	81
1991 LFS	Male	53	41	66	9	50	68	12	9	36	5
	Mixed	25	19	20	17	21	20	22	13	24	11
	Female	22	40	14	74	29	12	66	78	40	84

Note: Occupational groups are based on an implicit 40% average female share of the workforce, with mixed jobs defined as 40% ±15% as follows:

Male occupations are those with <25% female workers in each year;

Mixed occupations are those with 25%–55% female workers in each year;

Female occupations are those with >55% female workers in each year.

This typology was applied separately to the two datasets, which employed slightly different definitions of part-time work and different occupational classifications, identifying 223 and 371 occupations respectively in 1971 and 1991.

Source: Hakim (1993b: 297) Table 2 reporting 1971 Census 10% sample and 1991 LFS data for people in employment.

Table 6.5 Feminisation and polarisation of the workforce 1971–1991

		Occupational group:			
		Male	Mixed	Female	All
% female	1971	7	36	78	37
	1981	7	36	80	40
	1991	9	40	81	44
% part-time	1971	3	11	30	15
	1981	3	11	36	18
	1991	5	15	43	22

Source: Hakim (1993b: 298) Table 3 reporting 1971 Census 10% sample data for Britain for 223 occupations; 1981 Census 10% sample data for Britain aggregated to 350 occupations from 550; and 1991 LFS data for Britain for 371 occupations.

occupations provide a source of short-term employment on the edge of the labour market for young people who are still in transition from school to employment and for older workers who are withdrawing gradually from the labour market. The similarity of male and female occupations in terms of social class composition is completely overturned as regards location in the primary and secondary sectors within a labour market segmentation perspective.

This conclusion about the polarisation of the workforce into a female-dominated secondary labour market with many part-time jobs and high labour turnover, and a primary labour market consisting mainly of full-time jobs, low turnover rates, and male or mixed occupations is echoed in many other studies of women's employment in modern societies. For example, Humphries and Rubery (1992: 251) concluded that the female workforce was polarising, so that by the end of the 1980s it had become almost essential to distinguish between groups of women workers, for example, between managerial and professional women and women in other occupations, or between full-time and part-time workers, in analyses of women's evolving position in the labour market. Trends in Britain may be further advanced than elsewhere because of the earlier development of the part-time workforce (although the Dutch part-time workforce caught up very quickly), but recent research on modern economies has repeatedly observed a polarisation of women's employment, by qualifications or occupational grade, into what can broadly be labelled full-time long term careers and less-qualified short term jobs (Hakim, 2000: 102–27; Cantillon et al, 2001).

Long term trends 1891–1991

These findings overturn the idea of female occupations as stereotypically *feminine*. Closer examination of the nature of female occupations today confirms that their dominant feature now is low-skill. This contrasts sharply with the distinctively domestic and feminine characteristics of female occupations a century ago. Even if the overall *level* of occupational segregation changes little over time, the character and social functions of occupational segregation have been rewritten. In effect, the pattern of occupational segregation is being constantly reinvented and renewed by men and women at work.

Economic and social historians agree that the late 19th century was a key period for the study of occupational segregation, as it was in this period that the sexual division of labour and the sex-typing of jobs were socially constructed. Humphries (1987) states that the period after 1850 was crucial, with a *rising* trend in occupational segregation as gainful work was transferred from the home to separate workplaces, and jobs were rearranged so as to physically segregate unrelated men and women in the workplace. The concern about the moral propriety of men and women working together, beyond the social controls of the family environment, was illustrated by the Gangs Act of 1867 which prohibited the employment of women or girls in gangs in which men worked, and required a gang-mistress wherever females were employed. This explanation for the creation and development of occupational segregation in the late 19th century emphasises the physical and social segregation of men and women at work, especially unmarried young women and men, far more than attempts to specify the particular jobs done by women or a concern with economic segregation. This meant all occupations could be open to both sexes so long as they were employed in separate offices or workplaces men or women (Hakim, 1980: 567–68; Matthaei, 1982:.189). Humphries' conclusions, and her research results, are consistent with, or on different shifts, as illustrated by Post Office policy (Grint, 1988: 88). This also explains large regional variations in the jobs done by Lerner's (1986) theory that patriarchy has always been concerned primarily with the control of women's sexuality and childbearing, rather than the control of women's employment.

Other social historians claim that contemporary accounts reveal a desire to construct separate, 'feminine' jobs for girls and women, if they worked at all, as well as to restrict contact between men and women at work. Holcombe (1973) describes the patriarchal ideas which, whether believed or not, were used to legitimate restrictions on women's work after marriage, and restrictions on the types of occupation considered suitable for middle class ladies. Bradley (1989: 223–24) emphasises continuities in the social definitions of men's and women's jobs which were designed into the division of labour within mechanised mass production systems developed in America in the 1880s, and subsequently exported to Britain and the rest of the world. Matthaei (1982: 194) asserts that the sex-typing of jobs in the late 19th century in the USA was prompted by the desires of men and women to assert their sexual identities by undertaking work reserved for their sex alone, that occupational segregation was actively sought as a means of asserting and reaffirming manhood and womanhood. She also notes that this sex-typing is now breaking down, as androgynous styles become popular.

In 1891, the most common female occupation (employing 35% of all women) was the domestic servant working in a private household and subject to the employing family's supervision of her private life as well as her work, followed by dressmaking and sewing, often carried out in homes or in all-female contexts, which employed 17% of women. Thus, the two most important female occupations, employing half of all working women, combined feminine activity and relative seclusion. Similarly, half of all working women in the USA, and one-third in France, were in domestic service in 1870 (Grossman, 1980; Matthaei, 1982: 197–203, 281–85; Fine, 1992: 124). Women's much commented-on concentration in service sector industries and occupations is not as new as statisticians claim. The key change is that service jobs have been transferred out of households into public commercial locations (Hakim, 1994: 444, 450).

By 1991, the link to women's non-market domestic work had totally disappeared. The most important female-dominated occupations are now gender-neutral white-collar jobs rather than feminine in character (Hakim, 1998a: 45, 236, 242). Half of all working women are employed in a variety of clerical and sales occupations, as secretaries (8%), sales assistants (9%), clerks (5%), cashiers (7%), miscellaneous occupations in sales and services (9%) and miscellaneous other secretarial, clerical and sales jobs (9%), greatly outnumbering women's employment in childcare (3%), catering (3%) and teaching (5%). The social factors which shape occupational choices, and notions of what is 'appropriate' work for women, have changed radically over the century. Female occupations are now typically gender-neutral and low-skill rather than typically-female and drawing on undervalued feminine skills (Hakim, 1994: 445). This finding undermines the feminist idea that the *main* reason for women's low earnings is the devaluation of feminine skills (Phillips and Taylor, 1980) which would be remedied by equal value policies (Treiman and Hartmann, 1981). It is consistent with recent studies (reviewed below) finding that a devaluation of nurturant feminine skills is not an important factor in female low earnings (Kilbourne *et al*, 1994: 706; Macpherson and Hirsch, 1995; Tam, 1997).

A similar observation is made by Blitz who argues that we are wrong to regard the contemporary situation as a major advance on the past: women's high share of schoolteaching professions was just as important in its time, as a source of status and prestige, as the newer professions are today. He goes further to argue that in the USA women's representation in professional occupations peaked in the 1920s and 1930s, at the same time as the proportion of college and university degrees earned by women, so that recent 'advances' pale in comparison with achievements prior to World War Two (Blitz, 1974; see also Goldin, 1990: 74–75). We can conclude that the dominant feature of female occupations today has become relatively low-skill work which can easily be organised on a part-time basis (see Chapter 3) and allows the short term work horizons found in intermittent employment profiles (see Chapter 5). Thus, occupational segregation was restructured in the late 20th century to provide separate occupations and jobs for women who seek jobs rather than a career, who work intermittently, taking jobs which remain conditional and contingent on wives' non-market activities. The search for universal economic explanations for trends and changes in occupational segregation (as illustrated by Reskin and Roos, 1990) is far too narrow. Occupational segregation is pronounced even in contexts where employers' prejudices are eliminated, such as crime, so supply side factors and self-selection are clearly equally, if not more, important (Chiplin, 1976).

Another notable finding from this historical comparison is that this fundamental restructuring of work took place without any major changes in the relative female share of total employment. Over the 100 years 1891–1991, the female contribution to the workforce changed very little (Table 6.6), especially when a Full-Time

Equivalent (FTE) measure is used for 1991. (The FTE measure takes account of the hours worked to count two part-time jobs as equivalent to one full-time job, thus measuring the volume of female employment in 1991 on the same basis as in 1891.) The DI suggests a large fall in horizontal segregation over the period, and substantial change is indicated also by the re-distribution of workers across segregated and mixed occupations. Between 1891 and 1991, the proportion of the workforce in mixed occupations rose from 13% to 27% if a consistent definition is applied (Table 6.6). Clearly, there was too little change in women's share of total employment for this to be an important driving force for consequential changes in the degree or pattern of occupational segregation, so other social factors must provide the main explanation. Similarly, cross-national comparisons (reviewed below) have found that there is no association between female employment rates, or the female share of employment, and the level of occupational segregation, which is shaped by other factors (Boserup, 1970; Lane, 1983; Nuss and Majka, 1983; OECD,

Table 6.6 Changes in occupational segregation 1891–1991

	1891	1991	1991b
Women's share of the workforce:			
% of all working aged 15 and over	31%	..	
% of economically active aged 16 and over	..	43%	
% of economically active – FTE measure	..	39%	
Number of occupations in classification	93	78	
Dissimilarity Index	74	58	
Percentage of all occupations that are:			
Male occupations	62	46	31
Mixed occupations	18	28	36
Female occupations	19	26	33
Percentage of all workforce in:			
Male occupations	53	40	29
Mixed occupations	13	22	27
Female occupations	34	38	44
Percentage of men working in:			
Male occupations	75	63	48
Mixed occupations	13	23	33
Female occupations	12	14	19
Percentage of women working in:			
Male occupations	5	9	4
Mixed occupations	11	21	19
Female occupation	84	70	77

Notes: The FTE measure is based on counting two part-time jobs as equivalent to one full-time job.

Mixed occupations are those 15–45% female (30% ±15%) in 1891 and 1991b.

Mixed occupations are those 25–55% female (40% ±15%) in 1991.

Source: Hakim (1994: 440) Table 2, using 100% census counts from the 1891 Population Census for England and Wales and 10% sample data from the 1991 Census for Britain.

1985: 44; 1988: 148; Charles, 1992; Jacobs and Lim, 1992; Lewin-Epstein and Semyonov, 1992; Sorensen and Trappe, 1995).

The sex differential in earnings

While the pattern of occupational segregation changed fundamentally over the 20th century, the sex differential in earnings remained stable and unvarying for a century, until sex discrimination laws took effect. This contrast alone argues against any association between occupational segregation and the pay gap, let alone a close connection.

The sex differential in earnings, or pay gap, is the difference between *average* female and male hourly earnings. In practice, most studies quote average female earnings as a percentage of male earnings, the obverse of the pay gap. The measure is not weighted to take account of the different occupations of men and women, nor for changes in the occupational or industrial structure. This is a simple measure which can meaningfully be applied to large and small populations, time series and cross-national studies, and to comparisons of the full-time and part-time workforces. However, precisely because it is so simple, it is important to ensure that we compare like with like. Normally, comparisons are drawn between the *hourly* earnings of men and women working *full-time* whose pay is not affected by absence from work (on sick leave for example) and usually excluding any extra pay for overtime hours. Among full-time workers, male manual workers in Britain did an average of six hours overtime per week in the period 1971–1994, compared to three hours a week for female manual workers. Non-manual men did an average of one hour overtime compared to less than half an hour for women. Thus, overtime pay is an important boost to male earnings, particularly in manual jobs (Beatson, 1995: 40), and comparisons of weekly earnings are misleading. One of the most misleading comparisons is between male full-time weekly earnings and female part-time weekly pay; this is often used to 'prove' the shocking degree of pay discrimination women suffer. The lower earnings of part-time workers can be explained by their short hours and human capital factors.

In some countries, such as the USA, Germany, Britain and Austria, sex differences in earnings are less important than the *family gap*: the difference in earnings between mothers and childless women, especially single childless women, whose earnings can be identical to men's (Harkness and Waldfogel, 1999; OECD, 2002; Bayard *et al*, 2003).

Trends in earnings in Britain have been monitored since 1968 through the specially designed New Earnings Survey (NES) which provides nationally representative annual data and panel data on pay rates and earnings for the entire workforce (except for marginal workers), and is the basis for detailed analyses of the pattern and determinants of earnings (Gregory and Thomson, 1990). The NES replaced a variety of earlier surveys of employers (Routh, 1965, 1980). Most other countries rely on data from household surveys instead, such as the LFS and the European Community Household Panel (ECHP), initiated in 1994. These provide less detailed information on overall earnings and hours worked, often with substantial non-response and proxy information affecting representativeness. Other countries obtain pay data for the manufacturing sector or the private sector only. Britain is one of the few countries with detailed information about pay in every part of the economy and on the composition of earnings (Saunders and Marsden, 1981; Rubery and Fagan, 1994). Some comparative studies of the pay gap in Europe cover *all* workers, merging full-time and part-time workers, which distorts results.

Weekly earnings are quoted for 19th century Britain because full-time work was the norm, typically with far longer hours than are worked today. From 1886 to 1970, female earnings stood at half male earnings for manual work in Britain (Table 6.7). From the mid-19th century, and long before that (Middleton, 1988: 36–39), men were paid twice as much as women, even for identical jobs. A more detailed analysis for the period 1913–1978 reveals small fluctuations over time, but women's average pay was half men's average pay in 1913 and 1970 (Routh, 1965, 1980: 123).

The first major change in the sex differential in earnings was forced by equal pay legislation, which pushed women's earnings up very suddenly by 10%, from 64% of male earnings in 1970 to 74% by 1976 (Tzannatos and Zabalza, 1984; Zabalza and Tzannatos, 1985a, b; 1988; IRRR, 1991; Spence, 1992: 581–82). Women's earnings remained at this level for a decade, then rose slowly to 80% by 1995 (Table 6.7), and have since remained around this level. Seen in the context of the long term stability in the relative pay of men and women, this recent narrowing of the pay gap was exceptional.

Table 6.7 The declining sex differential in earnings 1886–2003

| | Female earnings as % of male earnings | | | | |
| | Adult FT workers: hourly earnings excluding overtime | | | Adult manual workers | |
	All	Non-manual	Manual	hourly earnings	weekly earnings
1886					52
1960				61	51
1970	64	53	62	60	50
1976	74	63	71	71	61
1984	74	62	69	70	61
1987	74	62	71	70	61
1989	77	63	70		
1991	78	67	71		
1993	79	68	71		
1995	80	68	73		
1999	81	69	74		
2003	82	..	..		

Source: Zabalza and Tzannatos (1988: 841) Table 2 updated with annual NES data for Britain.

There was a similar pattern in the USA. In 1883, employers paid women less than half, sometimes only one-third or one-quarter, of what they paid men (Pinchbeck, 1930: 193–94, quoted in Padavic and Reskin, 2002: 122). On average, manual jobs in agriculture and manufacturing initially paid women 29% to 37% of male wages, but female earnings rose quickly to 50% of male wages by 1850, as machinery made sex differences in physical strength less important, and then rose again to 60% of male earnings by 1930 (Goldin, 1989: 62; 1990: 63–65). With some variation, female earnings stayed at 60% of male earnings until 1985, despite the 1963 Equal Pay Act and the 1964 Civil Rights Act, and then rose to 72% by 2000, leaving a pay gap of 28% (Padavic and Reskin, 2002: 123). Legislation does not seem to have had the same immediate impact in the USA as in Britain, and the pay gap remains larger than the 18% observed in Britain in 2002. The USA pay gap is larger in male occupations and lowest in female occupations (Rytina, 1981), no doubt due to the paucity of higher-grade jobs in the female sector.

The long term stability in the sex differential in earnings, especially in Britain, over a period when there were considerable changes in the pattern of women's employment and in job segregation undermines Hartmann's and Walby's theory outlined in Chapter 1 that job segregation has been, or is now, the key mechanism for ensuring women's subordination and economic dependence on men; it suggests instead that unequal pay was always the principal mechanism for keeping women low-paid. Despite the Trades Union Congress's (TUC) nominal support for equal pay from 1888 onwards, British trade unions were content to allow men to be paid twice as much as women for their work, right up to the mid-1970s when there were sudden and huge pay increases for women (IRRR, 1991: 3). Patriarchal theory's emphasis on job segregation can be seen as a variant of the economic theory that the concentration of women into a small number of occupations produces an oversupply of labour that reduces their wage rates (Fawcett, 1918; Edgeworth, 1922). While this is plausible, the evidence goes against it. Scholars have repeatedly noted the absence of any link between the sex differential in earnings and the pattern of job segregation (Chiplin and Sloane, 1974; Joseph, 1983: 175; Grint, 1988: 89–92; Sorensen and Trappe, 1995; Hakim, 1998a; Joshi and Paci, 1998; Hakim, 2000: 136–38). Employers colluded with male trade unions to maintain earning differences directly, with or without job segregation, until equal pay laws made this illegal.

The argument from economic theory that raising women's wages relative to men's through equal pay laws would result in fewer jobs for women, all other things being equal, was similarly proven wrong by events. Clearly, all other things are not equal quite a lot of the time. In this case, job segregation ensured that demand for female labour continued to rise despite the rise in women's pay rates – in Britain (Joshi et al, 1985: S170–72; Zabalza and Tzannatos, 1985a, b; 1988), in Europe (Saunders and Marsden, 1981: 222) and in industrial societies generally (OECD, 1985: 72), to the discomfiture of some economists. Manning (1996) argues that this theoretically impossible outcome disproves the economic demand curve model; shows that competition between male and female workers does not happen, partly because of women's concentration in narrow local labour markets and their higher turnover rates; and suggests that the female labour market is at least partly monopsonistic (in practice, there is a single buyer for female labour). In other words, occupational segregation protects women's jobs and women's employment, and confers benefits as well as disadvantages (Rubery *et al*, 1998: 289). This is also why male and female unemployment rates tend to be largely independent of each other. The advantages of largely separate labour markets for men and women are never mentioned in discussions of occupational segregation and the pay gap.

The pay gap has fallen (or risen) to a stable level of around 20% in most modern industrial societies after the implementation of equal pay and opportunities policies, but it varies from a low of around 10% in southern Europe to a high of 30% in West Germany and the USA. Even higher levels of 25%–50% have been found in Japan and in East Germany under socialism (Sorensen and Trappe, 1995; OECD, 2001: 139). Cross-national comparisons yield some surprises.

Cross-national comparisons

Occupational segregation and the pay gap undoubtedly declined after equal pay and opportunities legislation. It seems to follow logically that job segregation and the pay gap were higher in the past, are higher in less industrialised countries, and fall as female employment rises. All these assumptions are proven wrong by recent cross-national comparative studies by the International Labour Office of the United Nations (ILO) in Geneva, the EC in Brussels, and the Organisation for Economic Development and Co-operation (OECD) in Paris.

The most comprehensive cross-national comparative study of the sex segregation of occupations was completed by the ILO in 1998 (Anker, 1997; 1998; Melkas and Anker, 1997; 1998). The study used data on occupations in 41 countries for the two decades 1970–1990 from population censuses or labour force surveys. Unlike earlier studies, that used aggregated classifications with only nine to 20 occupation groups, this study employed detailed occupational data, identifying 187–461 separate occupational groups. Several measures of occupational segregation were employed, and the study explored vertical segregation and the pay gap as well as horizontal segregation. Like the EC, the ILO insists that occupational segregation is an important measure of gender equality in the workforce; that it produces serious inefficiencies in the economy; and that policy should aim to repudiate, if not eradicate it in all civilised societies (Anker, 1998: 5–9).

The results showed that, after excluding agricultural occupations (which are never finely differentiated, and usually employ men and women), the level of occupational segregation in Nordic countries was substantially higher than in other OECD countries, and substantially higher than in Asian countries such as China, Hong Kong, Malaysia and India. Only the predominantly Islamic Middle East and North Africa, and certain developing countries, had similar or higher levels of occupational segregation (Anker, 1998: 176–78). These unexpected results led the ILO to carry out fuller analyses of the data for Sweden, Norway and Finland, which were presented within the context of Nordic gender equality policies (Melkas and Anker, 1997; 1998). By restricting comparisons to the OECD countries, these reports avoided the embarrassing conclusion that in some respects sex equality in the Nordic labour markets is equal to that in developing countries such as Angola and Senegal, but they still show that Nordic countries have the highest level of job segregation, while the USA has the lowest level.

What this means in practice is that about half of Nordic women are in female-dominated occupations compared to about one-quarter of women workers in other industrialised countries. In this study, female-dominated occupations are those with 80%+ female workers. They generally constitute lower status, less qualified and lower-paid jobs in any industry – even in the Nordic countries. Women are nurses while men are doctors; women are primary school teachers while men are university lecturers; women are secretaries while men are managers, and these patterns are much stronger in the Nordic countries than in other OECD countries. In sum, both the horizontal and vertical sex segregation of occupations are higher in the Nordic countries, despite, or because of, welfare state policies that promote sex equality and allow women to combine paid work with family work.

The ILO reports claim that the pay gap is smaller in Nordic countries than in other European countries (Anker, 1998: 34; Melkas and Anker, 1998: 19). However, this is due to cheating by using earnings data only for manual workers in manufacturing industries, where few women work. Other studies show that when earnings data for *all* workers are obtained (from household surveys), the pay gap in Sweden and Norway is very close to that in Italy, Austria, West Germany and Australia (Blau and Kahn, 2003). Petersen *et al* (1997) report a pay gap of 21% in 1990 in Norway, which was due mainly to the high level of occupational segregation. They point out that the pay gap in Norway thus differs little from that in the USA, despite institutional and ideological differences. An analysis of hourly pay statistics for full-time employees in the 1990s found pay gaps of about 20% in Norway, Britain, France and Australia, about 25% in the USA and Canada, and about 30% in West Germany (Grimshaw and Rubery, 1997: Table 7). Thus, the pay gap in Nordic countries is no different from that in other advanced economies. One study identified a pay threshold in the Nordic countries below which are eight out of 10 women, and above which are eight out of 10 men (Anttalainen, 1986, quoted in Melkas and Anker, 1998: 19). In short, Nordic women benefit from substantial family-friendly pro-natalist policies, but the effect of these is to impede equality with men in the labour market, in terms of access to the top jobs, occupations with authority, or higher pay. This is finally being admitted openly (Hakim, 2000: 240; Nermo, 2000; Breen and García-Peñalosa, 2002).

The ILO found that the USA and Canada had the lowest levels of occupational segregation within the OECD. These are liberal and *laissez-faire* economies with few welfare state and family-friendly policies, but with a fierce commitment to the sex and race equality that is the hallmark of meritocracies. The country with the lowest level of occupational segregation in the world is China; Swaziland and Sri Lanka have the lowest pay gaps in the world (Anker, 1998: Tables 2.2 and 9.1). The ILO concluded that the sex segregation of occupations does not decline with socio-economic development, and that social, cultural and historical factors are the main determinants of the sexual division of labour (Anker, 1998: 409). The same conclusion seems to apply to the pay gap also.

The findings of this major study are corroborated by smaller academic studies. A study of Sweden, Britain, Belgium, France, Luxembourg, Germany, Switzerland, Italy and Portugal in the 1990s (Charles, 1998) concluded that gender-equality norms facilitate the integration of women into professional and managerial occupations, but high levels of female employment are associated with greater segregation of women into female-dominated service sector occupations, which are generally low status. The Nordic countries' failure to achieve sex equality in the workforce, despite high female workrates, is duplicated in the socialist USSR (Lapidus, 1988) and egalitarian Israeli *kibbutzim* (Agassi, 1989), but not in socialist China. Clearly, egalitarian policies can work, but not when combined with family-friendly pro-natalist policies (Hakim, 2000: 241).

The OECD (2002: 89–110) study of industrialised countries confirmed the ILO results, showing that higher female employment rates often lead to higher levels of job segregation and a larger pay gap, because women with lower levels of education and less careerist attitudes are pulled into the workforce. Countries with low female workrates, such as Spain, can have a low pay gap (12%) because working women are a highly selective minority with strong work commitment. The largest pay gaps are in Switzerland (24%), the USA (21%), and Austria (21%), as shown in Table 6.8.

Table 6.8 The pay gap in OECD countries

	Hourly earnings wage and salary employees	
	Full-time	All
Australia	91	89
Austria	79	79
Belgium	91	93
Canada (2000)	82	81
Denmark	89	89
Finland	82	82
France	87	89
Germany	80	81
Greece	80	87
Ireland	81	79
Italy	85	91
Netherlands	80	79
New Zealand	86	84
Portugal	92	95
Spain	88	86
Sweden (2000)	86	83
Switzerland (2001)	76	78
United Kingdom	80	75
Unites States (1999)	79	78
OECD unweighted average	84	84

Source: extracted from Table 2.15 in OECD (2002) 'Women at work'. Data for wage and salary employees for 1998, except where specified. People aged 20–64 years, except for Australia, Canada, New Zealand and Sweden (18–64 years) and Switzerland (15–64 years). Average female earnings as a percentage of average male earnings.

The OECD study found that occupational segregation was substantially lower among younger women, but rose over the life cycle, partly due to women's discontinuous work histories. A further analysis of the same data by the EC (2002) looked at EU countries more closely. It reiterated the importance of career interruptions in reducing (women's) earnings, and generally confirms the OECD results: the pay gap in the EU is lowest in Italy, Belgium and Portugal, and highest in countries with large part-time workforces. It also noted the importance of vertical occupational segregation, a factor ignored in the OECD study. Consistent results are reported by academic studies. For example, Blau and Kahn (2003) studied 22 countries in Europe and North America, plus Japan, Australia and New Zealand, to show that countries with lower female employment generally had a smaller pay gap between men and women. In a narrower study of Australia, Canada, and the USA as well as Europe, Grimshaw and Rubery (2001: 27) concluded that the size of the pay gap is not correlated with female employment rates, or women's educational levels; but this is the only dissenting voice. A study of nine OECD countries by Rosenfeld and Kalleberg (1991: 217) was the first to show that the link between occupational segregation and the pay gap is coincidental, not causal. We now know why: both are pushed up by rising female employment.

Case studies of occupations that are fully integrated, employing men and women in equal numbers, provide the most conclusive evidence that it is not segregation itself that causes the pay gap. Studies of pharmacists in Britain, the USA, Canada and France reveal large sex differences in pay and job grade, even in this fully integrated occupation. In Britain, the 27% pay gap in pharmacy is due to sex differences in hours worked, work histories, and types of job chosen, not to sex (or race) discrimination, which has been eliminated in the profession (Hakim, 1998a: 221–34).

Hunt's (2002) study of developments in East Germany after reunification shows that declining female workrates were accompanied by a 10% shrinking of the pay gap, from 26% under communism to 16% under capitalism. She also found that reduced childcare services played no part at all in falling female workrates. So work orientations must have been the main factor here.

Finally, McCall (2001) confirmed the lack of any causal link between occupational segregation and the pay gap in her study of over 500 labour markets in the USA in the 1990s. She concluded that the elimination of occupational segregation is not a sufficient, nor even a necessary, condition for closing the pay gap (McCall, 2001: 118).

In short, there is no evidence for a causal link between horizontal occupational segregation and the pay gap, even though such a link has long been assumed, and is fixed in policy-makers' thinking. It is now clear that high female workrates are more likely to cause a widening of the pay gap and an increase in job segregation. High female workrates and gender equality in the workforce seem to be mutually exclusive policy goals, contrary to EC, and feminist assumptions. It appears that a search for explanations of the pay gap must now look to other factors that are often overlooked in research.

The devaluation of women's work

The theory that job segregation is a principal cause of women's lower pay takes various forms. The first is the argument from economics that crowding women into a smaller number of female occupations forces down their pay, due to excess supply. As noted above, Manning (1996) points out that standard economic theory about supply and demand simply does not work here, and women's employment actually increased after their pay was forced up by equal pay laws. However, studies continue to underline the small correlation between women's share of an occupation and occupational earnings. For example, in a study without information on work experience, subject of qualifications and other relevant factors, Boraas and Rodgers (2003) found earnings were around 5% lower than might otherwise be expected in female occupations in 1999, a lower impact than they found in earlier decades. The second argument is that, irrespective of what particular jobs women do, such work will always become devalued, as soon as women do it. For example, Reskin and Roos (1990) draw this conclusion from their study of occupations which feminised in the 1970s and 1980s in the USA. However, they admit that their research results also permit the opposite conclusion: that men quit occupations where wages are declining, while women readily move into the lower-paid jobs thus vacated. The stronger version of this thesis is that women's work is devalued because caring work and women's special skills are devalued.

The evidence suggests that women themselves, as well as women's work, have been devalued in the past, as illustrated by the integrated occupation of acting. Top female filmstars in Hollywood are routinely paid less for each film than their male co-stars. They have fought a long-running battle to get the same $10 to $50 million fees for co-starring in the same film. By the 21st century, film fees for men and women are beginning to equalise.

An experimental study in the 1960s showed that female undergraduates in the USA regarded men as more competent and able than women, *even for identical performances*, especially if they worked in typically male occupations (Goldberg, 1968). However, recent replications of this study failed to find the same strong pattern of female prejudice against women; the devaluation of female performance is now small, and limited to activities such as leadership and typically-male activities (Deaux and LaFrance, 1998: 797–98), as noted in Chapter 4. Men who excel in women's occupations (such as the dress designers Armani and Versace, or male top chefs) are just as highly regarded (and wealthy) as men who excel in male management jobs, so female occupations are not necessarily a barrier to success and high status.

The most recent studies generally fail to support the devaluation thesis. An analysis of earnings among young people in their 20s and 30s in full-time employment showed work experience to be the only important explanation of the pay gap, accounting for one-quarter in this age group, two to four times larger than the impact of the % female in occupations, and dwarfing the impact of the authors' favoured thesis of a significant bias against occupations employing nurturant feminine skills which are devalued in the market economy (Kilbourne *et al*, 1994). Tam's most recent and detailed test of the devaluation of caring work in analyses of the pay gap concludes that there is no longer any devaluation of female skills, at least in the USA. Lower wages in female occupations are fully explained by education and other human capital variables, industry wage differences, and a mark-up for vocational training (Tam, 1997; see also England *et al*, 2000; Tam, 2000; Cohen and Huffman, 2003). Similarly, Macpherson and Hirsch (1995) found that lower wages in female occupations can now be fully explained by the training needed, working part-time or not, and people self-selecting themselves into female jobs.

Furthermore, as noted earlier, caring work has ceased to be the principal characteristic of female occupations, if it ever was. Today, most female jobs are in white-collar work that utilises general schooling.

Finally, some economists are now offering an alternative explanation for lower earnings in jobs that involve personal services. Technological developments have greatly increased the productivity of many manual and service occupations. Film, television, the internet, and sound recording have increased the audiences for entertainers to millions worldwide instead of a few hundred people in one room. Some singers, actors, writers, sports people and others who would previously have had limited audiences and customers are now wealthy international superstars. Rosen (1981) points out that in certain services quality does not decline with reproduction. However, other services do not allow perfect duplication at constant or declining cost. Childcarers cannot properly deal with more than three to four small children at a time. Hairdressers can only cut one head of hair at a time. Earnings have increased in those services that are able to take advantage of technological developments, but have remained stable (and low) in services that remain local, small-scale and personal. On this new analysis, it is the more circumscribed scale of certain services that reduces their earning power, plus the lower visibility of any variations in quality. It is more difficult to identify a good childminder, or hairdresser, than a Maria Callas.

The returns to education

Human capital theory argues that higher earnings (rightfully) accrue to those who invest in relevant qualifications, training and work experience, as these skills increase their value to employers. All other correlates of earnings are treated as discriminatory. However, most of the datasets used to analyse the causes and correlates of the pay gap do not have information on work experience and the exact subjects studied in secondary or tertiary education. As a result, the 'discrimination' element in the pay gap has always been overestimated. Education has generally been measured more crudely as years of schooling, age of leaving full-time education, or the highest qualification attained. When more detailed information on education was collected, especially in longitudinal studies, it became clear that the subjects studied in higher education, and sometimes those studied in secondary school, have a powerful impact on earnings, and hence help to explain sex differences in earnings. Doctors earn more than nurses, although both have tertiary education. In most countries, engineers and lawyers earn more than graduates in humanities and languages. In most countries, elimination of sex differences in educational levels has not altered profound sex differences in subjects studied. This fact alone tends to undermine the argument that women (especially those working part-time) are often 'overqualified' for the jobs they do. Because of qualifications inflation, men and women are routinely 'overqualified' for the jobs they do, whether full-time or part-time (Hakim, 1998a: 37–38). When used in appropriate jobs, the earnings benefits of teaching and nursing qualifications rise continuously throughout women's lives (McIntosh, 2002).

Segregation in the subjects studied at tertiary level carries over into adult occupations and careers. In Britain, for example, men outnumber women two to one in most of the vocational subjects which lead to specific professional careers: medicine, dentistry, law, accounting and finance, architecture, and veterinary studies. Dale and Egerton (1997) found substantial earnings differences across subjects, and a small pay gap after controlling for level of qualification and hours worked: only 10% for graduates, rising to 15% for those with no qualifications at all. Some studies report that secondary school subjects also affect adult earnings. For example, Dolton and Vignoles (2002a, b) found that mathematics (which girls are less likely to study) produced a notable mark-up to earnings in later employment.

At least one study has found the field of study to be so important among college graduates that this factor, plus a few others, explains the entire wage gap (Black *et al*, 2003). This study validates human capital theory as a sufficient explanation for sex differences in earnings without any reference to job segregation or other details. Black *et al* (2003) were able to fully explain the pay gap among college graduates in the USA in 1993 with just five factors: age, highest degree, field of study, years of full-time work experience, and (for Hispanic and Asian people) whether English was spoken at home (an indicator of linguistic fluency). When the sample was restricted to childless, unmarried women (to eliminate sex differences in work commitment), the pay gap was almost entirely explained for white and black women. Similar results are reported by other studies of college-educated women (Hecker, 1998). However, Brown and Corcoran (1997) and the OECD (2002: 76) point out that choice of subject at college may in practice be an indicator of other, hidden differences in aspirations, workplans and life goals.

If human capital theory is extended slightly to consider careerist versus noncareerist attitudes to work, motivation and aspirations, it is likely that the pay gap could be completely explained. Filer (1983) found that these factors (not measured in most studies) contributed significantly to earnings differences among graduates.

Contextual factors

Economists regard 'human capital' correlates of earnings as legitimate, and label everything else as non-legitimate, potentially discriminatory. If occupation or industry (hence occupational segregation) influences earnings, this too is treated as discriminatory. This approach is over-simplistic. First, it does not allow people to choose occupations according to taste and personal preference. More important, there is a long list of contextual factors that influence earnings (and hence the pay gap) to some degree, which cannot be rejected as non-legitimate. They simply reflect real-world contexts.

Contextual factors include hours worked (generally longer among men, even among full-time workers); public or private sector location (the pay gap is almost invariably smaller in the public sector, which has centralised wage setting); industry (financial services has a larger pay gap, due to bonuses *inter alia*, than construction, where bonuses are rare); region of a country (regions with a long tradition of female employment usually have a smaller pay gap); rural/urban location of a workplace (pay is highest in big cities, lowest in rural areas); length of journey to work (which often reflects commuting into city centre jobs); and size of firm (small firms generally have lower wages than big firms, and they tend to employ more women). In addition, employers sometimes have to pay higher wages than usual to compensate for jobs being dirty or dangerous, having unsocial hours, shiftwork systems, long absences from home, or working in difficult or foreign locations. Men are more likely to take such jobs than are women. Workplaces that have trade unions tend to have higher earnings than similar non-unionised establishments, but the trade union mark-up varies a good deal. Some of the negative impact of occupational segregation on wages is actually due to closely linked contextual factors. Yet another factor, which helps to explain international variation in the size of the pay gap, is the national wage structure. Some countries (such as the USA) have a wide dispersion of earnings and substantial income inequality, while other countries (such as Sweden) have a compressed male earnings distribution and low income inequality. The pay gap is larger and smaller in each case, simply due to the overall earnings distribution (Blau and Kahn, 2003). Similarly, the age structure of the working population can affect cross-national comparisons. For example, most Dutch women working full-time are young, single and less experienced; older married women tend to work part-time hours. This pushes up the pay gap. Finally, the pay gap tends to be smaller in workplaces with transparent pay systems, which allow comparisons between colleagues; it is higher in workplaces that forbid workers from disclosing their salaries (and bonuses) to colleagues. (In Britain, one in five employers has such a rule.) The pay gap is lower in workplaces with job evaluation systems that expose the actual tasks done and skills needed, instead of relying on stereotypes and out-dated assumptions. For example, power-steering on vehicles now means that drivers do not need physical strength any more.

Contextual factors cannot easily be disregarded, yet they cannot be classified as obviously discriminatory, as human capital theory insists. In Sweden, for example, three-quarters of employed men work in the private sector while two-thirds of employed women work in public services, but it would be difficult to claim that this was due entirely to sex discrimination. In Britain, many women choose jobs that are close to home, especially if they work part-time, and local jobs tend to offer less choice, are often lower status and lower-paid than city centre jobs that require long commuting times (Hakim, 1998a: 187–91). Here too, it is hard to see that anyone is discriminating against women specifically. Even before we start to examine the impact of gender, personal characteristics (such as childcare responsibilities), motivation and aspirations on earnings, there is a wide array of factors that are important in explanations of the pay gap, yet are rarely included in studies. Data limitations mean that it is effectively impossible for one study to examine the influence of *all* relevant factors, yet if any relevant factors are omitted, the 'residual' pay gap that is not explained, and hence attributed to discrimination, is larger than it would be in an accurate and complete analysis. This means that studies always overestimate the contribution of sex discrimination; they never underestimate it. Of the four theories reviewed in Chapter 1, only preference theory gives proper consideration to contextual factors, arguing that they have the greatest impact on adaptive women.

Among the numerous studies of the pay gap, Sorensen (1989) includes the widest range of detailed variables, including work experience, job tenure, part-time work, years of education, qualifications (crudely classified) and a range of contextual variables, as well as occupational sex ratios. She finds that education and experience explain one-quarter of the pay gap; industry and other contextual variables explain another quarter; the % female variable another quarter; leaving one quarter of the pay gap to be explained by omitted variables such as job grade, field of study, motivation and workplans. Occupational segregation variables are often interpreted as measuring discrimination, or the devaluation of women's occupations. But this is not yet proven. Given the pattern of occupational segregation shown in Table 6.2, this result could arise because of the absence of any female-dominated occupations at professional level.

The glass ceiling and the glass escalator

As noted above, vertical job segregation *within* specific occupations can account for all, or almost all of the sex difference in earnings after equal pay rules have been implemented. The clearest example was the study of teachers' pay (Employment Department, 1976). So the best way to interpret studies that explain earnings and the reasons for the differences between men and women is to read them as analyses of the social processes that enable men to attain jobs with higher status and pay more often than women. In effect, the analyses are explaining occupational attainment or career progression, with earnings used as economists' favoured indicator of status or grade. The key issue is whether there is a glass ceiling preventing women from reaching the top jobs and the highest pay.

The term *glass ceiling* has become the popular term for the (invisible) barriers to women's access to the highest-grade jobs in their profession, and more specifically women's access to senior management positions. Some studies look at promotion rates, while others analyse the pay gap at the top of the earnings distribution.

A study by Albrecht *et al* (2003) of the glass ceiling in Sweden concludes that the problem is substantially larger than in the USA, and that it has emerged recently. Between 1968 and 1981, the overall pay gap in Sweden fell from 33% to 18%, but has been rising gradually since then. In 1968, there was no glass ceiling; by 1998, it was large and prominent. In contrast, the pay gap in 1999 in the USA was roughly the same at all levels of earnings, just over 20%, so there is no glass ceiling there. The authors conclude that Swedish family-friendly social policies pull women into the labour market even when they have little interest in careers. Extensive use of parental leave, time off to care for sick children, and reduced work hours also make female workers less attractive to employers. So the private sector mostly employs men while the public sector mostly employs women. These results are consistent with those of the international studies which found that higher levels of female employment tend to generate higher levels of occupational segregation and a larger pay gap, and explained the apparent link between the two. It appears that women-friendly policies push up women's employment rates and create a glass ceiling for women.

Studies generally show that the pay gap increases over the life cycle, and that the age-earnings profiles for men and women differ (Gregory and Thomson, 1990; European Commission, 2002), although there is convergence across age cohorts (Ferri *et al*, 2003: 158–61). There are many reasons for this, especially the discontinuity of women's work histories, noted in Chapter 5, which means they accumulate less work experience and are less likely to achieve promotion within an occupation. Another factor is women's different job values, which leads many women to prioritise non-pay job characteristics, as noted in Chapter 4. Studies of the glass ceiling need to control first for all these more obvious explanations. A study of the pay gap among engineers (Morgan, 1998) provides a strategic test of the existence of a glass ceiling after proper controls for work experience and job type. Women make up only 8% of all engineers in the USA, but they earn 97% of male earnings, so the pay gap is effectively non-existent here, but it does appear to increase with age. Morgan showed that the pay gap remained relatively constant in each of three age cohorts. Younger cohorts of women (entering the workforce after 1972) had the same earnings as their male colleagues. The older women had a pay gap, but this had not changed over time. Morgan (1998) dismissed the glass ceiling thesis as unfounded, confirming an earlier study by Petersen and Morgan (1995).

The equal opportunities revolution has led women to enter jobs in management more often than in the past. Jacobs (1992) shows this is a slow trend observed across all industries. Although the pay gap in management jobs has been above the average, the pay gap is steadily declining as more women get into management. As Jacobs found no evidence of changes in managerial women's attitudes over 1972–1989, it appears that the changes are due primarily to improved gender equality policies rather than greater ambition among women.

Studies of the glass ceiling for women in male-dominated occupations are now complemented by studies of what some people call the *glass escalator* for men in female-dominated occupations such as nursing, elementary school teaching, hairdressing, librarianship and social work. Williams (1992) points out the key difference between the two situations: men dominate administrative and management positions in all occupations, so that men in sex-atypical jobs still have a male boss in most cases. Partly for this reason, and partly because men generally display more ambition than women, men in sex-atypical occupations do not report any serious disadvantages or difficulties in these jobs, and they tend to get promoted quickly into jobs in administration and management. Nonetheless, men in sex-atypical jobs do experience discrimination from customers, and this can also help to push them out of the most female-identified types of work up into male-dominated management (Williams, 1992).

However, another study by Budig (2002) challenges the glass escalator thesis. She found that it made no difference whether men worked in male-dominated, female-dominated, or mixed occupations: in all three types of job, men's wages grew faster than women's. This was a general phenomenon, not concentrated in sex-atypical jobs. However, men's pay advantage is very small. The study also found that family responsibilities are a key factor in men being more likely, and women less likely to get promotion (Budig, 2002). Which brings us back to the link between sex-roles and employment choices.

A brilliant case study by Hinze (2000) shows that, even among young spouses who are (almost) equally well-qualified, a substantial pay gap emerges because men concentrate on their careers, while women concentrate on their family work. She studied 321 couples who were both physicians, often because they met at medical school. Even these high-earning young professional wives were in practice secondary earners who retained the main responsibility for the family, and chose jobs accordingly. Even today, middle class professional couples give priority to the husband's career, especially if he has better qualifications than his wife (Moen, 2003: 174–75, 198, 200). Bowlus (1997) shows that women's distinctive employment patterns emerge in early adulthood, and are a major cause of the widening pay gap among young people. This is consistent with studies showing a 25% 'marriage premium' in men's earnings at the start of the 21st century (Cohen, 2002), which gay and bisexual men do not enjoy (Blandford, 2003). Conversely, lesbian and bisexual women enjoy a wage premium of about 20% because they do not take on the family work of heterosexual women (Blandford, 2003). In most Western European countries, the preferred family division of labour is the same as the actual division of labour, on average (Väisänen and Nätti, 2002). As Sen (1990) pointed out, conflicts of interest between men and women are co-operative conflicts, because they share a household and joint interests. These studies confirm preference theory as well as human capital theory, and suggest that sex discrimination is no longer a factor in the pay gap in the 21st century.

Some of the most important processes that contribute to easier career success among men than women are invisible, not just unmeasured but unmeasurable (Smith, 2002). One example is the 'freezing out' process employed by men and women, consciously or otherwise, to people in sex-atypical jobs. This matters most in senior positions, and management and professional occupations are often male-dominated. Another problem is the unstated, and perhaps unconscious, stereotype of what a manager looks like, as the following example demonstrates.

Analyses of records in British national government administration revealed that when promotion boards included a female member, the proportion of female applicants passed for promotion was significantly higher than with all-male promotion boards. Promotion boards are nationwide exercises, with standardised and transparent procedures for interviewing and grading the promotability of candidates on the basis of general criteria of proven competence and future potential. The promotions procedures were as impersonal and free from gender bias as anyone could make them, unconnected from particular job vacancies and any personal preferences of managers seeking to fill vacancies in their sections. Nonetheless, personnel department analyses of the results showed that the sex composition of the promotion board that interviewed candidates made a significant difference to the outcome for women. Promotion boards were then required to include at least one female member. The proportion of women sweeping through the barriers into senior levels started to rise sharply, to the discomfiture of men of average talent who previously benefitted from the sex-role stereotyping that profiled managers in masculine terms. No study is available to explain exactly what was changed by the presence of a single female member. We only know that a single female on every board makes a difference to outcomes. Personnel managers also report that men tend to be promoted on the basis of their future potential, whereas women are promoted on the basis of past achievements only. Survey datasets never contain information on these hidden social processes that hinder women's career success.

Some women escape the restrictions of large organisations, where other people (usually men) define their abilities and potential (usually narrowly), by becoming self-employed consultants, an option that is especially accessible to professionals and technical experts. They escape the sex stereotyping of colleagues for that of customers, as illustrated by F International, a home-based company set up to employ homeworking computing specialists, especially programmers. F International started small, and stayed small, until its owner changed her name from Stephanie Shirley (a recognisably female name) to Steve Shirley (a recognisably male name), after which work flowed in and business boomed. The greater success of male self-employed entrepreneurs is due in part to this hidden discrimination which always gives men the benefit of the doubt and rarely gives women an even chance.

Analyses of earnings and of the pay gap can offer few pointers for policy innovations, as well as being routinely partial and inconclusive. Case studies seem to offer a far more promising method for explanatory research in this field. Economists rarely use this research design; it is popular among sociologists who rarely study quantitative topics such as earnings. Wood et al (1993) analysed the work histories and earnings of law school graduates 15 years after graduation, at age 40 and over. They showed that hours worked and employment history variables, in particular working part-time for a short period to care for children (three years on average) and frequent job changes, accounted for over half the wage gap between men and women. If differences in the types of job held are treated as personal choices, three-quarters of the earnings gap was explained. Most important, variables were already controlled by comparing the graduates of a single law school, so this study provides strong evidence that earnings differences observed 15 years later are due partly to preferences for particular types of work or career, partly due to women choosing to take time out to care for small children, and partly to work history characteristics such as number of years practising as a lawyer and annual hours worked. Men chose private practice more often, which involved extremely long hours as well as rapid salary growth. Women more often chose public sector employment, with shorter hours and lower earnings. Having children did not, of itself, affect a woman's earnings, only if she took time out to care for them herself, despite the fact that she could clearly afford quality childcare. However, 40% of the female graduates remained childless by age 40. The authors note that some of these outcomes may reflect discrimination rather than choice, especially for the childless women. On the other hand, these women earned enough for them to make real choices between higher earnings and more time for other activities. Baker (2002) reports consistent findings on female lawyers.

A study of MBA graduates showed that earnings differences were fully explained by human capital factors, plus an allowance for performance-related pay additions which pushed up male earnings. Women tended to choose jobs with fixed or predictable earnings, whereas men more often chose jobs with a substantial element of pay contingent on performance, consistent with research showing sex differences in risk aversion (Chauvin and Ash, 1994). On the other hand, employers may choose men for certain jobs because they believe men to be more highly motivated to succeed than are women. Without personal interview information on motives and plans, the interpretation of multivariate analyses is pure speculation, whether theory-driven or not.

Results of these and other case studies tend to confirm Halaby's (2003) theory of two distinct career strategies reviewed in Chapter 4. The 'entrepreneurial' strategy is most often chosen by men, while the 'bureaucratic' strategy is commonly chosen by women. On average, the two strategies produce sex differences in earnings in the long run.

Conclusions

The pattern of occupational segregation, and its functions, have changed substantially over time. It is not a simple case of men being concentrated in the higher-grade and higher-paid occupations while women are concentrated in lower-grade and low-paid occupations. Women's occupations today are not stereotypically feminine, and do not always involve caring work. Many female occupations are now gender-neutral, low-skill, lower-grade jobs that permit part-time work and high turnover rates, and do not demand a long term career commitment. Integrated occupations, employing men and women in equal numbers, tend to be the most highly qualified, yet still have large sex differences in earnings. The sex differential in earnings may be distributed evenly throughout the workforce in the USA, but it increases as one moves up the occupational structure in Britain (Sloane, 1990: 134) and generally in Europe (Rubery and Fagan, 1994: xxix, 191; OECD, 2002). Our analysis has also clarified that it is mainly in the higher grades of professional and managerial occupations that women lose out. Lower female earnings are otherwise due more to part-time jobs and intermittent employment than to job segregation. This is probably why comparable worth (equal value) policies implemented by employers in the USA and in Australia have generally raised women's earnings by only 5% to 6%, after allowance is made for contemporary pay upratings, and rarely exceed 10% (Steinberg, 1988: 207; Ehrenberg, 1989; Willborn, 1989: 140, 147; Killingsworth, 1990: 277; Kahn and Meehan, 1992: 13; Gunderson, 1994). Patriarchy may still contribute part of the explanation for women's position in society, but occupational segregation does not appear to be quite so important an economic weapon as Hartmann and Walby believed it to be. Human capital theory provides a more powerful explanation of changes in earnings and earnings differences between men and women: recent falls in the pay gap are generally due to women improving their educational qualifications, work experience, and tenure with an employer (O'Neill, 1985; O'Neill and Polachek, 1993).

Attempts to explain the pay gap are numerous but invariably partial. Almost all the pay gap can be explained by women's failure to attain the higher grades within occupations, leading to the thesis of a glass ceiling for women. The question is, why does this happen? The general drift of research results is that the main explanation for this outcome is that men are more likely to put in the longer hours, the more continuous employment and the longer tenures with an employer that lead to the top jobs. Another factor seems to be the contrasting career strategies of men and women: ambitious and high-risk versus low-risk and focused on predictable rewards. This factor, and related motivational or personality characteristics, are rarely studied, so their contribution to explaining the pay gap remains hidden, and the contribution of discrimination is thereby overestimated. Undoubtedly, sex discrimination remains a factor, in particular workplaces, or with particular managers. However, discrimination seems to be no longer a major factor, across the whole workforce, as it has been in the past. Even in cases where it is, the methods used for pay gap decompositions mean that it is never measured directly, and reliably. The most recent studies indicate that the importance of sex discrimination has shrunk now, to a tiny fraction of the pay gap. This is the result for the USA and Britain, and presumably for other modern countries in due course.

Recent cross-national comparative studies have finally eliminated the most popular feminist argument about occupational segregation and the pay gap: the idea that family-friendly policies would somehow eliminate all the problems, allowing women to return to work after childbirth, and break the glass ceiling. We now know that family-friendly policies increase women's employment rates – but they also increase occupational segregation, the pay gap, and the glass ceiling excluding women from the top jobs and highest pay, as a direct result of higher employment rates. The country with the lowest level of occupational segregation in the world (and possibly the lowest pay gap also) is China, not Sweden, a country with a one-child policy rather than pro-natalist policies. Sweden has the highest level of occupational segregation among industrial countries, and the largest glass ceiling. It has become clear that economic progress does not engender equality, as Goldin (1990: 212) already concluded.

Preference theory is the only theory that can make sense of these unexpected findings, because it identifies the differentiated responses of lifestyle preference groups to public policies (Hakim, 2000: 223–53). Policies supporting work-centred women can eliminate gender differences in labour market outcomes for this particular group. This is illustrated already by the USA, where women are far more likely to achieve senior management positions than in Sweden, for example: 11% and 1.5% respectively of senior posts are held by women (Rosenfeld and Kalleberg, 1990; Wright et al, 1995). Family-friendly policies supporting adaptive women (and men) provide them with a good work-life balance, and a real option of combining family work with paid employment. The sex difference in employment rates can be eliminated in this group (OECD, 2001: 153), but it would not contribute to any narrowing of the pay gap at the national level – on the contrary, it would increase it. Social policy cannot square the circle. Female (and male) heterogeneity in lifestyle preferences means that the two sets of policies are mutually incompatible, appeal to different groups of women, and have distinct outcomes.

One policy response to these results is to accept that women will never move into the top jobs and hence focus on comparable worth (USA) or equal value (UK) initiatives to raise women's pay in lower grade jobs. The other response is to find ways of breaking down the barriers to women's promotion into higher-grade and better-paid jobs. As shown in Chapter 7, EU employment law and policy encourages both approaches (Rubery and Fagan, 1994).

Chapter 7
Social Engineering: The Role of the Law

Social policies, such as those intended to redesign sex-roles and re-distribute paid and unpaid work between adults, can use four mechanisms of social engineering: ideological reform and moral exhortation; legislation; fiscal policy; and institutional change. Most commonly, some combination of these tools is used. In large pluralist societies, such as the USA and Britain, where competing interests and ideologies have to be accommodated, there can be contradictions between the implicit policies of the four tools of social engineering, so that social change is slow and uneven.

Four mechanisms of social engineering

The power of *ideological reform and moral exhortation* is illustrated by the effectiveness of government campaigns to pull women into the workforce during World War Two, to do manual jobs in factories that had previously been classified as men's work. The ideology of domesticity was then revived after the war, to reinstate the pre-war sexual division of labour, against some resistance from women (Summerfield, 1984; Milkman, 1987: 99–152). In China, where the strong tradition of collective adherence to the common ideology of Confucianism was transferred to communism, ideology and moral exhortation constitute a powerful tool of social engineering, as illustrated in Chapter 4 by the relatively successful transformation of sex-roles after 1950, and by the success of the one child per couple policy in a country where it had traditionally been regarded as imperative to have at least one son. By 1993, four-fifths of men and women in Beijing said a son or daughter were equally acceptable as their only child (Ma *et al*, 1994: 248).

In Europe, *legislation* prohibiting sex discrimination, and promoting equal treatment of men and women in the labour force, is the main tool of social engineering. It is the only mechanism common to all Member States of the EU. Legislation promoting equality between men and women in the labour market, health and safety regulations, and proposals for minimum standards for employment contracts, have in practice been the principal integrationist measures of European social policy. By the start of the 21st century, equal opportunity laws were extended to prohibit discrimination on the basis of age, sexual orientation, racial or ethnic origin, religion or belief, and disability, as well as EU nationality and sex, with the aim of ensuring equal access to jobs for all EU citizens. Beyond this, there is as yet no common European social policy because nation states have so far not wanted it. In particular, there is no agreement to harmonise direct taxation on earnings, and state social welfare systems, that are not employment-related (McCrudden, 1987: 20–22, 119–21, 186; Tsoukalis, 1993: 148–74). European sex discrimination legislation is having a major impact on all member countries, although lawyers often demand additional regulation (Fredman, 1997; 2002).

After countries have introduced equal opportunities legislation, further activities are needed to implement and enforce social engineering laws. The failure to fully enforce equality legislation is the main source of international variation in its impact. In Europe, for example, only two other countries have a public body charged with enforcing equal opportunities laws, similar to the two UK Equal Opportunities Commissions and the Race Relations Commission (for equivalent race discrimination issues): the Netherlands and Ireland (although Sweden has an Equal Opportunities Ombudsperson and Finland has an Ombudsman for Equality). France and Sweden have always taken the view that such bodies, and even the laws, were completely redundant in their cases, yet they have been taken to court by the Commission. Britain also has an extensive network of informal and free labour courts that hear sex (and other) discrimination cases. In many countries, such claims have to be pursued through the general civil courts, which deters most applicants. Employment tribunals in Britain have heard more equal value/comparable worth cases than all the other EU Member States put together, and equal pay court cases are very rare in France (Gregory *et al*, 1999: 5, 208). The British equality Commissions have the power to take employers to court to enforce equal pay and equal treatment, and have repeatedly taken the British Government, and government bodies, to court. In the Netherlands, the Equal Treatment Commission adjudicates on cases itself, to avoid the need for a court hearing.

Fiscal policy influences the employment decisions of secondary earners and, to a lesser extent, the hours worked by primary earners, by changing income tax rules and social welfare benefit rules to alter the net benefits from different quantities of wage work by one or both persons in a couple (Kay and King, 1978: 37). For example, husband and wife may be taxed separately as individuals, or jointly as a couple; tax allowances and benefits may be transferable or not. At present, home production of goods and services by a non-working wife is untaxed, but that too is a policy by default. Eligibility for key welfare benefits, such as pensions, may be dependent on a person's own employment record and contributions (as in Britain), or wives may be allowed to benefit from their husband's work record (as in Japan), or full-time homemakers may be credited with pension rights despite not working (as in the Netherlands). In Sweden, fiscal policy proved an effective mechanism for virtually eliminating the full-time homemaker with no market work and financially dependent on her husband: only 10% of wives remain in this category. Benefit rules also push Swedish women into full-time jobs, as important benefits are dependent on a record of full-time employment.

There is some debate as to whether taxation systems and welfare benefits have any important influence on work effort and spouses' employment decisions (O'Donoghue and Sutherland, 1999; OECD, 2001: 141–43), or on fertility and family formation (Gauthier, 1996a, b). Cross-national comparisons often fail to identify any clear, measurable impact. On the other hand, single-nation studies regularly find that important changes in fiscal policy have an immediate, visible impact on behaviour in that country, especially in small and socially homogeneous countries. Sweden, for example, has successfully used fiscal policy as an instrument of social engineering, to mould women's behaviour, although it has so far failed to persuade fathers to use paternal leave and get involved in childcare. Men appear to be less malleable than women. Another example is the introduction of a homecare allowance in Finland, Norway and France, for full-time mothers of new babies who do not use public childcare services. These schemes became controversial, despite their immediate success and popularity, because they reduced employment rates among young women (Ilmakunnas, 1997; Drew *et al*, 1998; Hantrais, 2000: 84–87; Ellingsæter, 2003). Fiscal policies that are effective can be controversial. Most changes to tax and welfare benefits are too marginal to have an observable effect.

Social institutions are influential everywhere, but almost never decisive factors in social change. Just one example is the relative importance of childcare services in facilitating women's employment. As Humphries and Rubery noted (1992: 253), female employment, in particular full-time female employment, rose in the late 1980s in Britain despite no change at all in the relative absence of childcare services. In the USA, universal no-cost childcare is estimated to increase women's labour force participation rate by just 10 percentage points (Connelly, 1991: 110). Portugal has always had very high female full-time employment rates, despite the absence of public childcare services. Social institutions change relatively slowly – except in small city states like Singapore, where social policy can shift sharply and quickly in response to changing needs. The choices made by individuals and couples can change much faster than social institutions, and thus need to be explained by other factors.

There is a fifth factor which affects female employment rates: the choice between a low-wage full employment economy and a high-wage, high productivity and low employment economy, as illustrated by the contrast between East and West Germany before 1989, or between China and Japan. In low-wage economies, families usually need two incomes to attain an adequate and secure income. However, this is a general, long term choice of economic policy which is not aimed specifically at women, although it has an impact on the number of women entering the workforce (Fine, 1992: 152).

This chapter examines the role of law in helping to redefine women's position in the labour market. It does not provide a general review of recent developments in labour law, sex discrimination law and their implications for women, which are discussed more fully by other writers (Davies and Freedland, 1984; 1993; Lewis, 1986; McCrudden, 1987; Prechal and Burrows, 1990; Ellis, 1991; Nielsen and Szyszczak, 1991; Pitt, 1992; Fredman, 1997; 2002). The focus here is on the impact of equal opportunities legislation on the sexual division of labour in the workplace; its role in creating fairer competition between male and female workers, as well as between Member States of the EU; and on the contribution of social science evidence to the analysis of indirect discrimination issues.

The development of discrimination law

Sex and race discrimination are often discussed together by labour lawyers, but they pose quite different problems from a social engineering perspective. Women are a fully integrated majority in society as a whole. Differential treatment of women in the labour market derives primarily from widely accepted norms on the family division of labour and sex roles that are now being challenged and rewritten. Racial and ethnic minorities are small groups. They are sometimes better integrated in the labour market than in society as a whole, but exclusion is their main problem. Policies have the general aim of achieving social inclusion by prohibiting what is most often overt prejudice, and direct discrimination. In the EU, ethnic minorities may be migrant workers who are not EU nationals and citizens, as illustrated (at present) by Turkish workers in Germany, or they may be nationals and citizens, as illustrated by the Asian, black and Chinese minorities in Britain. EU law prohibiting discrimination on grounds of nationality and sex developed into two of the foundation stones of the EU, whereas there is no prohibition on discrimination against non-EU citizens. Racial discrimination was dealt with only by national law (McCrudden et al, 1991; Hepple, 1996), until the 1997 Treaty of Amsterdam extended equal opportunities policy to cover all social groups and minorities. The Treaty of Rome signed by 'the Six' (Germany, France, Italy, Belgium, the Netherlands and Luxembourg) in 1957 laid the foundation stone for the development of the current EU, setting out aims and objectives, creating the legislation and key institutions of the EU, including the European Court of Justice (ECJ). Under the title of Social Policy, Art 119 of the Treaty of Rome laid down the principle that men and women should receive equal pay for equal work, an adaptation of the International Labour Office of the United Nations (ILO) Convention No 100 of 1951 which declared the principle of equal remuneration for men and women workers for work of equal value (which the UK ratified only in 1971). It is clear that the original intention of Art 119 was to specify equal pay for people doing the same job, narrowly defined. As EU policy developed over time, the intention was clarified and broadened to include work of equal value, as set out in the Equal Pay Directive (EEC Council Directive 75/117 of 1975), and this wider interpretation was confirmed by the ECJ in 1982 (Davies and Freedland, 1984: 381; 1993: 217). The EU 'principle of equal pay' means, for the same work or work to which equal value is attributed, the elimination of all discrimination on grounds of sex with regard to all aspects and conditions of remuneration. This was followed by the Equal Treatment Directive (EEC Council Directive 76/207 of 1976) which laid down the 'principle of non-discrimination' as regards access to employment, promotion, vocational training, working conditions, termination of employment and employment-related social security benefits. The European courts (like the USA courts before them) interpreted this to encompass indirect discrimination, and the principle of equal treatment is now read as excluding all discrimination in the labour market on grounds of sex, either directly or indirectly, by reference in particular to marital or family status. The Social Security Directive (No 79/7 of December 1978) further clarified the progressive implementation of the principle of equal treatment for men and women in matters of employment-related social security; it allowed Member States to treat favourably persons with family responsibilities, but it did not oblige them to do so. Two further Council Directives on Equal Treatment in Pension Schemes (Nos 79/7 and 86/378) and a series of ECJ decisions on pension issues following on from the 1990 decision on the *Barber v Guardian Royal Exchange Assurance Group* case clarified the application of the principles of equal pay and non-discrimination to pensions. For example, the widespread practice, in state and employer pension schemes, of allowing women to retire with a pension at a younger age than men (typically 60 versus 65 in Britain) was ruled to discriminate in favour of women, and had to be abandoned.

The Amsterdam Treaty, adopted in June 1997, updated the Treaty of Rome to include 'equality between men and women' as one of the aims of the EU; to redefine the equal pay principle to cover equal pay for work of equal value (comparable worth); and to permit some forms of affirmative action that stop short of positive discrimination. It also extended equal opportunities policy beyond sex and nationality to cover race and ethnic origin, religion or belief, disability, age and sexual orientation.

In the USA, Title 7 of the 1964 Civil Rights Act and its amendments prohibit employment discrimination based on race, national origin, religion, sex, pregnancy, age, and disability. The Equal Employment Opportunity Commission (EEOC) and federal courts have responsibility for enforcing the law. For most of its history, the EEOC was seen as giving a free hand to employers. In 1971, the Supreme Court greatly extended the impact of equal opportunity law by introducing the concept of disparate adverse impact (indirect discrimination) into its rulings, but federal courts varied in their interpretations. In 1991, Congress amended Title 7 to explicitly ban disparate impact discrimination, but federal courts continued with varied interpretations of the law. In 1991 also, Congress strengthened Title 7 discrimination lawsuits by giving plaintiffs the right to compensatory and punitive damages. In less than a decade, the annual number of lawsuits tripled from fewer than 7,000 to over 21,000 (Reskin, 2003: 12). In contrast, there were over 100,000 labour court cases in Britain in 2003, of which about 7,000 were sex discrimination cases. However, the main difference between USA and European law is that collective *class action* lawsuits were always available in the US, so that damages awarded frequently amounted to $ millions for the group of people bringing the case (Darity and Mason, 1998). The other important difference is that certain occupations and industries tend to be dominated by members of particular ethnic/cultural groups in the USA, so that social networks and discrimination in favour of the ingroup are probably as important as discrimination against outgroups (Tilly and Tilly, 1998; see also Bonacich, 1994).

When the UK joined the EU in 1973, along with Denmark and Ireland, it became bound by the Treaty of Rome and the principles of equal pay and equal treatment, along with other EU legislation, given that European legislation over-rides conflicting national law. In 1982, the ECJ ruled that the British Government's Equal Pay Act 1970 was deficient, in not making provision for equal value claims. The UK was obliged to amend national legislation through the Equal Pay (Amendment) Regulations 1983 which allow claims for equal pay between men and women for work which can be shown to be of equal value carried out within the same workplace or for the same employer (Davies and Freedland, 1993: 211–18, 581–83). This case was of enormous importance in making people aware of the force of European legislation prohibiting sex discrimination in all its forms, both direct and indirect, and that national legislation would have to implement the equal pay principle. This first ECJ decision against the British Government was followed by a second in 1983 which ruled that the UK Sex Discrimination Act 1975 failed to comply with the European Equal Treatment Directive: first, in that the Act's exemption for small firms was not permissible; secondly, in failing to declare void discriminatory provisions in collective agreements. This led to the

Sex Discrimination Act 1986 which combined necessary amendments to sex discrimination legislation; the repeal of legislation dating back to the 1930s which imposed restrictions on women's working hours, especially nightwork; and the equalisation of retirement ages (Davies and Freedland, 1993: 583–85).

It may appear from these two cases that Britain had difficulty in establishing the general principles of equal pay and non-discrimination in national legislation. There is no doubt that the Conservative Government's enthusiasm for European law in the 1980s was minimal. But it is inappropriate to present the problem in party political terms, as academics often do (Fredman, 1992: 119; Davies and Freedland, 1993: 583), given that the original legislation was passed by a Labour government, and the European Commission sued not only Britain but also Belgium, Denmark, France, West Germany, Luxembourg and the Netherlands for violating Art 119. (In fact, the Commission has probably taken every Member State to court at some point, to force them to include some aspect of European law.) All Member States of the EU experience genuine difficulty in implementing the simple but broad principles of equal pay and non-discrimination, since the differential treatment of men and women has long been written into most labour market practices, norms and labour law, often linked to assumptions about the sexual division of labour in the home. Implementation of the two principles thus involves a continuing process of re-examining existing practices and norms, with the courts providing a public forum for debate as to their fairness or discriminatory effects, whether intended or not. For example, in the 1970s and early 1980s, the courts in Britain (also in the USA and Canada) decided it could be lawful to dismiss a pregnant woman. Following ECJ rulings, such dismissals have invariably been judged discriminatory and unlawful in recent court cases (Fredman, 1992: 121–22; Sohrab, 1993: 146–47; Fredman, 1997). Substantial compensation has been paid to women dismissed from careers in the British armed services, or from lucrative careers in City law firms, due to pregnancy (over £1 million in one 2004 industrial tribunal case).

Discriminatory practices may be ruled lawful, if the employer can provide objective justification for them in national courts. One difficulty is that proof of *indirect* discrimination requires assessment of social scientific and statistical evidence which goes contrary to British law's traditional focus on the circumstances of individual cases. There are also major practical problems in rewriting rules and redesigning practices so as to pass the non-discrimination tests. These are illustrated by a series of ECJ rulings in the 1990s on pensions which, as a form of deferred pay, are subject to the equal pay principle. Redesigning pension schemes that have been running for decades on the basis of differential treatment is no easy matter, and while the courts can decide what is unlawful, they rarely offer constructive advice on the design of new arrangements.

European non-discrimination principles do not invariably benefit women. For example, the ECJ approved the abolition of unequal pension ages in Europe by raising women's pension age to that of men without compensation to those affected, and some commentators objected to the repeal of 'protective' laws controlling women's work hours in Britain. The principle of non-discrimination means that women become subject to the same competitive market forces as men, and it does not permit any reverse discrimination at all. For example, in the 1987 decision on the *Bilka-Kaufhaus* case, and in several other cases, the ECJ has rejected arguments that employers should take into account women's family responsibilities and be obliged to make special arrangements for them, such as providing childcare facilities, special working hours or special pension arrangements. Employers only have an obligation not to discriminate. Similarly, special advantages granted to working mothers by the French state, including leave when a child is ill and an allowance for childcare costs, were ruled discriminatory and unlawful by the ECJ in 1988 when the Commission took France to court. French men have used EU law to challenge the special privileges given to female workers, and to demand similar allowances for childcare and leave for family reasons, and they have won their cases. Although France was the originator of the EU equality laws, France has had just as many problems implementing EU laws as other countries (Hantrais, 2000: 20, 68–88).

Positive discrimination (for example, preferring a woman in job recruitment) is ruled out by European law. This question produced a long struggle between the Commission, politicians and the ECJ, centred on two German cases in the mid-1990s, *Kalanke* and *Marschall*, which are still debated (Fredman, 2002: 125–60). Affirmative action is permitted by the Treaty of Amsterdam, and is allowed in British race relations and sex discrimination law, for example in relation to training. It is the function of the Commission for Racial Equality and the Equal Opportunities Commission to promote equality of opportunity through positive action *inter alia* (Pitt, 1992: 31). In any event, the effectiveness of positive discrimination is doubtful (Hepple and Szyszczak, 1992). European lawyers look enviously at USA positive discrimination policies and Supreme Court decisions, and regularly present the case for positive discrimination, as well as affirmative action, in order to achieve substantive equality as well as equality of opportunity (Fredman, 1997; 2002: 125–60). However, American positive discrimination rulings have been most prominent in cases of racial discrimination rather than sex discrimination. An early example is the bussing experiment aimed at eliminating the racial segregation of schools in southern American states.

Finally, European 'social policy' was prompted initially by concern with fair competition, and it deals almost exclusively with the labour market and workers (Bercusson, 1990; Hepple, 1990; Nielsen and Szyszczak, 1991; Tsoukalis, 1993: 151; Hepple, 1996). It does not extend to other areas, which remain subject to national law and regulations. However, the EU Race Discrimination Directive that followed the Treaty of Amsterdam does go wider, to prohibit race discrimination in relation to health care and housing, as well as in the labour market.

Hoskyns' (1996; 1999) history of EU policy on women's rights identifies the key actors and officials who pushed things forward, and reviews the 80 plus legal cases on equal treatment decided by the ECJ. She points out that women's groups sought to use legislation as a central instrument of social engineering, to achieve changes through EU law that they could not achieve through the normal political process within their own countries. They have thus brought up wider issues of sexual politics that fall outside the remit of the Commission, EU law and the ECJ. As she points out, politicians and the ECJ have allowed the scope of EU social policy to be gradually broadened, beyond the narrow original focus on ensuring the free movement of labour and fair competition in the European labour market, but they have also resisted pressure for EU law to be used as a multi-purpose tool to address all gender equality issues. Thus, the ECJ has insisted that the EU Directive on equal treatment 'was not designed to settle questions concerning the organisation of the family, or to alter the division of responsibility between parents' (Fredman, 1997: 195; Hoskyns, 1999: 30). There will always be critics who claim that European law does not go far enough, and needs to be strengthened – in effect demanding that lawyers be given the role of change agents (Fredman, 1997).

After the Treaty of Amsterdam, the emphasis in EU policy has changed to 'mainstreaming gender' in all areas of EU policy-making, and the reconciliation of employment and family life for all workers (Hantrais, 2000), despite the fact that the Commission has no role in family policy. This means that non-working women are currently left out of the picture in EU policy-making (Threlfall, 2000). EU social policy is now shifting focus, towards issues raised by immigration from non-EU countries, and internal migration resulting from the accession of new Member States in Central and Eastern Europe. It is possible that the EU's development of sex equality policies has effectively come to an end. Human rights legislation, and the European Court of Human Rights (ECHR) may become more important in the 21st century, because they have a potentially wider application than discrimination laws. The Treaty of Amsterdam also prompted the British Government to move to a single Equality Commission to cover all types of discrimination, as is the practice in Australia, for example. Sex discrimination will in future be addressed alongside competing claims for social equality.

Social science evidence on indirect discrimination

The prohibition of *indirect* sex discrimination is the most important innovation of USA and European labour law (Redmond, 1986; Pitt, 1992; Hepple, 1996), and it is also the most problematic. Courts have generally adapted slowly to dealing with discrimination cases that are not based on overt prejudice. Indirect discrimination cases necessarily involve arguments about an employer's rules having a differential, or disproportionate, impact on women compared to men, and hence statistical evidence on the proportions affected by a rule. Yet there are no arrangements for judges to have access to relevant social science or statistical advice. This has undoubtedly been one factor in the courts' reluctance to address statistical evidence, in judgments that appear ill-informed to the social scientist, and controversy over decisions (Barnard and Hepple, 1999). The absence of social science expertise in the European courts, and even in the ECJ, is in marked contrast to North America, where indirect discrimination cases frequently involve consideration of regression analyses of large datasets of a kind more common in social science journals than law journals (Redmond, 1986; Willborn, 1989). The gulf separating labour lawyers and labour sociologists in Europe is illustrated by a debate in the *Industrial Law Journal* on the employment rights of full-time and part-time employees under British legislation then applying: statistical comparisons of the characteristics of the full-time and part-time workforces clashed with the labour lawyer's focus on the rights of individual workers (Hakim, 1989a; Disney and Szyszczak, 1989).

Sometimes, the statistical evidence is simple. A landmark decision by the House of Lords in 1994 in favour of the Equal Opportunities Commission, against the Secretary of State for Employment, ruled that British laws excluding part-timers working fewer than 16 hours a week from certain statutory employment rights failed the European non-discrimination principle. Indirect discrimination was easily proven in this case, as the majority of employees working over 16 hours a week are men and the great majority of those working less than 16 hours a week are women. The decision thus rested on whether there was any objective justification for the exclusion of part-timers working fewer than 16 hours. As the British Government chose to rely on economic theory, with no supporting factual evidence that the exclusion resulted in greater availability of part-time jobs, the government lost. The irony of this case is that the House of Lords decision forced the government to accept more extensive employment rights for part-time employees than had been proposed by the EC's Social Charter, and Directives on atypical workers, that the government had previously rejected (Hakim, 1995a: 440–41). Similarly, in 1989, in the *Rinner-Kühn* case, the ECJ ruled that the German Government failed to offer objective justification for the exclusion from sick pay schemes of part-timers working less than 10 hours a week or less than 45 hours a month, the majority of whom are women.

In other cases, the statistical evidence becomes slightly more sophisticated: for example, it must be shown that the proportion of women (or part-timers) fulfilling certain conditions are 'considerably smaller' than the proportion of men, or that a 'much lower' proportion of women work full-time. As yet there is no agreement on appropriate measures, for example on whether a 20 percentage point difference constitutes sufficient evidence of a differential impact, or of differential eligibility. Some British courts have rejected a 8–9 percentage point difference in eligibility rates as not proving indirect discrimination, while others have accepted such evidence as adequate. In 1995, in the *Seymour-Smith* case, the Court of Appeal ruled that the government's decision to increase the qualifying period for unfair dismissal rights from one year to two years in 1985 was in breach of the non-discrimination principle, as the two year qualifying period excluded a third of women but only a quarter of men in employment (Hantrais, 2000: 21–22, 196–207). This means an average 9 percentage point difference between men and women was accepted as sufficient proof of indirect discrimination, over-ruling the Divisional Court in a judicial review proceeding. Table 5.5 shows an 11 percentage point difference between men and women in the proportion with less than two years' tenure (41% versus 30%), but it also shows roughly the same difference in the proportions with less than one year's tenure with their employer (27% versus 19%), so that raising the qualifying period from one to two years (or lowering it to one year) did not significantly change the situation. Most social scientists would regard a 10 percentage point difference as too small to constitute a 'considerable' difference and proof of indirect discrimination. Tests of statistical significance are irrelevant here, as the issue is substantive significance (Hakim, 1987a: 6–7), a distinction that few labour lawyers appreciate, and Labour Force Surveys (LFS) samples are large enough to ensure statistical significance for even a 3–5 percentage point difference between working men and women. In the event, the ECJ decided that the 10 percentage point gap was too small to be proof of indirect discrimination, a decision that met with some criticism (Barnard and Hepple, 1999). In general, the statistical evidence employed in British courts (and the ECJ) is simple, and the criteria applied to prove indirect discrimination seem to be haphazard, in contrast with the hairsplitting finesse of assessments of points of law. This is in marked contrast with the contribution of complex social science evidence in comparable worth lawsuits and policies in the USA.

Paradoxically, comparable worth policies were introduced in the USA as a result of inadequate social science evidence. Equal pay was introduced in 1963 and enforced, but women's average earnings remained stubbornly at an unvarying 60% of male earnings among full-time year-round workers, a pay gap of 40% (Goldin, 1990: 59). In the late 1970s, the EEOC requested a study of comparable worth as an alternative route to reducing the pay gap. The report of the committee duly concluded that job segregation and the practice of paying lower wages for women's occupations were the main causes of the pay gap, so that equalising earnings on the basis of comparable worth (equal value) represented the only way of closing the pay gap (Treiman and Hartmann, 1981). The report stated, on the basis of the research evidence then available, that human capital factors failed to explain the pay gap, even though one study by Corcoran (1979) showed that half the pay gap was explained by work history and job tenure variables, and other studies showed vertical job segregation to explain one-third or more (Treiman and Hartmann, 1981: 22–23, 32–33, 55–56). Although comparable worth remained controversial in the USA, both politically and among economists, the report was persuasive enough for some 20 states and employers to adopt pay systems based on comparable worth principles that Congress had explicitly excluded from equal pay laws. This often entailed detailed analyses of the correlates of earnings within the organisation, or across all state employees. As noted in Chapter 6, comparable worth pay policies typically increase female earnings by only 5% to 6%, far less than was suggested by Treiman and Hartmann's report, leading some to conclude that even the most carefully constructed job evaluation systems may not be entirely free from sexism, with a bias in favour of work done by men.

An alternative explanation is that Treiman and Hartmann's analysis was mistaken, completely overlooking psychological capital (Feinstein, 2000), and failing to identify the full importance of human capital variables alongside sex discrimination as determinants of earnings. Historical analyses by Smith and Ward (1984) and Goldin show that female heterogeneity was the hidden factor that led to incorrect analyses. Female workrates rose after 1950 because women with little work experience were pulled into the labour market. The pay gap stayed constant after equal pay was introduced because there was no change in average female work experience from the 1920s to the 1980s (Goldin, 1989; 1990: 30–42, 214). The pay gap then declined steadily throughout the 1980s due to increases in women's work experience, job tenure, qualifications and related human capital variables (O'Neill, and Polachek, 1993). While Treiman and Hartmann were right to conclude that women's jobs were undervalued at that time, they were wrong to conclude that sex discrimination was a more important explanatory factor than human capital variables.

Willborn (1989) compares the legal processes, and outcomes, of comparable worth lawsuits in the USA and equal value cases in Britain, focusing on two case studies: Helen Castrilli, the secretary who was the central plaintiff in the larger class action against the State of Washington in 1982, and Julie Hayward, the cook in the Cammell Laird shipyard who successfully brought the first equal value claim in Britain in 1984. He shows how the contribution of statistical evidence to prove indirect discrimination differs between class actions and individual claims, and how different are the outcomes of the two types of case in terms of wage adjustments, and in terms of the breadth of application of the judgments. In class actions, the court case concerns a group of people with some common characteristic that gives rise to a common legal claim. Class actions were originally restricted to the North American courts. From the 1990s onwards, British courts began to accept such cases, for example to consider collective claims arising from a collective event, such as a train crash, or a pension fund becoming insolvent.

In some cases, it is social science concepts, rather than statistics, that are used to prove indirect discrimination. The *Meade-Hill* case is of interest for this reason, and also because it shows how women are using the law to *prevent* equal treatment with men. In 1990, Mrs Meade-Hill, a public official in London, was promoted from a clerical grade to the rank of Executive Officer (EO), the lowest managerial grade in white-collar work. The contractual terms for this grade, like all managerial grades, included a mobility rule requiring people to work anywhere in Britain, if so directed by the employer. Her employers did not in fact ask her to work outside London, but she sought to have the mobility rule judged unlawful anyway, just in case. Her argument, which was accepted by all parties as common ground, was that the mobility clause was acceptable to men, who are primary earners, but was a condition that women could not easily comply with, as most women are secondary earners – hence was indirectly discriminatory. Secondary earners were defined very simply as women earning less than their husbands or partners. In her case, her husband was a computer engineer who earned considerably more than she did, although she worked full-time.

The case is interesting because the secondary earner label was the key, indeed only argument for refusing to accept the usual terms and conditions of a management position, albeit the lowest grade of management. Executive Officers were a national career grade in government service, with a London salary scale of £13,500–£16,700, right on the average weekly earnings for full-time employees in Britain in 1994, when the case was heard. The grade was large enough to be separately identified in the 1991 Census results, which showed 82,000 EOs, of whom 54% were men, and 91% worked full-time. Thus, Mrs Meade-Hill was an entirely representative full-time employee in an integrated career grade attracting national average earnings of the sort that constitute a breadwinner wage for men supporting a family. Because she earned less than her husband, an almost universal characteristic of wives (as noted in Chapter 3), she was classified as a secondary earner, who could legitimately be exempted from employment conditions routinely applied to men in the same occupational grade. The mobility rule is in fact disliked just as much by men, who can no longer assume their wives will necessarily be agreeable to moving with them. The case demonstrates that the law can be used to institutionalise the concept of secondary earner, and to legitimise preferential treatment for women which is not entirely dissimilar from earlier protectionist legislation. This case stereotypes all working wives as secondary earners, disregarding female heterogeneity.

The problem of female heterogeneity

The equal treatment principle implicitly treats working women as a homogeneous group in the same way that men are treated as a homogeneous group, insisting that the same rules, conditions and benefits should be applied to all workers, male and female (unless there is objective justification for doing otherwise). Given that the female adult population is heterogeneous in its work orientations and labour market behaviour, and given increasing polarisation of the female workforce, the equal treatment principle is problematic, and can have unpredictable or surprising effects. One example has been given above, in a court ruling accepting that secondary earners should be treated differently from primary earners in order to avoid indirect discrimination. Another example is the ECJ's 1994 decision that part-timers cannot have their own separate overtime rates.

In *Stadt Lengerich v Helmig* (1994) the ECJ ruled that there is no discrimination contrary to European law where a collective agreement provides overtime supplements will be paid only when the normal working hours for full-time workers are exceeded. This decision involved six joined cases from Germany on whether Art 119 requires employers to pay part-timers overtime supplements when they work in excess of their own, shorter contractual hours. Angelika Helmig, a married women with two young children, was employed as a tutor in the town of Lengerich's youth centre, normally working 19.5 hours a week compared to full-timers' 38.5 hours a week. Collective agreements for public service workers provided for 25% overtime supplements to hourly pay for people in her grade, which her employer argued were not required in her case. The ECJ decided that, as part-time and full-time workers were paid the same overtime rates, there was no unequal treatment and no discrimination. There was thus no need to consider whether discrimination could be justified, for example by the fact that overtime hours have a greater impact on the discretionary free time of full-timers than of part-timers.

The Advocate General's Opinion which preceded the ECJ ruling noted that full-time hours were uniform and fixed, by statute or collective agreement, whereas part-time hours can vary from 5 hours a week to 30 hours a week. Paying an overtime supplement to part-timers on an individual basis would create inequality of treatment, since one part-timer might be paid an overtime supplement for working an extra hour that was part of normal hours for another part-timer, as well as for full-timers. Part-timers would thus be treated more favourably than full-timers, progressively so, the shorter their normal hours.

The ECJ has generally ruled that employers must give part-timers the same employment benefits as they offer to full-time workers, but it has also consistently refused to allow part-timers better than *pro rata* benefits, or any transitional arrangements, that would leave part-timers advantaged compared with full-timers. For example, in the group of decisions in late 1994 on occupational pensions, the ECJ confirmed that part-timers had the right to join employers' pension schemes, with retrospective effect, but also that part-timers would have to pay in the appropriate backdated employee contributions, in order to benefit retrospectively. There is extensive evidence that, even when they are eligible to join employers' pension schemes, part-timers are much less likely to join: no more than half do so (Martin and Roberts, 1984: Table 5.14; Rubery *et al*, 1994: Table 6.7). Similarly, as noted in Chapter 2, part-time workers often limit their hours and earnings so as to ensure that there are no income tax or social security deductions from their earnings (Hakim, 1987b: 109–12, 192–96; 1989b: 473, 493). Given the relatively small *pro rata* pensions earned by part-timers, this may be economically rational behaviour.

In summary, the non-discrimination principle, applied as between men and women, treats all women uniformly, ignoring the differences noted in Chapters 3 and 5 between employment-centred women who work continuously and home-centred secondary earners. Women who work part-time, and intermittently, are getting improved employment rights and benefits as a result of ECJ rulings, but these benefits will not put them on an equal level with people who work full-time, and continuously, in long term careers. Some feminist lawyers reacted with surprise and anger at the ECJ ruling that part-time workers could not be paid overtime supplements on an individual basis. They overlook the fact that laws prohibiting sex discrimination do not alter the pre-existing diversity of the female population, the polarisation of the female workforce, and their economic consequences.

Legal textbooks on women's employment, and sex discrimination, frequently attempt to review the social scientific research evidence on female employment and the pay gap, as background information to a discussion of the law (for example, see Fredman, 1997). Inevitably, labour lawyers cannot bring the same skill to this task as do social scientists, and European lawyers routinely trip up on technical questions such as the distinction between the substantive importance and the statistical significance of research results. Even this brief review of the use of statistical evidence in indirect discrimination cases suggests that female heterogeneity, which is increasing over time, poses a fundamental problem for law in this area. It is a problem that labour lawyers have so far failed completely to recognise, or get to grips with. In the USA, lawyers' use of statistical evidence on indirect discrimination is far more sophisticated and skilful, but female heterogeneity still poses a fundamental substantive problem for law in this field.

Conclusions

In sex discrimination cases, the ECJ only adjudicates on basic principles in the application of the Treaty of Rome, Treaty of Amsterdam, and EC Directives, leaving national courts to deal with factual matters, including the crucial decision on whether an employer's reasons for a given practice constitute objectively justified economic reasons unrelated to sex, correspond to a real need in the enterprise, are appropriate and necessary to the objective pursued, and are thus justified. National differences in employment practices will thus remain. However, there is no doubt that the rigorous application of non-discrimination principles is forcing everyone to review and rethink rules, customs and practices that may have been applied for decades, and were widely accepted, but are nonetheless discriminatory, such as unequal retirement ages for men and women. Within Europe, legislation is an important tool of social engineering. The process was strengthened by the controversial 1991 *Francovich* case in which the ECJ ruled that a Member State could be forced to pay damages for any harm or loss caused to individuals as a result of the state's failure to implement an EC Directive properly. However, legislation is only one policy tool among the many available, and it has its limits, as feminist lawyers are beginning to recognise (Hepple and Szyszczak, 1992; Fredman, 1992; 1997; 2002; More, 1993; Sohrab, 1993; Fenwick and Hervey, 1995).

The law sets out the (new) rules of the game, but it is not pro-active: it only comes into play when a conflict has arisen, and discussions are conducted in an adversarial context. There is a huge range of issues that cannot be addressed through legislation, and require other tools of social engineering. One example is the 'freezing out' process which can exclude people from sex-atypical occupations as noted in Chapter 6: the law can address overt acts of prejudice, but not silent poor co-operation from colleagues. Another example is the social and psychological processes in the workplace that inhibit women functioning effectively in senior positions and management posts, as noted in Chapter 4. Most important of all, European law only covers education, employment, and the provision of services, and even national law is restricted to roles and activities in the public sphere. Neither European nor national law address the sexual division of labour in the household, which is taken to be a private matter in Western democracies, subject to private bargaining between partners. Employment law has no interest in these private arrangements and employers are not required to take account of them. It seems to follow that labour law currently has no role in sorting out any problems caused by the diversity of women's lifestyle choices and the polarisation of women's employment. The principles of equal pay and equal treatment are powerful, but limited, instruments for redesigning sex-roles, and the opportunities open to men and women. The law can change the treatment of women in the workforce; it cannot change women themselves.

Feminist activists and lawyers campaign for the goal of substantive equality rather than the 'formal equality' of equal opportunities. Given the hard evidence of female heterogeneity reviewed in this book, and elsewhere (Hakim, 2000; 2003a), substantive equality appears technically impossible, even in the labour market, even if policy-makers were persuaded that this should be the goal. It has certainly not been achieved in Scandinavia. It is hard to see how the law could square the circle, and produce substantive equality between primary and secondary earners, even in the context of a minimum wage that provides a living wage, as some argue (Gregory *et al*, 1999).

Chapter 8
Conclusions: Female Diversity and Workforce Polarisation

What has been demonstrated by this review of the theory and empirical evidence on women's employment? First, that a great many true lies are told about women's employment in modern society. Secondly, that the most effective mechanism for subordinating women is neither exclusion from the workforce nor segregation within it, but the ideology of the sexual division of labour in the home, and the ideology of sexual differences. Prisons of the mind are always more effective than prisons of the body. Thirdly, because most women are eager to raise their own children personally, it is women who are the main propagators, and the main beneficiaries, of the ideology of the sexual division of labour, both by precept and example. How many mothers tell their daughters that they should never marry, never have children, because they will live to regret it bitterly? And how many daughters, faced with a daily demonstration of what marriage and motherhood does to women, recoil in horror to say, 'No! Never! Not I!' and rush to enrol at the nearest college to enable themselves to be self-supporting? Fourthly, social attitude surveys that reveal more positive views on working wives and working mothers are reflecting increasing tolerance in pluralist societies, not necessarily women's personal preferences. Fifthly, the heterogeneity of women's preferences for homemaking or employment careers is pronounced, and seems to be increasing rather than fading. Sixthly, this heterogeneity is the main source of the polarisation in women's labour market behaviour. Seventhly, sex differences and the polarisation of women's employment are larger, and most clearly visible among graduates, and at the top of the occupational structure. Case studies of women in the professions, and in management, show that a minority of women conform to the male employment profile of continuous full-time employment; the majority of women are secondary earners who balance employment with family life. As a result, the pay gap is often larger in the professions and in management than in the workforce as a whole, because the rewards for people committed to their careers are substantially greater at this level. Eighthly, paradoxically, it is also at the top of the occupational hierarchy that the potential for sex (and other) discrimination remains the greatest. It is easily hidden at this level, partly because work tasks and performance are more variable, but also because they are more difficult to measure reliably in a situation where almost every job is unique. In addition, there is minimal information on professional and managerial women, or even on graduates, in national datasets, and a focus on the manufacturing sector in industrial relations research (Rubery and Fagan, 1995b), so the research spotlight is weak for this group. Ninthly, there is evidence to support all four main theories explaining why women are less likely than men to achieve positions offering wealth, power and status, so that they should be seen as complementary rather than competing, partly because they apply at different points in historical time.

True lies

A great many true lies are told about women. It is said that women's work is invisible in industrial society because women are family helpers, do home-based work, work in the informal economy, do voluntary work. All of this is true. The lie is the unstated implication that women are distinctive in engaging in these activities; that their important contribution to the economy is hidden by not being recorded in national statistical surveys; that the activities are devalued by being excluded from the definition of economic activity. All of these assumptions are untrue. Men also do a great variety of informal and unrecorded work, sometimes displaying the same level and pattern of activity as women (as in voluntary work), sometimes doing more than women (in the case of home-based work), sometimes less than women (as illustrated by family helpers). Men and women are equally likely to have caring responsibilities for elderly or infirm people, although women devote more time to childcare. Household work is shared by men and women, currently in the ratio of 40% to 60% on average. However, men do more hours of market work than women, in addition to all their other informal work activities. Time use surveys now show that men and women do exactly the same overall number of hours of work, using the term in its wide sense of activities producing goods and services. Employment statistics do not give the complete picture, but they are not entirely misleading on the balance of work between men and women. In addition, women have the benefit of a degree of autonomy in household work that is commonly absent in paid work. This may be part of the explanation for women living longer than men, despite the fact that women wear themselves out in childbirth. In practice, men still work harder, with longer hours of employment, and wear out faster. The most telling inequality in society today is the sex difference in average life expectancy, which is increasing over time. Life expectancy at birth has almost doubled in Britain, from 40 years for men and 42 years for women in 1838–54, to 74 years for men and 79 years for women in 1990–95. The sex difference in average life expectancy has more than doubled, from just under 2 years to 5.4 years in favour of women in Britain, with even higher sex differences in France (8 years), the USA (7 years), Germany, Sweden and Japan (6 years). The EU average is 7 years, and the sex difference shows no signs of shrinking (European Commission, 1995b: 36). The sex differential in life expectancy is almost as large as the social class differential, yet only the latter is treated as inegalitarian. Women in developing countries have heavy workloads; most women in industrial society do not. Case studies that focus on the short phase when women have young children at home have given a misleading picture of the average housewife's workload. They also show that many full-time homemakers make their own misery: those with the longest hours include a substantial volume of unnecessary make-work. As an occupation, the job of full-time homemaker is hard to beat: short hours (compared to people in paid work), reasonable job security, and average rewards in terms of status and income. It may be boring, but so are most jobs. The price is dependence on another person, but most housewives value their autonomy in comparison with the subservience of waged labour in the market economy. The choice is finely balanced.

Women do not make completely free choices, it is argued, hence are forced into low-paid part-time jobs, or are forced into marriage, instead of the financial independence of wage labour. This is true in part. The implication is that men have real choices, and more choices to make. This is the lie. Most men have little choice in how to spend their lives, being forced into the full-time continuous life-long employment career whether they like it or not, whether they take on the breadwinner role for a wife and children or not. Public disapproval for the househusband role is reflected in a status score so low that it scrapes the very bottom of the prestige scale, whereas the housewife's score is right in the middle of the scale. Women can choose to drop out of the labour market and become homemakers, full-time or in combination with a part-time job, and retain a social status not very different from the status of typically-female occupations in the market economy (such as secretary), or else they can rely on the borrowed glory of their husband's social status, as most women do (Sobel *et al*, 2004). No such choice is open to men. It is indicative that even career women refuse to marry and maintain househusbands: women who earn enough to be breadwinners themselves, who can afford to keep a non-earning or low-paid husband, and who constantly bemoan the fact that most men have the support services of a wife at home whereas they do not, even these women refuse to contemplate role reversal and become economic supporters, rather than joint earners in a dual-career household (Hakim, 2000: 153). The closest approximation to this is the young woman who works as the main breadwinner while her husband goes through law, medical or business school. However, she is investing in her husband's career with a view to being financially dependent for the rest of her life after he qualifies, so her role is the same as that of all wives contributing to two-person careers, whatever the nature of the career (Papanek, 1973; Finch, 1983). Goldberg (1993: 152, 192) and Buss (1995) are right to underline this *joint* refusal of men and women to contemplate genuine role reversal at home, as telling us something important about relations between the sexes.

Sample selection bias provides one of the most fruitful sources of true lies. Choose an unrepresentative minority group that demonstrates your point, study it in detail, then broadcast the results as if they concerned women generally, rather than the particular minority group in question. Interestingly, economists are far more likely to be aware of, and seek to correct, sample selection bias than are sociologists.

Sex and gender

Some doubt that the Western distinction between sex and gender is universally meaningful, theoretically and empirically. All human societies recognise biological differences between men and women, and the differentiation of masculine and feminine social roles seems to be universal, with or without the possibility of an intermediate position, temporary or permanent (Moore, 1994). The most powerful evidence of what it means to be male and female in everyday life comes not from social science research but from real life natural experiments (Hakim, 1987a: 109–10): the accounts of people who undergo sex changes. These are not 'ordinary' people. They already believe, strongly enough to persuade doctors to help, that their true personality lies on the other side, and requires a physiological sex change to match. Yet even they are shocked when they cross over to the other side. Men who change over to being women discover they have become second-class citizens, are ignored, kept waiting, are treated dismissively and belittled in a never-ending stream of small daily humiliations; they also find themselves not protesting as they would when they were men. Women who change over to being men are amazed to discover that they go out into the world charged with aggressive energy and consumed with lust when they start the testosterone injections. People who cross over to the other side *in real life* confirm the fluidity of the boundaries between male and female, in terms of sex and gender. They also reveal how dramatic the differences are, in terms of feelings and lived experience. These real life cases also underline the fact that sex and gender almost invariably go together in real life, even if it requires physiological change to get the match right, so that there is little point in the artful distinction between biology and social roles, for most people most of the time. These and other natural experiments (Stoller, 1975; Imperato-McGinley *et al*, 1979; Goldberg, 1993: 167–68) contrast interestingly with the mind-games that feminists like to play around sex and gender (Butler, 1990; 1993; Moore, 1994: 135–50). It seems perverse for feminists to argue that sex and gender are exclusively ideological constructs that can easily be discarded, but at the same time to focus on gender inequality in the labour market, and the politics of gender.

Sex and gender are central concepts in patriarchy theory, in all its forms. Sex and gender are not central concepts in rational choice theory. Becker argues that any division of labour in the family, any specialisation in family work or in market work, is efficient. Role reversal, with a female full-time breadwinner and a male full-time homemaker can be just as efficient as the more conventional arrangement. So sex-roles are not important. Preference theory is also a unisex theory. It claims that lifestyle preferences are replacing sex and gender as the central determinant of activities and social roles.

Female heterogeneity

Ideas generally have a material base. But once created, ideas have a life and vigour of their own, as illustrated by feminist ideology itself.

Patriarchal ideology promoted the idea of bourgeois domestic femininity, which contradicted the reality of most working class women's lives, but provided an ideal for everyone to aspire to. Patriarchal ideology also developed the idea of the sexual division of labour in the family, which gave responsibility for the home and children to the wife-mother, while the husband-father was responsible for income-earning market work. Cross-national comparisons show there is no necessary connection between these two ideas. The sexual division of labour in the home seems to be a universally attractive idea, unconnected with other ideas on sex-roles, the personalities and abilities of men and women. This suggests that the idea is accepted because it is demonstrably efficient and fruitful for most couples, as Becker argues. But the exact specification of the family division of labour is changing. By the start of the 21st century, the *complete* division of labour, which encouraged wives to refrain altogether from employment outside the home, had been replaced by the *modern* family division of labour in which the wife's employment is fitted around her family work, as illustrated by part-time and/or part-year work, or a job that is less demanding than her husband's.

Modern women are more heterogeneous than men in their values and lifegoals. Men are divided into two main groups: roughly half are work-centred and roughly half seek a balance between family life and paid jobs. Women are more differentiated: a two-thirds majority seek a balance between family work and paid employment, but another third divide into two distinctive minorities of work-centred and home-centred (or family-centred) women (Hakim, 2003a: 84–87). A four-fifths majority of women prefer to be secondary earners, while at least half of men choose to be primary earners.

No-one doubts that the work orientations of the full-time homemaker who stops work soon after marriage differ from the work orientations of the career woman who works all her life. It is much easier to overlook the fact that the motivations of the career woman and the secondary earner are also quite different. The career woman challenges the sexual division of labour, and the sex-stereotyping of jobs, that constrain her choice of occupation. In contrast, the secondary earner, even when working full-time, does not challenge the sexual division of labour, and often works in female-dominated occupations. Wage work is an extension of her homemaking role, not an alternative to it; she seeks additional family income, whereas the career woman seeks personal development and personal fulfilment, competing on equal terms with men (Matthaei, 1982: 278–79).

The USA is distinctive in being the only Western society to exhibit a sustained long term increase in female workrates (OECD, 1988: 129–30; Goldin, 1990: 119), so it might be expected to prove that women's diversity is a new phenomenon. On the contrary, Goldin's historical analysis of female employment reveals that female heterogeneity is of such long duration that it must be a permanent feature of the female population. It was the key (hidden) factor explaining the absence of any change in the pay gap for 15 years after equal pay was introduced in the USA, until the 1980s (Goldin, 1990: 28–35; see also Smith and Ward, 1984; O'Neill and Polachek, 1993). Female heterogeneity can no longer be ignored, as it is the source of increasing polarisation within the female workforce, and has social and economic consequences that are not altered by sex discrimination legislation.

Polarisation within the workforce

As a group, women are heterogeneous, diverse and divided. They have genuine choices to make between different lifestyles, and the choice has widened since the contraceptive revolution made voluntary childlessness accessible. Having made one choice early in life, some change their minds and turn off onto another road. A great many women 'hang loose' and refuse to choose fixed objectives, drifting with events and opportunities as they arise, pretending they can keep all their options open by refusing to close the door on any of them. This itself is an important choice, one men do not have, even if it leads to chaotically unplanned careers.

There has always been a minority of women who worked continuously throughout life: 15% of women of working age in Britain in 1965 falling to less than 10% by 1980. In the past, career women were often those who never married. The modern employment career is far less socially restrictive and far more attractive. One-quarter of women working full-time are in professional and managerial jobs.

Most of them will marry and many will have children, some dropping out of the workforce into full-time domesticity at this stage, usually temporarily.

The homemaker career narrowly defined, which involves a permanent cessation of work early in adult life, on marriage or when children are born, is on the decline, replaced by the modern homemaker career, chosen by over two-thirds of women of working age in Britain. This group is the most dominant, in terms of numbers, though it is not the most vociferous. The attitudes, behaviour and interests of this group are in sharp contrast to the attitudes, behaviour and interests of the small minority of employment career women. These two contrasting groups are producing a polarisation of female employment in the 21st century, in Europe, the USA and other industrial societies (Jenson et al, 1988; Rubery, 1988: 44, 96, 127, 145, 159, 278; Humphries and Rubery, 1992; Coleman and Pencavel, 1993; Hakim, 2000: 84–127). In Australia, the polarisation of employment is accompanied by a polarisation of partnership-formation and fertility, leading to fundamental differences in lifestyle between dual-earner couples with children and other types of household (Birrell et al, 2004).

Women in senior grades have invested in qualifications, work continuously and full-time, are as ambitious and determined as men, are concentrated in integrated or male-dominated occupations and have high earnings. Women who pursue the modern homemaker career are secondary earners, do not fully utilise any qualifications they may have, choose jobs for their convenience factors and social interest rather than with a view to a long term career, are often concentrated in female occupations and have lower earnings. When the earnings dispersion increases, as it did in most countries in the 1980s, especially in Britain and the USA, the two groups polarise further. The current focus on low earnings as an indicator of discrimination has distracted attention from the fact that career women confront far more discrimination than secondary workers, because they compete as equals with men, but are often treated as uncommitted secondary earners.

This diversity makes women's employment patterns more interesting, but also much harder to study. Studies of male employment produced only a small labour economics literature until women were pulled into the picture (Blau and Ferber, 1992). Averages and measures of central tendency hide more than they reveal in relation to working women, often concealing divergent trends, as illustrated by trends in occupational segregation. At present, men are forced into a careerist lifestyle even if they would prefer a more even balance between family life and paid work. The absence of choice for men is highlighted by their obligation to work even during recessions, when unemployment becomes a regular experience for many. The pressure on men to seek and obtain employment does not diminish even in these circumstances. Even men who have taken early retirement can be embarrassed at not having a job, even if there is no financial need (Alcock et al, 2003). Women may take refuge, willingly or otherwise, in the alternative identity and social role of homemaker or mother, but this is not possible for men. Research shows that men are less likely to share domestic work when they are unemployed than when they have a job (Pahl, 1984: 269, 273, 276, 327; Brines, 1994). Despite the fact that they have more time available, domestic work poses more of a threat to their male identity than when they have the security of the main income-earning role in the household. Unemployment creates more social and psychological stress for men than women (Hakim, 1982b: 449; Charles and James, 2003).

Sex differentials

Even if sex discrimination were completely eliminated, sex differentials in employment would continue, mainly due to female secondary earners, but also due to women who quit the labour market almost permanently around marriage or childbirth.

This conclusion relies in part on case studies of graduates in professional and managerial occupations, in particular those that are fully integrated (employing men and women in equal numbers), and where sex and race discrimination are eliminated by long-standing labour shortages. These case studies provide strong proof that it is not sex discrimination that is the *principal* cause of sex differences in labour mobility, turnover rates, work experience, hours worked and earnings. Sex discrimination will still be a factor in some occupations (those dominated by one sex for example), and with some employers.

This conclusion is rejected as 'complacent' by feminists who insist that the goal is equality of outcomes, not equality of opportunity, especially in the labour market, and that fully symmetrical family roles are essential for achieving equality in the labour market. Like many other feminist theorists, Phillips (2004) claims that equality of outcomes is the appropriate measure of equality of opportunity, implying that the entire body of social science research on sex differences reviewed in this book simply does not exist, or does not count. Lawyers and political philosophers are most likely to sidestep the relevant research evidence, to rely instead on normative theory and *a priori* arguments. In essence, they argue that all paid occupations should have a 50:50 ratio of men and women, that all household and childcare work should be split 50:50 between men and women, and that convergence on perfectly symmetrical lifestyles is the only outcome that is ethically acceptable. Some go further to demand that differences of social class are also eliminated, along with gender and racial differences. They insist that private life cannot be treated as a separate domain, and should be regulated in the same way as activities in the public sphere. In particular, they problematise the ideas of 'choice' and 'preference', insisting that these are invariably socially constructed and socially determined. Those who disagree with them are effectively accused of false consciousness, *mauvaise foi* and complacency. In effect, they claim superior knowledge of what women want, brushing aside the voices of women themselves.

Preference theory accepts that women's choices were socially determined in the past, and still are in many societies. However, recent social and economic changes are creating a new scenario in some societies, in which women and men can make genuine choices. It does not make sense to argue that no society could ever exist in which preferences and choices were authentic. In this respect, much feminist theory is backward-looking, and not historically informed.

Graduate couples are of particular interest here, because they have incomes that permit wider choices than among less qualified couples. They can afford quality childcare and domestic services, if both spouses choose to pursue careers. They can also afford to live well on just one income. At the same time, graduate jobs are often more demanding jobs, and can require long hours of overtime. Case studies of graduate couples, and of graduates more generally, often reveal larger sex differences, and a greater polarisation of primary and secondary earners, than in jobs lower down the occupational ladder, or at the national level. Women's improved educational qualifications do not eliminate sex differences in achievement. On the contrary, they illuminate the importance of lifestyle preferences and values in outcomes even more clearly.

A pay gap of about 20% seems likely to be an enduring feature of the labour market. Of course, it could be eliminated overnight, simply by paying all workers a single, flat-rate salary, irrespective of qualifications, effort, or hours worked. In the context of capitalist economies with differential pay, and pay incentives, women are unlikely to achieve the same average earnings as men, simply because most women regard themselves as secondary earners, even when they are working full-time in jobs that provide men with a breadwinner wage. Men and women who regard themselves as primary earners invest that much greater time and effort in their work, so we can expect a tiny pay gap in this group. This is already apparent among young workers, childless women, and lesbian women (Blandford, 2003).

Instead of trying to eliminate the pay gap in national statistics, policy should target specific areas where sex discrimination survives. The substantial pay gap in higher grade and graduate jobs is an obvious target, especially in fields where tasks and performance are nebulous enough to conceal an unthinking bias in favour of male employees.

Feminism and public attitude

As noted in Chapter 1, stereotypes of male and female personality and behaviour are well-informed: they match social science research findings pretty closely. Overall, the media do a good job of keeping people informed of new research findings, and stereotypes have changed a good deal. In contrast, feminist theory today seems to be disconnected from the huge stream of new social science research evidence on women's work produced in the last two or three decades. There also appears to be a gulf between public opinion and feminism, or as some see it, feminism gets a bad press these days.

Feminists remain a minority group. In the USA, for example, only one-quarter of women and one in eight men identify themselves as feminist (Schnittker et al, 2003). On the other hand, feminist ideas and expectations have become received wisdom, 'common sense', within public opinion. Today, any departure from gender-neutral treatment is readily identified as objectionable, especially by young women (Antecol and Kuhn, 2000). On every available objective measure, young women suffer far less discrimination than older women; indeed they benefit from substantial *advantages* in the labour market, compared to older women. However, younger women are more sensitive to differential treatment, and raise objections more readily.

At the same time, younger women do not share the same ideas and values as older women, even when they claim feminist identities (Schnittker et al, 2003). The second wave of feminism produced a cohort of (now older) women with specific social attitudes that are not shared by younger feminists. In addition, feminist attitudes do not shape views on the sexual division of labour in the family. The authors conclude that there is a decreasing consensus among younger cohorts about what feminism entails. Generational differences are pronounced (Schnittker *et al*, 2003).

Research on trends in public opinion does not show (as some have claimed) a steady shift towards a preference for symmetrical roles at home and in the workplace. In fact, there are no stable trends in sex-role ideology (Hakim, 2000: 85–94). It is more appropriate to interpret changes in social attitudes as reflecting increasing *tolerance* for women's diverse lifestyle choices, including full-time careers as one option. Public opinion polls and social attitude surveys generally collect data on public morality rather than on personal preferences, on what is good for society in general, rather than what is preferred by the respondent for their own life (Hakim, 2003b; 2004). What may appear to be increasing personal interest in careers among women is in reality increasing tolerance of working women and career women. This is why Scott and Duncombe (1991) were unable to produce an overall traditional versus egalitarian gender-role index with data for the USA and Britain. Attitudes are more complex than that.

Education has the strongest impact on attitudes and values, generally producing increasing tolerance and liberalism (Davis, 1982). As populations become better-educated, there is a general rise in tolerance in societies, that is, acceptance of different lifestyle choices, of differences in ascribed characteristics, of differences in political beliefs (Evans, 2002). Conflicting beliefs and disliked viewpoints are tolerated rather than challenged. Indeed, De Graaf and Evans (1996) argue that the swing towards postmaterialistic values in modern societies is in reality a swing towards the liberalism and tolerance that results from an increasingly educated population. Thus, we would argue that it is tolerance that is reflected in social attitude survey findings on widespread acceptance of working mothers, not necessarily a personal choice of this lifestyle.

This explains why we now see many cases of women who have achieved the highest ranks in management, politics or the professions, voluntarily resigning from their jobs to spend time with their young children (Moen, 2003: 1). Some become full-time mothers for a few years; others turn to part-time self-employment to gain more time flexibility, and more free time. This is a choice that is inconceivable for most prime age men, and inconceivable also for older career women who came of age during the second wave of feminism. Younger women believe they have choices, and they are using the freedom to choose. Eventually, men will catch up. At present, young women, even when immensely successful in the labour market, often prefer family work, even if this confirms stereotypes about women attaching greater importance to relationships and to private life than to success in the public sphere.

Political scientists study the core beliefs and values (such as equality versus freedom) that structure and inform all other, more volatile, political attitudes, evaluations of politicians, and policy dispositions (Feldman, 1988). Core beliefs and values may not be sufficiently well-organised to constitute an ideology, but they still provide the central framework for people's thinking about politics. Obviously, there are rough edges, contradictions and inconsistencies in day-to-day thinking. Similarly, sex-role ideology and a preference for a competitive career in the public sphere or a life centred on home and family, are core values and beliefs among women, that inform more volatile day-to-day attitudes, opinions, and choices. We can expect contradictions and inconsistencies, but this does not invalidate the idea of core values. At present, social attitude surveys pay little attention to women's core values and personal preferences. Feminist thought seems to ignore them altogether, largely because modern feminist political theory generally ignores social science research evidence, especially research on women's position in the labour market.

Rethinking patriarchy and male dominance

The major theoretical contribution of modern feminism has been to elaborate the concept of patriarchy, and attempt to explain the success of patriarchy.

Goldberg's theory of patriarchy and male dominance rests on the idea that men are without malice towards women. Faced with a race, men run harder than women, and win the top prizes more often. He explains the sex difference in competitiveness and aggression as driven by psychophysiological factors within the boundaries set by socialisation processes. Recent research on the impact of testosterone and other hormones supports his thesis. But it also shows that high testosterone, relative to the female average, has the same impact on women as it does on men. Within-sex variations are important for women as well as men, and influence behaviour. Male high achievers do not invariably have high testosterone; testosterone seems to matter more in occupations with a large element of 'public performance', such as politicians and actors; and high testosterone increases risk-taking, so can be disadvantageous. It is not yet clear whether within-sex variation is more, or less, important than between-sex variation. Goldberg's thesis has yet to be fully proven as a sufficient explanation for the subordinate position of women throughout history.

Hartmann's and Walby's theories of patriarchy imply a streak of collective malice in men which seeks to ensure that the male *team* always wins the race, so that women are kept from the prize, by fair means or foul. But neither Hartmann nor Walby provide any explanation for the male malice that is implicit in their idea of patriarchy. Why should men seek to put women down? Hartmann and Walby describe mechanisms but not motives. Even Walby's (1990) most sophisticated account is essentially just description (Fine, 1992: 42). As Goldberg points out (1993: 148), and Bryson (1992: 188) admits, patriarchy theory has so far failed to identify a cause for patriarchy, male dominance and male solidarity. The second problem with the Hartmann-Walby theory of patriarchy is that the historical evidence just does not support many of the central elements of the argument. For example, women's earnings were kept lower than men's by openly paying women less for the same job, sometimes only half as much, not as a result of occupational segregation.

Although it has attracted little attention among feminists (Bryson, 1992: 187), Lerner's (1986) historically-based theory of patriarchy has the virtue of simplicity, and is consistent with the evidence. She argues that men have always sought to control women's sexuality and childbearing, in order to safeguard the inheritance of private property. (In other words, the key problem was the fact that a man could never be certain that a child was his, in the way women were certain.) Male control of women's paid work, and other activities outside the home, was an accidental side-effect, not the main aim. This is consistent with Humphries' (1987) exploration of the origins of occupational segregation in the late 19th century: the aim was the physical segregation of men and women in the workplace, rather than economic segregation. Lerner's theory suggests that Hartmann and Walby were wrong to focus on women's position in the labour market, rather than family life. Lerner provides a clear and forceful explanation for the development of patriarchy, and at the same time opens the door to change in the future. DNA tests to check the paternity of babies avoid the need for men to control women's movements and activities directly, so as to ensure valid maintenance and inheritance claims. If Lerner's theory is right, patriarchy is already on its way out in modern societies, due to DNA testing rather than equal opportunities laws. However, a residual form of patriarchy could remain, due to the sex differences Goldberg underlines.

If Goldberg is right in saying men bear no malice towards women, then, arguably, patriarchal institutions and social processes are not inevitable; they are malleable and reversible. Male solidarity rests on the natural instinct for people with similar interests, similar styles of behaviour and conversation to group together. Male managers select male applicants for jobs because they feel comfortable with them, know they can communicate effectively, will understand each other even if they disagree at times. Women are visibly different, talk differently, behave differently, so can be harder to understand or trust as colleagues. This explanation places the emphasis on social styles, communication styles and life interests providing the basis for the assumption of shared interests, and hence a distinct bias towards persons of the same sex as colleagues and friends in the workplace, as well as non-work contexts. This turns our attention to the source of such well-defined differences in personal style.

Clearly, women as mothers play a large role in laying the foundations of sex-role ideologies and behaviours. The separation of the workplace from the home in modern industrial society means that children do not have any regular access to the labour market, to roles in the workplace and their father's activities. All children witness the roles of men and women in the home, in particular the female role. Women are the first to give dolls to their daughters and guns to their sons, to encourage independence in their sons and conformity in their daughters. It is mothers who create homemakers and mothers in their own image. Women treat their children as extensions of themselves, especially girl children. Whether they like them or not, men treat their children as independent social beings, who may well resist attempts to influence or persuade. Gilligan emphasises women's voice, insists it is benign rather than incapacitating, and claims it would be revolutionary to incorporate women's voice in the management of society. Another view is that it is precisely this women's voice, so sensitive to other voices, that handicaps girls and women, allowing them to be easily swayed by others, initially their mothers, later men, in a world view in which everything is relative anyway, so why should women insist on their interests taking priority? Male solidarity wins because women are swayed by the dominant male voice, are uncertain in their judgments and, ultimately, because women are divided in their preferences and interests. Even feminists cannot agree on the main goals (Bryson, 1992: 263).

The key reason why male solidarity and male organisation are so effective (despite the fact that men are not more able than women) is that women are diverse and divided. If men are the enemy, women make a hopeless adversary. Men gain a huge structural advantage from women's diversity. The heterogeneity of female preferences – for a life centred on the family, or a career, or some combination of the two – opens up a fatal weakness in women's representation of their interests. The trouble is that there are at least two sets of interests, as reflected in the two women's movements in the USA, for example, with paler parallels in Britain. With the opposition so fundamentally divided *within itself*, men race to the winning line without much imagination, effort or talent. This bothers employment career women, who see men of average ability succeeding in occupations (especially management) where women barely get through the door. It is entirely acceptable to women following the homemaker career, who are spending their spouse's earnings and profits. Women's failure to organise, and lack of solidarity, *vis a vis* men is due to their having two avenues of upward mobility and achievement in life, through the marriage market or through the labour market. At present, men are limited to the labour market, though that might conceivably change, if employment career women learn to value toyboys and househusbands in the same way that men value trophy wives and housewives. Looking at it from the male perspective, the bias is in favour of women who become homemakers. Men see housewives living a life of relative comfort and low stress, winning positions of financial dependency without necessarily displaying much competence, effort or talent for the job of wife and mother. This bothers employment career men, who see women succeeding in a role where men fail even to get through the door. Some men would make far better parents than women do, especially for adolescent children, but women currently have a monopoly on the homemaker role and, to a large extent, on parenting, while the male monopoly on employment careers has been declared unlawful.

Female heterogeneity of lifestyle preferences and values provides the missing link between the concept of patriarchy (since it is not really a theory) and Goldberg's theory of male dominance. Male patriarchal solidarity and male organisation to promote male interests are disproportionately successful because women are sharply divided in their life goals, activities and interests.

Patriarchy in the sense of male institutions that dominate society, and hence structure women's lives and activities, could thus be a historically specific social development that is already fading away in modern societies. Patriarchy in the sense of male dominance in public life and in private relationships could continue, because of the sex differences in competitiveness noted by Goldberg and social psychologists, and the sex differences in mate selection preferences and in private heterosexual relationships noted by numerous social scientists (including Goldberg, Buss, Gerson, Bozon and Héran, and Hakim, *inter alia*). These differences can be attenuated by socialisation processes and cultural pressures that disregard them. Hofstede (1980; 1991) identified societies as having a more male or more female culture and values, which exaggerate or minimise sex differences respectively. However, it seems that these particular sex differences are unlikely to disappear completely. On the other hand, these differences are balanced by a huge array of other characteristics where there are no sex differences at all, such as ability and cognitive functioning. So in occupations where competitiveness, aggressive energy and public performance are not important, we might eventually see women rise to the top jobs as easily as men.

One-fifth of the workforce now works in integrated occupations that employ equal numbers of men and women. Certain professional occupations are already fully integrated, but it is notable that they tend to be occupations without a major 'public performance' element, such as pharmacist, personnel manager, and administrator. Occupations that reward aggressive energy and competitiveness, and are most demanding, in terms of long hours and so on, will probably continue to be dominated by men, with women a minority of one-third, or even one-quarter. Senior management, especially in the private sector, is one field where women are likely to remain a minority, even in the absence of sex discrimination. One factor here is the problem of women being more unco-operative with female bosses than male bosses: this hinders women's career progression, even though the problem ceases to matter at the higher levels of hierarchies, which are male-dominated.

Explaining women's subordination

Our reformulated version of patriarchy theory is consistent with the historical evidence, and provides a powerful explanation for *why* men sought to control and subordinate women, as well as how they did it. The Western ideal of bourgeois domestic femininity can now be seen as an updated 19th century version of the older ideal of the secluded wife and mother who rarely left her home, a higher status ideal that was found from China to Europe. Our reformulated patriarchy theory is also historically-specific, and outdated, in the context of prosperous modern societies. It remains useful for understanding women's subordination in less developed countries. In particular, it points out how women's employment can be made socially acceptable in such societies, by ensuring it takes place in a safe setting, with no risk of heterosexual liaisons.

Goldberg's theory of male dominance and Becker's rational choice theory have a more universal application. Both are supported by substantial amounts of evidence, and can be seen as complementary. Becker points out the rationality of the family division of labour, with one spouse specialising in market work and the other specialising in family work, in terms of the mutual benefits of increased efficiency and outputs. However, he cannot explain why it is usually the male who goes out to work and the female who stays at home with the babies. Goldberg provides an answer here, to explain why men will always dominate competitive activities in the public sphere, while women will concentrate on communal, sharing and caring activities in the private sphere. Childless couples provide a strategic test here, showing that the conventional family division of labour persists even when there are no childcare responsibilities to constrain women's choices. The principal weakness of these two theories is that they assume women and men are homogeneous groups, that everyone makes the same choices. There is evidence this is not so.

A report on the 50 wealthiest people in Britain found that there were more women than men in the group. The explanation is simple. Some women, like men, are wealthy through their own efforts, as writers, entertainers, or entrepreneurs. Some women are the wealthy widows of men who were high achievers. Women can still achieve positions of wealth and status through the marriage market, as well as through the labour market. Women today still use both, sometimes in combination. Men can only use the labour market.

Preference theory builds on rational choice theory, human capital theory, the theory of male dominance, chaos theory, and person-centred analysis, to present a predictive theory of likely trends in the future. It is thus consistent with earlier theories, but looks forward rather than backward. In addition, it is historically situated. It specifies the social and economic conditions necessary for women to gain genuine choices, and sets out the pattern of preferences that will guide choices in the future. Unlike the other theories, it shows how preferences interact with the social context to produce patterns of female employment that vary between countries, and it allows the possibility of change. The past does not always predict the future.

Looking ahead

Everything may change. Social science research results can give a misleading sense of inevitability: the current pattern of behaviour is readily interpreted as inevitable, institutionally determined and unchangeable rather than volatile, chosen and changeable. Without hard proof of causal connections, contemporary coincidences are nothing more than that. And most research goes no further than contemporary coincidences, especially in the case of multivariate analyses where even the direction of causality is left completely open. However, natural experiments and large-scale real-life social experiments show that there are limits to what social engineering can achieve.

There is nothing 'traditional' about women's restriction to the domestic sphere – quite the contrary. In Britain, women were as likely to be in the workforce in 1871 as in 1971. The domestication of women was a social experiment that did not last even a century, three generations. The Chinese social experiment at encouraging all women into social work outside the home achieved greater success within half a century. However, even in the context of a policy of one child per couple, one-quarter to one-third of women are now inclined to return to the sexual division of labour in the home and drop out of paid work. It appears that the diversity of women's preferences for employment careers or for homemaking careers is a permanent feature which resists attempts to squeeze everyone into a single lifestyle. Public policy has to allow both options, even if it is difficult to design policies that are completely neutral between the two (Hakim, 2000: 223–53). The fact that socialisation processes exist in all societies does not guarantee their success. Like men, women can always say 'No'. Some women are prepared to swim against the current; others prefer to go with the flow. Women's preferences are malleable, to some extent. But on current evidence there is a substantial minority of women (about 20%) who will never want to have and raise children, and there is a substantial minority of women (about 20%) who would prefer to have four or more children and devote their life to family activities mainly. Perhaps public policy should encourage this more efficient division of labour and polarisation of fertility patterns.

Preferences help to determine choices, but they do not predict performance. Women who choose to compete with men in the public arena, not just in the market economy but also in politics and other public activities, will not necessarily have the ability to make it to the top, any more often than men do. Most men do not attain the top positions, even in the absence of discrimination. So it is not a sign of discrimination if equally few women are successful. Similarly, women who choose not to join the rat race may have to confront the possibility that they are no better as mothers and homemakers than they were (or would be) as workers. One of the great myths is that all women have a natural and benign talent for nurturance, that the mother's influence in never noxious. From a feminist perspective, it is arguable that mothers should not be allowed to raise girls or boys beyond the age of about 12 years. Adolescents of both sexes need to break away from the mother to achieve autonomy and adult identities, not only boys as assumed by Chodorow (1978).

This review suggests that research should now focus on particular issues in women's employment. The invisible, and often unconscious, social processes that prevent women from obtaining, and flourishing, in senior-grade posts merit far more attention than they have so far received. More generally, we should look more closely at the work and life histories of women committed to full-time continuous employment, including those in less prestigious occupations than the easily identified professional and managerial women, and including studies of sex differences in earnings. Research on occupational segregation should now move away from the long-standing concern with historical trends, and fruitless obsession with measurement issues, to address the causes and consequences of occupational segregation, its meaning for different groups of women, and whether its meaning for men is changing. Integrated or mixed occupations, employing both men and women, are of particular interest, both from a theoretical and a policy perspective. Lessons for the future must surely be found most often in this minority group of occupations in the workforce. Most challenging of all is the relationship between vertical job segregation, movement between segregated and integrated occupations across the life cycle, and the three employment profiles identified in Chapter 5. We need to know if the highest achievements are accessible to, even if restricted to, women following the male employment profile, or whether it still takes more than that to succeed in male-dominated careers. There are now enough women sweeping into senior positions in the labour market, if not in the political arena, to enable us to consider general patterns rather than uniquely individual cases. We also need more qualitative research on the difficulties encountered by female managers with *female* subordinates, a problem that has been overlooked because it does not fit assumptions about sex discrimination.

The key conclusion is that the 21st century is bringing significant restructuring of women's social and economic position. The report on the 1980 Women and Employment Survey concluded that, despite important changes in women's attitudes to employment since Hunt's 1965 survey, work was still less central to women's lives than to men's; that most women were still primarily homemakers and secondary wage earners, while husbands were primary wage earners; that a majority of women regarded a home and children as women's prime aim and main job, so that children took priority over a career; and that there was little evidence that women saw themselves becoming equal or joint wage earners on the same terms as their husbands (Martin and Roberts, 1984: 191–92). All these conclusions remain valid today in the early 21st century, but only for one section of the female adult population. The polarisation process that started in the 1980s has produced a sharp divide between these home-centred women and the minority of career-oriented women for whom employment is just as central to their lives as it is for men; who do not regard a home and children as their primary aims in life; and who see themselves as independent wage earners whether or not they marry. This means that there will always be evidence to support both the gloomy view and the optimistic view of women's position in the labour market. Modern industrial society creates the conditions for women to make genuine choices between two polarised lifestyles, so their preferences become an important new social factor, potentially over-riding the demographic, social, economic and institutional factors that have historically been so important. Difference and diversity are now the key features of the female population, with the likelihood of increasing polarisation between work-centred and home-centred women in the 21st century. And in a civilised society difference and diversity are positively valued, and welcomed.

Bibliography

Agassi JB (1989) 'Theories of gender equality: lessons from the kibbutz', *Gender and Society*, 3: 160–86.

Albrecht J, Björklund A and Vroman S (2003) 'Is there a glass ceiling in Sweden?', *Journal of Labor Economics*, 21: 145–77.

Alcock P, Beatty C, Fothergill S, Macmillan R and Yeandle S (2003) *Work to Welfare: How Men Become Detached from the Labour Market*, Cambridge: Cambridge University Press.

Alexander MJ and Mohanty CT (eds) (1997) *Feminist Genealogies, Colonial Legacies, Democratic Futures*, New York: Routledge.

Allen S and Wolkowitz C (1987) *Homeworking: Myths and Realities*, London: Macmillan.

Almond GA and Verba S (1965) *The Civic Culture: Political Attitudes and Democracy in Five Nations*, Boston and Toronto: Little Brown.

Althauser RP and Kalleberg AL (1981) 'Firms, occupations and the structure of labour markets' in Berg I (ed), *Sociological Perspectives on Labour Markets*, New York: Academic Press.

Alwin DF, Braun M and Scott J (1992) 'The separation of work and the family: attitudes towards women's labour-force participation in Germany, Great Britain and the United States', *European Sociological Review*, 8: 13–37.

Anderson M, Bechhofer F and Gershuny J (eds) (1994) *The Social and Political Economy of the Household*, Oxford: Oxford University Press.

Andorka R (1987) 'Time budgets and their uses', *Annual Review of Sociology*, 13: 149–64.

Anker R (1997) 'Theories of occupational segregation by sex: an overview', *International Labour Review*, 136: 315–39.

Anker R (1998) *Gender and Jobs: Sex Segregation of Occupations in the World*, Geneva: ILO.

Antecol H and Kuhn P (2000) 'Gender as an impediment to labor market success: why do young women report greater harm?', *Journal of Labor Economics*, 18: 702–28.

Anttalainen M-L (1986) *Sukupuolen Mukaan Kahtiajakautuneet Työmarkkinat Pohjois-Maissa* (Gender-based labour market segmentation in the Nordic countries), Working Paper Naistutkimusmonisteita 1: 1986, Helsinki: Tasa-arvoasiain Neuvottlukunta (Council for Equality between Men and Women).

Applebaum E (1987) 'Restructuring work: temporary, part-time and at-home work' in Hartmann HI (ed), *Computer Chips and Paper Clips*, Washington DC: National Academy Press, pp 268–310.

Arber S and Ginn J (1995) 'Gender differences in the relationship between paid employment and informal care', *Work, Employment and Society*, 9: 445–71.

Babcock L and Laschever S (2003) *Women Don't Ask: Negotiation and the Gender Divide*, Princeton NJ: Princeton University Press.

Badinter E (1981) *The Myth of Motherhood: An Historical View of the Maternal Instinct*, trans DeGaris R, London: Souvenir Press.

Baker JG (2002) 'The influx of women into legal professions: an economic analysis', *Monthly Labor Review*, 125/8: 14–24.

Baker P and Eversley J (eds) (2000) *Multilingual Capital*, London: University of Westminster Press.

Barnard C and Hepple B (1999) 'Indirect discrimination: interpreting *Seymour-Smith*', *Cambridge Law Journal*, 58(2): 399–412.

Barron RD and Norris GM (1976) 'Sexual divisions and the dual labour market' in Barker DL and Allen S (eds), *Dependence and Exploitation in Work and Marriage*, London: Longman, pp 47–69.

Bayard K, Hellerstein J, Neumark D and Troske K (2003) 'New evidence on sex segregation and sex differences in wages from matched employee-employer data', *Journal of Labor Economics*, 21: 887–922.

Beatson M (1995) *Labour Market Flexibility*, Research Series No 48, London: Employment Department.

Beatson M and Butcher S (1993) 'Union density across the employed workforce', *Employment Gazette*, 101: 673–89.

Becker GS (1981, 1991) *A Treatise on the Family*, Cambridge MA: Harvard University Press.

Becker GS (1985) 'Human capital, effort and the sexual division of labour', *Journal of Labor Economics*, 3: S33–S58.

Beechey V and Perkins T (1987) *A Matter of Hours: Women, Part-Time Work and the Labour Market*, Cambridge: Polity.

Beller AH (1982) 'Occupational segregation by sex: determinants and changes', *Journal of Human Resources*, 17: 371–92.

Benería L (1981) 'Conceptualising the labour force: the underestimation of women's economic activities', *Journal of Development Studies*, 17: 10–28. Reprinted in Pahl RE (ed), *On Work*, 1988, Oxford: Blackwell, pp 372–91.

Benería L and Sen G (1981) 'Accumulation, reproduction and women's role in economic development: Boserup revisited', *Signs*, 7: 279–98. Reprinted in Pahl RE (ed), *On Work*, 1988, Oxford: Blackwell, pp 355–71.

Bercusson B (1990) 'The European Community's Charter of Fundamental Social Rights of Workers', *Modern Law Review*, 53: 624–42.

Berk R (1983) 'An introduction to sample selection bias in sociological data', *American Sociological Review*, 48: 386–98.

Beutel AM and Marini MM (1995) 'Gender and values', *American Sociological Review*, 60: 436–48.

Bhavnani R (1994) *Black Women in the Labour Market: A Research Review*, Manchester: Equal Opportunities Commission.

Bielby DD and Bielby WT (1984) 'Work commitment, sex-role attitudes and women's employment', *American Sociological Review*, 49: 234–47.

Bielby DD and Bielby WT (1988) 'She works hard for the money: household responsibilities and the allocation of work effort', *American Journal of Sociology*, 93: 1031–59.

Bielby WT and Baron JN (1984) 'A woman's place is with other women: sex segregation within organisations' in Reskin BF (ed), *Sex Segregation in the Workplace: Trends, Explanations, Remedies*, Washington DC: National Academy Press, pp 27–55.

Birrell B, Rapson V and Hourigan C (2004) *Men and Women Apart: The Decline of Partnering in Australia*, Melbourne: Monash University Centre for Population and Urban Research.

Bittman M and Wajcman J (2000) 'The rush hour: the character of leisure time and gender equity', *Social Forces*, 79: 165–89.

Black D, Haviland A, Sanders S and Taylor L (2003) 'Gender wage disparities among the highly educated', paper presented to the Centre for Economic Performance, London School of Economics.

Blandford JM (2003) 'The nexus of sexual orientation and gender in the determination of earnings', *Industrial and Labor Relations Review*, 56: 622–42.

Blanpain R and Rojot J (eds) (1997) *Legal and Contractual Limitations to Working Time in the European Union*, Leuven: Peeters Press.

Blau FD and Ferber MA (1992) *The Economics of Women, Men and Work*, Englewood Cliffs NJ: Prentice-Hall.

Blau FD and Kahn LM (2003) 'Understanding international differences in the gender pay gap', *Journal of Labor Economics*, 21: 106–44.

Blaxall M and Reagan B (eds) (1976) *Women and the Workplace: The Implications of Occupational Segregation*, Chicago and London: University of Chicago Press. Reprint of supplement to Spring 1976 issue of *Signs*.

Blitz RC (1974) 'Women in the professions: 1870–1970', *Monthly Labor Review*, 97, May, 34–39.

Blossfeld H-P (1987) 'Labour market entry and the sexual segregation of careers in the Federal Republic of Germany', *American Journal of Sociology*, 93: 89–118.

Blossfeld H-P and Mayer KU (1988) 'Labor market segmentation in the Federal Republic of Germany: an empirical study of segmentation theories from a life course perspective', *European Sociological Review*, 4: 123–40.

Blossfeld H-P and Hakim C (eds) (1997) *Between Equalization and Marginalization: Women Working Part-Time in Europe and the USA*, Oxford: Oxford University Press.

Blossfeld H-P and Drobnic S (eds) (2001) *Careers of Couples in Contemporary Society: From Male Breadwinner to Dual-Earner Families*, Oxford: Oxford University Press.

Bonacich E (1994) 'A theory of ethnic antagonism: the split labor market' in Grusky DB (ed), *Social Stratification: Class, Race and Gender in Sociological Perspective*, Boulder CO: Westview Press, pp 474–86. Originally published in *American Sociological Review*, 1972.

Bonney N (1988) 'Dual earning couples: trends of change in Great Britain', *Work, Employment and Society*, 2: 89–102.

Bonney N and Reinach E (1993) 'Housework reconsidered: the Oakley thesis twenty years later', *Work, Employment and Society*, 7: 615–27.

Boraas S and Rodgers WM (2003) 'How does gender play a role in the earnings gap? and update', *Monthly Labor Review*, 126/3: 9–15.

Boris E and Daniels CR (eds) (1989) *Homework: Historical and Contemporary Perspectives on Paid Labor at Home*, Urbana and Chicago: University of Illinois Press.

Bosch G, Dawkins P and Michon F (1994) *Times are Changing: Working Time in 14 Industrialised Countries*, Geneva: International Labour Office International Institute for Labor Studies.

Bose CE (1985) *Jobs and Gender: A Study of Occupational Prestige*, New York: Praeger.

Bose CE (1987) 'Devaluing women's work: the undercount of women's employment in 1900 and 1980' in Bose C et al (eds), *The Hidden Aspects of Women's Work*, New York: Praeger, pp 95–115.

Bose CE (2001) *Women in 1900: Gateway to the Political Economy of the 20th Century*, Philadelphia: Temple University Press.

Bose CE and Rossi PH (1983) 'Gender and jobs: prestige standings of occupations as affected by gender', *American Sociological Review*, 48: 316–30.

Boserup E (1970) *Women's Role in Economic Development*, London: Allen & Unwin.

Bottero W (1992) 'The changing face of the professions? Gender and explanations of women's entry into pharmacy', *Work, Employment and Society*, 6: 329–46.

Bowlus AJ (1997) 'A search interpretation of male-female wage differentials', *Journal of Labor Economics*, 15: 625–57.

Bozon M and Héran F (1988) 'La découverte du conjoint – II – les scènes de rencontre dans l'espace social', *Population*, 43: 121–50.

Bozon M and Héran F (1990a) 'Les femmes et l'écart d'âge entre conjoints: une domination consentie – I – Types d'union et attentes en matiere d'écart d'âge', *Population*, 45: 327–60.

Bozon M and Héran F (1990b) 'Les femmes et l'écart d'âge entre conjoints: une domination consentie – II – modes d'entrée dans la vie adulte et représentations du conjoint', *Population*, 45: 565–602.

Bradley H (1989) *Men's Work, Women's Work: A Sociological History of the Sexual Division of Labour in Employment*, Cambridge: Polity Press.

Brannen J (1991) 'Money, marriage and motherhood: dual earner households after maternity leave' in Arber S and Gilbert N (eds), *Women and Working Lives*, London: Macmillan, pp 54–70.

Breen R and García-Peñalosa C (2002) 'Bayesian learning and gender segregation', *Journal of Labor Economics*, 20: 899–922.

Brewer MB and Brown RJ (1998) 'Intergroup relations' in Gilbert DT, Fiske ST and Lindzey G (eds), *Handbook of Social Psychology*, New York: McGraw-Hill, pp 554–94.

Brines J (1994) 'Economic dependency, gender and the division of labour at home', *American Journal of Sociology*, 100: 652–88.

Britton M and Edison N (1986) 'The changing balance of the sexes in England and Wales, 1851–2001', *Population Trends*, 46: 22–25.

Brown C and Corcoran M (1997) 'Sex-based differences in school content and the male/female wage gap', *Journal of Labor Economics*, 15: 431–65.

Bruegel I (1979) 'Women as a reserve army of labour: a note on recent British experience', *Feminist Review*, 3: 12–23.

Bruyn-Hundt M (1996) *The Economics of Unpaid Work*, Amsterdam: Thesis Publishers.

Bryson V (1992) *Feminist Political Theory*, London: Macmillan.

Buckley JE (1985) 'Wage differences among workers in the same job and establishment', *Monthly Labor Review*, 108/3: 11–16.

Budig MJ (2002) 'Male advantage and the gender composition of jobs: who rides the glass escalator?', *Social Problems* 49: 258–77.

Bulman J (2003) 'Patterns of pay: results of the 2003 New Earnings Survey', *Labour Market Trends*, 111: 601–12.

Burchell B and Rubery J (1994) 'Divided women: labour market segmentation and gender segregation' in Scott AM (ed), *Gender Segregation and Social Change*, Oxford: Oxford University Press, pp 80–120.

Burgess S and Rees H (1994) 'Lifetime jobs and transient jobs: job tenure in Britain 1975–1991', *mimeo*, University of Bristol, Department of Economics.

Buss DM (1989) 'Sex differences in human mate preferences: evolutionary hypotheses tested in 37 cultures', *Behavioural and Brain Sciences*, 12: 1–49.

Buss DM (1995) 'Psychological sex differences: origins through sexual selection', *American Psychologist*, 50: 164–68.

Butcher S and Hart D (1995) 'An analysis of working time 1979–1994', *Employment Gazette*, 103: 211–22.

Butler J (1990) *Gender Trouble: Feminism and the Subversion of Identity*, New York: Routledge.

Butler J (1993) *Bodies That Matter: On the Discursive Limits of 'Sex'*, New York: Routledge.

Cain GG (1986) 'The economic analysis of labour market discrimination: a survey' in Ashenfelter O and Layard R (eds), *Handbook of Labor Economics* Amsterdam: North Holland, pp 693–785.

Cairns RB, Bergman LR and Kagan J (eds) (1998) *Methods and Models for Studying the Individual*, London and Thousand Oaks CA: Sage.

Callender C, Millward N, Lissenburgh S and Forth J (1997) *Maternity Rights and Benefits in Britain*, DSS Research Series No 67, London: Stationery Office for Department of Social Security.

Campbell B (1993) *Goliath: Britain's Dangerous Places*, London: Methuen.

Campbell E (1985) *The Childless Marriage*, London and New York: Tavistock.

Cantillon B, Ghysels J, Mussche N and Van Dam R (2001) 'Female employment differences, poverty and care provisions', *European Societies*, 3: 447–69.

Caputo RK and Cianni M (2001) 'Correlates of voluntary vs involuntary part-time employment among US women', *Gender, Work and Organisation*, 8(3): 311–25.

Carrier S (1995) 'Family status and career situation for professional women', *Work, Employment and Society*, 9: 343–58.

Cassirer N and Reskin B (2000) 'High hopes: organizational position, employment experiences, and women's and men's promotion aspirations', *Work and Occupations*, 27: 438–63.

Castle B (1993) *Fighting All The Way*, London: Macmillan.

Chamberlain E and Purdie E (1992) 'The Quarterly Labour Force Survey: a new dimension to labour market statistics', *Employment Gazette*, 100: 483–90.

Charles M (1992) 'Cross-national variations in occupational sex segregation', *American Sociological Review*, 57: 483–502.

Charles M (1998) 'Structure, culture, and sex segregation in Europe', *Research in Social Stratification and Mobility*, 16: 89–116.

Charles M and Grusky DB (1995) 'Models for describing the underlying structure of sex segregation', *American Journal of Sociology*, 100: 931–71.

Charles N and James E (2003) 'The gender dimensions of job insecurity in a local labour market', *Work, Employment and Society*, 17: 531–52.

Chauvin KW and Ash RA (1994) 'Gender earnings differentials in total pay, base pay and contingent pay', *Industrial and Labor Relations Review*, 47: 634–49.

Chiplin B (1976) 'Sexual discrimination: are there any lessons from criminal behaviour?', *Applied Economics*, 8: 121–33.

Chiplin B and Sloane PJ (1974) 'Sexual discrimination in the labour market', *British Journal of Industrial Relations*, 12: 371–402.

Chiplin B and Sloane PJ (1976) 'Male-female earnings differences: a further analysis', *British Journal of Industrial Relations*, 14: 77–81.

Chodorow N (1978) *The Reproduction of Mothering*, Berkeley: University of California Press.

Christiansen SL and Palkovitz R (2001) 'Why the good provider role still matters', *Journal of Family Issues*, 22: 84–106.

Clark AE (1997) 'Job satisfaction and gender: why are women so happy at work?', *Labour Economics*, 4: 341–72.

Clogg CC, Eliason SR and Wahl RJ (1990) 'Labour market experiences and labor-force outcomes', *American Journal of Sociology*, 95: 1536–76.

Cockburn C (1983) *Brothers: Male Dominance and Technological Change*, London: Pluto Press.

Cohen PN (2002) 'Cohabitation and the declining marriage premium for men', *Work and Occupations*, 29: 346–63.

Cohen PN and Huffman ML (2003) 'Individuals, jobs and labor markets: the devaluation of women's work', *American Sociological Review*, 68: 443–63.

Cohn S (1985) *The Process of Occupational Sex-Typing: The Feminisation of Clerical Work in Great Britain*, Philadelphia: Temple University Press.

Cole S and Fiorentine R (1991) 'Discrimination against women in science: the confusion of outcome with process' in Zuckerman H, Cole JR and Bruer JT (eds), *The Outer Circle: Women in the Scientific Community*, New York: WW Norton, pp 205–26.

Coleman MT and Pencavel J (1993) 'Trends in market work behaviour of women since 1940', *Industrial and Labor Relations Review*, 46: 653–77.

Connelly R (1991) 'The importance of child care costs to women's decision-making' in Blau DM (ed), *The Economics of Childcare*, New York: Russell Sage Foundation.

Corcoran L (1995) 'Trade union membership and recognition: 1994 Labour Force Survey data', *Employment Gazette*, 103: 191–203.

Corcoran ME (1979) 'Work experience, labor force withdrawal and women's wages: empirical results using the 1976 Panel Study of Income Dynamics' in Lloyd CB, Andrews ES and Gilroy CL (eds), *Women in the Labor Market*, New York: Columbia University Press, pp 216–45.

Corcoran M and Duncan GJ (1979) 'Work history, labor force attachment and earnings differences between the races and sexes', *Journal of Human Resources*, 14: 3–20.

Corcoran M, Duncan GJ and Ponza M (1984) 'Work experience, job segregation and wages' in Reskin BF (ed), *Sex Segregation in the Workplace: Trends, Explanations, Remedies*, Washington DC: National Academy Press, pp 171–91.

Corti L and Dex S (1995) 'Informal carers and employment', *Employment Gazette*, 103: 101–07.

Cousins C (1998) 'Social exclusion in Europe: paradigms of social disadvantage in Germany, Spain, Sweden and the United Kingdom', *Policy and Politics*, 26: 128–46.

Cragg A and Dawson T (1981) *Qualitative Research Among Homeworkers*, Research Paper No 21, London: Department of Employment.

Cragg A and Dawson T (1984) *Unemployed Women: A Study of Attitudes and Experiences*, Research Paper No 47, London: Department of Employment.

Crompton R (1997) *Women and Work in Modern Britain*, Oxford: Oxford University Press.

Crompton R and Harris F (1998) 'Explaining women's employment patterns: orientations to work revisited', *British Journal of Sociology*, 49: 148–70.

Crompton R and Sanderson K (1990) *Gendered Jobs and Social Change*, London: Unwin Hyman.

Crull P (1987) 'Searching for the causes of sexual harassment: an examination of two prototypes' in Bose C, Feldberg R and Sokoloff N (eds), *Hidden Aspects of Women's Work*, New York and London: Praeger, pp 225–44.

Cully M, O'Reilly A, Millward N and Forth J (1998) *The 1998 Workplace Employee Relations Survey: First Findings*, London: Department of Trade and Industry.

Cully M, Woodland S, O'Reilly A and Dix J (1999) *Britain at Work*, London: Routledge.

Curtice J (1993) 'Satisfying work – if you can get it' in Jowell R (ed), *International Social Attitudes: the 10th BSA Report*, Aldershot: Gower.

Dabbs JM (2000) *Heroes, Rogues, and Lovers: Testosterone and Behaviour*, New York: McGraw-Hill.

Dale A and Egerton M (1997) *Highly Educated Women: Evidence from the National Child Development Study*, RS25, London: Department for Education and Employment.

Daly PA (1981) 'Unpaid family workers: long-term decline continues', *Monthly Labor Review*, 105/10: 3–5.

Darity WA and Mason PL (1998) 'Evidence on discrimination in employment: codes of colour, codes of gender', *Journal of Economic Perspectives*, 12: 63–90.

Davidson MJ and Cooper CL (eds) (1993) *European Women in Business and Management*, London: Paul Chapman.

Davies C (1980) 'Making sense of the census in Britain and the USA: the changing occupational classification and the position of nurses', *Sociological Review*, 28: 581–609.

Davies P and Freedland M (1984) *Labour Law: Text and Materials*, 2nd edn, London: Weidenfeld & Nicolson.

Davies P and Freedland M (1993) *Labour Legislation and Public Policy*, Oxford: Clarendon.

Davis JA (1982) 'Achievement variables and class cultures: family, schooling, job, and forty-nine dependent variables in the cumulative GSS', *American Sociological Review*, 47: 569–86.

Deaux K and LaFrance M (1998) 'Gender' in Gilbert DT, Fiske ST and Lindzey G (eds), *Handbook of Social Psychology*, New York: McGraw-Hill, pp 788–827.

De Graaf ND and Evans G (1996) 'Why are the young more postmaterialist? A cross-national analysis of individual and contextual influences on postmaterialist values', *Comparative Political Studies*, 28: 608–35.

De Grazia R (1980) 'Clandestine employment: a problem of our times', *International Labour Review*, 119: 549–63.

De Grazia R (1984) *Clandestine Employment: The Situation in Industrialised Market Economy Countries*, Geneva: ILO.

de Neubourg C (1985) 'Part-time work: an international quantitative comparison', *International Labour Review*, 124: 559–76.

Department of Employment (1992) 'Women and the labour market', *Employment Gazette*, 100/9: 433–59.

Desai S and Waite LJ (1991) 'Women's employment during pregnancy and after the first birth: occupational characteristics and work commitment', *American Sociological Review*, 56: 551–66.

Deutsch FM, Lassier JB, and Servic LJ (1993) 'Husbands at home: predictors of paternal participation in childcare and housework', *Journal of Personality and Social Psychology*, 65: 1154–66.

de Vaus D and McAllister I (1991) 'Gender and work orientation: values and satisfaction in Western Europe', *Work and Occupations*, 18: 72–93.

Dex S (1985) *The Sexual Division of Work*, Brighton: Harvester Press.

Dex S (1987) *Women's Occupational Mobility: A Lifetime Perspective*, London: Macmillan.

Disney R and Szyszczak EM (1989) 'Part-time work: reply to Catherine Hakim', *Industrial Law Journal*, 18: 223–29.

Dolton P and Vignoles A (2002a) 'The returns on post-compulsory school mathematics study', *Economica*, 69: 113–41.

Dolton P and Vignoles A (2002b) 'Is a broader curriculum better?', *Economics of Education Review*, 21: 415–29.

Downes D and Rock P (1988) *Understanding Deviance*, Oxford: Clarendon.

Drew E, Emerek R and Mahon E (eds) (1998) *Women, Work and Family in Europe*, London and New York: Routledge.

Dubin R (1956) 'Industrial workers' worlds: a study of the central life interests of industrial workers', *Social Problems*, 3: 131–42.

Duncan OD and Duncan B (1955) 'A methodological analysis of segregation indices', *American Sociological Review*, 20: 200–17.

Dunnell K (1979) *Family Formation 1976*, London: HMSO.

Dupre MT, Hussmanns R and Mehran F (1987) 'The concept and boundary of economic activity for the measurement of the economically active population' in *ILO Bulletin of Labour Statistics*, No 1987-3, Geneva: ILO, pp IX–XVIII.

Eagly AH (1995) 'The science and politics of comparing women and men', *American Psychologist*, 50: 145–58 (with comments by Hyde and Plant, Marecek, and Buss, and response by Eagly, pp 159–71).

Eagly AH and Crowley M (1986) 'Gender and helping behaviour: a meta-analytic review of the social psychological literature', *Psychological Bulletin*, 100: 283–308.

Edgeworth FY (1922) 'Equal pay to men and women for equal work', *Economic Journal*, 32: 431–57.

Eggebeen DJ and Hawkins AJ (1990) 'Economic need and wives' employment', *Journal of Family Issues*, 11: 48–66.

Ehrenberg RG (1989) 'Empirical consequences of comparable worth' in Hill MA and Killingsworth MR (eds), *Comparable Worth – Analyses and Evidence*, Ithaca NY: ILR Press, pp 90–116.

Elias P (1988) 'Family formation, occupational mobility and part-time work' in Hunt, A (ed), *Women and Paid Work*, London: Macmillan, pp 83–104.

Elias P and Gregory M (1994) *The Changing Structure of Occupations and Earnings in Great Britain, 1975–1990 – An Analysis Based on the New Earnings Survey Panel Dataset*, Research Series No 27, London: Employment Department.

Elias P and Main B (1982) *Women's Working Lives: Evidence from the National Training Survey*, Coventry: University of Warwick Institute for Employment Research.

Elias P and White M (1991) *Recruitment in Local Labour Markets*, Research Paper No 86, London: Employment Department.

Ellingsæter AL (2003) 'The complexity of family policy reform', *European Societies*, 5: 419–43.

Ellis E (1991) *European Community Sex Equality Law*, Oxford: Clarendon.

Ellison R (1994) 'British labour force projections: 1994 to 2006', *Employment Gazette*, 102: 111–21.

Employment Committee of the House of Commons, Session 1994–95 (1995) *Unemployment and Employment Statistics – Minutes of Evidence: Tuesday 2 May 1995, 411–i*, London: HMSO.

Employment Department (1976) 'Teachers' pay – how and why men and women's earnings differ', *Employment Gazette*, 84: 963–68.

Employment Department (1992) 'Economic activity and qualifications: results from the Labour Force Survey', *Employment Gazette*, 100: 101–33.

England P (1981) 'Assessing trends in occupational sex segregation 1900–1976' in Berg I (ed), *Sociological Perspectives on Labor Markets*, New York: Academic Press, pp 273–95.

England P (1982) 'The failure of human capital theory to explain occupational sex segregation', *Journal of Human Resources*, 17: 358–70.

England P (1984) 'Wage appreciation and depreciation: a test of neoclassical economic explanations of occupational sex segregation', *Social Forces*, 62: 726–49.

England P, Hermesen JM and Cotter DA (2000) 'The devaluation of women's work: a comment on Tam', *American Journal of Sociology*, 105: 1741–60.

England P and McCreary L (1987) 'Integrating sociology and economics to study gender and work' in Stromberg AH *et al* (eds), *Women and Work: An Annual Review*, Beverly Hills and London: Sage, pp 143–72.

England P, Reid LL and Kilbourne BS (1996) 'The effect of the sex composition of jobs on starting wages in an organisation: findings from the NLSY', *Demography*, 33: 511–21.

Erikson K and Vallas S (eds) (1990) *The Nature of Work: Sociological Perspectives*, New Haven CT and London: Yale University Press.

Erikson R and Goldthorpe JH (1993) *The Constant Flux: A Study of Class Mobility in Industrial Societies*, Oxford: Clarendon.

Esping-Andersen, G (1990) *The Three Worlds of Welfare Capitalism*, Cambridge: Polity Press/Princeton NJ: Princeton University Press.

European Commission (1984) *European Men and Women in 1983*, Brussels: Commission of the European Communities.

European Commission (1994) *Employment in Europe 1994*, Luxembourg. OOPEC.

European Commission (1995a) *Employment in Europe 1995*, Luxembourg: OOPEC.

European Commission (1995b) *The Demographic Situation in the European Union*, DG V-COM(94)595, Luxembourg: OOPEC.

European Commission/Eurostat (2000) *The Social Situation in the European Union*, Luxembourg: OOPEC.

European Commission (2002) *Employment in Europe*, Luxembourg: OOPEC.

European Commission (2003) *Employment in Europe*, Luxembourg: OOPEC.

Evans G (2002) 'In search of tolerance' in Park A *et al* (eds), *British Social Attitudes – 19th Report*, London: Sage.

Evans J (1995) *Feminist Theory Today*, London: Sage, pp 213–30.

Fagan C and Rubery J (1996) 'The salience of the part-time divide in the European Union', *European Sociological Review*, 12: 227–50.

Fawcett MG (1918) 'Equal pay for equal work', *Economic Journal*, 28: 1–6.

Feingold A (1992) 'Gender differences in mate selection preferences: a test of the parental investment model', *Psychological Bulletin*, 112: 125–39.

Feinstein, L (2000) *The Relative Economic Importance of Academic, Psychological and Behavioural Attributes Developed in Childhood*, Discussion Paper 443, London School of Economics Centre for Economic Performance.

Feldman S (1988) 'Structure and consistency in public opinion: the role of core beliefs and values', *American Journal of Political Science*, 32: 416–40.

Felstead A and Jewson N (1995) 'Working at home: estimates from the 1991 Census', *Employment Gazette*, 103: 95–99.

Fenton-O'Creevy M (1995) 'Moderators of differences in job satisfaction between full-time and part-time female employees: a research note', *Human Resource Management Journal*, 5/5: 75–81.

Fenwick H and Hervey T (1995) 'Sex equality in the single market: new directions for the European Court of Justice', *Common Market Law Review*, 32: 443–70.

Ferri E, Bynner J and Wadsworth M (2003) *Changing Britain, Changing Lives: Three Generations at the Turn of the Century*, London: Institute of Education.

Filer RK (1981) 'The influence of affective human capital on the wage equation' in Ehrenberg RG (ed), *Research in Labor Economics*, vol 3, Greenwich CT: JAI Press, pp 367–409.

Filer RK (1983) 'Sexual differences in earnings: the role of individual personalities and tastes', *Journal of Human Resources*, 18: 82–99.

Finch J (1983) *Married to the Job: Wives' Incorporation in Men's Work*, London: Allen & Unwin.

Fine B (1992) *Women's Employment and the Capitalist Family*, London and New York: Routledge.

Fiorentine R (1987) 'Men, women and the premed persistence gap: a normative alternatives approach', *American Journal of Sociology*, 92: 1118–39.

Fiorentine R and Cole S (1988) 'The confusion of outcome with process: reply to Gross', *American Journal of Sociology*, 94: 856–63.

Fiorentine R and Cole S (1992) 'Why fewer women become physicians: explaining the premed persistence gap', *Sociological Forum*, 7: 469–96.

Firestone S (1974) *The Dialectic of Sex: The Case for Feminist Revolution*, New York: Morrow.

Fiske ST (1998) 'Stereotyping, prejudice and discrimination' in Gilbert DT, Fiske ST and Lindzey G (eds), *Handbook of Social Psychology*, New York: McGraw-Hill, pp 357–411.

Fitzenberger B, Schnabel R and Wunderlich G (2004) 'The gender gap in labor market participation and employment: a cohort analysis for West Germany', *Journal of Population Economics*, 17: 83–116.

Fogarty M (1985) 'British attitudes to work' in Abrams M, Gerard D and Timms N (eds), *Values and Social Change in Britain*, London: Macmillan, pp 173–200.

Fogarty M, Allen AJ, Allen I and Walters P (1971) *Women in Top Jobs*, London: Allen & Unwin for Political and Economic Planning.

Fredman S (1992) 'European Community discrimination law: a critique', *Industrial Law Journal*, 21: 119–34.

Fredman S (1997) *Women and the Law*, Oxford: Clarendon.

Fredman S (2002) *Discrimination Law*, Oxford: Clarendon.

Friedan B (1963) *The Feminine Mystique*, New York: Norton.

Fuchs VR (1986) 'His and hers: gender differences in work and income, 1959–1979', *Journal of Labor Economics*, 4: S245–S277.

Furnham A (1990) *The Protestant Work Ethic: The Psychology of Work-Related Beliefs and Behaviours*, London: Routledge.

Galbraith JK (1975) *Economics and the Public Purpose*, Harmondsworth: Penguin.

Gallie D and White M (1993) *Employee Commitment and the Skills Revolution*, London: Policy Studies Institute.

Gauthier AH (1996a) 'The measured and unmeasured effects of welfare benefits on families: implications for Europe's demographic trends' in Coleman D (ed), *Europe's Population in the 1990s*, Oxford: Oxford University Press, pp 295–331.

Gauthier H (1996b) *The State and the Family*, Oxford: Clarendon.

Gerhart B (1990) 'Gender differences in current and starting salaries: the role of performance, college major, and job title', *Industrial and Labor Relations Review*, 43: 418–33.

Gershuny J (1983a) *Social Innovation and the Division of Labour*, Oxford: Oxford University Press.

Gershuny J (1983b) 'Technical change and social limits' in Ellis A and Kumar K (eds), *Dilemmas of Liberal Democracies*, London: Tavistock, pp 23–44.

Gershuny J (1988) 'Time, technology and the informal economy' in Pahl R (ed), *On Work*, Oxford: Blackwell, pp 579–97.

Gershuny J (1992) 'Are we running out of time?', *Futures*, 3–22.

Gershuny J (1993) 'Post-industrial convergence in time allocation', *Futures*, 578–86.

Gershuny J (2000) *Changing Times: Work and Leisure in Postindustrial Society*, Oxford: Oxford University Press.

Gershuny J, Godwin M and Jones S (1994) 'The domestic labour revolution: a process of lagged adaptation' in Anderson M, Bechhofer F and Gershuny J (eds), *The Social and Political Economy of the Household*, Oxford: Oxford University Press, pp 151–97.

Gershuny J and Sullivan O (1998) 'The sociological uses of time-use diary analysis', *European Sociological Review*, 14: 69–85.

Gerson K (1985) *Hard Choices: How Women Decide about Work, Career and Motherhood*, Berkeley and Los Angeles: University of California Press.

Gilligan C (1982, 1993) *In a Different Voice: Psychological Theory and Women's Development*, Cambridge MA and London: Harvard University Press.

Ginn J, Arber S, Brannen J, Dale A, Dex S, Elias P, Moss P, Pahl J, Roberts C, Rubery J and Breugel I (1996) 'Feminist fallacies: a reply to Hakim on women's employment' and 'Whose myths are they anyway: a comment', *British Journal of Sociology*, 47: 167–77.

Glaser BG and Strauss AL (1967) *The Discovery of Grounded Theory*, Chicago: Aldine.

Glass J and Camarigg V (1992) 'Gender, parenthood and job-family compatibility', *American Journal of Sociology*, 98: 131–51.

Glezer H (1988) *Maternity Leave in Australia*, Melbourne: Australian Institute of Family Studies.

Goddard E (1994) *Voluntary Work*, London: HMSO for OPCS.

Goldberg P (1968) 'Are women prejudiced against women?', *Trans-Action*, 5(5): 28–30.

Goldberg S (1973) *The Inevitability of Patriarchy*, New York: William Morrow.

Goldberg S (1993) *Why Men Rule: A Theory of Male Dominance*, Chicago: Open Court.

Goldin C (1987) 'The gender gap in historical perspective' in Kilby P (ed), *Quantity and Quiddity: Essays in Honour of Stanley Lebergott*, Middletown, CT: Wesleyan University Press, pp 135–70.

Goldin C (1989) 'Life-cycle labor force participation of married women: historical evidence and implications', *Journal of Labor Economics*, 7: 20–47.

Goldin C (1990) *Understanding the Gender Gap*, New York: Oxford University Press.

Goldin C (1997) 'Career and family: college women look to the past', with discussion, in Blau F and Ehrenberg G (eds), *Gender and Family Issues in the Workplace*, New York: Russell Sage Foundation, pp 20–64.

Goldin C and Polachek S (1987) 'Residual differences by sex: perspectives on the gender gap in earnings', *American Economic Review*, 77: 143–51.

Goldschmidt-Clermont L (1982) *Unpaid Work in the Household: A Review of Economic Evaluation Methods*, Women, Work and Development Series No 1, Geneva: ILO.

Goldschmidt-Clermont L (1987) *Economic Evaluations of Unpaid Household Work: Africa, Asia, Latin America and Oceania*, Women, Work and Development Series No 14, Geneva: ILO.

Goldschmidt-Clermont L (1989) 'Valuing domestic activities', *ILO Bulletin of Labour Statistics*, No 1989-4, Geneva: ILO.

Goldschmidt-Clermont L (1990) 'Economic measurement of non-market household activities', *International Labour Review*, 129: 279–99.

Goldthorpe JH (1987) 'The class mobility of women' in Goldthorpe JH, *Social Mobility and Class Structure in Modern Britain*, Oxford: Clarendon, pp 277–301.

Goldthorpe JH (1990) 'A response' in Clark J, Modgil C and Modgil S (eds), *John H Goldthorpe: Consensus and Controversy*, London: Falmer Press, pp 399–438.

Goldthorpe JH and Hope K (1972) 'Occupational grading and occupational prestige' in Hope K (ed), *The Analysis of Social Mobility*, Oxford: Clarendon.

Goldthorpe JH and Hope K (1974) *The Social Grading of Occupations: A New Approach and Scale*, Oxford: Clarendon.

Green H (1988) *Informal Carers*, London: HMSO for OPCS.

Gregg P and Wadsworth J (1995) 'A short history of labour turnover, job tenure and job security, 1975–93', *Oxford Review of Economic Policy*, 11: 73–90.

Gregory J, Sales R and Hegewisch A (1999) *Women, Work and Inequality: The Challenge of Equal Pay in a Deregulated Labour Market*, London: Macmillan/New York: St Martin's Press.

Gregory MB and Thomson AWJ (eds) (1990) *A Portrait of Pay 1970–1982: An Analysis of the New Earnings Survey*, Oxford: Clarendon.

Grimshaw D and Rubery J (1997) *The Concentration of Women's Employment and Relative Occupational Pay: A Statistical Framework for Comparative Analysis*, Labour Market and Social Policy Occasional Papers No 26, Paris OECD.

Grimshaw D and Rubery J (2001) *The Gender Pay Gap: A Research Review*, Manchester: Equal Opportunities Commission.

Grint K (1988) 'Women and equality: the acquisition of equal pay in the Post Office 1870–1961', *Sociology*, 22: 87–108.

Gronau R (1980) 'Home production: a forgotten industry', *Review of Economics and Statistics*, 62: 408–14.

Gronau R (1986) 'Home production, a survey' in Ashenfelter O and Layard R (eds), *Handbook of Labour Economics*, Amsterdam: North Holland, pp 273–304.

Grossman AS (1980) 'Women in domestic work: yesterday and today', *Monthly Labor Review*, 103/8: 17–21.

Gunderson V (1994) *Comparable Worth and Sex Discrimination*, Geneva: ILO.

Hakim C (1979) *Occupational Segregation: A Study of the Separation of Men and Women's Work in Britain, the United States and Other Countries*, Research Paper No 9, London: Department of Employment.

Hakim C (1980) 'Census reports as documentary evidence: the census commentaries 1801–1951', *Sociological Review*, 28: 551–80.

Hakim C (1981) 'Job segregation: trends in the 1970s', *Employment Gazette*, 89: 521–29.

Hakim C (1982a) *Secondary Analysis*, London: Allen & Unwin.

Hakim C (1982b) 'The social consequences of high unemployment', *Journal of Social Policy*, 11: 433–67.

Hakim C (1985) *Employers' Use of Outwork: A Study Using the 1980 Workplace Industrial Relations Survey and the 1981 National Survey of Homeworking*, Research Paper No 44, London: Department of Employment.

Hakim C (1987a) *Research Design*, London: Allen & Unwin/Routledge.

Hakim C (1987b) *Home-Based Work in Britain: A Report on the 1981 National Homeworking Survey and the DE Research Programme on Homework*, Research Paper No 60, London: Department of Employment.

Hakim C (1987c) 'Trends in the flexible workforce', *Employment Gazette*, 95: 549–60.

Hakim C (1988a) 'Self-employment in Britain: recent trends and current issues', *Work, Employment and Society*, 2: 421–50.

Hakim C (1988b) 'Homeworking in Britain' in Pahl R (ed), *On Work: Historical, Comparative and Theoretical Approaches*, Oxford: Blackwell, pp 609–32.

Hakim C (1989a) 'Employment rights: a comparison of part-time and full-time employees', *Industrial Law Journal*, 18: 69–83.

Hakim C (1989b) 'Workforce restructuring, social insurance coverage and the black economy', *Journal of Social Policy*, 18: 471–503.

Hakim C (1990a) 'Workforce restructuring in Europe in the 1980s', *International Journal of Comparative Labour Law and Industrial Relations*, 5/4: 167–203.

Hakim C (1990b) 'Core and periphery in employers' workforce strategies: evidence from the 1987 ELUS survey', *Work, Employment and Society*, 4: 157–88.

Hakim C (1991) 'Grateful slaves and self-made women: fact and fantasy in women's work orientations', *European Sociological Review*, 7: 101–21.

Hakim C (1992) 'Explaining trends in occupational segregation: the measurement, causes and consequences of the sexual division of labour', *European Sociological Review*, 8: 127–52.

Hakim C (1993a) 'The myth of rising female employment', *Work, Employment and Society*, 7: 97–120.

Hakim C (1993b) 'Segregated and integrated occupations: a new framework for analysing social change', *European Sociological Review*, 9: 289–314.

Hakim C (1993c) 'Refocusing research on occupational segregation: reply to Watts', *European Sociological Review*, 9: 321–24.

Hakim C (1994) 'A century of change in occupational segregation 1891–1991', *Journal of Historical Sociology*, 7: 435–54.

Hakim C (1995a) 'Five feminist myths about women's employment', *British Journal of Sociology*, 46: 429–55.

Hakim C (1995b) 'Theoretical and measurement issues in the analysis of occupational segregation' in *Beiträge zur Arbeitsmarkt- und Berufsforschung* (Monographs on Employment Research) No 186, Nürnberg: Federal Employment Services (IAB), pp 67–88.

Hakim C (1996a) *Key Issues in Women's Work*, 1st edn, London: Athlone.

Hakim C (1996b) 'The sexual division of labour and women's heterogeneity', *British Journal of Sociology*, 47: 178–88.

Hakim C (1996c) 'Labour mobility and employment stability: rhetoric and reality on the sex differential in labour market behaviour?', *European Sociological Review*, 12: 45–69.

Hakim C (1997) 'A sociological perspective on part-time work' in Blossfeld H-P and Hakim C (eds), *Between Equalization and Marginalization: Women Working Part-Time in Europe and the USA*, Oxford: Oxford University Press, pp 22–70.

Hakim C (1998a) *Social Change and Innovation in the Labour Market*, Oxford: Oxford University Press.

Hakim C (1998b) 'Developing a sociology for the 21st century: preference theory', *British Journal of Sociology*, 49: 150–62.

Hakim C (1999) 'Models of the family, women's role and social policy: a new perspective from preference theory', *European Societies*, 1: 25–50.

Hakim C (2000) *Work-Lifestyle Choices in the 21st Century: Preference Theory*, Oxford: Oxford University Press.

Hakim C (2001) '*Les femmes obtiennent-elles ce qu'elles veulent ou se contentent-elles de ce qu'on leur propose?*' (Do women get what they want, or accept what they are given?), *Revue de l'OFCE – Observations et Diagnostics Economiques*, No 77: 297–306, Paris: Observatoire Francais des Conjonctures Economiques. Reprinted July 2001 in *Problèmes Economiques*, No 2721: 25–28.

Hakim C (2002) 'Lifestyle preferences as determinants of women's differentiated labour market careers', *Work and Occupations*, 29: 428–59.

Hakim C (2003a) *Models of the Family in Modern Societies: Ideals and Realities*, Aldershot: Ashgate.

Hakim C (2003b) 'Public morality versus personal choice: the failure of social attitude surveys', *British Journal of Sociology*, 54: 339–45.

Hakim C (2003c) 'A new approach to explaining fertility patterns: preference theory', *Population and Development Review*, 29: 349–74.

Hakim C (2004) 'Lifestyle preferences versus patriarchal values: causal and non-causal attitudes' in Giele JZ and Holst E (eds), *Changing Life Patterns in Western Industrial Societies*, Oxford: Elsevier, pp 69–91.

Hakim C and Dennis R (1982) *Homeworking in Wages Council Industries: A Study of Pay and Earnings Based on Wages Inspectorate Records*, Research Paper No 37, London: Department of Employment.

Halaby CN (2003) 'Where job values come from: family and schooling background, cognitive ability, and gender', *American Sociological Review*, 68: 251–78.

Hall M, Knighton T, Reed P, Bussiere P, Macrae D and Bowen P (1998) *Caring Canadians, Involved Canadians*, Ottawa: Statistics Canada.

Haller M and Hoellinger F (1994) 'Female employment and the change of gender roles: the conflictual relationship between participation and attitudes in international comparison', *International Sociology*, 9: 87–112.

Haller M and Rosenmayr L (1971) 'The pluridimensionality of work commitment', *Human Relations*, 24: 501–18.

Han S-K and Moen P (2001) 'Coupled careers: pathways through work and marriage in the United States' in Blossfeld H-P and Drobnic S (eds), *Careers of Couples in Contemporary Society*, Oxford: Oxford University Press, pp 201–31.

Hansard Society (1990) *Women at the Top*, London: Hansard Society.

Hantrais L (ed) (2000) *Gendered Policies in Europe: Reconciling Employment and Family Life*, London: Macmillan/New York: St Martin's Press.

Harding P and Jenkins R (1989) *The Myth of the Hidden Economy*, Milton Keynes: Open University Press.

Harding S, Phillips D and Fogarty M (1986) *Contrasting Values in Western Europe: Unity, Diversity and Change*, London: Macmillan.

Hargreaves-Heap S and Varoufakis Y (2002) 'Some experimental evidence on the evolution of discrimination, co-operation and perceptions of fairness', *Economic Journal*, 112: 679–703.

Harkness S (1996) 'The gender earnings gap: evidence from the UK', *Fiscal Studies*, 17: 1–36.

Harkness S and Waldfogel J (1999) *The Family Gap in Pay: Evidence from Seven Industrialised Countries*, London School of Economics: Centre for Analysis of Social Exclusion.

Harman J (1982) *Volunteerism in the Eighties*, Washington DC: University Press of America.

Harper B (2000) 'Beauty, stature and the labour market: a British cohort study', *Oxford Bulletin of Economics and Statistics*, 62 (special issue): 771–800.

Hartmann H (1976) 'Capitalism, patriarchy and job segregation by sex' in Blaxall M and Reagan B, *Women and the Workplace: The Implications of Occupational Segregation*, Chicago: University of Chicago Press, pp 137–79. Reprinted 1976, *Signs*, 1: 137–69. Reprinted in Eisenstein ZR (ed), *Capitalist Patriarchy and the Case for Socialist Feminism*, 1979, New York and London: Monthly Review Press.

Hartmann H (1979) 'The unhappy marriage of Marxism and feminism: towards a more progressive union', *Capital and Class*, 8: 1–33. Reprinted in Sargent L (ed), *Women and Revolution*, 1981, London: Pluto Press.

Hartmann H (1981) 'The family as the locus of gender, class and political struggle: the example of housework', *Signs*, 16: 366–94.

Hatton TJ and Bailey RE (2001) 'Women's work in census and survey, 1911–1931', *Economic History Review*, 54: 87–107.

Hawrylyshyn O (1977) 'Towards a definition of non-market activities', *Review of Income and Wealth*, 23: 78–96.

Hecker D (1998) 'Earnings of college graduates: women compared with men', *Monthly Labor Review*, 121/3: 62–71.

Heckman JJ (1976) 'The common structure of statistical models of truncation, sample selection and limited dependent variables and a simple estimator for such models', *Annals of Economic and Social Measurement*, 5: 475–92.

Heckman JJ (1979) 'Sample selection bias as a specification error', *Econometrica*, 45: 153–61.

Hennig M and Jardim A (1978) *The Managerial Woman*, London: Marion Boyars.

Hepple BA (1990) 'The implementation of the Community Charter of Fundamental Social Rights', *Modern Law Review*, 53: 643–54.

Hepple BA (1996) 'Equality and discrimination' in Davies P, Schiarra S and Simitis SS (eds), *Comparative Principles and Perspectives of European Community Labour Law*, Oxford: Oxford University Press.

Hepple BA and Hakim C (1997) 'Working time in the United Kingdom' in Blanpain R, Rojot J and Kohler E (eds), *Legal and Contractual Limitations on Working Time*, Antwerp: Kluwer, pp 659–93.

Hepple BA and Szyszczak E (eds) (1992) *Discrimination: The Limits of the Law*, London: Mansell.

Hibbett A and Meager N (2003) 'Key indicators of women's position in Britain', *Labour Market Trends*, 111: 503–11.

Higgs E (1987) 'Women, occupations and work in the nineteenth-century censuses', *History Workshop*, 23: 59–80.

Hill ET (2002) 'The labor force participation of older women: retired? working? both?', *Monthly Labor Review*, 125/9: 39–48.

Hinze SW (2000) 'Inside medical marriages: the effect of gender on income', *Work and Occupations*, 27: 464–99.

Hobson B (1990) 'No exit, no voice: women's economic dependency and the welfare state', *Acta Sociologica*, 33: 235–50.

Hochschild A (1990) *The Second Shift: Working Parents and the Revolution at Home*, London: Piatkus.

Hochschild A (2003) *The Managed Heart*, Berkeley CA: University of California Press.

Hodgkinson V and Weitzman M (1996) *Giving and Volunteering in the United States*, Washington DC: Independent Sector.

Hofstede G (1980, 1994) *Culture's Consequences: International Differences in Work-Related Values*, Beverly Hills and New York: Sage.

Hofstede G (1991) *Cultures and Organisations*, London: HarperCollins.

Holcombe L (1973) *Victorian Ladies at Work: Middle Class Working Women in England and Wales 1850–1914*, Hamden, CT: Archon Books.

Holloway S, Short S and Tamplin S (2002) *Household Satellite Account (Experimental) Methodology*, London: Office for National Statistics.

Hörning KH, Gerhard A and Michailow M (1995) *Time Pioneers: Flexible Working Time and New Lifestyles*, Cambridge: Polity Press.

Horrell S (1994) 'Household time allocation and women's labour force participation' in Anderson M, Bechofer F and Gershuny J (eds), *The Social and Political Economy of the Household*, Oxford: Oxford University Press, pp 198–224.

Horrell S and Humphries J (1995) 'Women's labour force participation and the transition to the male-breadwinner family, 1790–1865', *Economic History Review*, 48: 89–117.

Hoskyns C (1996) *Integrating Gender: Women, Law and Politics in the European Union*, London: Verso.

Hoskyns C (1999) 'Then and now: equal pay in European Union politics' in Gregory J *et al* (eds), *Women, Work and Inequality*, London: Macmillan, pp 27–43.

Howard JA (2000) 'Social psychology of identities', *Annual Review of Sociology*, 26: 367–93.

Humphries J (1981) 'Protective legislation, the capitalist state and working-class men: the case of the 1842 Mines Regulation Act', *Feminist Review*, 7: 1–35. Reprinted in Pahl RE (ed), *On Work*, 1988, Oxford: Basil Blackwell, pp 95–124.

Humphries J (1987) 'The most free from objection ... the sexual division of labour and women's work in nineteenth-century England', *Journal of Economic History*, 47: 929–49.

Humphries J and Rubery J (1992) 'The legacy for women's employment: integration, differentiation and polarisation' in Michie J (ed), *The Economic Legacy of Thatcherism*, London: Academic Press, pp 236–55.

Hunt A (1968a, b) *A Survey of Women's Employment: Report and Tables*, 2 vols, London: HMSO.

Hunt A (1975) *Management Attitudes and Practices Towards Women at Work*, London: HMSO.

Hunt J (2002) 'The transition in East Germany: when is a ten-point fall in the gender wage gap bad news?', *Journal of Labor Economics*, 20: 148–69.

Husbands R (1992) 'Sexual harassment law in employment: an international perspective', *International Labour Review*, 131: 535–59.

Hussmanns R (1989) 'International standards on the measurement of economic activity, employment, unemployment and underemployment', *ILO Bulletin of Labour Statistics*, No 1989-1: IX–XX.

Hutson S and Cheung W (1991) 'Saturday jobs: sixth-formers in the labour market and in the family' in Arber S and Marsh C (eds), *Household and Family: Divisions and Change*, London: Macmillan.

Huws U (1984) 'New technology homeworkers', *Employment Gazette*, 92: 13–17.

Hyde JS (1996) 'Where are the gender differences? Where are the gender similarities?' in Buss DM and Malamuth NM (eds), *Sex, Power, Conflict*, New York: Oxford University Press, pp 107–18.

IER (1995) *Review of the Economy and Employment: Occupational Assessment*, Coventry: University of Warwick Institute for Employment Research.

Ilmakunnas S (1997) 'Public policy and childcare choice' in Persson I and Jonung C (eds), *The Economics of the Family and Family Policies*, London: Routledge, pp 178–93.

ILO (1962) 'Discrimination in employment or occupations on the basis of marital status', *International Labour Review*, 85: 368–89.

ILO (1990a) *Statistical Sources and Methods: Economically Active Population, Employment and Hours of Work*, Geneva: ILO.

ILO (1990b) 'Methodology of labour force surveys in 70 countries', *ILO Bulletin of Labour Statistics*, No 1990-2: XVIII–XXIV.

Imperato-McGinley J *et al* (1979) 'Androgens and the evolution of male-gender identity among male pseudohermaphrodites with 5a reductase deficiency', *New England Journal of Medicine*, 300/22: 1233–37.

Inglehart R (1990) *Culture Shift in Advanced Industrial Society*, Princeton NJ: Princeton University Press.

Inglehart R (1997) *Modernization and Postmodernization: Cultural, Economic, and Political Change in 43 Societies*, Princeton NJ: Princeton University Press.

Inglehart R and Baker WE (2000) 'Modernization, cultural change, and the persistence of traditional values', *American Sociological Review*, 65: 19–51.

IRRR (1991) 'Long-term earnings trends 1971–91', *Industrial Relations Review and Report*, No 500: 2–8.

Irvine J, Miles I and Evans J (eds) (1979) *Demystifying Social Statistics*, London: Pluto Press.

Jacobs JA (1989a) 'Long-term trends in occupational segregation by sex', *American Journal of Sociology*, 95: 160–73.

Jacobs JA (1989b) *Revolving Doors: Sex Segregation and Women's Careers*, Stanford CA: Stanford University Press.

Jacobs JA (1992) 'Women's entry into management: trends in earnings, authority, and values among salaried managers', *Administrative Science Quarterly*, 37: 282–301.

Jacobs JA and Lim ST (1992) 'Trends in occupational and industrial sex segregation in 56 countries, 1960–1980', *Work and Occupations*, 19: 450–86. Reprinted in Jacobs J (ed), *Gender Inequality at Work*, 1994, Thousand Oaks CA: Sage, pp 259–93.

Jacobs S (1995) 'Changing patterns of sex segregated occupations throughout the life-course', *European Sociological Review*, 11: 157–71.

Jacobsen, JP (1994) *The Economics of Gender*, Cambridge MA and Oxford: Blackwell.

James DR and Taeuber KE (1985) 'Measures of segregation' in Tuma NB (ed), *Sociological Methodology*, San Francisco: Jossey-Bass, pp 1–31.

Jenson J, Hagen E and Reddy C (eds) (1988) *Feminization of the Labour Force: Paradoxes and Promises*, New York: Oxford University Press.

Jones RM (1971) *Absenteeism*, Manpower Paper No 4, London: HMSO.

Jonung C and Persson I (1993) 'Women and market work: the misleading tale of participation rates in international comparisons', *Work, Employment and Society*, 7: 259–74.

Joseph G (1983) *Women at Work*, Oxford: Philip Allen.

Joshi HE (1981) 'Secondary workers in the employment cycle: Great Britain, 1961–1974', *Economica*, No 189, 48: 29–44.

Joshi HE, Layard R and Owen SJ (1985) 'Why are more women working in Britain?', *Journal of Labor Economics*, special issue on *Trends in Women's Work, Education and Family Building*, Layard R and Mincer J (eds), 3: S147–S176.

Joshi HE and Owen S (1987) 'How long is a piece of elastic? The measurement of female activity rates in British censuses, 1951–1981', *Cambridge Journal of Economics*, 11: 55–74.

Joshi H and Paci P (1998) *Unequal Pay for Women and Men*, Cambridge MA: MIT Press.

Kahn P and Meehan E (eds) (1992) *Equal Value/Comparable Worth in the UK and the USA*, London: Macmillan.

Kalleberg AL (1977) 'Work values and job rewards: a theory of job satisfaction', *American Sociological Review*, 42: 124–43.

Kanter RM (1977) *Men and Women of the Corporation*, New York: Basic Books.

Kay H (1984) 'Is childminding real work?', *Employment Gazette*, 92: 483–86.

Kay JA and King MA (1978) *The British Tax System*, Oxford: Oxford University Press.

Kiecolt, KJ (2003) 'Satisfaction with work and family life: no evidence of a cultural reversal', *Journal of Marriage and the Family*, 65: 23–35.

Kiernan K (1992) 'Men and women at work and at home' in Jowell R *et al* (eds), *British Social Attitudes: the 9th Report*, Aldershot: Dartmouth, pp 89–112.

Kilbourne BS, England P, Farkas G, Beron K and Weir D (1994) 'Returns to skill, compensating differentials and gender bias: effects of occupational characteristics on the wages of white women and men', *American Journal of Sociology*, 100: 689–719.

Killingsworth MR (1990) *The Economics of Comparable Worth*, Kalamazoo MA: WE Upjohn Institute.

King MC (1992) 'Occupational segregation by race and sex, 1940–88', *Monthly Labor Review*, 115/4: 30–37.

Kunhikrishnan K and Manikandan K (1995) 'Sex differences in locus of control: an analysis based on Calicut LOC scale', *Psychological Studies*, 37: 121–25.

Lane C (1983) 'Women in socialist society with special reference to the German Democratic Republic', *Sociology*, 17: 489–505.

Lapidus GW (1988) 'The interaction of women's work and family roles in the USSR' in Gutek BA, Stromberg AH and Larwood L (eds), *Women and Work: An Annual Review*, vol 3, Newbury Park CA and London: Sage, pp 87–121.

Laufer J (1993) 'Women in business and management – France' in Davidson MJ and Cooper CL (eds), *European Women in Business and Management*, London: Paul Chapman, pp 107–32.

Leete L and Schor JB (1994) 'Assessing the time-squeeze hypothesis: hours worked in the United States, 1969–89', *Industrial Relations*, 33: 25–43.

Leighton P (1983) *Contractual Arrangements in Selected Industries: A Study of Employment Relationships in Industries with Outwork*, Research Paper No 39, London: Department of Employment.

Lerner G (1986) *The Creation of Patriarchy*, New York and Oxford: Oxford University Press.

Letablier M-T (2004) 'Work and family balance: a new challenge for policies in France' in Giele JZ and Holst E (eds), *Changing Life Patterns in Western Industrial Societies*, Oxford: Elsevier, pp 189–209.

Lewin-Epstein N and Semyonov M (1992) 'Modernization and subordination: Arab women in the Israeli labour-force', *European Sociological Review*, 8: 39–51.

Lewis J (1984) *Women in England 1870–1950: Sexual Divisions and Social Change*, Brighton: Wheatsheaf/Bloomington: Indiana University Press.

Lewis J (1992) *Women in Britain Since 1945 – Women, Family, Work and the State*, Oxford: Blackwell.

Lewis R (1986) *Labour Law in Britain*, Oxford: Blackwell.

Lipset SM, Trow MA and Coleman JS (1956) *Union Democracy: The Internal Politics of the International Typographical Union*, Garden City NY: Anchor Books.

Lopata H (1971) *Occupation Housewife*, New York: Oxford University Press.

Lorenzi-Cioldi F (1988) *Individus Dominants et Groupes Dominés: Images Masculines et Feminines*, Grenoble: Presses Universitaires de Grenoble.

Lorenzi-Cioldi F (1991) 'Self-stereotyping and self-enhancement in gender groups', *European Journal of Social Psychology*, 21: 403–17.

Loveridge R (1983) 'Labour market segmentation and the firm' in Edwards J *et al* (eds), *Manpower Planning: Strategy and Techniques in an Organisational Context*, Chichester: John Wiley & Sons, pp 155–75.

Loveridge R (1987) 'Stigma – the manufacture of disadvantage' and 'Social accommodation and technological transformations – the case of gender' in Lee G and Loveridge R (eds), *The Manufacture of Disadvantage: Stigma and Social Closure*, Milton Keynes: Open University Press, pp 2–17 and 76–197.

Lucas JW (2003) 'Status processes and the institutionalization of women as leaders', *American Sociological Review*, 68: 464–80.

Ma Youcai, Wang Zhenyu, Sheng Xuewen and Shinozaki Masami (1994) *A Study of Life and Consciousness of the Contemporary Urban Family in China: A Study in Beijing with Comparisons with Bangkok, Seoul and Fukuoka*, Beijing: Chinese Academy of Social Sciences with Kitakyushu Forum on Asian Women.

Macarov D (1982a) 'The work personality: a neglected element in research', *International Journal of Manpower*, 3(4): 2–8.

Macarov D (1982b) *Worker Productivity: Myths and Reality*, Beverly Hills: Sage.

Macaulay C (2003) 'Job mobility and job tenure in the UK', *Labour Market Trends*, 111: 541–50.

Macpherson DA and Hirsch BT (1995) 'Wages and gender composition: why do women's jobs pay less?', *Journal of Labour Economics*, 13: 426–71.

Madden JF (1981) 'Why women work closer to home', *Urban Studies*, 18: 181–94.

Magnusson D (1998) 'The logic and implications of a person-oriented approach' in Cairns RB, Bergamn LR and Kagan J (eds), *Methods and Models for Studying the Individual*, London and Thousand Oaks CA: Sage (pp 33–64).

Magnusson D and Bergman LR (1988) 'Individual and variable-based approaches to longitudinal research on early risk factors' in Rutter M (ed), *Studies of Psychosocial Risk: The Power of Longitudinal Data*, Cambridge and New York: Cambridge University Press, pp 45–61.

Main B (1988a) 'The lifetime attachment of women to the labour market' in Hunt A (ed), *Women and Paid Work*, London: Macmillan, pp 23–51.

Main B (1988b) 'Women's hourly earnings: the influence of work histories on rates of pay' in Hunt A (ed), *Women and Paid Work*, London: Macmillan, pp 105–22.

Manning A (1996) 'The Equal Pay Act as an experiment to test theories of the labour market', *Economica*, 63: 191–212.

Maret E (1983) *Women's Career Patterns*, Lanham MD: University Press of America.

Marsh C (1991) *Hours of Work of Women and Men in Britain*, EOC Research Series, London: HMSO for the Equal Opportunities Commission.

Marshall H (1993) *Not Having Children*, Melbourne: Oxford University Press Australia.

Martin J and Roberts C (1984) *Women and Employment: A Lifetime Perspective*, London: HMSO.

Martin JK and Hanson SL (1985) 'Sex, family wage-earning status and satisfaction with work', *Work and Occupations*, 12: 91–109.

Matheson J (1990) *Voluntary Work*, GHS-17/A, London: HMSO for OPCS.

Matthaei JA (1982) *An Economic History of Women in America: Women's Work, the Sexual Division of Labour and the Development of Capitalism*, New York: Schocken/Brighton: Harvester.

Mavin S (2004) *Venus Envy: Daring to Raise Female Misogyny*, Newcastle: Northumbria University Business School.

Mayer KU (2003) 'Small children should have their mother at home! Culture, institutions and policies shaping women's work-family interface in West and East Germany', paper presented to the American Sociological Association annual conference, Atlanta, 16–19 August.

Mayhew K and Rosewell B (1978) 'Immigrants and occupational crowding in Great Britain', *Oxford Bulletin of Economics and Statistics*, 40: 223–48.

McCall L (2001) *Complex Inequality: Gender, Class and Race in the New Economy*, New York: Routledge.

McCrudden C (ed) (1987) *Women, Employment and European Equality Law*, London: Eclipse.

McCrudden C, Smith DJ and Brown C (1991) *Racial Justice at Work: The Enforcement of the Race Relations Act 1976 in Employment*, London: Policy Studies Institute.

McIntosh S (2002) *Further Analysis of the Returns to Academic and Vocational Qualifications 1993–2001*, Research Report No 370, London: Department for Education and Skills.

McOrmond T (2004) 'Changes in working trends over the past decade', *Labour Market Trends*, 112: 25–35.

McRae S (1991) *Maternity Rights in Britain*, London: Policy Studies Institute.

McRae S (1996) *Women's Employment During Family Formation*, London: Policy Studies Institute.

McRae S (2003) 'Constraints and choices in mothers' employment careers: a consideration of Hakim's preference theory', *British Journal of Sociology*, 54: 317–38.

Melkas H and Anker R (1997) 'Occupational segregation by sex in Nordic countries: an empirical investigation', *International Labour Review*, 136: 341–63.

Melkas H and Anker R (1998) *Gender Equality and Occupational Segregation in Nordic Labour Markets*, Geneva: ILO.

Mellor EF and Parks W (1988) 'A year's work: labor force activity from a different perspective', *Monthly Labor Review*, 111/9: 13–18.

Meulders D, Plasman R and Vander Stricht V (1993) *The Position of Women on the Labour Market in the European Community*, Aldershot: Dartmouth.

Meulders D, Plasman O and Plasman R (1994) *Atypical Employment in the EC*, Aldershot: Dartmouth.

Middleton C (1988) 'The familiar fate of the *Famulae*: gender divisions in the history of wage labour' in Pahl R (ed), *On Work*, Oxford: Blackwell, pp 21–47.

Mikes G (1966) *How to be an Alien: A Handbook for Beginners and Advanced Pupils*, Harmondsworth: Penguin.

Milkman R (1987) *Gender at Work: The Dynamics of Job Segregation by Sex During World War II*, Urbana and Chicago: University of Illinois Press.

Miller JB (1976) *Toward a New Psychology of Women*, Boston MA: Beacon.

Millward N, Stevens M, Smart D and Hawes WR (1992) *Workplace Industrial Relations in Transition: The ED/ESRC/PSI/ACAS Surveys*, Aldershot: Dartmouth.

Millward N, Bryson A and Forth J (2000) *All Change at Work?*, London: Routledge.

Mincer J (1962) 'Labor force participation of married women: a study of labor supply' in *Aspects of Labor Economics*, Princeton NJ: Princeton University Press, pp 63–73. Reprinted in Amsden AH (ed), *The Economics of Women and Work*, 1980, Harmondsworth: Penguin, pp 41–51.

Mincer J (1985) 'Intercountry comparisons of labor force trends and of related developments: an overview', *Journal of Labor Economics*, special issue on *Trends in Women's Work, Education and Family Building*, S1–S32.

Mincer J and Ofek H (1982) 'Interrupted work careers: depreciation and restoration of human capital', *Journal of Human Resources*, 17: 3–24.

Mincer J and Polachek S (1974) 'Family investments in human capital: earnings of women', *Journal of Political Economy*, 82: S76–S110.

Mirowsky, J (1985) 'Depression and marital power: an equity model', *American Journal of Sociology*, 91: 557–92.

Moen P (1992) *Women's Two Roles: A Contemporary Dilemma*, Westport CT: Auburn House.

Moen P (ed) (2003) *It's About Time: Couples and Careers*, Ithaca NY and London: ILR Press.

Mogensen GV (ed) (1990) *Time and Consumption*, Copenhagen: Danmarks Statistik.

Molm LD (1986) 'Gender, power and legitimation: a test of three theories', *American Journal of Sociology*, 91: 1356–86.

Moore HL (1994) *A Passion for Difference: Essays in Anthropology and Gender*, Cambridge: Polity Press.

More GC (1993) 'Equal treatment of the sexes in European Community law: what does "equal" mean?', *Feminist Legal Studies*, 1: 45–74.

Morell CM (1994) *Unwomanly Conduct: The Challenges of Intentional Childlessness*, New York and London: Routledge.

Morgan LA (1998) 'Glass ceiling effect or cohort effect? A longitudinal study of the gender earnings gap for engineers, 1982–1989', *American Sociological Review*, 63: 479–93.

Morgan SP and Waite LJ (1987) 'Parenthood and the attitudes of young adults', *American Sociological Review*, 52: 541–47.

Morse NC and Weiss RS (1955) 'The function and meaning of work and the job', *American Sociological Review*, 20: 191–98.

Mósesdóttir L (1995) 'The state and the egalitarian, ecclesiastical and liberal regimes of gender relations', *British Journal of Sociology*, 46: 622–42.

Mott FL (ed) (1978) *Women, Work and Family*, Lexington MA: DC Heath.

Mott FL (ed) (1982) *The Employment Revolution: Young American Women of the 1970s*, Cambridge MA: MIT Press.

MOW (Meaning of Work) International Research Team (1987) *The Meaning of Working*, London: Academic Press.

Murgatroyd L and Neuburger H (1997) 'A household satellite account for the UK', *Economic Trends*, No 527: 63–71.

Mueller CW, Wallace JE and Price JL (1992) 'Employee commitment: resolving some issues', *Work and Occupations*, 19: 211–36.

Myrdal A and Klein V (1956, 1968) *Women's Two Roles: Home and Work*, London: Routledge.

Naylor K (1994) 'Part-time working in Great Britain – an historical analysis', *Employment Gazette*, 102: 473–84.

Naylor M and Purdie E (1992) 'Results of the 1991 Labour Force Survey', *Employment Gazette*, 100: 153–72.

Nermo M (2000) 'Models of cross-national variation in occupational sex segregation', *European Societies*, 2: 295–333.

Nielsen R and Szyszczak E (1991) *The Social Dimension of the European Community*, Copenhagen: Handelshojskolens Forlag.

Nock SL (2001) 'The marriages of equally dependent spouses', *Journal of Family Issues*, 22: 755–75.

Nuss S and Majka L (1983) 'The economic integration of women: a cross-national investigation', *Work and Occupations*, 10: 29–48.

Nyberg A (1994) 'The social construction of married women's labour-force participation: the case of Sweden in the twentieth century', *Continuity and Change*, 9: 145–56.

Oakley A (1974, 1985) *The Sociology of Housework*, Oxford: Blackwell.

Oakley A (1976) *Housewife*, Harmondsworth: Penguin.

O'Donoghue C and Sutherland H (1999) 'Accounting for the family in European income tax systems', *Cambridge Journal of Economics*, 23: 565–98.

OECD (1984) 'Employment turnover and job tenure', *Employment Outlook*, Paris: OECD.

OECD (1985) *The Integration of Women into the Economy*, Paris: OECD.

OECD (1987) 'Occupational differentials in earnings and labour demand', *Employment Outlook*, Paris: OECD.

OECD (1988) 'Women's activity, employment and earnings: a review of recent developments', *Employment Outlook*, Paris: OECD.

OECD (1989) 'Job tenure by industry', *Employment Outlook*, Paris: OECD.

OECD (1990) 'Maternity and parental leave', *Employment Outlook*, Paris: OECD.

OECD (1991) 'Absence from work reported in labour force surveys', *Employment Outlook*, Paris: OECD.

OECD (1993) 'Enterprise tenure, labour turnover and skill training' and 'Earnings inequality: changes in the 1980s', *Employment Outlook*, Paris: OECD.

OECD (1994) *Women and Structural Change: New Perspectives*, Paris: OECD.

OECD (2001) 'Balancing work and family life: helping parents into paid employment', *Employment Outlook*, Paris: OECD, pp 129–66.

OECD (2002) 'Women at work', *Employment Outlook*, Paris: OECD, pp 61–125.

O'Leary B and McGarry J (1993) *The Politics of Antagonism: Understanding Northern Ireland*, London: Athlone.

O'Leary VE (1988) 'Women's relationships with women in the workplace' in Gutek B *et al*, *Women and Work: An Annual Review*, Thousand Oaks CA: Sage, pp 189–213.

O'Neill J (1985) 'The trend in the male-female wage gap in the United States', *Journal of Labor Economics*, 3: S91–S116.

O'Neill J and Polachek S (1993) 'Why the gender gap in wages narrowed in the 1980s', *Journal of Labor Economics*, 11: 205–28.

ONS (1998) *Living in Britain 1996*, London: HMSO.

ONS (2003a) *The UK 2000 Time Use Survey*, available only online through ONS website www.statistics.gov.uk/timeuse/background.asp.

ONS (2003b) *Household Satellite Account (Experimental)*, available only online through ONS website www.statistics.gov.uk/hhsa.

ONS (2003, continuing) 'The UK 2000 Time Use Survey', available only on the website www.statistics.gov.uk/timeuse/background.asp.

OPCS (1973) *Cohort Studies – New Developments*, Studies on Medical and Population Subjects No 25, London: HMSO.

OPCS (1983) *General Household Survey 1981*, London: HMSO for OPCS.

OPCS (1988) *Census 1971–1981: The Longitudinal Study – England and Wales*, CEN81LS, London: HMSO for OPCS.

OPCS (1991) *Standard Occupational Classification, Vol 3: Social Classifications and Coding Methodology*, London: HMSO for OPCS.

OPCS (1992) *GHS: Carers in 1990*, OPCS Monitor SS92/2, London: OPCS.

OPCS (1994) *1991 Census – Economic Activity Great Britain*, London: HMSO.

OPCS (1995) *General Household Survey 1993*, London: HMSO.

Oppenheimer VK (1970) *The Female Labor Force in the United States*, Westport, CT: Greenwood Press.

O'Reilly J and Fagan C (eds) (1998) *Part-Time Prospects: An International Comparison of Part-Time Work in Europe, North America and the Pacific Rim*, London: Routledge.

Osmond MW and Martin PY (1975) 'Sex and sexism: a comparison of male and female sex-role attitudes', *Journal of Marriage and the Family*, 37: 744–58.

Owen D (1994) *Ethnic Minority Women and the Labour Market: Analysis of the 1991 Census*, Manchester: Equal Opportunities Commission.

Owen SJ and Joshi H (1987) 'Does elastic retract: the effect of recession on women's labour force participation', *British Journal of Industrial Relations*, 25: 125–43.

Paci P and Joshi H (1996) *Wage Differentials Between Men and Women: Evidence from Cohort Studies*, Research Series No 71, London: Department for Education and Employment.

Padavic I and Reskin B (2002) *Women and Men at Work*, 2nd edn, Thousand Oaks CA: Pine Forge Press.

Pahl JM and Pahl RE (1971) *Managers and their Wives*, Harmondsworth: Penguin.

Pahl RE (1984) *Divisions of Labour*, Oxford: Blackwell.

Pahl RE (ed) (1988) *On Work: Historical, Comparative and Theoretical Approaches*, Oxford: Basil Blackwell.

Papanek H (1973) 'Men, women and work: reflections on the two-person career' in Huber J (ed), *Changing Women in a Changing Society*, Chicago and London: University of Chicago Press, pp 90–110.

Parsons T and Bales RF (1955) *Family Socialization and Interaction Process*, New York: Free Press.

Payne M (1995) 'Patterns of pay: results of the 1995 New Earnings Survey', *Labour Market Trends*, 103: 405–12.

Petersen T and Morgan L (1995) 'Separate and unequal: occupation-establishment sex segregation and the gender wage gap', *American Journal of Sociology*, 101: 329–65.

Petersen T, Snartland V, Becken L-E and Olsen KM (1997) 'Within-job wage discrimination and the gender wage gap: the case of Norway', *European Sociological Review*, 13: 199–213.

Pfau-Effinger B (1993) 'Modernisation, culture and part-time employment: the example of Finland and West Germany', *Work, Employment and Society*, 7: 383–410.

Pfau-Effinger B (1998) 'Culture or structure as explanations for differences in part-time work in Germany, Finland and the Netherlands' in O'Reilly J and Fagan C (eds), *Part-Time Prospects*, London: Routledge, pp 177–98.

Phelps ES (1972) 'The statistical theory of racism and sexism', *American Economic Review*, 62: 659–61.

Phillips A (2004) 'Defending equality of outcome', *Journal of Political Philosophy*, 12: 1–19.

Phillips A and Taylor B (1980) 'Sex and skill: notes towards a feminist economics', *Feminist Review*, 6: 79–88.

Pilling D (1990) *Escape from Disadvantage*, London: Falmer.

Pinchbeck I (1930, 1981) *Women Workers and the Industrial Revolution, 1750–1850*, London: Virago.

Pinker S (2002) *The Blank Slate: The Modern Denial of Human Nature*, London: Allen Lane.

Pitt G (1992) *Employment Law*, London: Sweet & Maxwell.

Plaisance, E (1986) *L'Enfant, la Maternelle, la Societé*, Paris: Presses Universitaires de France.

Polachek SW (1979) 'Occupational segregation among women: theory, evidence and a prognosis' in Lloyd CB, Andrews ES and Gilroy CL (eds), *Women in the Labor Market*, New York: Columbia University Press, pp 137–70.

Pollert A (1981) *Girls, Wives, Factory Lives*, London: Macmillan.

Pott-Buter HA (1993) *Facts and Fairy Tales about Female Labor, Family and Fertility: A Seven-Country Comparison, 1850–1990*, Amsterdam: Amsterdam University Press.

Power M (1988) 'Women, the state and the family in the US: Reaganomics and the experience of women' in Rubery J (ed), *Women and Recession*, London: Routledge & Kegan Paul, pp 140–62.

Prechal S and Burrows N (1990) *Gender Discrimination Law of the European Community*, Aldershot: Gower.

Pringle R (1988, 1989) *Secretaries Talk: Sexuality, Power and Work*, London and New York: Verso.

Purcell J (1993) 'The end of institutional industrial relations', *Political Quarterly*, 64: 6–23.

Redclift N (1985) 'Gender, accumulation and the labour process' in Mingione E and Redclift N (eds), *Beyond Employment*, Oxford: Blackwell. Reprinted in Pahl RE (ed), *On Work*, 1988, Oxford: Blackwell, pp 428–48.

Redmond M (1986) 'Women and minorities' in Lewis R (ed), *Labour Law in Britain*, Oxford: Blackwell, pp 472–502.

Reskin BF (ed) (1984) *Sex Segregation in the Workplace: Trends, Explanations, Remedies*, Washington DC: National Academy Press.

Reskin BF (2003) 'Including mechanisms in our models of ascriptive inequality', *American Sociological Review*, 68: 1–21.

Reskin BF and Hartmann HI (eds) (1986) *Women's Work, Men's Work: Sex Segregation on the Job*, Washington DC: National Academy Press.

Reskin BF and Padavic I (1994) *Women and Men at Work*, Thousand Oaks CA: Pine Forge.

Reskin BF and Roos PA (1990) *Job Queues, Gender Queues: Explaining Women's Inroads into Male Occupations*, Philadelphia: Temple University Press.

Rexroat C (1992) 'Changes in the employment continuity of succeeding cohorts of young women', *Work and Occupations*, 19: 18–34.

Rexroat C and Shehan C (1984) 'Expected versus actual work roles of women', *American Sociological Review*, 49: 349–58.

Riboud M (1985) 'An analysis of women's labour force participation in France: cross-section estimates and time series evidence', *Journal of Labor Economics*, special issue on *Trends in Women's Work, Education and Family Building*, 3: S177–S200.

Roberts E (1984) *A Woman's Place: An Oral History of Working Class Women 1890–1940*, Oxford: Blackwell.

Robinson JP and Gershuny J (1994) 'Measuring hours of paid work: time-diary vs estimate questions' in *Bulletin of Labour Statistics*, No 1994-1, Geneva: ILO, pp xi–xvii.

Rodgers G and Rodgers J (eds) (1989) *Precarious Jobs in Labour Market Regulation*, International Institute for Labour Studies, Geneva: ILO.

Rogers B (1981) *The Domestication of Women: Discrimination in Developing Societies*, London: Tavistock.

Roos PA (1983) 'Marriage and women's occupational attainment in cross-cultural perspective', *American Sociological Review*, 48: 852–64.

Rose M (1994) 'Skill and Samuel Smiles: changing the British work ethic' in Penn R, Rose M and Rubery J (eds), *Skill and Occupational Change*, Oxford: Oxford University Press, pp 281–335.

Rosen S (1981) 'The economics of superstars', *American Economic Review*, 71: 845–48.

Rosenfeld R (1983) 'Sex segregation and sectors', *American Sociological Review*, 48: 637–56.

Rosenfeld RA and Birkelund GE (1995) 'Women's part-time employment: a cross-national comparison', *European Sociological Review*, 11: 111–34.

Rosenfeld RA and Kalleberg AL (1990) 'A cross-national comparison of the gender gap in income', *American Journal of Sociology*, 96: 69–106.

Rosenfeld RA and Kalleberg AL (1991) 'Gender inequality in the labour market', *Acta Sociologica*, 34: 207–25.

Rosenfeld RA and Spenner KI (1992) 'Occupational segregation and women's early career job shifts', *Work and Occupations*, 19: 424–49. Reprinted in Jacobs JA (ed), *Gender Inequality at Work*, 1995, London: Sage, pp 231–58.

Rossi A (1977) 'A biosocial perspective on parenting', *Daedalus*, 106: 1–31.

Rotter JB (1966) 'Generalised expectancies for internal versus external control of reinforcement', *Psychological Monographs*, 80(1): 1–28.

Routh G (1965, 1980) *Occupation and Pay in Great Britain 1906–79*, London: Macmillan.

Routh G (1987) *Occupations of the People of Great Britain, 1801–1981*, London: Macmillan.

Rubery J (ed) (1988) *Women and Recession*, London: Routledge & Kegan Paul.

Rubery J and Fagan C (1993) *Occupational Segregation of Women and Men in the European Community, Social Europe*, Supplement 3/93, Luxembourg: Office for Official Publications of the European Communities.

Rubery J and Fagan C (1994) *Wage Determination and Sex Segregation in Employment in the European Community, Social Europe*, Supplement 4/94, Luxembourg: Office for Official Publications of the European Communities.

Rubery J and Fagan C (1995a) 'Gender segregation in societal context', *Work, Employment and Society*, 9: 213–40.

Rubery and Fagan C (1995b) 'Comparative industrial relations research: towards reversing the gender bias', *British Journal of Industrial Relations*, 33: 209–36.

Rubery J, Horrell S and Burchell B (1994) 'Part-time work and gender inequality in the labour market' in Scott AM (ed), *Gender Segregation and Social Change*, Oxford: Oxford University Press, pp 205–34.

Rubery J, Smith M, Fagan C and Grimshaw D (1998) *Women and European Employment*, London: Routledge.

Rytina NF (1981) 'Occupational segregation and earnings differences by sex', *Monthly Labor Review*, 104/1: 49–53.

Sainsbury, D (1996) *Gender Equality and Welfare States*, Cambridge: Cambridge University Press.

Sandell S and Shapiro D (1980) 'Work expectations, human capital accumulation and the wages of young women', *Journal of Human Resources*, 15: 335–53.

Saunders C and Marsden D (1981) *Pay Inequalities in the European Communities*, London: Butterworths.

Sayer A (1984) *Method in Social Science: A Realist Approach*, London: Routledge.

Schnittker J, Freese J and Powell B (2003) 'Who are feminists and what do they believe? The role of generations', *American Sociological Review*, 68: 607–22.

Schoon I and Parsons S (2002) 'Teenage aspirations for future careers and occupational outcomes', *Journal of Vocational Behaviour*, 60: 262–88.

Scott AM (ed) (1994) *Gender Segregation and Social Change*, Oxford: Oxford University Press.

Scott AM and Burchell B (1994) 'And never the twain shall meet? – Gender segregation and work histories' in Scott AM (ed), *Gender Segregation and Social Change*, Oxford: Oxford University Press, pp 121–56.

Scott J (1990) 'Women and the family' in Jowell R et al (eds), *British Social Attitudes: the 7th Report*, Aldershot: Gower, pp 51–76.

Scott J, Braun M and Alwin D (1993) 'The family way' in Jowell R et al (eds), *International Social Attitudes: The 10th BSA Report*, Aldershot: Dartmouth, pp 23–47.

Scott, J and Duncombe, J (1991) 'Gender-role attitudes in Britain and the USA' in Arber S and Gilbert N (eds), *Women and Working Lives*, London: Macmillan, pp 36–53.

Sen AK (1990) 'Gender and cooperative conflicts' in Tinker I (ed), *Persistent Inequalities: Women and World Development*, New York: Oxford University Press, pp 123–291.

Shavit Y and Blossfeld H-P (eds) (1993) *Persistent Inequality: Changing Educational Attainment in Thirteen Countries*, Boulder CO: Westview Press.

Shaw LB (ed) (1983) *Unplanned Careers*, Lexington MA: DC Heath.

Shaw LB and Shapiro D (1987) 'Women's work plans: contrasting expectations and actual work experience', *Monthly Labor Review*, 110/11: 7–13.

Short S (2000) 'Time use data in the household satellite account – October 2000', *Economic Trends*, No 563: 47–55.

Sieling MS (1984) 'Staffing patterns prominent in female-male earnings gap', *Monthly Labor Review*, 107/6: 29–33.

Siltanen J (1994) *Locating Gender: Occupational Segregation, Wages and Domestic Responsibilities*, London: UCL Press.

Sloane PJ (1990) 'Sex differentials: structure, stability and change' in Gregory MB and Thomson AWJ (eds), *A Portrait of Pay, 1970–1982: An Analysis of the New Earnings Survey*, Oxford: Clarendon, pp 125–71.

Sly F (1993) 'Women in the labour market', *Employment Gazette*, 101: 483–502.

Sly F (1994) 'Mothers in the labour market', *Employment Gazette*, 102: 403–13.

Smart C (1976) *Women, Crime and Criminology: A Feminist Critique*, London: Routledge.

Smart C and Smart B (eds) (1978) *Women, Sexuality and Social Control*, London: Routledge.

Smith JD (1998) *The 1997 National Survey of Volunteering*, London: National Centre for Volunteering.

Smith JP and Ward MP (1984) *Women's Wages and Work in the Twentieth Century*, Santa Monica CA: Rand Corporation.

Smith PB, Dugan S and Trompenaars F (1997) 'Locus of control and affectivity by gender and occupational status', *Sex Roles*, 36: 51–77.

Smith RA (2002) 'Race, gender, and authority in the workplace: theory and research', *Annual Review of Sociology*, 28: 509–42.

Smith SJ (1982) 'New worklife estimates reflect changing profile of labor force', *Monthly Labor Review*, 105/3: 15–20.

Smith SJ (1983) 'Estimating annual hours of labor force activity', *Monthly Labor Review*, 106/2: 13–22.

Sobel MF, De Graaf ND, Heath A and Zou Y (2004) 'Men matter more: the social class identity of married British women, 1985–1991', *Journal of the Royal Statistical Society – A*, 167: 37–52.

Sohrab JA (1993) 'Avoiding the exquisite trap: a critical look at the equal treatment/special treatment debate in law', *Feminist Legal Studies*, 1: 141–62.

Sorensen, A (1994) 'Women's economic risk and the economic position of single mothers', *European Sociological Review*, 10: 173–88.

Sorensen A (2004) 'Economic relations between women and men: new realities and the re-interpretation of dependence' in Giele JZ and Holst E (eds), *Changing Life Patterns in Western Industrial Societies*, Oxford: Elsevier, pp 281–97.

Sorensen A and McLanahan S (1987) 'Married women's economic dependency, 1940–1980', *American Journal of Sociology*, 93: 659–87.

Sorensen A and Trappe H (1995) 'The persistence of gender inequality in earnings in the German Democratic Republic', *American Sociological Review*, 60: 398–406.

Sorensen E (1989) 'The wage effects of occupational sex composition: a review and new findings' in Hill MA and Killingsworth MR (eds), *Comparable Worth: Analyses and Evidence*, Ithaca NY: ILR Press, pp 57–89.

Sorensen JB (1990) 'Perceptions of women's opportunity in five industrialised nations', *European Sociological Review*, 6: 151–64.

Sorokin PA and Berger CQ (1939) *Time Budgets of Human Behaviour*, Cambridge MA: Harvard University Press.

Sousa-Poza A and Sousa-Poza A (2000) 'Well-being at work: a cross-national analysis of the levels and determinants of job satisfaction', *Journal of Socio-Economics*, 29: 517–38.

Spence A (1992) 'Patterns of pay: results of the 1992 New Earnings Survey', *Employment Gazette*, 100: 579–91.

Spitze GD and Waite LJ (1980) 'Labor force and work attitudes', *Work and Occupations*, 7: 3–32.

Stafford FP (1980) 'Women's use of time converging with men's', *Monthly Labor Review*, 103/12: 57–59.

Statistics Sweden (1995) *Women and Men in Sweden*, Orebro: Statistics Sweden Publication Services.

Steinberg R (1988) 'The unsubtle revolution: women, the state and equal employment' in Jenson J, Hagen E and Reddy C (eds), *Feminisation of the Labour Force: Paradoxes and Promises*, New York: Oxford University Press, pp 189–213.

Stephan PE and Schroeder LD (1979) 'Career decisions and labour force participation of married women' in Lloyd CB *et al* (eds), *Women in the Labor Market*, New York: Columbia University Press, pp 119–35.

Stewart MB and Greenhalgh CA (1984) 'Work history patterns and the occupational attainment of women', *Economic Journal*, 94: 493–519.

Stinson JF (1990) 'Multiple jobholding up sharply in the 1980s', *Monthly Labor Review*, 113/7: 3–10.

Stockman N, Bonney N and Sheng Xuewen (1995) *Women's Work in East and West: The Dual Burden of Employment and Family Life*, London: UCL.

Stoller RJ (1975) *The Transsexual Experiment*, London: Hogarth Press.

Stolzenberg RM and Waite LJ (1977) 'Age, fertility expectations and plans for employment', *American Sociological Review*, 42: 769–83.

Stolzenberg RM and Relles DA (1997) 'Tools for intuition about sample selection bias and its correction', *American Sociological Review*, 62: 494–507.

Strickland BR and Haley WE (1980) 'Sex differences on the Rotter I-E scale', *Journal of Personality and Social Psychology*, 39(5): 930–39.

Strom SH (1989) 'Light manufacturing: the feminisation of American office work, 1900–1930', *Industrial Labor Relations Review*, 43: 53–71.

Stubbings P and Humble S (1984) 'Voluntary work, unemployment and the labour market in Britain' in *Voluntary Work and Unemployment: A Study in the Countries of the European Community*, London: Policy Studies Institute, pp 1–63.

Summerfield P (1984) *Women Workers in the Second World War*, London: Croom Helm.

Sutherland S (1978) 'The unambitious female: women's low professional aspirations', *Signs*, 3: 774–94.

Swaffield J (2000) *Gender, Motivation, Experience and Wages*, London: Centre for Economic Performance.

Swim JK (1994) 'Perceived versus meta-analytic effect sizes: an assessment of the accuracy of gender stereotypes', *Journal of Personality and Social Psychology*, 66: 21–36.

Swim JK and Sanna LJ (1996) 'He's skilled, she's lucky: a meta-analysis of observer's attributions for women's and men's successes and failures', *Personality and Social Psychology Bulletin*, 22: 507–19.

Szalai A (ed) (1972) *The Use of Time*, The Hague: Mouton.

Tajfel H (1970) 'Experiments in intergroup discrimination', *Scientific American*, 223: 96–102.

Tajfel H (1978) 'Interindividual behaviour and intergroup behaviour' in Tajfel H (ed), *Differentiation Between Social Groups: Studies in the Social Psychology of Intergroup Relations*, London: Academic Press, pp 27–60.

Tajfel H (1982) 'Social psychology of intergroup relations', *Annual Review of Psychology*, 33: 1–30.

Tajfel H, Billig MG, Bundy RP and Flament C (1971) 'Social categorization and intergroup behaviour', *European Journal of Social Psychology*, 1: 149–78.

Tam T (1997) 'Sex segregation and occupational gender inequality in the United States: devaluation or specialised training?', *American Journal of Sociology*, 102: 1652–92.

Tam T (2000) 'Occupational wage inequality and devaluation: a cautionary tale of measurement error', *American Journal of Sociology*, 105: 1752–60.

Thomas JJ (1992) *Informal Economic Activity*, LSE Handbooks in Economics, Herts: Harvester Wheatsheaf.

Threlfall M (2000) 'Taking stock and looking ahead', in Hantrais L (ed), *Gendered Policies in Europe*, London: Macmillan, pp 180–200.

Tijdens K (1993) 'Women in business and management – the Netherlands' in Davidson MJ and Cooper CL (eds), *European Women in Business and Management*, London: Paul Chapman, pp 79–92.

Tilly C and Tilly C (1998) 'Inequality at work: hiring' in Tilly C and Tilly C (eds), *Work Under Capitalism*, Boulder CO: Westview Press, pp 177–98.

Tilly LA and Scott JW (1990) *Women, Work and Family*, London: Routledge.

Tokyo Metropolitan Government (1994) *International Comparative Survey of Issues Confronting Women*, Tokyo: Tokyo Metropolitan Government.

Tomaskovic-Devey D (1993) *Gender & Racial Inequality at Work: The Sources and Consequences of Job Segregation*, Ithaca NY: ILR Press.

Townsend J (1998) *What Women Want – What Men Want, Why the Sexes Still See Love and Commitment so Differently*, New York: Oxford University Press.

Townsend JM and Jankowiak W (1986) 'Sex differences in mate choice and sexuality: a comparison of the United States and China', *Human Mosaic*, 20: 39–76.

Treadwell P (1987) 'Biologic influences on masculinity' in Brod H (ed), *The Making of Masculinities*, Boston YMA and London: Allen & Unwin, pp 259–85.

Treas J (1987) 'The effect of women's labor force participation on the distribution of income in the United States', *Annual Review of Sociology*, 13: 259–88.

Treiman DJ and Hartmann HI (eds) (1981) *Women, Work and Wages: Equal Pay for Jobs of Equal Value*, Washington DC: National Academy Press.

Tsoukalis L (1993) *The New European Economy: The Politics and Economics of Integration*, Oxford: Oxford University Press.

Tzannatos Z and Zabalza A (1984) 'The anatomy of the rise of British female relative wages in the 1970s: evidence from the New Earnings Survey', *British Journal of Industrial Relations*, 22: 177–94.

United Nations (1995) *Human Development Report 1995*, Oxford: Oxford University Press.

Vaessen M (1984) *Childlessness and Infecundity*, World Fertility Survey Comparative Studies No 31, Voorburg: International Statistical Institute.

Väisänen M and Nätti J (2002) 'Working time preferences in dual-earning households', *European Societies*, 4: 307–29.

Van Berkel M and De Graaf ND (1998) 'Married women's economic dependency in the Netherlands, 1979–1991', *British Journal of Sociology*, 49: 97–117.

van der Lippe T and van Dijk L (2002) 'Comparative research on women's employment', *Annual Review of Sociology*, 28: 221–41.

Vanek J (1974) 'Time spent in housework', *Scientific American*, 231: 116–20. Reprinted in Amsden AH (ed), *The Economics of Women and Work*, 1980, Harmondsworth: Penguin, pp 82–90.

Van Klaveren M and Tijdens K (2003) 'Substitution or segregation? The impact of changes in employment, production and product on gender composition in Dutch manufacturing 1899–1999', *Economic and Industrial Democracy*, 24: 595–629.

Veevers JE (1973) 'Voluntarily childless wives: an exploratory study', *Sociology and Social Research*, 57: 356–66.

Vella F (1994) 'Gender roles and human capital investment: the relationship between traditional attitudes and female labour market performance', *Economica*, 61: 191–211.

Visser J and Hemerijck A (1997) *A Dutch Miracle – Job Growth, Welfare Reform and Corporatism in the Netherlands*, Amsterdam: Amsterdam University Press.

Vogler C (1994a) 'Segregation, sexism and labour supply' in Scott AM (ed), *Gender Segregation and Social Change*, Oxford: Oxford University Press, pp 39–79.

Vogler C (1994b) 'Money in the household' in Anderson M, Bechhofer F and Gershuny J (eds), *The Social and Political Economy of the Household*, Oxford: Oxford University Press, pp 225–66.

Wade TJ (1996) 'An examination of locus of control/fatalism for blacks, whites, boys and girls over a two-year period of adolescence', *Social Behaviour and Personality*, 24: 239–48.

Waite LJ and Berryman SE (1986) 'Job stability among young women: a comparison of traditional and non-traditional occupations', *American Journal of Sociology*, 92: 568–95.

Waite LJ and Stolzenberg RM (1976) 'Intended childbearing and labor force participation of young women: insights from nonrecursive models', *American Sociological Review*, 41: 235–52.

Waite LJ, Haggstrom GW and Kanouse D (1986) 'The consequences of parenthood for the marital stability of young adults', *American Sociological Review*, 50: 850–57.

Wajcman J (1996) 'Desperately seeking differences: is management style gendered?', *British Journal of Industrial Relations*, 34: 333–49.

Wajcman J (1998) *Managing Like a Man: Women and Men in Corporate Management*, Philadelphia: Pennsylvania University Press.

Walby S (1986) *Patriarchy at Work: Patriarchal and Capitalist Relations in Employment*, Cambridge: Polity Press.

Walby S (1990) *Theorising Patriarchy*, Oxford: Blackwell.

Waring M (1988) *Counting for Nothing: What Men Value and What Women are Worth*, Wellington: Allen & Unwin/Port Nicholson.

Warr P (1982) 'A national study of non-financial employment commitment', *Journal of Occupational Psychology*, 55: 297–312.

Warr P (2002) 'The study of well-being, behaviour and attitudes' in Warr P (ed), *Psychology at Work*, London: Penguin, pp 1–25.

Warr P and Yearta S (1995) 'Health and motivational factors in sickness absence', *Human Resource Management Journal*, 5/5: 33–48.

Watson G (1992) 'Hours of work in Great Britain and Europe: evidence from the UK and European Labour Force Surveys', *Employment Gazette*, 100: 539–57.

Watson G (1994) 'The flexible workforce and patterns of working hours in the UK', *Employment Gazette*, 102: 239–47.

Watson G and Fothergill B (1993) 'Part-time employment and attitudes to part-time work', *Employment Gazette*, 101: 213–20.

Weir G (2002) 'The economically inactive who look after the family or home', *Labour Market Trends*, 110: 577–87.

Wellington AJ (1994) 'Accounting for the male/female wage gap among whites: 1976 and 1985', *American Sociological Review*, 59: 839–48.

Wells T (1999) 'Changes in occupational sex segregation during the 1980s and 1990s', *Social Science Quarterly*, 80: 370–80.

Werner B (1986) 'Family building intentions of different generations of women: results from the General Household Survey', *Population Trends*, 44: 17–23.

Werner B and Chalk S (1986) 'Projections of first, second, third and later births', *Population Trends*, 46: 26–34.

Wicker A (1969) 'Attitudes versus actions: the relationship of verbal and overt behavioral responses to attitude objects', *Journal of Social Issues*, 25: 41–78.

Willborn SL (1989) *A Secretary and a Cook: Challenging Women's Wages in the Courts of the United States and Great Britain*, Ithaca NY. ILR Press.

Williams CL (1989) *Gender Differences at Work: Women and Men in Nontraditional Occupations*, Berkeley and London: University of California Press.

Williams CL (1992) 'The glass escalator: hidden advantages for men in the female professions', *Social Problems*, 39: 253–67.

Williams G (1976) 'Trends in occupational differentiation by sex', *Sociology of Work and Occupations*, 3: 38–62.

Williams RD (2004) 'An introduction to the UK Time Use Survey from a labour market perspective', *Labour Market Trends*, 112: 63–70.

Willis P (1977) *Learning to Labour: How Working Class Kids Get Working Class Jobs*, Farnborough: Saxon House.

Wilson J (2000) 'Volunteering', *Annual Review of Sociology*, 26: 215–40.

Witherspoon S (1988) 'Interim report: a woman's work' in Jowell R *et al* (eds), *British Social Attitudes: the 5th Report*, Aldershot: Gower, pp 175–200.

Witherspoon S and Prior S (1991) 'Working mothers: free to choose?' in Jowell R *et al* (eds), *British Social Attitudes: the 8th Report*, Aldershot: Gower, pp 131–54.

Wood RG, Corcoran ME and Courant PN (1993) 'Pay differences among the highly paid: the male-female earnings gap in lawyers' salaries', *Journal of Labor Economics*, 11: 417–41.

Wright EO, Baxter J and Birkelund GE (1995) 'The gender gap in workplace authority: a cross-national study', *American Sociological Review*, 60: 407–35.

Yankelovich D (1985) *The World at Work*, New York: Octagon Books.

Young M and Willmott P (1973) *The Symmetrical Family*, London: Routledge. Reprinted 1975, London: Penguin.

Zabalza A and Arrufat J (1985) 'The extent of sex discrimination in Great Britain' in Zabalza A and Tzannatos Z, *Women and Equal Pay: The Effects of Legislation on Female Employment and Wages in Britain*, Cambridge: Cambridge University Press, pp 70–96, 120–37.

Zabalza A and Tzannatos Z (1985a) 'The effect of Britain's anti-discriminatory legislation on relative pay and employment', *Economic Journal*, 95: 679–99.

Zabalza A and Tzannatos Z (1985b) *Women and Equal Pay: The Effects of Legislation on Female Employment and Wages*, Cambridge: Cambridge University Press.

Zabalza A and Tzannatos Z (1988) 'Reply to comments on the effects of Britain's anti-discrimination legislation on relative pay and employment', *Economic Journal*, 98: 839–43.

Zelizer VA (1989) 'The social meaning of money: special monies', *American Journal of Sociology*, 95: 342–77.

Author Index

Subject Index